, John

s history of the world

A

# DISASTROUS
# HISTORY
## OF THE
# WORLD

# A
# DISASTROUS
# HISTORY
## OF THE
# WORLD

### CHRONICLES OF WAR,
### EARTHQUAKE, PLAGUE AND FLOOD

## JOHN WITHINGTON

PIATKUS

PIATKUS

First published in Great Britain in 2008 by Piatkus Books

ISBN 978-0-7499-0978-9

Edited by Philip Parr
Text design by Paul Saunders
Typeset in Minion by M Rules
Printed and bound in Great Britain by
MPG Books, Bodmin, Cornwall

Papers used by Piatkus are natural, renewable and recyclable
products made from wood grown in sustainable forests and certified
in accordance with the rules of the Forest Stewardship Council.

**Mixed Sources**
Product group from well-managed
forests and other controlled sources
www.fsc.org  Cert no. SGS-COC-004081
© 1996 Forest Stewardship Council
FSC

Piatkus Books
An imprint of
Little, Brown Book Group
100 Victoria Embankment
London EC4Y 0DY

An Hachette Livre UK Company
www.hachettelivre.co.uk

www.piatkus.co.uk

# CONTENTS

# INTRODUCTION

Tune into a news bulletin, with its stories of tsunamis, earthquakes, monsoon floods, bird flu and international terrorism, and you would be forgiven for thinking that the world was getting more dangerous by the day. In fact, we have always lived with disasters. They might be natural, as with diseases, hurricanes or volcanic eruptions; accidental, such as fires and shipwrecks; or deliberately inflicted, like wars or massacres. The human race had barely got going before it was almost wiped out by a volcanic eruption 74,000 years ago. More recently, in the fourteenth century, the Black Death made many of our ancestors think we faced extinction. Then, in the twentieth century, the great tyrants – Hitler, Stalin and Mao – seemed to vie with each other to see who could exterminate the most people. This book tells the story of the world's worst disasters, ancient and modern, which have blighted the lives of many millions of people, but which have also shown human beings at their bravest and most generous. So far, we have managed to survive all of them.

# 1

## VOLCANOES

### · LAKE TOBA ·

One of the earliest disasters we know about was also probably the one that came closest to wiping out the human race. About 74,000 years ago, there was a huge volcanic eruption at what is now Lake Toba on the Indonesian island of Sumatra. According to some recently advanced theories, it reduced the earth's existing human population of about one million to just 10,000. The eruption was one of the biggest ever, perhaps twenty-eight times as powerful as Mount Tambora's in 1815 (see below), which was the fiercest of modern times. Vulcanologists think it went on for as long as ten days, but as so often happens with volcanoes, the deadliest effect came not from the eruption itself but from the enormous volume of ash flung into the atmosphere, and the effect it had on the weather. Today we worry about global warming, but Toba produced catastrophic global cooling, spewing out an estimated 670 cubic miles of rock that prevented the sun's rays getting through to the earth, and plunged the planet into a dark, six-year volcanic winter, with temperatures plunging by up to five degrees.* There was also severe acid rain, and plants, animals and our human ancestors died all over the globe as the world was tipped into its last ice age. At one site in central India twenty feet of debris from Toba can still be detected today, while parts of Malaysia were covered to a depth of nearly thirty feet.

* This and all other temperatures are in Celsius.

Lake Toba lies near a fault line that runs along the centre of Sumatra, one of the weak points in the earth's crust, and Indonesia remains probably the most volcanically active country on earth. The ancient eruption gouged out a huge crater which filled with water to create the lake, the biggest in Indonesia and one of the world's deepest. Fifty miles long, with cliffs up to 800 feet high, today it is a lovely, tranquil stretch of water, and one of the most beautiful features of Sumatra. Sediment from the eruption also formed the picturesque island of Samosir in its centre, now a favourite holiday resort.

## · SANTORINI ·

Another of today's tourist paradises is Santorini, a small ring of volcanic islands in the Aegean Sea about 125 miles from the Greek mainland, famous for the spectacular sunsets that can be seen across its circular bay. The bay is actually the rim of a crater, created by a catastrophic volcanic explosion about 3,500 years ago. In those days, Santorini was a single island, ten miles in diameter, rising nearly a mile high to a handsomely symmetrical mountain peak. Along with Crete, it formed one of the ancient world's greatest civilisations, dominating the eastern Mediterranean for a millennium and a half during the Bronze Age. The Minoans who lived there were a cultured and sophisticated people, who loved sculpture, paintings and jewellery, and had houses with hot and cold running water, toilets and bathrooms.

One dreadful day, their pleasant existence was rudely interrupted by an earthquake. Walls cracked and crumbled, houses collapsed. At this point, many may have departed, perhaps for the Greek mainland, but more likely for Crete, seventy miles away. Not everyone left, though, or perhaps some who did returned later, for there is evidence of paths being cleared and rubble neatly piled up. Someone set up an improvised cooking hearth outside a ruined building; someone else hauled a bathtub on to a roof to collect rainwater. We do not know exactly how long it was after the earthquake, but the reconstruction project would come to an abrupt end. The first suggestion that something was amiss was probably another series of tremors. At this point, did the Minoans take flight again? Certainly, there is some evidence that they did. When archaeologists discovered their houses, there were few signs of human remains, or of gold, silver or other valuables, while household utensils and supplies were found in basement storerooms.

For any who did stay, the outlook would have been bleak. A first eruption covered the island with a light fall of pumice, rather like snow. Next came bigger lumps of rock. Then the top of that handsome, symmetrical mountain burst open, and a pillar of smoke and ash rose more than twenty miles into the air, with a bang that could be heard from Central Africa to Scandinavia, and from the Persian Gulf to Gibraltar. The explosion produced a great crater into which the sea flowed, forming the bay that is such a distinctive feature of Santorini today, with its towering cliffs coloured black, grey, pink and rust, around a 1,300-foot-deep sea bed. Thirty-two cubic miles of the island went up in smoke, and a white-hot avalanche descended from the sky on anything left alive on Santorini, covering the island with pumice and debris to a depth of 100 feet. Any of its inhabitants who had taken refuge on Crete would also have been in grave danger as the eruption sent giant waves up to 300 feet high dashing against its coast. Great palaces like the one at Knossos suffered terrible damage. Homes were wrecked, ships sank, and the land was choked and poisoned by vast clouds of pumice and ash, slashing food production. Many believe this disaster marked the beginning of the end of the Minoan civilisation.

It was one of the most powerful eruptions of all time, perhaps second only to Mount Tambora (see below) during the last 5,000 years. For centuries, Santorini remained unoccupied, until the Phoenicians settled there in about 1200 BC, but the area is still volcanically active. Today Thera, the biggest island of the archipelago, has two smaller neighbours nestling in its eight-mile bay – Palea Kameni ('Old Burned') and Nea Kameni ('New Burned') – both created by undersea eruptions. It was only in 1966 that archaeologists uncovered, almost intact, an ancient city near the modern town of Akrotiri. Entombed in solidified volcanic ash, it was dubbed 'the Pompeii of the Aegean'. There were streets and squares, three-storey houses with stone staircases, sewerage and drainage systems and beautiful wall paintings, showing wonderfully vivid and natural scenes of monkeys, fish merchants, elegant ladies and boxing children. Some believe Santorini was the lost land of Atlantis, described by Plato as a 'great and marvellous power, which held sway over all the island and many other islands', until one day 'there occurred portentous earthquakes and floods' so that 'the island of Atlantis was swallowed up by the sea and vanished'. And could the column of ash created by the eruption be the 'pillar of cloud' the Bible says God sent to guide Moses and the Israelites out of Egypt? Certainly, it would have been visible from the Nile as it stretched high into the atmosphere.

### · POMPEII ·

On Santorini, there is a well-preserved town frozen in time at the moment when disaster struck. But nobody knows for certain the fate of the inhabitants. Did they escape? If they did not, what did they think and feel as the cataclysm was about to engulf them? At Pompeii, there is another wonderfully preserved town on an even grander scale, but we also have a vivid account of how its people faced their doom.

By AD 79, a number of towns had sprung up around the base of Mount Vesuvius, thanks to the area's famously fertile soil. Few at the time seemed to suspect that the mountain was a volcano, even though it had actually erupted many times, once destroying a number of Bronze Age settlements. The area was also prone to earthquakes. One in AD 62 caused such widespread damage in Pompeii that seventeen years later it had not been completely repaired. But still the townsfolk refused to leave. Nor were they alarmed that the smoking caverns and volcanic steam geysers of the Phlegraean Fields, believed to be the doorway to Hades, were less than twenty miles from their homes. They were happy to go on harvesting the olives and fruit that grew in abundance on Vesuvius's slopes, while the brilliant sunshine tempered by cooling breezes tempted newcomers to build ever more opulent villas. The town boasted a 16,000-seat amphitheatre, magnificent public baths, and plush brothels and drinking houses.

The first signs of the disaster that was about to engulf them came in early August 79, when springs and wells started drying up. There were also reports of dogs, cats and livestock growing agitated. On 20 August, small earthquakes began shaking the ground. Pliny the Elder, Rome's greatest living expert on natural history, had arrived in the area a few weeks earlier to take command of the fleet stationed at Misenum, just over twenty miles from Vesuvius at the mouth of the Bay of Naples. Aged fifty-six, a little overweight and suffering from respiratory problems, he began 24 August in his usual way – an hour stretched out in the sun, followed by a quick plunge into cold water, then a hearty meal. He had just settled down to a few hours' reading when his sister burst in to say she had seen a huge, oddly shaped cloud in the sky to the north-east, and that it appeared to be going dark. His nephew, Pliny the Younger, then aged seventeen, would write that the cloud looked like 'a pine tree', shooting up to a great height and then spreading out at the top 'as though into branches'.

About midday, there was a roar like thunder as Vesuvius split open, belching out fire, ash, pumice and stones. Scientists now reckon that the eruption would have produced a column of smoke with a temperature of 850 degrees Celsius, soaring more than twenty miles into the sky. The explosion certainly would have set the ground shaking violently. A thick rain of ash fell, making the sun disappear and day turn to night. Pliny the Elder's reaction was just what his nephew would have expected: 'Like a true scholar, my uncle saw at once that it deserved closer study.' He decided to take a small flotilla out into the bay for a better view. The younger Pliny turned down an invitation to join him, saying he had to study. They set off eastwards across the bay and were soon being showered with thick clouds of hot cinders, while the admiral dictated his observations and comments to a scribe. As they tried to approach the shore, Pliny found the way blocked by pumice and rock from the eruption. The pilot urged him to turn back, but Pliny shouted, 'Fortune favours the brave!' and sailed on another three miles to Stabiae, where they landed. By now, many of the sailors were panicking, so, to try to calm them down, Pliny made a great show of taking a leisurely bath followed by a hearty dinner. The night, though, was even more terrifying than the day had been, with fearful booms and roars, and great sheets of fire flashing out of the mountain, while ash continued to fall.

By morning, 'the walls of the house were swaying with repeated violent shocks and seemed to move in one direction and then another'. Here was an agonising dilemma – should the sailors remain inside, and risk having the building collapse on top of them, or should they run the gauntlet of choking fumes and falling stones to reach their ships? They chose escape, trying to protect their heads with pillows. There was an overpowering stench of sulphur and so much ash in the air that they needed torches to see where they were going. When they arrived at the beach, the tremors were making the sea churn so violently that it tossed their ships around like toys. Twice the admiral called for water. Then he collapsed. Had the poisonous gas exacerbated his breathing problems, or was it a heart attack induced by his exertions? Whatever the cause, he died, but his comrades managed to escape and would tell the full story to his nephew. At Misenum, the younger Pliny and his mother had passed a restless night. The tremors had become 'so violent that it seemed the world was not only being shaken, but turned upside down', and the younger Pliny saw 'the sea sucked back, apparently by an earthquake, and many creatures were left stranded on the sand'.

Eventually they managed to flee along the coast, away from the vol-cano. Behind them, they saw 'a horrible black cloud ripped by sudden bursts of fire, writhing snakelike, and parting to reveal great tongues of fire larger than lightning', while the day grew as dark as 'a sealed room without lights'. They were nearly overwhelmed by a growing throng of groaning, crying and shouting fugitives: 'some loudly sought their par-ents, others their children, others again their spouses . . . many raised their arms to the gods, but still more said there were no more gods, and that this was the last night of the world'.

Pliny the Younger escaped to tell the tale, but many perished in Pompeii. Some must have been killed by direct hits from the eight-inch stones raining down on the town. Others would have been engulfed by the boiling mass of pumice and ash that coursed through the streets at sixty miles an hour. Others still were buried and suffocated in their own homes as ten-foot drifts of debris made their roofs collapse. The ash turned out to be an archaeologist's dream, forming a perfect mould of each corpse it encased, which was preserved even after the bodies them-selves had decayed. Such was the detail that facial expressions and even the folds of clothes were clearly visible. Remains of about 1,150 bodies have been found around Pompeii, out of a population of perhaps 20,000, suggesting that many realised the danger and fled in time. And this may have been one of those rare disasters in which the poor were more likely to survive than the rich, because those with least possessions to worry about were most likely to run away first. Vesuvius's wrath, though, afflicted a wide area of the countryside, so simply leaving Pompeii itself may not have been enough, and the turbulent sea whipped up by the volcano must also have drowned many.

Even nearer to Vesuvius than Pompeii was the seaside resort of Herculaneum, which had a population of about 5,000. It was probably engulfed by red-hot lava within five minutes of the great explosion. Scores, perhaps hundreds, of people took refuge in the town's celebrated baths which opened out on to the sea, only to find great waves crashing in on them just as the steaming avalanche from the mountain poured through the doors and windows of the town's buildings, ripping giant columns from their bases like matchsticks. Some parts of Herculaneum were buried fifty feet deep, but while Pompeii was covered with pumice and ash that could be shovelled away, the seaside town was left under a cement-like topping that could be removed only by laborious drilling and chiselling, protecting it from the treasure hunters who got to Pompeii before the archaeologists. A group of seven adults, four children and a baby were found huddled in a corner; one woman still had jewelled rings on her fingers. There were still loaves in bakers' ovens and family tables laden with eggs, fruit, walnuts and vegetables. A sick boy lay in bed with a plate of chicken untouched beside him. It is an astonishing picture of a community at the moment when disaster overtook it. Stabiae, where the elder Pliny spent his last night, was also buried by the eruption.

Vesuvius went on to erupt many more times, though not since 1944 and never so destructively as during that terrible August of AD 79.

## · ETNA ·

According to Greek legend, in a tale that may have been inspired by stories of the Santorini eruption (see above), Zeus once did battle with the great monster Typhon and 'the whole earth and firmament and sea boiled'. The myth ends with Zeus winning and imprisoning his adversary beneath Mount Etna on Sicily, only for Typhon to foment new volcanic mischief from his lair. Certainly, Etna has been one of the most active volcanoes in recorded history, erupting more than seventy times between

1500 BC and AD 1669. Its name comes from a Greek word meaning 'I burn'.

Etna stands nearly 11,000 feet high. One of the earliest descriptions we have of it comes from the Greek poet Pindar in 475 BC: 'The monster flings aloft the most fearsome fountains of fire, a marvel wondrous to behold or even to hear.' Seventy-nine years later, it was said to have halted the Carthaginian army then trying to conquer the island, while a particularly lethal outburst occurred in AD 1169, when 15,000 people were killed in the port of Catania alone.

The mountain's most violent known eruption, though, came precisely half a millennium later, in 1669. Etna had been spewing out stones and gas for weeks without causing any damage or injury. In March came an earthquake accompanied by what the Bishop of Catania called 'horrible roarings'. Then, three days later, there were 'three terrible eruptions'. Boulders shot into the air, and burning cinders and ash 'fell like a fiery rain'. The mountain had split open along a six-mile fissure. First in the firing line was the town of Nicolosi, though most of its inhabitants managed to escape. Before the end of the month two towns and several smaller settlements had been obliterated, and the mountain's thundering could be heard fifty miles away.

Refugees poured into Catania, where the people tried to appease an angry God by mounting a procession carrying holy relics, including those of St Agatha, the port's patron saint. Some lashed themselves with whips, but to no avail. By early April, the lava had reached the town's outskirts. On 23 April, it filled the harbour. More practical measures were needed, so a man named Diego Pappalardo assembled a task force of fifty locals, who wore wet cow-hides for protection against the intense heat and set off with shovels to try to divert the lava. It looked as though Catania's gain might be Paterno's loss, because if the course of the flow were successfully altered, it would threaten that town instead. The story goes that 500 Paterno men set on Pappalardo's 50 and forced them to abandon what was believed to be the first attempt in history to divert lava. It was quickly followed by a law forbidding any repetition.

The mission's failure meant that Catania once again lay at Etna's mercy. Lava piled up against the city walls until 30 April, when it breached them and they collapsed. Local people threw up barriers inside the town, which had some effect, but they could not save its western side from destruction. Officially, the death toll was 20,000, but many believe a figure of 100,000 is more realistic. Outside Catania, at least ten towns and villages were completely destroyed and many others were severely damaged. An area that had been full of rich orchards and fine villas for millennia was turned into a wasteland.

Since 1669, Etna has continued to erupt regularly. In 1852 it claimed many lives, while a four-month episode in 1983 alarmed the authorities so much they repealed the law forbidding interference with lava flows and tried to divert them with dynamite. An eruption of 2002–3 was used in the making of the *Star Wars* film *Revenge of the Sith*, with Etna cast as a feature of the fictional planet Mustafar.

## · LAKI ·

Like Toba (see above), the Laki volcano on Iceland killed people thousands of miles away when it erupted in 1783. Iceland has always been a land of spitting geysers and mysteriously grumbling mud. It sits on the mid-Atlantic ridge where two of the earth's great tectonic plates are pulling away from each other, and it has around 200 volcanoes. So the inhabitants may not have been particularly surprised when the first week of June brought a series of earthquakes. Then, at about nine o'clock on the morning of the day of Pentecost, Sunday 8 June, Laki began to erupt. A Lutheran pastor, Jon Steingrimsson, recorded his impressions: 'It began with the earth heaving upwards, with a great screaming and noise of wind from its depths, then splitting asunder, ripping and tearing as if a crazed animal were tearing something apart. Great slabs of rock were cast up indescribably high into the air.' There were crashes, flashes of fire, smoke and fumes. 'How fearsome it was', mused the pastor, 'to look upon the tokens and manifestations of God's wrath.'

The sides of the mountain had cracked open and lava was pouring out. One vulcanologist said it was as if the earth had been 'unzipped'. A stream of molten rock up to 600 feet deep filled up a nearby river gorge, then overflowed. On 18 June Laki ejected yet more lava at a temperature of 1,000 degrees Celsius, until the amount disgorged was reckoned to be as big as Mont Blanc. The fissure in the mountain was now fifteen miles

long, and Steingrimsson said the lava 'flowed with the speed of a great
river swollen with meltwater on a spring day . . . great cliffs and slabs of
rock were swept along, tumbling about like big whales swimming, red
hot and glowing'. Death came in many forms – from burning lava which
overwhelmed twenty villages, toxic fumes, or floods caused by blocked
rivers overflowing their banks. For Steingrimsson, though, the eruption
had one beneficial effect: it literally put the fear of God into people. He
noted that 'the worship of God and public church services were restored
to a much more respectable and religious order'. On 20 July the lava was
advancing menacingly on the village of Kirkjubæjarklaustur when the
pastor delivered what became famous as his 'fire sermon', while his flock
prayed earnestly for deliverance. When they emerged from the church,
they found that the flow had, astonishingly, stopped just one mile away.

However, this was not the miracle it first appeared to be. The eruptions
continued until the following February, by which time 218 square miles
were covered with lava. The volcano had also emitted a prodigious amount
of poison, including 120 million tons of sulphur dioxide – more than the
total emissions of every factory in modern-day Europe for three years – and
it fell to earth as sulphuric acid rain. 'The grass became yellow and pink
and withered down to the roots,' wrote Steingrimsson. 'The animals that
wandered around the fields got yellow-coloured feet with open wounds.'
Four-fifths of the sheep – about 190,000 of them – perished, as did half of
the cows and horses. Crops failed and fish disappeared from the polluted
coastal waters. People began to starve, with many reduced to gnawing on
boiled animal skins. In the end, about a quarter of Iceland's population –
perhaps 10,000 people – died as a direct result of Laki. Among them was
Steingrimsson's wife. It was decades before the island fully recovered.

But the volcano also claimed many more lives, far from the shores of
Iceland. As early as 10 June 1783, ash began to fall on Bergen in Norway;
then in Prague, a 'dry fog' was reported, while in Berlin the sun was
'coloured as if it had been soaked in blood'. Soon the fog had enveloped
France, and by the end of June it had reached Moscow and Baghdad. It
was first mentioned in Britain on 22 June. Twenty days later, the
*Edinburgh Advertiser* reported a 'thick dry fog' with an 'infectious smell'
that had covered 'the whole surface of Europe'. Ships could not venture
out from some ports because visibility was too poor, and the unnatural

haze was evident even high in the Alps. The fog also seemed to bring freak weather. From eastern England 'a most severe frost' was reported that severely damaged crops. Others spoke of a sun 'shorn of his beams'. The Hampshire clergyman and naturalist Gilbert White – one of the founding fathers of ecology in Britain – wrote that the summer of 1783 was 'an amazing and portentous one, and full of horrible phenomena'. The fog persisted for weeks, and White considered it 'unlike anything known within the memory of man. The sun at noon looked as blank as a clouded moon.' Benjamin Franklin, who was in Paris helping to negotiate the treaty that established the United States' independence, noted that when the sun's rays 'were collected in the focus of a burning glass, they would scarcely kindle brown paper'. Astutely, he suggested the 'vast quantity of smoke' emitted by Laki might be responsible. A French observer noticed that 'While the sun was obscured, there was a sickness that caused innumerable deaths.' A priest in a village near Chartres said a third of the men had been 'swept to their tombs'. At Broué, west of Paris, local people dragged their priest from his bed and made him perform an exorcism on the deadly cloud, while churches were said to be 'most unusually crowded'.

In England the poet William Cowper said people were asserting 'with great confidence' that the Day of Judgement was at hand. Workers began collapsing in the fields, and so many were ill, Cowper noted, that 'farmers have difficulty gathering their harvest; the labourers, having been almost every day carried out of the field, incapable of work, and many die'. It could be an agonising death, too. When sulphur dioxide is inhaled it turns into sulphuric acid, corroding the soft tissue of the lungs and causing the victim to choke. The death rate in Bedfordshire doubled in the autumn, and a similar picture began to emerge for the whole of eastern England. Meanwhile, all over Europe, there were torrential rains, flash floods, and huge hailstones that killed livestock – indeed, 'an almost universal perturbation in nature'. In faraway Alaska, the Kauwerak tribe would call 1783 'the year summer did not come'.

The turbulent summer and autumn were followed by one of the longest and most severe winters in 250 years, as the sulphur dioxide in the atmosphere continued to block the sun's rays. On 14 February 1784 Gilbert White said the frost had lasted twenty-eight days. On 4 April there was 'snow as deep as a horse's belly'. Then spring brought terrible floods of meltwater. The eastern United States also suffered one of its longest and coldest winters, with temperatures nearly five degrees below normal. Estimates for the number who died in Britain alone as a result of the Laki eruption range up to 30,000, with perhaps another 200,000 killed in the rest of Western Europe.

## · MOUNT ASAMA ·

On 5 August 1783, just two months after Laki went up in smoke, Mount Asama erupted on the main Japanese island of Honshu. Throughout the summer, the 8,000-foot volcano had been belching out smoke before it finally exploded with a terrifying roar, spewing lava, ash and rock over a wide area. The initial explosion killed perhaps 1,000 people, but the huge clouds of ash blotted out the sun and had temperatures plummeting across Japan for months after, bringing cold, wet weather and widespread crop failure. It was Asama's first major eruption since 1108, but now 1783 became known as the 'year without a summer' in Japan too.

Soon came reports of villagers living on roots and the bark of trees, and slaughtering their working animals for food, while there were many stories of desperate people eating human corpses. One military governor launched a mass relief effort, scrapping land taxes and bringing in rice and medicines. He saved many lives, but in other areas the authorities tried to increase taxation. Some villages lost up to a third of their inhabitants, and there was a riot in the port of Aomori as people tried to prevent rice being exported. Harvests did not recover until the end of the decade, and estimates for the number who died reach 1.2 million. Mount Asama remains active, erupting most recently in 2004.

## · TAMBORA ·

Indonesia has 150 volcanoes, and in 1815 one of them produced another 'year without a summer'. The people who lived on the island of Sumbawa, 1,500 miles from Lake Toba (see above), were famed for their honey, their horses, and their sandalwood, which was used in incense and medicine. Its 13,000-foot mountain, Tambora, was regarded as an extinct volcano by the Europeans who began to arrive in the islands in 1512. The first hint that they might have made a mistake came in 1812 as Tambora began to rumble. Two years later, it emitted small showers of ash. Then, on 5 April 1815, it erupted with a sound so thunderous it could be heard nearly 800 miles away on Java by Sir Stamford Raffles, at that time the military governor during a brief spell of British occupation. At first, everyone thought it was cannon fire, and a detachment of troops was sent to investigate.

Five days later, the bangs grew louder; now they could be heard on Sumatra, too. At seven o'clock that evening, three columns of flame rose from the mountain and merged into what seemed to be a mass of liquid fire. Eight-inch pumice stones rained down, and scorching lava flows cascaded to the sea on all sides, wiping out the tiny kingdom of Tambora, next to the mountain. The lava also destroyed all vegetation on Sumbawa. Uprooted trees were washed out to sea, making natural rafts up to three miles across. One was found off Calcutta (now Kolkota), 4,000 miles away, in October. The sky turned dark for more than 300 miles, and ash fell 800 miles away. The eruptions continued until July. Once they had finished, Tambora was 4,000 feet lower, having blasted about 1.7 million tons of ash and debris 28 miles into the air.

Raffles dispatched a Lieutenant Phillips to Sumbawa to investigate. He painted a grim picture: 'The extreme misery to which the inhabitants have been reduced is shocking to behold. There were still on the roadside the remains of several corpses, and the marks of where many others had been interred: the villages almost entirely deserted and the houses fallen down, the surviving inhabitants having dispersed in search of food.' A ship's captain in the area reported: 'a village was inundated, and had three fathoms of water over it. Great numbers of the miserable inhabitants have perished, and others die daily.' The rice crop had been 'utterly destroyed over a great part of the island, so that the situation of the unfortunate survivors will be really pitiable'. The immediate death toll on the island was about 12,000, but, as so often happens with volcanoes, worse was to come.

Tambora is now believed to have been the biggest volcanic eruption in recorded history – about four times as powerful as the much more famous one at Krakatoa (see below). Altogether, the starvation and disease that followed are thought to have accounted for perhaps 40,000 more victims on Sumbawa, and anything up to another 40,000 on the neighbouring island of Lombok.

Like Laki and Toba, it also affected weather patterns all over the world. Brown snow fell in Hungary and Maryland, red snow in Italy – all attributed to volcanic ash in the atmosphere. Many countries experienced spectacular sunsets, and in Britain they inspired the painter J.M.W. Turner. Meanwhile, the 'wet, ungenial summer' in Switzerland generated a great horror classic. Their holiday ruined, Percy and Mary Shelley and their friends had to find something to do to while away the long hours indoors at Lord Byron's house. They came up with a scary story competition, and eighteen-year-old Mary's entry was *Frankenstein*. The dreadful weather that contributed to Napoleon's defeat at Waterloo was also put down to Tambora.

The effects continued into the following year. Snow fell in England in July, and poor harvests brought bread riots in East Anglia and Dundee. In Wales, families had to leave their homes to go begging for food, and famine hit Ireland. French farmers taking their grain to market needed armed escorts to protect them from hungry mobs, and riots broke out in Poitiers, Toulouse and the Loire Valley. Across the Atlantic, a newspaper in Washington, D.C., complained that the sun's rays had lost 'their usual power', while June saw snowstorms in eastern Canada and New England that killed many people. Amid severe food shortages, soup kitchens had to be opened in Manhattan. Famine struck China's Yunnan province as the rice harvest was devastated; while in India poor harvests led to hunger and cholera. It is thought that global temperatures may have declined by as much as three degrees. According to one estimate, in Europe alone 200,000 people might have died as a result of the great chill, which was perhaps made worse by the eruptions of two other volcanoes – La Soufrière on St Vincent in the Caribbean and Mayon in the Philippines, which had both been active in the three years before Tambora exploded.

During the last few years, a team of American and Indonesian scientists has unearthed evidence of the 'lost kingdom of Tambora'. In 2006, buried under ten feet of debris, they found bronze bowls, ceramic pots, fine china, glass, and iron tools. They also discovered the frame of a house with two human skeletons: a woman in the kitchen, her hand next to some melted glass bottles, and a man just outside clutching a large knife. One of the team claimed Tambora could turn out to be 'the Pompeii of the East'.

Meanwhile, the volcano has demonstrated that it is only sleeping: its most recent, mercifully minor, eruption occurred in 1967.

## · KRAKATOA ·

Sixty-eight years after Tambora, Indonesia was rocked by another deadly eruption. And this one sent a whole island up in thin air. Tambora might have been more powerful, but Krakatoa was more deadly and became more famous. As with Tambora, most Europeans in what were then the Dutch East Indies believed Krakatoa, in the busy Sunda Strait between Java and Sumatra, was extinct. After all, there had been no recorded activity from the island's three cones since 1680, but early on the morning of 10 May 1883, the lighthouse keeper at First Point, standing at the Java entrance to the strait, felt a tremor, and the building shifted on its foundations. Five days later there was another, stronger tremor, which awoke Willem Beyerinck, a Dutch colonial official in the Sumatran town of Ketimbang. Before long, powerful tremors were being felt continuously on the Sumatran side of the strait.

Then, on the hot, cloudless morning of 20 May, the captain of a German warship saw a white cloud 'rising fast' from Krakatoa. After half an hour he reckoned it had reached a height of seven miles, before it 'spread like an umbrella so that soon only a small patch of blue sky was seen on the horizon'. Ash began to fall, and before long the ship was covered. To local people, it seemed obvious what had happened. They believed the mountain was home to a fire-breathing god, who must have grown angry. Eight fishermen had been on the island gathering wood to make boats when they heard loud bangs. They told Beyerinck's wife that at first they thought it was a Dutch man o' war on exercises in the strait, but then suddenly the beach had split open, and jets of black ash and red-hot stones had flown into the air. They had run for their lives and managed to swim out to their boats to escape.

After Beyerinck heard the story, he and his boss took out a launch to investigate. They had to fight their way through choking gas and huge waves tossing about broken trees. Perboewatan, the most northerly of the island's three cones, was erupting, the beach was belching fire and smoke, and the forests were ablaze. By now Krakatoa could be heard 500 miles away, while ash had already travelled 1,300 miles to Timor.

A week later, though, the volcano seemed to have quietened down, and eighty-six curious folk crowded on to the mail packet *Gouverneur-Generaal Loudon* to take a look. They found the island's rich tropical forests wiped out except for a few bare tree stumps, and smoke rising as if from an oven. Some of the more intrepid went ashore in a small boat, and found themselves wading calf-deep through hot ash. A few even climbed up to look at the crater, from which a column of smoke was rising.

For the next few weeks smoke continued to pour from Perboewatan, and ash blew into the skies. On 11 August the Dutch authorities sent an army captain, H.J.G. Ferzenaar, to investigate. By then, all three craters were erupting, and smoke was escaping from at least fourteen holes. The captain spent two days on the island, and would be the last human being to set foot there before it was changed for ever.

Over the next fortnight, ships in the strait continued to report alarming tremors, falls of ash turning the sea 'milk-white', and columns of smoke. By the afternoon of Sunday, 26 August, the ash was so thick that the town of Anjer on Java was plunged into premature night. For six hours, pumice rained down, and boats broke loose from their moorings. The British ship *Medea* reported the column of smoke was now seventeen miles high, and, even though she was eighty miles away, explosions shook her every ten minutes or so. To the east, in Jakarta, houses were shaking and windows shattering. Foul-smelling smoke choked the city, and people began to flee.

For a time on that Sunday, a British cargo ship en route to Hong Kong, the *Charles Bal*, was only ten miles from the volcano. Those on board were probably the closest human beings to survive the explosion that would destroy Krakatoa. The commander, Captain Watson, reported hearing what sounded like 'the discharge of heavy artillery at one or two seconds' interval'. At five o'clock debris began to pelt down. It was a 'fearful' night: 'the blinding fall of sand and stones, the intense blackness above and around us, broken only by the incessant glare of various kinds of lightning, and the continued explosive roars of Krakatoa'. At eleven o'clock, the volcano shone out of the darkness as 'chains of fire appeared to ascend and descend between it and the sky'. Fortunately, by the next morning the ship was thirty miles away, but missiles continued to rain down on her, and at noon it was so dark that the crew had to grope their way around the deck. Twelve hours later, they had managed to put seventy-five miles between themselves and the volcano, but they could still hear its roar. Miraculously, no one on board was hurt, but those on shore were undergoing a terrible ordeal.

Krakatoa's convulsions tugged the sea back and forth, producing tsunamis with waves 130 feet high. Their first victims were probably a group of Chinese labourers still stoically hewing stone in a quarry near Merak on Java despite the terrifying noises, the flames and the clouds of ash. At half past seven on Sunday evening, the quarry was flooded and they all drowned. During the evening and night, the water also swept away a number of villages, and by early Monday morning Ketimbang was completely flooded. Beyerinck's family and servants escaped by shinning up coconut palms as the surge came, then fleeing inland when the waters receded, to escape the next wave. One man who had been asleep at home was said to have awoken in his bed on top of a hill.

At dawn, an elderly Dutch pilot at Anjer saw a 'low range of hills rising out of the sea'. As the great wave burst upon the shore, he too survived by climbing a palm tree, but others were not so lucky: 'there floated past the dead bodies of many a friend and neighbour. Only a handful of the population escaped'. Meanwhile, the *Gouverneur-Generaal Loudon* was being bounced up and down by the sea off Sumatra. A passenger said the ship would make 'a formidable leap, and immediately afterwards we felt as though we had plunged into the abyss'. Around this time the biggest port in south Sumatra disappeared: 'where a few moments ago lived Telok Betong was nothing but the open sea'. One European ran for his life and survived, but he saw many others who failed. One was a woman who stumbled and dropped her baby. As she stooped to pick up the infant, both were washed away. The wave grabbed hold of a gunboat and dumped it a mile and a half inland, killing all twenty-eight crew on board. The *Loudon* eventually made it back to Anjer, but the port was nowhere to be seen. She picked up whatever survivors she could find. At nine o'clock, the wave hit Merak and killed all but two of the town's 2,700 inhabitants. Among those who died were hundreds sheltering in stone buildings on top of a 115-foot-high hill.

A 600-ton lump of coral was dashed against the lighthouse at Anjer, demolishing it and killing the keeper's wife and child. He stayed at his post, hanging out a lantern for any passing ships. Sebesi Island to the north of Krakatoa was submerged, and all its 3,000 inhabitants drowned. A rice farmer, five miles from the sea on Java, was caught up in a frantic battle to survive. There was a dreadful noise, then he saw 'a great black thing' coming towards him. 'It was very high and very strong, and we soon saw that it was water. Trees and houses were washed away.' Everyone tried to scramble up high ground to escape, but many drowned as they got wedged together in the rush. People 'struggled and fought, screaming and crying out all the time. Those below tried to make those above them move on again by biting their heels . . . some dragged others down with them'.

At two minutes past ten came Krakatoa's final eruption, said to be the loudest noise ever heard by modern man. Equivalent to the power of 1,000 atomic bombs, it rang out over one-twelfth of the globe. In Singapore, 500 miles away, the locals could not hear themselves speak because of 'a perfect roar, as of a waterfall'. The bang could also be heard nearly 3,000 miles away on the island of Rodrigues in the Indian Ocean – the longest distance such a sound has ever travelled. It took four hours to get there, and the local police chief reported hearing 'the distant roar of heavy guns'. Clouds of smoke and white-hot pumice were hurled twenty-four miles into the air, and came to rest over an area bigger than France, giving the tropical city of Jakarta a strange wintry hue. Krakatoa itself disappeared as eleven cubic miles of rock were vaporised.

There have been at least four volcanic eruptions bigger than Krakatoa, but it was the most deadly because of the tsunamis it generated. The tallest waves were higher than those of 2004's Boxing Day tsunami (see Chapter 3), though they did not travel such great distances. In all, 165 villages were devastated and more than 36,000 people were killed; only 37 of them were Europeans. The disaster virtually wiped out the population on the shores of the Sunda Strait, and 6,500 boats were sunk. Willem Beyerinck and his wife survived, but their child died from the burning heat and the poisonous gas. A crewman on one ship said that for two days after passing Anjer, they were sailing through bodies – 'groups of 50 and 100 all packed together'. The waves carried death as far away as Sri Lanka, where a woman was swept into a harbour and drowned. Great chunks of pumice, sometimes forming natural rafts with the skeletons of victims, floated around the seas, bringing havoc to shipping lanes up to 7,500 miles away. On the beach at Zanzibar, human bones and the remains of two Sumatran tigers were washed ashore.

While it took months for some parts of the outside world to hear about Tambora, news of Krakatoa was on the front page of the *Boston Globe* within four hours. The intervening years had witnessed a telecommunications revolution, with undersea telegraph cables carrying Morse code across oceans, and a Lloyd's agent had managed to get word of the eruption out just before the tsunami snapped the connection.

In 1928 a new volcano began to rise from the sea where Krakatoa had once stood. By 2000, Anak Krakatoa, 'Krakatoa's child', had grown to 1,300 feet, and scientists believe that one day it will erupt just as violently as its fearsome parent did. They now monitor all Indonesia's volcanic activity very carefully. With the population much greater than it was in the nineteenth century, any repeat of Tambora or Krakatoa would be even more catastrophic.

## · MONTAGNE PELÉE ·

At the beginning of the twentieth century, St Pierre on the Caribbean island of Martinique was known as 'the Paris of the West Indies'. The biggest town on the island, it boasted an imposing cathedral, a prestigious school and 26,000 inhabitants – whites, blacks, mulattos; some very rich, some very poor. There were cafés, dance halls and a theatre to which producers from the original Paris brought their shows. St Pierre had become a popular resort for Europeans and Americans; one visitor called it 'the sweetest, queerest, darlingest little city'. It featured brightly coloured stucco houses with palm trees that rose into the clear blue sky from gardens and back yards. Women in vivid robes negotiated steep alleys with exotic names like Climb-to-Heaven Street, while clear mountain water tinkled along in little streams, and the air was scented with cinnamon, mango and coconut.

One of the many delightful things to do on a sunny day was to picnic on the slopes of Montagne Pelée, 'Bald Mountain', which rose steeply above the town. The local Carib people had another name for it, though: they called it 'Fire Mountain' because in ancient times it had been a volcano. Now the town's 4,000-foot neighbour steamed and puffed occasionally like an old man smoking a pipe, and a minor eruption in 1851 had dusted St Pierre's prosperous suburbs with ash, but the locals regarded it rather like a tamed beast. In April 1902, though, the beast started to grumble, and sulphurous fumes began seeping from small holes near its summit. On 23 April there were earth tremors. Over the next two days, Pelée started blasting rocks and ash high into the sky, and on the 26th St Pierre again found itself under a light covering of ash.

The following day, a few brave souls ventured up the mountain and heard ominous sounds, like a giant cauldron bubbling underground. By now, St Pierre smelled more of rotten eggs than of coconut and mango. On 2 May there were louder bangs and fiercer tremors, a huge pillar of black smoke began rising, and ash covered the whole northern half of the island. Farm animals started to die as grass and water were contaminated: the wife of the US consul complained the fumes were so strong that horses were dropping dead in their harnesses. Wild creatures, meanwhile, grew restless: the local sugar factory was invaded by a great swarm of ants and foot-long centipedes, which bit the horses, while poisonous snakes began slithering through the streets. Soldiers were called in to shoot them, but not before dozens of people had been bitten.

Now the island's governor, Louis Mouttet, appeared in town, ostensibly to assess the situation. In fact, he had a hidden agenda. Important local elections were due to be held in a week's time, and he did not want them disrupted by people fleeing St Pierre, so he appointed a commission to investigate the volcano. Although the only person on the commission with any scientific experience was a local schoolteacher, it confidently reported that 'the safety of St Pierre is completely assured'. The local newspaper, *Les Colonies*, did its bit by printing soothing editorials, but, as ash continued to fall and the mountain carried on rumbling, not everyone was convinced. Shops and businesses started to shut down, while thousands of terrified refugees who lived on the mountain's slopes appeared in the town's bars and hotels demanding shelter. On 5 May the electricity supply failed, and dead birds were seen bobbing about in the sea. Then boiling mud began to flow down Mt Pelée, towards the local sugar works. The owner, Auguste Guerin, said he heard 'an immense noise – like the devil on earth! A black avalanche, beneath white smoke, an enormous mass, full of huge blocks,' 30 feet high and 150 yards wide was coming down the mountain. The steaming mud passed within ten yards of him. He felt 'its deathly breath. There was a great crashing sound. Everything was crushed, drowned and submerged.' His son, daughter-in-law and thirty other people were killed. The factory was buried beneath 'an expanse of mud forming a black shroud for my son, his wife and my workmen'. But this was only the beginning.

Despite the efforts of the port authorities to detain the ship, a barque had already left the harbour with only half of her cargo loaded, and some of St Pierre's wealthier citizens were starting to flee. But the next day the governor stationed troops on the roads out of town to stop the exodus, while *Les Colonies* managed to unearth a tame professor who told everyone once again that there was no danger. Mt Pelée did not appear to have heard, though, and all through 7 May its unruliness continued. Now news came through that the volcano La Soufrière had erupted on nearby St Vincent, killing 1,600 people.

The next day was Ascension Day, and it dawned bright and sunny, but as one of Martinique's leading planters, Fernand Clerc, was having breakfast with his wife, four children and friends, he noticed the needle on the barometer swinging wildly. Just after seven o'clock, he and his family fled St Pierre in a carriage. His friends accused him of being alarmist, and insisted on staying. Forty-five minutes later, the Clercs reached their country house, three miles away. In St Pierre, people were gathering in the churches for eight o'clock mass. There were eighteen vessels in the harbour, including the Canadian steamship *Roraima*, with sixty-eight people aboard. The captain was anxious to leave, but his passengers crowded on the deck to watch Pelée in action. It was quite a show, with enormous clouds of black smoke hanging over the mountain, and flames spurting up, accompanied by a constant muffled roar.

At eight minutes to eight, in Clerc's words, the cloud on top of Pelée 'seemed to topple over with a loud noise and tumble into the city'. It was like 'a great torrent of black fog', and in its wake came a sheet of flame.

The terrifying sight was accompanied by staccato beats, 'something like the throbbing, pulsating roar of a Gatling-gun battery going into action'. Hot ash began to rain down the hillside, blotting out the sun. Pelée had exploded. By now, the *Roraima* was 400 yards from shore. Assistant Purser Thompson recounted: 'There was no warning. The side of the volcano was ripped out and then hurled towards us like a solid wall of flame. It sounded like 1,000 cannons. The wave of fire was on us and over us like a lightning flash . . . The town vanished before our eyes.' As people in church heard the roar, they ran out and knelt in the street. There had actually been two explosions: one that shot upwards from the main crater, and a second that blew out sideways. The 1,000-degree cloud had reached St Pierre in less than a minute, igniting everything it touched. On the quay, thousands of bottles of rum exploded. People were killed instantly. According to Thompson, 'After the explosion, not one living being was seen on land,' and the mushroom cloud covered the sky with a fifty-mile-wide umbrella of darkness.

In the harbour, more than a dozen ships were destroyed, burned by the blast or sunk by the great wave that followed it. Chief Officer Ellery Scott said the *Roraima* heeled right over to port, 'then with a sudden jerk she went to starboard, plunging her lee rail far under water'. The ship's masts and funnel were removed 'as if they had been cut by a knife', and fires broke out on her deck. Thompson survived by burying himself under bedding in his cabin. A lady's maid told of how her mistress had seen two of her three children burned to death before she 'handed me some money, told me to take Rita [the surviving child] to her aunt, and sucked a piece of ice before she died'. Scott looked for the captain, but at first did not recognise him because he was so badly burned. The skipper told him to compile a report on the state of the ship, but Scott never saw him again. Although many of the surviving crew members had had the flesh burned from their hands, the chief officer managed to assemble a team of four who carried buckets between their elbows to fight the flames. Only about twenty of those on-board survived. On other ships, boiling ash coated men's clothes from head to foot and baked them alive. Some jumped overboard, sizzling as they entered the water.

The Comte de Fitz-James was fortunate to be on a vessel further out to sea, and he saw it all: 'From the depths of the earth came rumblings, an awful music that cannot be described.' Some ships were destroyed 'by a breath of fire', while others like the cable ship *Grappler* 'keeled over in the whirlwind, and sank as though drawn down into the waters of the harbour by some force from below'. The following day Fitz-James joined a landing party hoping to help those on shore, but they could find no one alive – 'we called aloud, and only the echo of our voices answered us'. They came upon bodies with their clothes ripped from them as if by a cyclone; some were burned beyond recognition; others had not a mark on them. St Pierre had been reduced to a mass of smoking rubble, with trees stripped of their bark, and metal roofs ripped off and crumpled like paper. Everywhere there were huge stones 'that seemed to be marvels of strength, but when touched with the toe of a boot, they crumbled into impalpable dust'.

There were survivors, though – just three of them. A twenty-eight-year-old shoemaker, Léon Compère-Léandre, had been sitting on his doorstep when he felt a terrible wind: 'the earth began to tremble, and the sky suddenly became dark'. It was only three or four strides into the house, but he found them a terrible struggle. His whole body seemed to be burning. Three or four other people came in 'crying and writhing with pain', but soon they were all dead. 'Crazed and almost overcome', he threw himself on the bed, 'inert and awaiting death'. A few minutes later, he had recovered enough to see the roof was on fire, and although his legs were bleeding and he was covered in burns, he managed to drag himself the four miles to a neighbouring village and safety. He probably survived because his house was on the edge of the scorching cloud.

An even more astonishing escape was that of a young girl named Havivra Da Ifrile. She had been running an errand for her mother when she noticed lava coming from a small crater on the side of the volcano: 'it followed the road first, but then as the stream got bigger, it ate up the houses on both sides of the road'. Then she saw 'a boiling red river' that was coming from another part of the hill and cutting off the escape of people who were trying to run away. She raced to the shore and jumped into a small boat. When she looked back, 'the whole side of the mountain which was near the town seemed to open and boil down on the screaming people'. Burned by falling stones and ash, she passed out but was eventually plucked from her charred boat by a French cruiser two miles out at sea.

The most amazing story of all, though, concerns Auguste Cyparis, a twenty-five-year-old stevedore, who was in solitary confinement in St Pierre's jail, waiting to be executed for murder. He suddenly heard people screaming: 'Help! Help! I'm burning! I'm dying!' Five minutes later, he said, 'Nobody was crying out any more – except me.' A cloud of scalding smoke rushed in through the tiny window of his cell, and burned him: 'I was dancing up and down, left and right – everywhere – to get out of its way . . . I listened and shouted for help, but nobody answered.' For three days, he said, 'I smelled nothing but my own body burning . . . I heard nothing but my own unanswered cries for help.' Then his moaning reached the ears of rescuers, who found him. The door of Ciparis's cell was so low it could be entered only on all fours, while the solitary window was small and heavily grilled, and quickly got blocked by fallen debris as the prison walls collapsed. It was this high-security construction that probably saved the convict's life. After his ordeal, the authorities freed him, and he began a new career with Barnum & Bailey's circus, sitting in a replica of his cell as the 'lone' survivor of the 'Silent City of Death'.

It took days for the fires to stop, and weeks to bury the dead. Then nature took over, with luxuriant vegetation covering much of what had been the Paris of the West Indies. There was some rebuilding: fishermen erected huts along the waterfront and a small village grew up; but it was nothing like the old St Pierre. Pelée erupted again in 1929, and undid most of the new inhabitants' handiwork. Today the town has only about 5,000 inhabitants.

### · NEVADO DEL RUIZ ·

The snow-capped Nevado del Ruiz stands 18,000 feet high in the Colombian Andes and forms part of the notorious 'Ring of Fire' around the Pacific, which contains three-quarters of the world's active volcanoes. In 1845 it triggered mudslides and floods in the surrounding valleys, killing about 1,000 people. But that eruption provided fertile soil for cotton, rice, coffee and other crops, and the region prospered. The volcano then behaved impeccably for well over a century, yet some local people still called it 'the sleeping lion', and in 1984 a group of mountaineers said they had felt minor tremors and seen fumes rising from its peak. Throughout the spring and summer of 1985, it continued to shake, then in September it spat out a mixture of steam, rock and ash, causing a fifteen-mile mudslide.

The prosperous farming community of Armero lay thirty miles east of the volcano. In October, Colombian geologists produced a report saying it and other towns around the mountain's base were in imminent danger, while a team of Italian vulcanologists urged the government to begin civil defence preparations, warning that 'the worst may be yet to come', but as the days went by and nothing sinister happened, interest started to wane. Then, just after three o'clock on the afternoon of 13 November, Nevado del Ruiz exploded violently, showering pumice fragments and ash down on Armero. The citizens were pacified, though, by a reassuring radio broadcast from the mayor and calming messages from the local priest over a public address system. At seven o'clock, the Red Cross did order everyone to leave the town, but soon after the ash stopped falling and the evacuation was cancelled.

Just two hours later there were two very loud explosions, and within the next half hour a column of steam and ash shot nearly seven miles into the air. Molten rock began to pour out for the first time, and the ice cap started to melt. Unfortunately, clouds prevented the people in the villages below from seeing the melting ice and debris forming into fifty-foot-deep mudslides that began careering down the mountain at more than thirty miles an hour in all directions. One of these buried the village of Chinchina, killing nearly 2,000 people. A number of other villages were swept away. Armero lay defenceless on a plain by the side of the River Lagunilla, which was already swollen by three days of heavy rain. As the mudslide poured along its course, it burst its banks.

The water swept into town at eleven o'clock, when most people were either asleep or getting ready for bed. A geology student on a field trip, José Luis Restrepo, was staying at a hotel. He and his friends were listening to the local radio station that had broadcast the mayor's reassuring message when suddenly it fell silent. Fifteen seconds later, the lights went out. They ran outside into complete darkness. 'A river' came down the street, 'dragging along beds, overturning cars, sweeping people away'. They ran back to the hotel, which seemed sturdily built. Then, suddenly, they heard bangs and saw 'a wall of mud' which crashed into the back of the building. Walls and ceilings collapsed until it was completely destroyed. A sea of debris peppered with boulders razed Armero like 'a wall of tractors'. As he tried to get away, José Luis felt his feet sinking into hot mud, but he managed to escape.

Another survivor said the mudslide made 'a moaning sound like some sort of monster. It seemed like the end of the world.' It swallowed 80 per cent of the town's buildings, entombing many people who never knew what had hit them, and cut down those who tried to flee. Outside the town, a Reuters news agency correspondent described seeing survivors huddled on a cold, bare hilltop: 'deathly figures – old men, women, and children, caked in dried grey mud, their hair stiff, only their eyeballs visible in the night to suggest they were still alive'. When relief workers arrived in Armero the next day, they found a tangle of trees, cars and mutilated bodies in an ocean of mud. A few injured survivors lay moaning. Rescuers had to build bridges of corrugated iron on the mud to reach them. More than thirty-six hours after the disaster, thousands on the hilltop, terrified of what Nevado del Ruiz might do next, still had no food, water or medical help. Army helicopters started to airlift people out, with one woman nursing her baby as she was hoisted up. But the Reuters reporter reckoned he personally saw a dozen die as they waited to be rescued. The helicopters could only function during daylight hours, so as the skies darkened there was a desperate struggle for the last few places.

Altogether at least 25,000 people, including three-quarters of the population of Armero, were killed. The hot mud acted as a giant incubator for germs, so that many of those who survived the initial mudslide with no more than a few cuts later died from infected wounds. The eruption had been relatively small, but the mudslide turned it into the worst volcanic disaster of the twentieth century after Montagne Pelée. Eight thousand of those who died were children. Almost immediately bitter recriminations began, with survivors claiming that many lives could have been saved if the experts' warnings had been heeded. There were also complaints that the local rescue teams were poorly trained and equipped, lacking thermal imaging and sonar equipment to search for people buried in the mud.

# 2

## EARTHQUAKES

Antioch, now Antakya in Turkey, was once known as the 'Fair Crown of the Orient', a rich, cosmopolitan city perched on key trading routes between East and West. It was the third-biggest city in the Roman Empire, and later the commercial centre of the Byzantine Empire. Antioch had wide paved streets lit by oil lights, marble colonnades, ornate public baths and amphitheatres. Its richly decorated octagonal cathedral was the envy of the world, and beautiful mosaic floors adorned houses where people dined off silver plates and drank from crystal goblets. In Greek mythology, this was where Daphne, pursued by Apollo, saved her virtue by turning herself into a laurel tree. According to Christian tradition, Matthew wrote his gospel here, and it was where St Paul began his mission. It was also where the word 'Christian' was first applied to the followers of Jesus.

But Antioch had a major drawback. It was prone to earthquakes. One in AD 115 nearly killed the Emperor Trajan and the future Emperor Hadrian. Believing it had happened because Roman gods were angry about the spread of Christianity in the city, Trajan had Antioch's bishop taken in chains to Rome and thrown to wild animals in the Colosseum.

Four centuries later, the Christians were in charge, and on 29 May 526 Antioch was even livelier than usual because thousands of them had flocked there for the feast of the Ascension the following day. At six in the evening, according to the contemporary scholar Procopius, there was 'an exceedingly violent earthquake, which shook down the whole city'. It appears to have struck so suddenly that most people had no chance to escape. A wave of aftershocks followed, then fire enveloped the city, so that those who had survived the initial quake now risked being burned to death. Another chronicler, John Malalas, who survived the disaster, wrote that it was as if the fire 'had received a commandment from God that every living thing should be burned . . . Not a single dwelling, nor house of any sort, no church, nor monastery, nor any other holy place was left unruined.' The great cathedral stood against the flames for five days, 'after everything else had fallen by the wrath of God'. Then it too caught fire 'and collapsed to the ground'.

Up to 300,000 people died, many starving or bleeding to death trapped beneath the rubble, and some who escaped fell prey to bandits who, having stripped and robbed the dead, turned their attentions to the living, killing anyone who dared to resist. They also looted the ruins. The most infamous thief was said to have been a government official who used his slaves to amass a fortune during the days following the disaster. Then, suddenly, he collapsed and died without warning. There were also reportedly a series of miracles. Three days after the earthquake, survivors looked up to see a vision of the Holy Cross floating in the sky. It hovered for an hour as people fell to their knees and prayed. Malalas claimed that pregnant women who had been trapped now emerged 'with newborn infants unscathed'. There were many other extraordinary events 'which no human tongue can express, and of which only the immortal God knows the secret', but none of this altered the fact that 'Antioch the Great' had been flattened.

Malalas said that as soon as the Emperor, Justinian the Great, heard the news, 'he took off his crown and the purple robe . . . and wept'. He then embarked on a massive reconstruction project, but the aftershocks continued for a year, and people began to drift away. In November 528 there was another full-scale earthquake which killed a further 5,000 people and demolished buildings that had just been restored. Some survivors inscribed above their doors, 'Christ is with us – stand,' but most people fled. Justinian even tried changing Antioch's name to Theopolis, the City of God, but its misfortunes continued. In 540 it was captured and sacked by the Persians, and two years later it was ravaged by plague (see Chapter 7). After another four earthquakes, it was conquered by the Arabs in 636. Only in the 1930s was the true glory of the ancient city revealed as archaeologists discovered wonders that had lain buried for more than a thousand years.

## · IRAN AND SYRIA ·

The Middle East has suffered many devastating earthquakes. One in northern Iran on 22 December 856 is said to have killed 200,000 people along a 200-mile stretch of fertile land. The ancient city of Shahr-i-Qumis was flattened and probably abandoned, while at Damghan, a city still famous for producing almonds with paper-thin shells, more than 45,000 died. Two generations later, the damage was still apparent. Iran has often been devastated since then, too. A quake in the Tabriz region in 1780 killed another 200,000, while as recently as 2003 26,000 died in the city of Bam. The latter was the thirteenth major earthquake in the country in just thirty years.

Aleppo in Syria is one of the world's oldest cities. It also sits over the meeting point of two tectonic plates – the Arabian and the African. Three times in the tenth century it was shaken by earthquakes. Then, on 11 October 1138, came one of the most devastating the world has ever seen. It destroyed a huge crusader castle at Harim and a nearby church. A Muslim fort called Atharib was also flattened, killing 600 guards, though the governor and some of his servants managed to escape. Some of Aleppo's inhabitants had taken fright at tremors that preceded the main earthquake and left the city, which, according to contemporary accounts, was totally destroyed, as were a number of other towns. Altogether, 230,000 people are said to have died.

## · THE GREAT EARTHQUAKE OF 1202 ·

Perhaps the most destructive earthquake of all time struck the eastern Mediterranean in July 1202. According to some estimates, it killed up to 1.1 million people, devastating Upper Egypt, Syria, Iraq and Palestine, and it may have been felt as far away as Armenia and Cyprus. Damascus, Tyre and Nablus (where 30,000 are said to have been killed) were all severely damaged. The walls of Acre and Tripoli fell, while some of the wonderful Roman remains at Baalbek in Lebanon were damaged. Many crusaders thought it was the harbinger of the Last Judgement, especially as Jerusalem seemed to have been spared. When they found that Egypt was also being stalked by a fearful famine (see Chapter 9), some decided it was time to go home.

## · CHINA ·

China sits on the Pacific's 'Ring of Fire' – the site not just of most of the world's volcanoes, but also of many of its earthquakes. The first to be recorded there occurred in 1831 BC, while one of the deadliest came in AD 1556, devastating ten provinces and killing no fewer than 830,000 people. It happened on the morning of 23 January, with its epicentre in Shaanxi province, an important trading and financial area. Although there have been many stronger earthquakes in China, this one was particularly lethal because it struck a densely populated area where many people lived in man-made caves dug into soft cliffs. These collapsed immediately, killing up to 60 per cent of the population in some areas, but cave-dwellers were not the only victims. In the city of Huaxian, every single building came down, killing more than half the inhabitants, while elsewhere people fell into sixty-foot crevasses that opened in the earth or were buried under landslides. A chronicler in Hua county wrote: 'the ground suddenly rose up and formed new hills, or it sank in abruptly and became new valleys . . . Huts, official houses, temples and city walls collapsed.' A scholar named Qin Keda survived the earthquake. He deplored what he considered the foolishness of those who tried to escape. In his view, people should 'just crouch down and wait. Even if the nest is collapsed, some eggs may still be kept intact.' It is not clear whether those who sat tight did any better than those who tried to run for it. Fires burned for days after the quake, and with many people having to live out in the open, there was plenty of robbery and looting.

The earthquake that struck Gansu province on 16 December 1920 was more powerful – 8.6 on the Richter scale against an estimated 8.3 for the 1556 disaster – but it killed fewer people: 180,000. A further 20,000, though, are said to have perished through lack of shelter during the winter months that followed. At Ping-Liang one resident said, 'We thought all the artillery of Heaven was let loose, and the floor and the earth seemed as if they were big waves.' Just as in 1556, many of those killed had been living in man-made caves. Food stores were buried and flour mills destroyed, so hunger added to the suffering of survivors. Just seven years after this earthquake, another struck the region around Xining, claiming 200,000 victims.

## · SICILY ·

The same fault lines in the earth's crust generate volcanic eruptions and earthquakes, and Sicily has been the victim of both. The island has often suffered from the activities of Mount Etna (see Chapter 1), but in the dying days of 1908 it was an earthquake that caused devastation. The first tremor struck at twenty past five on the morning of 28 December. A London ship-broker staying at a hotel in the port of Messina was jolted awake, and felt he was 'falling through space'. Then came a series of awful crashes: 'I was smothered in brick and plaster . . . I felt for matches, struck a light, and was horrified to find my bed on the side of an abyss.' He managed to escape by knotting sheets together and climbing down. Other guests jumped out of the hotel's windows but did not survive the fall. Another guest woke up when the roof collapsed. He found himself trapped, unable to move his hands or his feet, but he noticed a faint ray of light near his head. It appeared to be blocked by a curtain, so he bit a hole through it, then managed to shout loud enough to attract the attention of rescuers. A local man named Francesco Calabresi said the earth 'rocked from side to side as if it were in pain'. His house collapsed, imprisoning him and his family, but he managed to crawl out through a small hole in the wall, then help the others escape.

The tremors' epicentre was under the Straits of Messina that divide Sicily from the Italian mainland. Messina's old cathedral and the military hospital collapsed, as did the army barracks, where 800 men died. Meanwhile, forty railway workers perished in the ruins of the station. When the walls of the jail fell down, many of the 650 prisoners were killed or injured; survivors made their escape. In spite of Sicily's history of earthquakes, many an ostentatious villa had been built with flimsy walls of pebbles and rubble bound with inferior cement, then faced with brick or stone. An American visitor wrote: 'The great palaces of the rich proved fatal deathtraps.' Sometimes, when they crashed down, they also destroyed more humble dwellings near by.

One survivor described seeing a family crazed with grief and terror huddling under an umbrella in the remains of their house. They refused all help, saying they preferred to die among the ruins, but, according to *The Times*, thousands of others abandoned their homes 'and remained in the torrential rain, half-naked, not daring to return into their tottering dwellings, and filling the air with their lamentations'. Some dashed into churches to save statues of saints and carry them in procession into the countryside. Others went to the mountains, where 'peasants, priests, soldiers and gentlefolk' could all be found sheltering together in caves.

Back in Messina, looters were pillaging shops and warehouses and rummaging through the pockets of corpses, but even law-abiding citizens had to forage wherever they could for food, water and clothing. Soldiers guarded any banks that had survived, but that did not deter two men who were shot dead trying to mount a robbery. British, Italian and Russian naval vessels arrived off Messina within a few hours of the disaster, and the sailors played a brave and crucial role in the rescue operation. Three generations of Francesco Calabresi's family had spent two days in the cold and rain without shelter when a group of Russian sailors – 'angels', according to Francesco – gave them food and clothing and arranged for them to be taken to the mainland. Russian sailors also joined with crewmen from a Welsh steamer to help people trapped in upper floors climb down ropes and ladders. Under a heap of rubble, the commander of a Russian cruiser found two babies safe and well, 'laughing and playing with the buttons on their clothes', while soldiers rescued a man, his wife and eight children who had been shivering for two days among the ruins. They had survived on bread, wine and a bottle of cognac salvaged from the ruins of a shop. A number of sailors were killed, including a Russian crushed by a collapsing wall as he carried a girl's body from the ruins of the town hall. Sometimes rescuers had to beat a retreat in the face of the 'desperadoes' who were pillaging the town, though the Russian sailors in particular were admired for their courage in standing up to the looters. Ships in the harbour found themselves surrounded by boats filled with desperate people begging for food or a passage to safety. One Russian cruiser picked up 1,000. Some were turned into floating hospitals, and sailors also put up tents for refugees on shore.

In Calabria, on the mainland, most of the town of Reggio was in ruins. Like Messina, it had to be put under martial law because of looters, and the townspeople killed all the dogs and cats in case they went mad with hunger and fright. The whole coast was covered with deep mud, and refugees were often found wandering half naked up to thirty miles from their homes, 'among them even delicate girls', as *The Times* put it. Many young children froze to death, and there were 'numerous cases of raving madness'. The newspaper also reported that along the road from Reggio to Lazzaro all the houses had disappeared, the orange groves had been destroyed, and huge areas were flooded by a tidal wave created by the quake. One of the places worst hit was Bagnara, a town of 10,000, which was completely destroyed. A number of ships were also sunk. Altogether, it is estimated that up to 90,000 died in Messina, 40,000 in Reggio di Calabria, and another 27,000 in the towns and villages on both sides of the straits.

Money for the relief effort poured in from all over Europe, and the Americans chartered a liner to distribute food and medical help. Two days after the disaster King Victor Emmanuel and Queen Elena of Italy both arrived in Messina to help. The queen 'rolled up her sleeves, put on her apron, and went to work' nursing the sick and injured. The city was rebuilt with wide streets and reinforced concrete buildings, but many of the survivors who had lost homes, friends and family were not there to see it, having departed to seek a new life in other parts of Italy or America.

## · TOKYO ·

Like China, Japan is also on the Pacific 'Ring of Fire', sitting on the meeting point of two great tectonic plates – the Philippine Sea and the North American. On the last day of 1703 Tokyo, then known as Edo, was hit by an earthquake that brought its wooden houses crashing to the ground and sent fires scorching through the ruins. It also precipitated a terrifying flood. Some believe that as many as 150,000 people were killed.

At two minutes before noon on Saturday, 1 September 1923, Tokyo began to shake again. The earth had shifted beneath Sagami Bay, fifty miles away, and the initial shock lasted for about five minutes. It was followed by two more. Huge chasms opened in the streets, swallowing people and even trams. Electric cables snapped like string then flailed about, electrocuting anyone unfortunate enough to be within reach. One lethal flick killed a whole tramload of passengers, leaving them frozen as they were at the moment of death. 'One woman's hand held out a coin as though she had been on the point of paying her fare,' said an eyewitness. Roderick Matheson, the *Chicago Tribune*'s Tokyo correspondent, reported: 'The ground swayed and swung, making a foothold almost impossible . . . The groaning of the swaying buildings rose to a roar, and then a deafening sound as the pitching structures began to crumble and fall.' Desperate people ran out, 'pallid with fright', banging into each other and falling over. Some fainted while others laughed hysterically.

The earthquake came as people were cooking lunch on the open charcoal braziers found in most Japanese homes at the time. As these fell over, they started hundreds of fires, which eventually did more damage than the quake. Within minutes, thousands of homes were ablaze, and those who had stayed inside at first came running out, carrying whatever they could. Tokyo had a few modern concrete blocks on broad streets, but most of the city was still like an enormous village, with narrow paths winding between densely packed single-storey houses, built of timber, paper and thatch. These alleys soon became blocked with desperate people, while the individual fires coalesced into great conflagrations that raced through the city, hurried on by high winds spinning off a typhoon raging off the coast. Devastating firestorms, fed by gas from fractured mains, sucked in air, objects and people, while broken water pipes made it almost impossible to fight them. A Japanese newspaper reporter said firemen were 'utterly helpless'. They tried blowing up buildings to deprive the flames of sustenance, but to no avail. 'The frequent dynamiting . . . strengthened the impression of war,' recorded *The Times*.

Nearly all the business quarter and most government offices were destroyed. A power station caved in, killing 600, and an arsenal exploded. Sixteen hundred people perished when a cotton mill caught fire. Hundreds more tried to shelter in the basement vault of a bank, only to die from heat and suffocation. Others fled to a wooden bridge spanning the Sumida River, but found themselves trapped as the fire took hold of each bank. Then the Sumida burst its banks, drowning hundreds more. Police and firemen designated a park as a refuge area, and by four o'clock in the afternoon 40,000 people had arrived. Then a firestorm coursed through it, killing an estimated 30,000. They were packed so tightly that many died standing up. Others were picked up by the roaring winds, lifted high in the air, then flung down to earth incinerated. Some people stood in canals for hours, only to die with their heads burned beyond recognition; though one woman was in water up to her neck for a whole day with a baby on her head, and both survived. Most of Japan's political leadership was wiped out when the floor collapsed in the room where the newly appointed prime minister was trying to form a cabinet, and twenty of them died.

It was Monday before firemen were able to bring the flames under control. Then the streets were filled with desperate, hungry people looking for missing loved ones, their mouths covered against the choking smoke. At night they carried paper lanterns on poles. Those whose throats were too parched for them to speak held out bits of paper on which they had written names, or wore signs hung around their necks. Altogether Tokyo lost more than 300,000 buildings, including 20,000 factories and warehouses, 5,000 banks, 150 Shinto shrines, more than 600 Buddhist temples, many beautiful gardens, and 1,500 schools and libraries, including the Imperial University Library – one of the oldest in the world, with an irreplaceable collection of rare books, documents and artefacts.

The port of Yokohama, eighteen miles away, also suffered dreadfully. *The Times'* correspondent reported: 'Yokohama is wiped off the map, and those of its population who are not dead are homeless.' A Japanese army airman who flew over the city said there was not a single building left standing. The quake tore chasms in the street, buckled quays, dismantled bridges, flung a hospital from a cliff and demolished two big hotels, burying 180 guests. Two hundred schoolchildren were entombed alive in a train when an embankment collapsed on it. As the second and third shocks struck, crowds raced for the shore to try to escape by boat, but oil storage tanks exploded, and many were burned to death. At that moment, the ocean liner *Empress of Australia* was being drawn out of the harbour by tugs. Thousands rowed out to her and took refuge aboard. A passenger on a Japanese steamer said dead bodies kept floating past, but they were able to take on 2,000 refugees, who were 'scattered all over the boat, in deck chairs and along the halls. They are the most pitiful sight imaginable . . . Mothers with babies strapped to their backs and some of them naked, many horribly burned and ill.' The smell was 'frightful . . . but we are told that many are the best families of Tokyo and Yokohama and if we had been in those cities before the earthquake we would have been proud to have gone to their homes.' There were children without their parents and victims whose broken limbs had still not been set when they were put ashore nine days after the earthquake: 'each with a slice of bread and an orange. They do not know where they are going or what may happen next.'

Roderick Matheson managed to reach Yokohama, travelling by sampan, car and on foot, through flattened villages on roads with twenty-foot cracks. He found survivors sleeping in the open while tremors still came every few minutes, some severe enough to bring down weakened walls. Sixty thousand buildings were destroyed, along with the docks and harbour, and an estimated 25,000 people had died. As in Tokyo, the flames had claimed most lives, while some had drowned trying to submerge as much of their bodies as they could in water or mud to protect themselves from the searing heat. Others had been drowned by a tsunami that hit the port. In the mountainous areas outside the cities, many houses were buried or swept away by landslides. At Nebukawa, a fifty-foot mudslide swept a passenger train into the sea, along with the station and the rest of the village, killing about 300.

Then came the clear-up. Rescue workers burned piled-up bodies, while pathetic groups of survivors, clutching the few belongings they had managed to salvage, were living on just one bowl of rice a day. At some relief stations the military had to draw their sabres to prevent desperate people stealing supplies, and soon there were reports of widespread robbery, looting, rape and murder. Fifteen hundred prisoners had been released when Ichigaya prison in Tokyo was on the verge of collapse, and inmates broke out from other jails. The disorder, though, was blamed on Koreans, several thousand of whom lived in the city. They were alleged to have bombs, or to be poisoning the water supply. Vigilante groups beat up or killed anyone they believed to be Korean, including a number of Chinese and even Japanese citizens with unfamiliar accents. The government declared martial law, and took more than 2,000 Koreans into protective custody, but mobs attacked some of the police stations where they were being kept, sometimes with the help of the supposed upholders of law and order. According to official figures, 231 Koreans were killed, though other estimates put the number in the thousands. More than 350 people were charged with murder, attempted murder and assault, but most of those convicted escaped with light sentences, and even those sent to jail were soon released under a general pardon. A number of leftist politicians were abducted and killed by police officers who claimed they had tried to use the crisis to overthrow the government.

Amid this brutality, observers remained impressed by the resilience shown by the Japanese people and the speed with which they recovered. *The Times* reported: 'There is no panic and marvellous patience is shown.' All day and night, there was an endless procession 'of people of all classes, carrying portable goods and their salved belongings, or using trunks and carts . . . a whole family pushing them along, often with the grandparents riding on the top of the pile . . . the weak were carried on the backs of the strong . . . they exhibited patience beyond praise. Many jested; some even began to rebuild their homes before the ashes of the old homes were cold.' Within days, businesses and shops were trading again. Nearly every country in Europe sent help, and less than forty-eight hours after the quake, the US Pacific Fleet had arrived with water, food and medicine.

Final estimates put the number killed at around 150,000, with another 100,000 seriously injured. Up to 1.9 million people were made homeless.

In the immediate aftermath, the government wondered whether the capital should be rebuilt elsewhere, but within seven years Tokyo and Yokohama had been completely restored with scarcely any visible scar. The latter emerged as a much better-designed city, but in Tokyo survivors wanted similar homes in similar places to those they had inhabited before, so the new capital became as cluttered, congested and inflammable as the old. Its ability to burn would be demonstrated twenty years later when the Americans who had helped so generously in the aftermath of the great earthquake would return as a deadly enemy (see Chapter 10).

## · ASHGABAT ·

While the Tokyo earthquake made immediate headline news around the globe, it was decades before the true story of the quake that devastated Ashgabat in Central Asia in 1948 reached the outside world. The region had a long history of earthquakes. In 1667 the silk-making town of Shemakha in modern-day Azerbaijan was flattened, and 80,000 people died. Almost three centuries later mistrust between the Soviet Union and the West was at its height, with the wartime alliance against Hitler transmuted into a paranoid cold war. So when an earthquake ripped through Ashgabat, then the capital of the Soviet republic of Turkmenistan, in October 1948, Russian leader Joseph Stalin would not accept any help from the outside world; and; indeed, he did his best to keep it a secret. It was only after President Gorbachev had brought in his policy of *glasnost* (openness) in the 1980s that the authorities admitted 110,000 people had been killed.

It emerged that most of Ashgabat's main buildings had been destroyed, including all its mosques, while many nearby villages were also flattened. One woman said she had been lying in bed in the maternity wing of the hospital. She heard a loud rumble, then everything started to shake until the walls and ceiling collapsed on her. For a long time she lay in pitch darkness, listening to terrible cries and moans all around. After she was pulled from the debris, she heard a doctor saying that only 14 out of 67 mothers had survived, and just 7 of the babies. When she saw the surviving children, she was overcome with relief: one had the number 37 inked on to its forehead. It matched the number written on her breast.

Among those killed were the mother and two brothers of Saparmurad Niyazov, who became Turkmenistan's first president after the break-up of the Soviet Union in 1990. Niyazov was heavily criticised for his human rights record, but he appears to have been a most dutiful son, erecting many memorials to his mother, and even renaming the month of April after her. He built a museum documenting the disaster, and a feature film, *Children of the Earthquake*, was also made, telling the story of a young boy living an idyllic life until the disaster orphaned him. The character was partly modelled on the young president, but the film was never shown after Niyazov stormed out of a private viewing because it did not cast the Turkmen people in a sufficiently heroic light.

## · TANGSHAN ·

In 1976 another earthquake caused embarrassment to another communist regime that also refused help from the outside world. This time, the victims were the 1.6 million inhabitants of the densely populated Chinese industrial city of Tangshan, about 100 miles south-east of Beijing. Tangshan was the site of one of China's biggest coal-mining complexes, and many of the city's giant chimneys bore Chairman Mao's instruction: 'Prepare for war and natural disasters.'

It was the 'year of the dragon', believed by many Chinese to be unlucky. In January Zhou Enlai, the elder statesman of Chinese communism, had died. Then, six months later, weird things started happening. Water in wells rose and fell, or gas spouted out of them. Animals grew restless, with chickens refusing to eat, dogs barking incessantly, and goldfish leaping out of their bowls.

Finally, at a quarter to four on the morning of 28 July, China was hit by its worst earthquake in four centuries. It struck directly beneath

Tangshan, and in just twenty seconds twenty square miles of the city was shaken into rubble. People were hurled into the air, buildings collapsed, railway tracks buckled, great craters opened in the earth. One survivor said the ground was 'like an ocean, everything moving'. Most people had been asleep in the stifling summer night. Ho Shu-shen, a senior police officer, was woken by his wife. He heard what sounded like a goods train underground, then 'the floor began jerking up and down'. His house collapsed: 'For two or three minutes, there was no sound. Then I heard people crying everywhere in the darkness.' Ho managed to rescue his wife and three sons, though his fourteen-year-old daughter died. Together they saved nineteen neighbours and organised them into a rescue team. Then Ho strode into the stricken city, dressed only in his underwear, but brandishing a pistol. He and his sons set up an emergency police station and arrested seventy looters over the next few days, locking them in makeshift cells.

Meng Jiahua was working on the night shift down one of the coal mines when he felt the earth begin to tremble around him. Terrified, he and the miners near him fled to the surface. They were stunned: 'Everything you could see around was in ruins. The living were lined up along one side of the roads and the corpses on the other.' Bizarrely, he said, hardly any of the miners working underground were killed. Official records confirm this: although three-quarters of the mine shafts were damaged, only 13 miners out of 15,000 perished. Some would survive below ground for fifteen days without food or clean water. When they emerged they believed they had been trapped for only three or four days, but their bodies told the true story – they were all reduced to just skin and bone, having each lost up to three stones.

The Communist Party's official newspaper, the *People's Daily*, printed an uplifting tale designed to illustrate perfectly the official maxim that 'Any grave natural disaster can be overcome with the guidance of Chairman Mao.' After the earthquake, Che Cheng-min, a Communist Party committee member, was dragging himself from the ruins of his wrecked house when he heard his son and daughter shout: 'Quick, Daddy, come and save us.' But just as he was about to try to rescue them, Che heard another call for help from the home of Chiu Kuang-yu, the local Communist Party secretary. What should he do when confronted by such an appalling dilemma? For a good party member it was no con-test: 'without any hesitation, Che told his wife: "I am going to rescue old Chiu first."' With the earth still shaking, he pulled out the secretary and his family. 'What about your children?' asked Chiu as he emerged. 'Let's not bother about them,' replied Che. 'You are secretary of the neigh-bourhood party committee and you have no time to lose. Go and organise the rescue work immediately.' Only then did Che allow himself to return home. When he arrived, the *People's Daily* reported, he 'found his two children dead. But he felt neither remorse nor grief. In the inter-ests of the people of the neighbourhood and in the majority interest, he did not hesitate to sacrifice his own children.'

Whether everyone behaved in this ideologically sound manner is not recorded. What is certain is that many who had survived the initial earth-quake were trapped under collapsed buildings, and killed by another shock that came fifteen hours later, though there were stories of people who survived for up to a week in the rubble. In Tangshan it was esti-mated that 95 per cent of official buildings and 80 per cent of industrial plants were severely damaged. Because the region had not been regarded as vulnerable to earthquakes, few buildings had been built to withstand one. The quake brought down some older buildings in Beijing, where about a hundred people were killed, and there was also considerable damage in Tientsin, then China's third-biggest city, sixty miles away.

The Chinese military mounted a huge rescue effort. Aircraft dropped food, clothing and medical supplies, and within two weeks there were 100,000 troops on the ground, plus 30,000 medical personnel and 30,000 building workers. In China there is a tradition that any trembling of the earth may be a sign that the ruling dynasty is about to be overthrown, so the official media handled the story very cautiously. For the first twenty-four hours, there was a news blackout. Then the central committee of the Communist Party said only that the quake had 'caused great losses to people's life and property'. In January 1977 the *South China Morning Post* in Hong Kong quoted what it claimed was a 'secret' Communist Party document saying that 655,237 people had died, and it was only two years later that the Chinese government finally issued what it said was the actual death toll – 242,000 – though many still believe the true figure is much higher.

Arguments raged over whether the people of Tangshan could have been warned before the disaster. Chinese scientists had developed a system for predicting earthquakes by monitoring animal behaviour and changes in the level and temperature of water in wells, which had been used successfully the previous year to anticipate a major quake in Liaoning province, where many lives were saved. In Qianlong county, forty miles from Tangshan, officials had listened to warnings from local seismologists and ordered people to sleep outside. Casualties were much lighter there than in Tangshan, even though many buildings were destroyed.

Six weeks after the disaster, Chairman Mao died, and the so-called Gang of Four mounted an abortive bid to seize power. The political order had indeed trembled. For three years the authorities agonised over the best course of action before deciding that Tangshan should be rebuilt. It took ten years to create a new city with wider streets and stronger buildings.

# 3

# TSUNAMIS

Tsunami is a Japanese word meaning 'harbour wave'. Tsunamis can be caused by volcanic eruptions or earthquakes on land, or similar events under the sea, which generate waves up to 120 miles long that can travel at 500 miles an hour. In the middle of the ocean, these waves are usually only a couple of feet high, making them almost unnoticeable, but the volume of water they carry is huge. They become deadly when they hit a harbour or coastline, and the water washes in and out from the shore with catastrophic force as if it were being shaken in a giant glass.

## · THE GREAT TSUNAMI OF 365 ·

One of the greatest disasters ever to strike the Roman Empire came early in the morning of 21 July AD 365, when an earthquake beneath the Mediterranean provoked a vicious tsunami. The contemporary Roman historian Ammianus Marcellinus wrote: 'The sea was driven back, and its waters flowed away . . . so that in the abyss of the deep thus revealed men saw many kinds of sea-creatures stuck fast in the slime; and vast mountains and deep valleys, which Nature, the creator, had hidden in the unplumbed depths.' Then the waters that had withdrawn so dramatically suddenly returned with terrifying force: 'The roaring sea, resenting, as it were, this forced retreat, rose . . . dashed mightily upon islands and broad stretches of the mainland, and levelled innumerable buildings.' These were 'horrible phenomena . . . such as are related to us neither in fable nor in truthful history'. The Christian scholar St Jerome put it in more apocalyptic terms: it seemed 'as though God was threatening a second deluge, or all things were returning to original chaos'.

One of the places that suffered most was Alexandria, the city Alexander the Great had founded 600 years earlier, and which had become a world-famous centre for learning. This was where Euclid wrote his famous treatise on geometry, where the circumference of the globe was first calculated, and where Cleopatra had seduced her lovers. Alexandria's lighthouse was one of the wonders of the world, and its library one of the greatest on earth. For a long time, it was the most important city in the empire after Rome. Ammianus said 'many thousands' were drowned, and 'some great ships were hurled by the fury of the waves on to rooftops and others were thrown up to two miles from the shore'. The lighthouse and the library survived (although both would later be destroyed), but about 50,000 people are thought to have died in the city and other parts of Egypt. There was also destruction on the coast of Greece, as well as in Sicily, Dalmatia, Libya and Cyprus. It is believed that the epicentre was close to Crete, where many cities were destroyed, but legend has it that the Greek town of Epidaurus, with its famous theatre, was more fortunate. As its people stood transfixed by the incoming wave, St Hilarion, a revered hermit, made the sign of the cross three times in the sand and stretched out his hands to the sea. The wave hesitated, bowed and retreated.

## · LISBON ·

It was All Saints' Day – 1 November – 1755. In Lisbon, a bustling city of 275,000 people and the proud, wealthy hub of Portugal's great empire, 'there never was a finer morning', the Reverend Charles Davy recalled. 'The sun shone out in its full lustre; the whole face of the sky was perfectly serene and clear.' At twenty to ten he was writing a letter when the table began to tremble, which surprised him, as there was not a breath of wind. While he was trying to puzzle out what was going on, 'the whole house began to shake from the very foundation'. At first he thought it might be the carriages in the busy street outside, but then came 'a strange frightful kind of noise under ground, resembling the hollow distant rumbling of thunder'. Now the clergyman realised what was happening. Seven years earlier, he had been on Madeira when similar events had been the first signs of an earthquake, though fortunately it had done little damage.

As Davy wondered whether he should stay in the house or get out, any hope that this might be a repeat of Madeira was dashed when there was 'a most horrid crash, as if every edifice in the city had tumbled down at once'. The upper storeys of his building collapsed, and in his first-floor apartment he was afraid he would be crushed to death, as the walls rocked 'to and fro in the frightfullest manner, opening in several places; large stones falling down on every side from the cracks'. Choking on the dust, Davy was plunged into almost complete darkness. Outside, people came rushing out of churches as chandeliers swayed alarmingly. Worshippers from the cathedral and the nearby church of St Anthony fell to their knees in the street to pray. Amazingly, it seemed to work: the earth stopped trembling, but this being All Saints' Day, there were even more candles than usual burning in the churches. Some had toppled over and started fires, while all over the city kitchen fires added to the conflagration. Shopkeepers tried to salvage their goods by carrying them to a great square by the River Tagus, but this only provided more fuel for the flames.

Davy decided his best option was to head for the river, where he found 'a prodigious concourse of people of both sexes, and of all ranks and conditions'. There were senior clergy in their purple robes, priests 'who had run from the altars in their sacerdotal vestments in the midst of their celebrating Mass', and ladies 'half dressed, and some without shoes'. All 'were on their knees at prayers, with the terrors of death in their countenances, every one striking his breast and crying out incessantly, "*Miserecordia meu Dios!*"' As they prayed there was a second earthquake. It was less violent, but many buildings weakened by the first now collapsed. Down came St Anthony's and much of the cathedral, burying many people. Chasms fifteen feet wide appeared in the city's centre, accompanied by more shrieks and cries of '*Miserecordia!*' A Portuguese eyewitness said the earth was moving like 'the billows in a storm'.

But worse was to come. Davy heard a shout: 'The sea is coming in, we shall all be lost.' He looked at the Tagus and saw it 'heaving and swelling in the most unaccountable manner, as no wind was stirring. In an instant there appeared, at some small distance, a large body of water, rising as it were like a mountain. It came on foaming and roaring, and rushed towards the shore with such impetuosity, that we all immediately ran for our lives.' Many were swept away, but Davy had a narrow escape, managing to cling to a beam lying on the ground until the water went back 'with equal rapidity'. Not knowing quite what to do next, he headed back to the area he had come from near St Paul's church.

As he went, he could see 'ships tumbling and tossing about as in a violent storm; some had broken their cables, and were carried to the other side of the Tagus; others were whirled around with incredible swiftness; several large boats were turned keel upwards'. People who had clambered into boats were 'swallowed up, as in a whirlpool, and nevermore appeared'. The fifty-foot tsunami demolished a new quay, killing the people who had taken refuge there. By the time Davy reached St Paul's, it lay in ruins, and he felt a third shock, less violent than the first two but enough to set the sea rushing in and out again. Fortunately, he was now on higher ground and the water only came up to his knees, but it was swirling about alarmingly, so he headed for the Mint, which he knew was sturdily built. There should have been a party of soldiers on guard, but the only one who had not fled his post was a young officer of about eighteen. Another survivor, a British merchant named Braddock, described how the streets were now full of victims shouting for help with 'their backs or thighs broken, others [with] vast stones on their breasts'.

By nightfall, wrote Davy, there were fires in 'at least a hundred different places' and the flames were bright enough to read by. They destroyed 'everything the earthquake had spared'. People were so dejected or terrified that few tried to salvage their goods. Most just stared 'with silent grief'. The fires would burn for six days and destroy up to 85 per cent of the city, including many churches, along with the patriarch's palace, the Inquisition's headquarters, thirty monasteries, and scores of convents. Meanwhile, the red-light district survived unscathed. The brand-new opera house, opened only six months before and named, ironically, the

Phoenix Opera, was levelled. The Royal Ribeira Palace was destroyed, along with its 70,000-volume library and pictures by Titian, Rubens and Correggio. The royal archives, with their priceless records of the journeys of Vasco da Gama and other great Portuguese explorers, were also lost. More than forty noble houses and warehouses full of silks and spices went up in smoke. Lisbon's biggest hospital was destroyed and hundreds of patients burned to death. In total, the city lost 17,000 houses, and as many as 90,000 people were killed.

The epicentre of the earthquake appears to have been somewhere out in the Atlantic, and it caused destruction in the Algarve and throughout southern Portugal, too. Up to 10,000 people are said to have been killed in Morocco as a huge fissure opened in a coastal village. Lives were also lost in Spain and Gibraltar, while a twenty-foot wave was seen across the Atlantic in the Lesser Antilles, and one measuring ten feet reached the south coast of England. Tremors continued for some time, and more than 300 people were killed on 21 December when a number of houses collapsed and the Tagus overflowed.

The King of Portugal just escaped the main disaster on All Saints' Day, having left the town after taking mass at sunrise. For a long time afterwards, he was afraid of living in a building, so he set up court in a huge complex of tents and pavilions. He put his prime minister, the Marquis of Pombal, in charge of reconstruction. Pombal turned his coach into an office in the middle of the ruins, and lived on soup brought in by his wife. As soon as the flames died down, he dispatched teams to remove tens of thousands of bodies from the streets, and persuaded the Church to agree to them being buried at sea to reduce the risk of disease. He hanged more than thirty looters in prominent places around the ruined city, leaving their bodies swinging in the air, and posted soldiers around Lisbon to prevent able-bodied men from fleeing. Then he pressed them into work on the clean-up. He also requisitioned grain from Portuguese and foreign ships and forced them to sell it at pre-tsunami prices. Tents and huts were erected for the homeless, and soup kitchens sprang up. Kilns were built at record speed to ensure a steady supply of bricks, and ships were dispatched to all corners of the empire with the message that Lisbon was still open for business. Pombal tried to get the clergy to stop going on about the disaster being punishment from God, but they leaned on the king, making him lead a penitential procession barefoot.

Pombal planned a new Lisbon with big squares and long avenues. Prototype buildings were tested by having troops march around them to attempt to mimic the effects of an earthquake. The Jesuits tried to prevent reconstruction on the grounds that the disaster was divine punishment, and after the king's death Pombal was sacked and sent away from the city. But he had the last laugh. The elegant capital of today is his memorial, and his statue on a tall column is one of its great landmarks.


## · SANRIKU ·

The coastal towns of Japan's Sanriku province were packed on 15 June 1896, as people celebrated a Shinto festival. At about half past seven in the evening, there was a deep rumbling underground. It did not cause much alarm as seismic activity was common in the area, and people did not realise they were hearing an earthquake ninety miles away under the sea. This would stir up a tsunami of similar ferocity to one in 1293 which had killed more than 20,000 people in the area, or another in 1703 that may have accounted for 100,000.

Twenty minutes after the tremors started, the water suddenly retreated from the shore, leaving fish flapping on the mud. Boats were torn from their moorings and washed out, while far away, over the sea, there was a loud boom. Some thought it was the sound of an approaching gale; others said it was a huge school of sardines; while one old soldier took it for cannon fire, and armed himself to face the enemy. When his battered body was found later, he was still gripping his sword.

What they had all heard was in fact a wall of water up to 100 feet high rushing in at terrifying speed. It left few survivors. According to *The Times*, the little seaside town of Kamaishi was 'virtually annihilated' in less than two minutes. Of more than 1,200 houses, only 140 were left standing, and 4,700 people died. At Yamada 3,000 perished from a population of 4,200. In Hongo a group of old men who had gone for a game of Go on a hilltop overlooking the sea were the only ones to escape. In another village only the babies survived. Their parents had fled the waters and dumped them on higher ground before, fatally, going back to try to rescue their older children. Another baby survived, amazingly, after being washed out to sea on a mat. Five children lived by climbing up on a roof beam. Their mother and father died. And an eight-year-old who managed to cling to a rock was the sole survivor from a family of ten.

Fishermen who had been well out at sea had seen nothing unusual, but when they set off for home, they began to find floating debris and bodies. One crew saw what they thought was a big fish, pulled it aboard and found it was a child, still alive. Another boat picked up three children, including one belonging to a crew member. When they got back, many of the fishermen found their homes destroyed and the corpses of their wives and children floating in the water. The wave struck 170 miles of coastline, sweeping away more than 10,600 houses and killing more than 27,000 people. A correspondent for *Harper's* magazine found no one alive during a thirty-mile trek up the coast. For days after, 'the unconquerable stench of death and the smoke of funeral fires' were everywhere.

*The Times* was horrified by the suddenness of the disaster: 'In the case of inundations, cyclones, or even earthquakes, there is a record of more or less continuous mischief and of more or less continuous struggle against the forces of destruction. But in the case of a seismic wave, one stupendous blow accomplishes the whole calamity in an instant.'

Sanriku would be hit by another tsunami in 1933, but a last-minute warning kept the death toll down to 3,000.

## · THE BOXING DAY TSUNAMI ·

The deadliest tsunami in history happened on 26 December 2004. It began just before eight o'clock in the morning with a huge earthquake under the Indian Ocean, its epicentre close to the island of Simeulue, about 100 miles west of Sumatra. Registering 9.3 on the Richter scale, it was the second-biggest ever recorded. It was also one of the longest, lasting ten minutes. Nearly 1,000 miles of fault-line slipped about fifty feet, pushing up the sea bed, displacing seven cubic miles of water, and triggering devastating waves, which reached as far as Mexico, Chile and the Arctic.

There had been a warning system for tsunamis in the Pacific Ring of Fire since 1948, but there was none in the Indian Ocean, so most victims were taken completely by surprise. As so often happens, the first sign of the tsunami was a dramatic retreat of the sea, leaving gasping fish and bemused, beached swimmers. Then, as it surged back, those who escaped drowning risked being smashed or impaled by tons of debris. The waves destroyed everything in their path: from the built-up tourist resorts of Thailand to isolated fishing villages in Indonesia and Sri Lanka.

The first wave hit Indonesia within fifteen minutes of the earthquake, reaching nearly 100 feet high in Aceh province on Sumatra, but others would continue to wreak havoc for the next seven hours. Walls of water slammed into the coasts of Malaysia, Myanmar, Thailand, Bangladesh, Sri Lanka, India and even Somalia, 4,500 miles away, where 176 people were killed and 50,000 made homeless. There were eight deaths in South Africa, and Durban harbour had to be closed. Low-lying 'paradises' like the Maldives and the Andaman and Nicobar islands were literally swamped, while great swathes of Asia and East Africa turned instantly from lush green to sludge brown.

Among the few people to get out of coastal areas in time to avoid destruction were the islanders of Simeulue. According to local folklore, there had been a tsunami there in 1907, and now people fled inland to the hills the moment they felt the earth shaking. On holiday at Phuket in Thailand, a ten-year-old British girl who had been studying tsunamis in her geography class recognised the danger signs of the receding ocean. She and her parents spread the word, and many people fled from the beach in time. At nearby Kamala Bay, a Scottish teacher also spotted what was happening and shepherded a busload of tourists and locals to the safety of higher ground.

Most people in the stricken areas were less fortunate. Among the many individual disasters of the tsunami was the worst rail accident in history. This being a Buddhist as well as a Christian holiday, Sri Lanka's most popular tourist train, the *Queen of the Sea*, was packed when it left Colombo for the southern city of Galle at half past seven in the morning. Many of the passengers were children. Two hours later the train was halted in the coastal village of Peraliya by a huge wave. As it stopped, with water surging around, hundreds of local people clambered aboard, hoping it would take them to safety. Others stood behind the eight coaches believing they would be shielded from any further waves. Instead, a twenty-foot wall of water flipped over the carriages, smashing them against the trees and houses that lined the track, crushing those sheltering behind them and leaving the rails a twisted tangle of metal. As the sea flooded into the carriages, a sixty-two-year-old restaurateur found himself separated from his son and daughter. For forty-five minutes he was trapped, convinced they would die: 'But we prayed to our god and because of that I got up to a window and escaped.' He found his son and daughter, and they trekked two miles uphill to safety. An Israeli tourist was trapped in the darkness of a flooded carriage: 'I held my breath. I thought, This is how you die.' Then the train flipped over again, the water ebbed away, and he escaped by wading towards the light.

At first, the Sri Lankan emergency services were overwhelmed by the scale of the tsunami; for several hours they did not even know where the train was. Then the wreckage was spotted from the air. Dozens of injured people died before help could reach them. The train driver's wife was one of many distraught relatives who rushed to the scene to search for their loved ones. She complained bitterly: 'Nobody helped us. I had to find his body myself.' Her brother pulled the driver's corpse from his cab, and they took him away in their car.

According to the authorities, just a few dozen people on the train survived, while probably more than 2,000 died. Only about 900 bodies were ever recovered, with the rest either swept out to sea or reclaimed by relatives. Buddhist monks buried scores of victims in a mass grave: 'This was the only thing we could do,' said a monk who performed the funeral rites for the dead of many faiths. 'The bodies were rotting. We gave them a decent burial.'

Peraliya was virtually destroyed, with only ten buildings left standing, but the town was rebuilt and the railway repaired. A year after the disaster, the train's guard was back at work on the same route.

The final death toll from the Boxing Day tsunami may never be known, and estimates range as high as 310,000, but the United Nations now puts the figure around 230,000. Sumatra lost 94,000 people; Sri Lanka more than 30,000; India nearly 9,000; and Thailand 6,000. Nine thousand of those killed were foreign tourists, with the Nordic countries particularly badly hit. In addition, 1.8 million people were left homeless. Relief agencies reported that about a third of those killed were children, while Oxfam said that in some areas most of the victims were women waiting on the beach for fishermen to return.

There were some miraculous escapes. A two-year-old Swedish toddler snatched by the waves from a beach in Thailand was found by an American couple on a road near the resort of Khao Lak, unhurt apart from a few cuts and bruises. His mother was never found, but he was eventually reunited with his father, who said they had been trying to run away from their hotel but had gone only twenty yards when they saw the wave coming, 'overturning telegraph poles and everything else in its path'. For a time he managed to hold on to his son, 'but finally the wave was too strong, so I lost my grip of him, and he floated away'.

A twenty-one-year-old man was picked up by a container ship after fifteen days adrift in the Indian Ocean. He had been swept out while working on a seaside building site in Aceh. He said he had lived on coconuts that floated by, tearing them open with his teeth. Then, five weeks after the tsunami, nine survivors were found wandering lost in the jungle of India's Nicobar Islands.

Ninety-one British people died, and an inquest into their deaths heard many complaints about the lack of warning. One survivor commented: 'There was not even a single phone call . . . not even someone running along with a Tannoy system.' A woman whose twenty-three-year-old daughter was killed said, 'If my daughter had had five minutes, she would have been alive today,' but some experts said an earthquake of this ferocity happened only once every 500 years, and nobody could have predicted such a big one in this region.

Humanity as a whole was praised for its prompt and generous response. The United Nations official in charge of relief, Jan Egeland, said, 'I think the world was great in the tsunami.' The response had been 'effective, swift and muscular' from a record ninety countries, many of them far from rich, but Egeland conceded that the longer-term task of reconstruction had gone less well. In Sri Lanka and Indonesia, political tension between governments and rebels hampered recovery. In Aceh a year after the disaster 150,000 people were still living in tents and other emergency shelters, while in Indonesia as a whole half a million depended on rations from the World Food Programme. In Sri Lanka about 80 per cent of the fishing boats in the areas affected were damaged and the fishermen could not afford to repair them. Many had been put up in temporary camps away from the sea and therefore cut off from their livelihood. Aid organisations said they had come across at least fifty cases of desperate fishermen's wives selling their kidneys, often for as little as £600.

# 4

## FLOODS

### · NOAH'S FLOOD ·

'In the six hundredth year of Noah's life, in the second month, the seventeenth day of the month, the same day were all the fountains of the great deep broken up, and the windows of heaven were opened. And the rain was upon the earth forty days and forty nights.' And everyone drowned apart from Noah, his family, and the animals who went two by two into his ark. Or at least that is what the Bible says.

As in so many of the disasters that would follow, the cause cited was the sinfulness of mankind: 'God saw that the wickedness of man was great in the earth and that every imagination of the thoughts of his heart was only evil continually.' The divine prescription was drastic: 'I will destroy man whom I have created from the face of the earth.' So God instructed Noah to build a ship for himself, his wife, his three sons and their wives, then 'of clean beasts, and of beasts that are not clean, and of fowls, and of every thing that creepeth upon the earth, there went in two . . . the male and the female'. The earth was flooded for 150 days, then Noah's ark came to rest 'upon the mountains of Ararat'. But it was another five months before the waters had subsided sufficiently for the occupants to disembark and start repopulating the earth.

This might be a useful story for keeping congregations on the straight and narrow, but is it any more than a myth? Even relatively minor floods leave behind thousands of tons of mud and silt, so anything on this scale should have created monstrous deposits. But excavations in Israel have found no evidence of a flood even in places like Jericho that have been inhabited for 10,000 years.

Intriguingly, the story of Noah is not unique. There are also ancient tales from Mesopotamia (modern-day Iraq) that describe the gods destroying mankind with a flood. In the epic of Gilgamesh, written about 1,000 years before Genesis, the water god warns Utnapishtim, the wise king of the city of Shuruppak, that a terrible flood is coming, and tells him to make a great boat to save himself, his family, and representatives of every species of animal. Sure enough, the flood comes, and the king and his passengers escape.

In 1929 the British archaeologist Sir Charles Woolley caused a sensation with his book *Ur of the Chaldees*, said to be the most widely read work on archaeology ever published. Woolley, the son of a clergyman, found a layer of silt without human remains which he took to be evidence of a major inundation about 3500 BC in the Mesopotamian city of Ur, site of one of the world's oldest civilisations. This, he believed, was Noah's flood. Other scholars, though, said it was just one of a number of floods of the Tigris and Euphrates rivers. Then two American geologists came up with another theory: there was a great flood around 5600 BC, perhaps 700 years before the date that many assign to Noah's flood, but it was centred on the Black Sea. They argued that this had originally been an inland freshwater lake that was considerably smaller than today's saltwater sea and that it lay perhaps 500 feet below the level of the Mediterranean. Then a minor earthquake, or perhaps just a prolonged period of rain, led the Mediterranean to burst through a natural dam at what is now the Bosporus. The water would have rushed into the Black Sea with two hundred times the power of Niagara Falls. The scientists reckoned the flood lasted about 300 days – like Noah's – while the waters inundated a huge area, driving people to flee south to the regions where the various flood stories would be written.

In 2000, the oceanographer Robert Ballard, who found the *Titanic* and a number of other famous wrecks, decided to trawl the Black Sea for evidence of the flood and even perhaps the remains of Noah's ark. His team believed they found evidence of a major inundation, but there was no sign of the ship. Although the Bible says it came to rest on the 'mountains of Ararat', many believe this does not mean Mount Ararat itself, the highest peak in modern-day Turkey. Even so, since the mountain was first climbed in 1829, explorers have been looking for remains of the ark. In 1955 a Frenchman found some wooden fragments 14,000 feet up, but excitement died down when carbon dating suggested they were no more than 1,300 years old. Then, in the 1990s, it was alleged that the CIA possessed a top-secret picture taken from space of an unexplored region close to the mountain that showed something like a ship in the snow.

Noah is also regarded as a prophet by Muslims, and some of them believe they found his ark as long ago as 1908, when a boat-like outline was spotted on a peak named El Judi, twenty miles from Ararat. In 1988 the American religious archaeologist Vendyl Jones investigated the site, and declared: 'There is very strong evidence it could well be Noah's ark.' The Turkish government promptly declared the site an area of outstanding historical interest, and even marked the ark on official maps. A number of Christian authors and scientists have gone on expeditions since, and some claim to have found traces of wood or nails, but the theory was dealt a severe blow in 1996 when a Californian professor declared that the supposed ark was actually a natural rock formation. In 2006 new satellite images of Mount Ararat were released which believers claimed showed a clearer image of a boat beneath the ice. Sceptics said it was merely a trick of the light. The mystery endures.

### · HOLLAND ·

'God created the earth,' goes the saying, 'but the Dutch made Holland.' Through their courage, energy and ingenuity, they wrested hundreds of square miles of land from the sea. But it came at a price. On 11 November 1099 an unusually high tide combined with a violent storm to bring flooding to the Netherlands and England. According to the *Anglo-Saxon Chronicle*, 'the incoming tide rushed up so strongly and did so much damage that no one remembered anything like it before'. About 100,000 people are said to have been killed.

Further serious floods followed. In 1212 perhaps 60,000 drowned around the Zuider Zee, much of which is below sea level, while just six-teen years later the death toll was again said to be 100,000. The response of the Dutch to each succeeding disaster was to roll up their sleeves and build stronger defences, but that meant the floods kept on claiming lives.

On 16 January 1362 there was the *Grote Mandrenke,* or 'Great Drowning of Men', as a massive Atlantic gale whipped up floods across England, the Netherlands, northern Germany and southern Denmark, causing at least 25,000 deaths. 'Evil Saturday' was the name given to 5 November 1530 as the sea dyke was breached again, and an estimated 400,000 people drowned.

Some of these casualty figures may be exaggerated, but one modern climatologist reckons that between 1099 and 1570 there were thirty major floods that destroyed at least 286 towns and villages and drowned 1.5 million people. As recently as 1953 Holland (and eastern England) suffered again when floods drowned 1,850 people.

## · THE YELLOW RIVER ·

The Yellow River, Huang He to the Chinese, is the world's muddiest. During its 2,877-mile journey to the sea it dumps about 1.6 billion tons of yellow silt. Dubbed 'China's sorrow', it has flooded about 1,500 times in the last 3,000 years. The Zhou emperors, who ruled from the twelfth to the third century BC, tried to stop the inundations by having young girls flung into rivers as sacrifices. Local people tried the more practical method of building dykes from silt reinforced with great bales of sorghum stalks, sometimes erected as far as eight miles from the river, to try to contain it in a wide corridor when it flooded. By the nineteenth century AD the dykes were often thirty feet high and a hundred feet wide at the base. Each flooding, though, raised the floor of the corridor, so, in spite of all the efforts of the Chinese, the river usually won.

In September 1887 many foresaw trouble. It had been very wet, and Huang He was rising ominously, but the official in charge of the dykes said it was an inauspicious time to act. At a bend near the city of Zhengzhou in Henan province there was a particularly decrepit section of dyke. As the water rose, it gave way on 28 September. At first, the breach was just a few feet, but soon it had widened to more than half a mile, and the river surged across the North China Plain. Whole towns disappeared. A visiting American reported seeing an expanse of water as big as Lake Ontario – more than 7,500 square miles. According to some estimates, the flood eventually covered 50,000.

News was slow to reach the rest of the world, but on 12 November a *Times* correspondent reported: 'the Yellow River has recently given fresh proof of its right to the title of "China's sorrow"'. Its waters had spread death and destruction 'to an unparalleled extent'. The journalist heard that the officials responsible for the dykes that were breached had been put in the pillory. Information remained thin, but in February 1888 a letter appeared in the newspaper from the Baptist mission in northern China asking for help. It said that 'some millions' were believed to have died as hundreds of villages were swept away. Many once-wealthy men were now paupers, and hundreds of thousands were in 'imminent danger of starvation'. The victims seemed resigned to their fate, behaving with a 'mute submissiveness which is extremely touching'.

When the waters finally receded, it became clear that at least 1,500 communities had been lost, and there followed two years of hunger and disease. In January 1889 *The Times* reported continuing famine, remarking that 'China, during the past 18 months, has suffered from calamity after calamity.' Many Chinese were reduced to eating coarse sorghum, which was usually shunned by all but the desperately poor. The number killed was put at between 900,000 and 2.5 million, with another 3 million made homeless. It was probably the deadliest flood the world has ever seen.

The Yellow River would flood many more times. In 1931 its waters covered 42,000 square miles, and up to 140,000 people drowned, while many more died in the famine that followed. Then, four years later, tens of thousands more perished. Perhaps the river's most bizarre flood came in 1938. China was locked in a desperate battle for survival against the invading Japanese, who controlled the northern part of the country (see Chapter 10 – The Rape of Nanking). By the spring, they were threatening the crucial railway junction of Zhengzhou. To the leader of the Chinese Nationalists, Chiang Kai-shek, this desperate situation called for desperate measures, so he took the extraordinary step of ordering General Shang Chen to blow up the dyke of the Yellow River near the city. Chiang decided it was crucial to surprise the Japanese, so no warning was given to the millions of inhabitants of the area who would now be in grave danger. This was not a new tactic. Back in 1642 about 300,000 people had been killed when the city of Kaifeng on the river's southern bank was deliberately flooded (see Chapter 10 – The Manchu Conquest of China). Shang, though, played for time, worried about whether he could get his troops safely out of the way. Then, on 11 May, the Japanese suddenly broke through into the area where Chinese engineers were planning to direct the flood, and the general felt he could delay no longer. That afternoon his men opened a 200-yard breach at Huayuankou. Water began to pour through, and by mid-afternoon it had swamped the advancing Japanese, drowning many soldiers and miring tanks and guns in the mud. Soon it covered 21,000 square miles of land, and it is estimated to have delayed the Japanese for three months. But the cost to the defenders was immense: more than 4,000 villages were destroyed and between 500,000 and 900,000 Chinese drowned, making this the deadliest man-made flood in history.

## · JOHNSTOWN ·

A journalist visiting Johnstown, Pennsylvania, in 1885 described it as 'new, rough, and busy, with the rush of huge mills and factories and the throb of perpetually passing trains'. The Little Conemaugh and Stony Creek rivers ran along the edges of the town and met to form the Conemaugh River at the western end. At least once a year they could be expected to flood the streets because of swiftly melting snow or heavy rain. Sometimes the water would lap at ground-floor windows, sending the townspeople scurrying home to salvage their belongings. The first five months of 1889 saw a hundred days of rain, and there was a lot of snow in April, so the rivers had become even more noisy and unruly than usual. On the afternoon of 30 May gentle rain began, but by ten o'clock that night it was pouring down.

When the waters started to rise the following day, most of Johns-town's 25,000 inhabitants were not too concerned as they gathered in the upper storeys of their homes, thinking they would just sit out the worst of it as they had done many times before, but they did not know what was happening at South Fork, fourteen miles upriver from the city. There what was believed to be the biggest earth dam in the world, 72 feet high and 300 yards wide, held back Lake Conemaugh, the biggest man-made lake in the country, a two-mile stretch of water used by the South Fork Fishing and Hunting Club. By the morning of 31 May, the creek that fed the lake was a raging torrent, and the water level had risen two feet. The resident engineer, John Parke, aged twenty-two and just three months into the job, was worried by water spilling through cracks in the dam so he assembled a group of workmen to try to clear debris clogging the main spillway. But the club's officials already feared that the whole thing might give way.

Parke decided to raise the alarm, so as fast as his horse would carry him, he galloped to the hamlet of South Fork, just two miles from the dam, and shouted to everyone to head for higher ground. Then he raced to the Pennsylvania Railroad's signal tower and asked the operator, Emma Ehrenfeld, to telegraph Johnstown. But he was too late: the rising waters had already washed away the lines. By the time Parke got back to the dam, a gap in the centre was widening by the minute. At about ten past three in the afternoon, as club officials, labourers and the people of South Fork watched in horror, it burst, and four billion gallons of water broke out into the valley with a roar that could be heard for miles. The proprietor of the fishing club's hotel said: 'The water seemed to leap, scarcely touching the ground. It bounded down the valley, crashing and roaring, carrying everything before it.' The Reverend W.G. Brown of the South Fork United Brethren church watched the flood sweeping by at treetop height, and prayed: 'God have mercy on the people below.' From the window of the railway signal tower, Emma Ehrenfeld saw what looked like a huge hill on the move. She ran for it, 'without thinking to get my hat or anything'. Four-fifths of the buildings in South Fork were swept away. Next came Mineral Point, then Conemaugh. Both were devastated.

The New York express was waiting to leave East Conemaugh when Charles Richwood saw 'a seething, turbulent wall of water, whose crests seemed mountain-high, filling the entire valley and carrying everything before it'. He grabbed Edith, his wife of a few hours, just before water filled their carriage, and they climbed on top. But the flood caught them and swept them along until some people floating past on a rooftop pulled them out. Then Richwood realised they were heading straight for a wire factory where furnaces were exploding. The couple grabbed a piece of driftwood and jumped off the roof, then somehow managed to steer away from the inferno just before the flood ripped free 100 tons of barbed wire that lacerated everything in its path. Eventually someone leapt into the water and pushed them to land.

Next in harm's way was the pleasant village of Woodvale, where virtually every building disappeared, and 300 people were sucked into the torrent. By the time the flood reached Johnstown it was swollen with wreckage. A local lawyer saw 'timber, trees, roofs, debris of every sort' advancing toward him. He managed to get up on the roof with his family. Meanwhile, said one eyewitness, the waters were carrying off goods wagons loaded 'with iron, cattle, and freight of all kinds' and locomotives 'like mere toys'. Thirty, weighing up to 100 tons each, would later be found wrecked.

John Fenn was helping his neighbours move their furniture out of the way of what everyone expected to be a normal Johnstown flood when he saw the torrent advancing. He tried to run back to his house but was swept away and lost. Inside, his pregnant wife had seven children clinging to her: 'The water rose and floated us until our heads nearly touched the ceiling.' It was dark and stifling. 'I could not tell just the moment the children had to give up and drown,' she said. 'What I suffered, with the bodies of my seven children floating around me in the gloom, can never be told.' Mrs Fenn survived, but asked her rescuers: 'What have I to live for?' She gave birth to a baby girl a few weeks later, but that child died too.

Six-year-old Gertrude Quinn Slattery was carried along the torrent on 'a wet, muddy mattress'. She saw a roof floating towards her with about twenty people clinging to it and shouted for help. A man came to the edge while the others tried to hold him back, but he struggled free and leapt into the water, then disappeared. Gertrude saw his head emerge for a moment, then vanish again. At last he reached the mattress and climbed on: 'I put both arms around his neck and held on to him like grim death. Together we went downstream . . . to the accompaniment of crunching, grinding, gurgling, splashing.' Her rescuer was a man named Maxwell McAchren. On they surged until they came to a building where two men with poles were trying to fish people out, but Gertrude could not reach. Then one shouted that McAchren should throw the girl to them. In desperation he complied and hurled her 'some say twenty feet, others fifteen. I could never find out, so I leave it to your imagination. It was considered a great feat in the town, I know.'

Sixteen-year-old Victor Heiser was with his father at an upstairs window as the waters crushed their home like an eggshell. His parents disappeared, and he was carried along in the flood, dodging all manner of hazards. He managed to clamber on to the roof of a house and spent the night in the attic with nineteen other survivors, praying it would not collapse. The rest of Victor's family were killed. He left Johnstown and went on to become a distinguished public health officer and doctor, developing the first effective treatment for leprosy.

Another family, named Waters, survived by balancing on the joists of their unfinished attic. Mrs Waters eventually fell off but managed not only to keep her head above the flood but also to hold her baby girl out of it.

The Reverend H.L. Chapman, a Methodist pastor, raced upstairs at the parsonage with his family just as the flood rushed in the front door. It flung over bookcases, causing terrifying noises but the Chapmans held on. 'I think none of us was afraid to meet God,' said Chapman, 'but we all felt willing to put it off until a more propitious time.'

Johnstown's tallest building was Alma Hall on Main Street, and 264 people sheltered on its upper floors, huddling together in the darkness. Among them were the Reverend David Beale from the Presbyterian church and his family. They had come from their home a block away by scrambling over floating wreckage. The clergyman led the refugees in prayer, while a local doctor tended the injured and even delivered two babies in spite of suffering broken ribs himself.

The next day the *New York Times* reported that Johnstown had 'been practically wiped out of existence'. The superintendent of the Pennsylvania Railroad had seen 200 people floating along clinging to wreckage of one sort or another, while a telegraph operator had counted 63 bodies carried past his office in just 20 minutes.

At least 2,200 people died, including nearly 400 children, though some believe the true total was more than 3,000. Bodies were found as far away as Cincinnati, and as late as 1911. About 1,600 homes were destroyed, and Johnstown lost its major municipal buildings. Its main bridge had to be blown up because the debris that had collected around it became a menace to health. But it was not all doom and gloom. A rescue crew heard noises from beneath a crushed goods wagon and found a cow quietly chewing the cud, along with five clucking hens and a small dog. Even more remarkably, a five-month-old baby was found alive on the floor of a wrecked house after being carried some seventy-five miles by the waters. Survivors had to live in tents for a time, and the *New York Times* reported 'attempts at disorder and violence by small gangs of tramps'. These, however, 'were vigorously suppressed, and several marauders have been lynched and shot to death, for the people in the solemn earnestness of their work of succour and rescue have not the patience to wait the tedious process of law'.

America rallied round. New York, Philadelphia and Pittsburgh each raised more than $500,000. Schoolchildren from California sent potatoes, while prison inmates baked 1,000 loaves of bread. By 1 July, stores were reopening on Main Street, and in 1926 the story of the disaster was told in an epic Hollywood silent film.

## · GALVESTON ·

At the end of the nineteenth century, Galveston was Texas's biggest port and wealthiest city as well as a popular holiday resort. Sited on a long, thin, sandy island just off the coast, and nicknamed 'the New York of the South', it had a population of 42,000. The downside was that it was only nine feet above sea level at high tide, and it was in the hurricane zone. Indeed, nearby Indianola, once its rival, had been reduced to a ghost town by storms in 1875 and 1886. As a result, many Galveston residents campaigned for a sea wall to protect their city, but the authorities dismissed them as alarmist. Since being founded in 1839 the city had weathered many storms, and the powers that be could see no reason why those assaulting it in the future would be any worse. In 1891 Isaac Cline from the Galveston Weather Bureau wrote an article for the local newspaper arguing that it would be impossible for a hurricane of any size to hit the city. So no wall was built, although sand was taken from dunes along the shore to fill low-lying areas around the city. Unfortunately, this just reduced the natural protection the dunes offered.

On Tuesday, 4 September 1900, Isaac Cline's office started to receive warnings from the US Weather Bureau in Washington of a tropical storm moving northwards over Cuba. They had no way of forecasting where it would go next, but storm warnings were common in early autumn, and the general belief was that it was heading for Florida. Three days later, though, Washington told Cline to hoist warning flags. This prompted a few people to leave for the mainland, but most of those enjoying Galveston's beaches seemed unconcerned, and rather welcomed the cool breeze as a relief from the sultry weather of the last few days. The barometer was falling, but the sky was clear, and the local paper wondered whether the storm was already a spent force. Then at four o'clock the following morning, Cline's brother Joseph, who also worked at the bureau, awoke to see the sea level about five feet higher than usual. He saddled his horse and went out to warn people living along the shore. A few headed for higher ground, but most stayed put, convinced it was just another 'overflow', as they were known locally, which would sweep across the island but soon clear, having done little damage.

Fairly typical was the reaction of a Bible teacher named Ida Austin, who told her niece: 'We have nothing to fear, the water has never been over our place.' Soon, though, the wind was getting up and pavements were under water. Then it crept into her yard. A light rain began to fall at about quarter to nine, and just after ten Joseph Cline hoisted another warning flag, but the wind tore it apart. Sister Elizabeth Ryan, from St Mary's orphanage, was in town that morning, picking up food from St Mary's infirmary for the children. At the hospital, they asked her to stay until the storm had passed, but she said she had to be on her way or the orphans would have nothing to eat. By noon, the wind was lashing in the rain with frightening power. Thousands of stay-putters had by now lost their nerve and were heading for higher ground, but it was not easy. The storm had got enough to knock down a grown man.

Mrs Austin was no longer so nonchalant, as 'planks and debris of every imaginable kind were being hurled through the air'. They had to bring their cow into the house, but before long it was standing in three feet of water. The flood had also reached the orphanage – two big dormitories just off the beach, behind a row of dunes. The sisters brought all the children into the chapel of the girls' dorm, which was newer and stronger, and got them to sing to try to keep up their spirits.

By mid-afternoon, any hope of escape for Galveston's citizens had disappeared as the causeways to the mainland were washed away. At half past three, before the storm snapped the wires, Joseph Cline managed to cable Houston: 'Gulf rising, water covers streets of about half of city.'

By evening, the wind was gusting to 120 miles an hour, streets were neck-deep in swirling water, and slate tiles were flying off buildings fast enough to remove a man's head. At St Mary's Infirmary, the flood now filled the ground floor, the windows were broken and the rain was lashing in. From the first-floor balcony, the sisters tried to pull people in as they were washed by. A thousand people took refuge in the Tremont Hotel on one of the highest points in the city, but by six o'clock the front desk was under water and the roof had been torn off. Half an hour later a storm surge toppled many houses, killing those inside. Among its other victims were passengers on the train from Beaumont to Galveston, trapped at the Bolivar Peninsula, where they would normally have caught a ferry. When the captain could not dock, the train tried to go back, but the tracks were flooded. Ten of the passengers sheltered at the Point Bolivar lighthouse with a couple of hundred local people and survived; the other eighty-five who stayed on the train all drowned.

In Galveston hundreds took refuge in churches but were killed when they collapsed. Fifty people were sheltering in the Clines' house but a section of tramline hit it like a battering ram and flung it on its side. Isaac was thrown into the water. Then he saw his six-year-old daughter Esther flailing and grabbed her. She asked for her mother, but Isaac did not know where his wife was, nor his two elder daughters, who had been standing by the window with his brother Joseph. After he and Esther had been buffeted in the water for a while, there was a flash of lightning, and he saw three figures clinging to wreckage: Joseph and the other two girls.

The two men used their bodies to shield the children from the debris constantly crashing into them, then they managed to climb on to the battered remains of a house that was floating by. Joseph had to use a knife to fend off a man who tried to push the children out of the way so he could board the raft himself. The Clines drifted for hours, first driven out to sea, then mercifully back as the wind changed direction. They heard cries coming from a two-storey house directly in front of them, but their makeshift raft just bulldozed it into the water.

Meanwhile, at the orphanage, the terrified children heard a fearful crash as the boys' dormitory collapsed and was carried off by the waters. Some of the older children climbed on to the roof of the girls' building, while the sisters cut a clothes line into sections and used it to tie half a dozen of the smaller children to each of them. Soon, though, the roof of the girls' dormitory collapsed, killing Elizabeth Ryan and all the other sisters. When their bodies were found, some still had children tied to them.

At ten o'clock the flood reached its highest level – fifteen feet above high tide. But as the waters ebbed they would do further damage, ripping buildings from their foundations. The Clines finally ran aground four blocks from their old home, with the children by now weeping over the loss of their mother. Three boys from the orphanage managed to escape by clinging to a floating tree for a whole day until it drifted back to Galveston. Those who had taken refuge at the Tremont Hotel also survived, but at the infirmary more than a hundred patients perished.

Dawn on Sunday, 9 September, brought clear skies. One woman was washed in to shore in the wooden bath-tub in which she had been swept out to sea the previous evening, but Galveston presented a scene of destruction almost beyond belief. More than 3,600 homes had been destroyed, and in some areas scarcely a single building was left standing. Food, water and medicine were all in short supply, but by that afternoon a relief committee had drafted men to clear away bodies and debris. Rescue workers were astonished to find a child nailed by its wrist to the roof of a house and alive, but their job was arduous and difficult, and many survivors of the initial disaster died in the wreckage before they could be saved. About 6,000 were killed in Galveston itself, with a similar number dying elsewhere along the Texas coast, and 5,000 families in the city were homeless. It was the greatest natural disaster ever to strike the United States.

At first, the dead were simply dumped at sea, but many were carried back to shore by the currents, so a decision was made to burn them on funeral pyres. The authorities issued free whiskey to workers who sometimes had to throw the bodies of friends and loved ones on to the flames. US Army tents were set up along the shore for survivors, and martial law was declared. *The Times* said that troops shot twenty-five looters, one of whom reportedly had twenty-three severed ring fingers in his pocket.

When the city was rebuilt, dredged sand was used to raise it by up to seventeen feet, and it got a new sea wall. A stronger bridge to the mainland was also constructed. These measures were put to the test in 1915 when a similar storm hit the town. There were casualties – 275 people died – but nothing like on the scale of 1900.

## · THE YANGTZE ·

The Yangtze is China's greatest river, and the third longest in the world. It rises on the Tibetan plateau, flows 4,000 miles through some of the richest parts of the country and enters the sea near Shanghai. While traditionally the Yellow River was 'China's sorrow', in the twentieth century the Yangtze became increasingly dangerous. After an exceptionally wet rainy season, in August 1931, just like the Yellow River it burst its banks. On the 22nd *The Times* reported that at Hankow it reached a record fifty-three feet above the normal high water mark, and many dykes had given way, including some that had been shamefully neglected 'due to official lethargy and mismanagement'. The river flooded thousands of square miles, ruining all the summer crops and destroying so much food that many people now faced starvation.

In mid-September *The Times*' correspondent said the countryside from Hankow to Shashi was a huge sheet of water 150 miles long, extending in places for 20 miles from the river, punctuated only by the occasional roof or hillock. A few inhabitants could be seen in sampans or junks. Another sheet of water stretched from Hankow to Jiujiang: 'Small spits of land, slightly higher than the rest, were peopled by two or three families and their livestock. There they remained, their last card played, until death brought release.' There were reports of whole districts being suddenly wiped out by the bursting of a dyke, with '7,000 drowned here, 5,000 there, while other areas are lucky to have lost only 500 or so'. China's then capital, Nanking, was flooded to a depth of three feet, while the streets of Hankow were under four feet of water, and sampans were a common sight, though rickshaws went on trying to ply their trade. The towns were crammed with refugees desperately looking for a few square feet of dry land. Hankow was estimated to have 70,000 of them, some camping on railway tracks.

The following April, *The Times* reported that an area larger than England was now devastated, with at least ten million people destitute in 'the greatest affliction that has befallen any nation in recent times'. The paper's reporter toured refugee camps and found 'thousands of men and women who have lost all but life itself sitting in patient expectation of death'. It was like a sodden Hades: 'Imagine a mud road three miles long and fifteen yards wide, with remains of mat sheds and bits of sacking as cover. People it so thickly in your imagination that there is only a path four feet wide down the middle. Remember that about a quarter of them are children under the age of six. To this hell add pigs, chickens, ducks and emaciated dogs. Now realise that for this vast, tightly packed multitude, there are no sanitary arrangements whatsoever.' The refugees lived in communal sheds about thirty yards long. In a 'pathetic attempt at privacy' some families had made little wigwams about three feet high from bamboo mats bent into a semicircle. Food supplies were under severe strain, with an estimated 70 per cent of the rice crop destroyed. Medicine was also scarce, so smallpox was raging, along with dysentery and influenza. A hundred people a day were dying of disease.

But even in these dreadful conditions the Chinese entrepreneurial spirit survived. There were food-sellers with oranges, peanuts, bean curd, fish and meat. Some of the refugees still seemed to have money and were able to prepare 'tolerable' meals. Others, though, lived on grass or rice husks. There were stories of corrupt officials stealing money meant to help the refugees, but some used the available funds with considerable resourcefulness. One mission group ran a bath-house for women, which was in great demand. Some were even prepared to miss out on eating to take their turn. As one put it: 'Food we may get another day, but not a bath.' In a Buddhist temple the reporter found 250 women and children attending school in the morning, sewing classes in the afternoon, and getting two meals a day: 'It was a relief to turn into the quiet busy cheerfulness of these temple courts where a giant gilded Buddha sits aloft and impartially surveys the scene.' There were estimated to be half a million people in the camps, but other refugees had crowded into schools and temples, seeming to fill every available corner of the cities. The authorities had put Hankow under martial law, but that did not prevent hundreds of robberies every night.

Altogether, at least 130,000 people drowned, and it is believed that up to three million more died from starvation and disease. By May more than a million people had joined in the repair of 3,000 miles of damaged dykes, but they were hampered by the civil war raging between Chiang Kai-shek's nationalists and Mao Zedong's communists, and at least 1,000 were said to have been killed in a month.

Heavy rains made the Yangtze flood again in 1935 and 1948, killing thousands more people.


## · HUARAZ ·

Huaraz is a picturesque colonial town 9,000 feet up in the Ancash region of Peru, about 200 miles north of Lima, with snow-capped mountains towering above it. In December 1941 it had been basking in a heatwave for days, with temperatures reaching thirty degrees. On Saturday, 13 December, a huge tongue of ice broke off the 20,575-foot Mount Palcaraju and crashed into a lake below that was already swollen with meltwater. As it overflowed, water gushed into a lower lake and, with a great explosion, burst through the natural moraine dam holding it back. Out poured a fifty-foot wall of water that careered through eight villages, picking up boulders and stones as it went, crushing everything in its path, before carving a great rocky scar through Huaraz, nine miles downstream.

Like most such floods, it arrived without warning, destroying about a quarter of the town and killing up to 7,000 of its 30,000 inhabitants. Three decades later, in May 1970, Huaraz was hit by an earthquake that killed half the population.

## · HENAN ·

Mao Zedong's 'Great Leap Forward' was meant to modernise China and make it one of the world's great powers. One bright idea was to get people all over the country to build dams, which they did with great enthusiasm, marching off to work with flags flying and martial music playing. The trouble was that the dams were often designed by untrained peasants and built with primitive tools, so within two or three years many were collapsing. The Shimantan dam on the Hong (or 'red') River and the Banqiao dam on the Ru, both in China's most heavily populated province of Henan, were probably among the better ones, but corners had still been cut. A hydrologist named Chen Xing tried to warn of the dangers, but he was purged for being a 'right-wing opportunist'.

At the beginning of August 1975 China was being buffeted by its third typhoon of the year, and a series of storms had dumped more than thirty-six inches of rain on Henan. 'The days were like nights as rain fell like arrows,' recalled one inhabitant. The two dams were designed to handle at most twenty inches over three days, but on 5 August alone a record seventeen inches fell. The next day brought a sixteen-hour downpour. Some suggested the Banqiao dam should be opened, but the authorities refused because there was already flooding in the areas below it. After more heavy rain on the 7th and 8th they finally tried to open the sluice gates, but by then they were blocked with sediment. Just after midnight on the 9th the Shimantan dam collapsed, emptying twenty-six billion gallons of water into the valley below in just five hours. Half an hour later, with people still trying to shore up the Banqiao dam, it started to crumble too. A woman shouted, 'The dragon is coming!' as the collapse unleashed a wall of water twenty feet high. According to a survivor, it was as though 'the sky was collapsing and the earth was cracking. Houses and trees disappeared in an instant . . . amid people's wailing for help.'

In all, more than sixty dams burst in the region, and flood waters travelling at thirty miles an hour spread over 4,000 square miles. The city of Huaibin, which stood where the Hong and Ru rivers meet, was completely washed away. Shahedian, just below Banquiao, was evacuated, so fewer than 1,000 of its 6,000 inhabitants were killed, but most neighbouring towns were caught completely unawares because the telecommunications system, such as it was, had been knocked out. More than 36,000 people perished in Wencheng commune, next to Shahedian, while Daowencheng was wiped from the map, with the loss of 9,600 lives. At Runan 100,000 people were left floating in improvised boats or on debris.

Tens of thousands of People's Liberation Army troops were deployed on relief work, but after nine days more than a million people were still trapped and dependent on air-drops of food. While the authorities had concentrated on building dams, they had not bothered to dredge rivers. Now much of the flood water could not escape, so some dams that had not been breached had to be bombed or dynamited as officials tried to direct water away from the most vulnerable areas. It was two weeks before the waters began to retreat, leaving mounds of corpses rotting in the sun. Now disease and hunger ripped through the survivors, striking more than a million people. In one commune it was reported that survivors ate all the leaves off the trees, while out of 500,000 people in Runan 320,000 were said to be ill, including 33,000 with dysentery. Now that Chen Xing had been so dramatically vindicated, Communist Party officials flew him over the disaster area to ask his advice.

China suppressed news of the disaster for a long time, and the first full account in English came from an American pressure group, Human Rights Watch, in 1995. It was only a decade later that the Chinese authorities finally started to lift the veil of official secrecy. They claimed that just 26,000 people had perished, but conceded that 'The number may be revised.' Many believe the true total was far higher. For instance, Human Rights Watch estimated that 85,000 were killed by the floods and another 145,000 died in the famine and epidemics that followed.

The Chinese had held a secret investigation soon after the floods in which they discovered a series of 'unexpected failures'. The country's Central Meteorological Observatory was not able to give an accurate prediction of rain, while the absence of any early warning system or evacuation plan meant the flooded areas had quickly descended into chaos. At an international seminar held in Henan in 2005, Li Zechun, a former weather forecaster who became an academician at the Chinese Academy of Engineering Sciences, declared the disaster was 'a man-made calamity rather than a natural one'.

## · VENEZUELA ·

Venezuela's coastal area has always suffered from flooding and mud-slides, but the deadliest came in December 1999. A 350-mile stretch from the capital, Caracas, to the Colombian border, where most of the country's twenty-three million people lived, would be devastated after fierce storms brought thirty-six inches of rain in just a few days. On 14 December rivers and streams burst their banks, setting off flash floods and mudslides which turned pretty Caribbean beaches into a mess of mud and rubble. In towns they engulfed even high-rise buildings, and effortlessly swept away the shanty towns perched precariously on tiny ridges around Caracas, burying them under stones, tree trunks and crushed concrete. Of the 4,000 people who had been living in one, Blandin, nearly a quarter were dead or missing.

A *Washington Post* reporter found one woman searching desperately for her father, but not expecting to find him alive. 'Death is everywhere now,' she said, 'under what is left of this place.' A fifty-two-year-old man lamented: 'I have survived an earthquake and other terrible things, but nothing in my life has compared to this. I will never forget the chaos and yelling . . . You can never forget something so savage.' A few miles away, the town of Los Corales, a collection of smart apartments near Caracas's La Guaira Airport, was buried under ten feet of mud and looked like a lunar landscape. Most of those caught up in the disaster complained that they had received no warning, though in the El Guapo area of Miranda state, south-east of the capital, the governor had ordered evacuations before a large dam broke. Even so, many people were killed in the subsequent floods.

More than 12,000 troops took part in the rescue operation, with helicopters plucking people from the flood waters and the mud. Major Jesus Rodriguez of the Venezuelan National Guard said everywhere desperate people were walking around 'like zombies'. He was making about eighty runs a day, delivering food, water and nappies. Every time they landed, dozens of people would surround them and carry off goods in wheelbarrows, wheelchairs or their bare hands. On one flight a woman gave birth. Down below, soldiers scoured the mountains on horseback and paratroopers leapt to deliver supplies into remote areas, while warships rescued people from the beaches. Twenty-three thousand homes had been destroyed, and an estimated 140,000 people were left homeless. Emergency shelters were soon overcrowded. Those for whom there was no room were often sent to Caracas, but there was scarcely a corner to spare. Three thousand people were living in the sports stadium, sleeping on mattresses covering every inch of space. President Hugo Chávez appealed to his fellow Venezuelans 'to show that we are all Christians' by taking people into their homes, and opened his own residence to children whose parents were missing.

Still, tens of thousands roamed the streets in search of food and water. Some broke into houses and stores. A reporter saw one young man carrying a huge frozen tuna on his back as armed soldiers looked on: 'This is an emergency, we need food, we take it,' he said. Hundreds of people, many of them barefoot, ransacked the cargo area at La Guaira, until troops fired in the air. Paratroopers also apprehended looters who had been stealing from the dead and the destitute. Most estimates put the number killed at about 30,000, but the authorities conceded that the true figure might never be known.

# 5

## STORMS

In the Caribbean, North Atlantic and eastern North Pacific severe tropical storms are called hurricanes. In the western North Pacific they are referred to as typhoons. In the western South Pacific and Indian Ocean they go by the name of cyclones. Gusts of wind can reach more than 200 miles an hour, and they are often accompanied by torrential rain and a storm surge that might raise the level of the sea by twenty feet. The first storm in this chapter, though, happened far from the tropics.

### · THE GREAT STORM ·

'No pen could describe it, nor tongue express it, nor thought conceive it unless by one in the extremity of it.' So wrote Daniel Defoe of the 'Great Storm' of 1703, the worst to hit Britain in recorded history. For weeks, fierce gales had been battering England and Wales, and by midnight on Friday, 26 November, the wind was blowing so fiercely that the vicar at St Keverne on Cornwall's Lizard Peninsula said people 'thought the great Day of Judgement was coming'.

Fourteen miles off Plymouth lay the jagged and treacherous Eddystone Rocks. Five years before, a shipowner named Henry Winstanley, two of whose vessels had been wrecked on them, had built a 120-foot lighthouse there. He believed it was indestructible, and said he hoped to be there during 'the greatest storm that ever was'. On 26 November he got his wish. He was supervising work on the building when a sixty-foot wave demolished it, killing Winstanley and five other people. Meanwhile, in London, Daniel Defoe looked at his barometer and saw a reading so low he assumed his children must have been tampering with it.

By now, winds of more than seventy miles an hour were devastating south Wales from Milford Haven to the Severn Estuary. In Swansea most houses lost their roofs, while the storm made a huge breach in Cardiff's city wall. The estuary rose to ten feet above high-tide level, flooding a wide area including Bristol, where the wind also brought down buildings, killing a number of people. Meanwhile, a chimney stack came crashing through the roof of the bishop's palace at Wells, striking dead the bishop and his wife as they slept. Coastal towns like Portsmouth 'looked as if the enemy had sacked them'. At Shoreham, the ancient Market House was flattened 'and all the town shattered', while Brighton seemed to have been 'bombarded' and more than 1,000 buildings were razed in Kent. Further north, waterspouts ripped through Oxfordshire, uprooting trees and haystacks, while in Northampton All Saints' and other churches were damaged and 'an honest yeoman, being up on a ladder to save his hovel, was blown off, and fell upon a plough, died outright and never spoke word more'. Everywhere barns, outhouses, sheds, haystacks and even men and animals were whisked into the air as winds accelerated to over 120 miles an hour.

London suffered severe damage, with the *Post Man* newspaper declaring: 'there is hardly any house but has had a share in the calamity'. Lead on the roof of Westminster Abbey was 'rolled up like parchment and blown clear of the building'. People were not sure what was more dangerous – staying inside and risking the house collapsing or going outside and facing an onslaught of roof tiles and other debris flying through the air at forty miles an hour. A carpenter and his wife decided to stay indoors. She asked him to read a chapter from the Bible but he refused. Whereupon the chimney promptly collapsed and killed him, leaving her 'miraculously' unhurt. Part of St James's Palace was blown down, killing a woman outside, while Queen Anne sheltered in the cellar. The wind smashed up boats on the Thames, and wreckage blocked the arches of London Bridge. Defoe reckoned he saw about 700 ships destroyed on the river, while about 20 people were drowned. The writer himself almost joined the casualty list when a chimney plummeted to the ground right next to him, but he was spared to become the great chronicler of the storm, gathering eyewitness accounts from all over the country.

His was not the only remarkable escape. As a chimney stack collapsed on a London house, a nurse, a maid and a baby all fell through three floors to the kitchen. The nurse and the maid suffered only bruises, and the baby was found hanging in the curtains unharmed. At Highbridge, on the Somerset levels, a man and his wife were drowned in their house, but their baby floated away in its cradle, and was found alive when the waters receded. A miller awoken by the storm at Charlwood, Surrey, went out to try to save his windmill, but he had to return home because he had forgotten the key. By the time he finally reached the windmill, there was nothing left of it. Altogether, on land, it is estimated that about 125 people were killed. At sea, though, things were much worse.

Many harbours were crammed with ships sheltering from the dreadful weather, while others were lying at anchor just outside. These included many naval vessels recently returned from the summer campaign against the French. People said they had never seen so many ships. There were 106 merchantmen anchored near the Goodwin Sands, and 20 heavily laden vessels from the West Indies waiting off Bristol. By 27 November, the winds were roaring through the Channel at 140 miles an hour. Many smaller vessels sank from the sheer weight of water washing over their decks, while bigger ones were set helplessly adrift. Soon they were crashing into each other. The warships *Prince George* and *Restoration* became hopelessly entangled and the latter went to the bottom with all 386 hands. A dozen ships were stranded on the Goodwin Sands, including the *Northumberland*, which would be lost with her entire crew of 253.

The sixty-gun *Mary* broke up, leaving a sole survivor from her crew of 273. He managed to cling to a piece of floating wreckage until a huge wave picked him up and dropped him on the deck of another man o' war, the *Stirling Castle*. As she was driven aground he was flung overboard again. This time he fell into one of the ship's boats – the only one that managed to float free – and reached the shore unconscious and suffering from exposure but alive. Nearly 280 other crewmen on the *Stirling*

*Castle* drowned. Altogether on the Goodwin Sands it is estimated that 1,200 men lost their lives. The *Reserve* was swamped at anchor off Yarmouth with the loss of 190 sailors, while 255 perished when the *Canterbury* sank near Bristol. The *Association* vanished after being driven from her anchorage at Harwich. Her rudder was ripped off by a sandbank, and with just a scrap of sail she was blown helplessly out to sea. As her stores ran out the crew were put on short rations and many fell ill. The Admiralty had given her up for lost when she suddenly appeared in the Medway the following January, having returned from Gothenburg, where she had been driven by the wind after the storm. Twenty-eight of her crew had died on the journey. Altogether, thirteen men o' war were lost and more than two thousand sailors.

Defoe accused the people of Deal and Walmer of failing to help sailors shipwrecked on the Goodwin Sands, claiming the townsfolk were more interested in gathering booty from the wrecks:

> They spare no hazard or no pain,
> But 'tis to save the Goods and not the Men.

The Mayor of Deal, Thomas Powell, commandeered boats by force and saved about 200 men who were 'almost dead with hunger and cold, naked and starving', but when he asked the queen's agent to help seamen injured in the storm, the agent 'would not relieve them with one penny'. The mayor had to dig into his own pocket to feed and lodge them, and if any died, Powell even had to pay to get them buried. It was the same story when the survivors needed funds to return to London. When the mayor tried to get his money back from the government he 'met with great obstructions and delays' before finally being reimbursed.

Merchant ships suffered too. The *John and Mary* was blown 150 miles from Great Yarmouth to Scarborough, with her master protesting: 'Such a tempest as this, there never was in the world.' Another cut away her masts and put out to sea to try to avoid being dashed against other vessels. Blown north for four days, the crew had no idea where they were until they met a pilot boat that guided them into a Norwegian port. Three ketches went down off Brighton with the loss of all hands, except for one man who clung to a floating mast for three days; and three merchantmen were sunk off Plymouth. At Grimsby nearly every vessel in the harbour was driven out to sea, and twenty never returned. Altogether, up to 8,000 died at sea.

Defoe not only gathered stories of the storm but catalogued the damage. On a journey through Kent he tried to count how many trees had been felled, but when he got to 17,000 he gave up. The diarist John Evelyn had 2,000 blown down at his house at Wotton, Surrey, and commented philosophically: 'I thank God for what are yet left standing.' Up to twenty-five miles inland farmers found their fields had been so badly contaminated with salt water that they were unfit for grazing. Most sheep on the South Downs turned their noses up at the grass; any that were desperate enough to eat it later 'drank like fishes'. The *Observator* newspaper wrote: 'never was such a storm of wind, such a hurricane and tempest known in the memory of man, nor the like to be found in the histories of England'.

Queen Anne felt it was important that the people should realise two things: the storm was their own fault for having been so sinful; and they were extremely lucky it had not been worse. It was decided that a national fast should be held on 19 January 1704 to thank God for deliverance from the tempest which Anne's subjects must 'humbly acknowledge' as 'a token of the Divine displeasure' while thanking God for His 'infinite mercy . . . that we and our people were not thereby wholly destroyed'. The churches were said to be 'so crowded few could get into them'.

Still, it is an ill wind that blows nobody any good, and tilers, bricklayers and glaziers saw their wages treble in the months that followed.

## · THE GREAT HURRICANE ·

The deadliest Atlantic hurricane of all time struck Barbados on 9 October 1780. For two days, winds of up to 200 miles an hour are said to have knocked down every house on the island, while most ships were torn from their moorings, and dozens of fishing boats failed to return to port. About 4,500 people died, with virtually every family losing someone.

Next the storm destroyed 584 out of 600 houses in Kingstown on St Vincent, while 19 Dutch ships were wrecked off Grenada. Early on 11 October it turned on St Lucia. A number of British warships, fighting against the American rebels, were taking refuge at Port Castries. The storm not only destroyed them, drowning most of the crews, but flattened the town's hospital by flinging a ship on top of it. Only two houses survived the hurricane's visit, and 6,000 people died. The next victim was Martinique, where twenty-five-foot waves killed 9,000 and flattened all the houses in St Pierre. At St Kitts another 100 ships were destroyed. The storm also caused severe damage in Guadeloupe, Antigua, Puerto Rico, the Dominican Republic, and Bermuda, where it drove fifty ships aground.

The total death toll on land was estimated at 24,000, and thousands more died at sea.

## · TWO DISASTROUS YEARS ·

On 16 July 1881 one of the deadliest typhoons in history devastated Haiphong, the main port of what is now Vietnam, stirring up great tidal waves that killed perhaps 300,000 people, including those who perished from disease and hunger in the aftermath.

Less than a year later, on 6 June 1882, it was the great Indian port of Bombay (now Mumbai) that found itself under assault, as a cyclone whipped up waves that drowned 100,000 people. This was not the first time India had found itself in harm's way. On 25 November 1839 a cyclone whipped up forty-foot waves that are said to have killed 300,000 people in Coringa at the mouth of the Ganges on the east coast. That port was never completely rebuilt.

## · VICIOUS VERA ·

Japan's fourth-biggest city, Nagoya, was heavily bombed during the Second World War, but by 1959 it had re-established itself as a major port and industrial centre, with a population of 1.3 million. On 21 September Typhoon Vera began its approach. It was the fifteenth tropical storm of the year and there was little alarm. Edwin O. Reischauer, later the US ambassador in Tokyo, remarked that the Japanese were accustomed 'to expect natural catastrophes and accept them with stoic resilience'. People even believed typhoons were good omens. In the thirteenth century Kublai Khan, the grandson of Genghis (see Chapter 10), twice had his Mongol armada scattered and sunk before he could launch an invasion by what the Japanese dubbed a 'divine wind' – a *kamikaze*. More often than not, typhoons died down before reaching land or veered out to sea, so even when the wind began to rattle the coast on Saturday, 26 September, residents just put up their storm shutters and brought in extra supplies.

Vera hit Nagoya with its full force late that night, bringing seventeen-foot waves that destroyed dams, wharves, bridges and buildings. A big apartment block collapsed, trapping eighty-four residents in the ruins. The sea quickly flooded low-lying areas that had been reclaimed from the sea, then swirled into timber yards, picking up logs and turning them into battering rams. Winds of up to 140 miles an hour tore roofs off houses and sent pieces of debris flying through the air like missiles. Many people were drowned before they could flee the raging waters, and the west bank of the Shonai River collapsed, killing more than 1,800 people as police braved the roaring wind and blinding rain to try to guide inhabitants to higher ground. For three hours Vera raged around the city before heading out to the Pacific and disappearing.

Sunday dawned with a third of Nagoya submerged, and the rest piled high with mud and rubble. The streets and the water of the bay were littered with bodies, and more than twenty ships had been driven ashore. Now the survivors faced a desperate struggle, often diving into the polluted water to try to retrieve scraps of food from submerged kitchens or gardens. Some refused to abandon their homes for fear of looters, while others carried bundles of bedding and clothing or a treasured possession, such as a television, as they searched for somewhere to shelter. The biggest emergency centre was at the racecourse, but the refugees there had nothing to drink for thirty hours. The dead, meanwhile, were being laid out on sodden fields or in temporary morgues, each covered with a reed mat. The mayor lamented: 'I feel as if my arms and legs have been cut off. All I can see is the whole town submerged under a sea and filled with the dead.' Many neighbouring towns and villages had also been severely damaged: at Handa a giant wave destroyed 250 houses, killing 300 people and carrying off hundreds more without trace.

Thirty-eight of Japan's forty-seven prefectures were hit, so assistance was sometimes slow to arrive, and rescue operations were hampered by the flood waters and the rain that continued to fall. US Navy helicopters dropped food and other supplies on to high ground, and winched people from the roofs of buildings. Many had not eaten for days. By 30 September, 9,000 Japanese soldiers were helping with the rescue, and tons of relief supplies had reached Nagoya, but the swirling waters still made it hard to pull out survivors. The flood had destroyed the Tsushima waterworks, and many people had been drinking polluted water or eating contaminated food. There were 800 cases of dysentery, and medicine was in short supply. Six days after the disaster, *The Times'* correspondent flew over the worst-hit areas in a helicopter. In the suburbs to the south-west all the landmarks had been obliterated. Buildings had collapsed like packs of cards, but many inhabitants were still clinging to roofs, and were dependent on supplies dropped from the air. Some seemed 'to have reached the extremity of starvation and exhaustion'.

The next day the reporter sailed to the village of Jushiyama. Nearly all its 900 buildings were still awash up to the eaves. He saw old men and women, mothers with infants, children and the sick forming an orderly queue as they waited to board a landing craft that was going to take them away with their bundles of belongings. Many younger men stayed behind to guard against looters.

Altogether, at least 5,000 people were killed by Vera, hundreds more were never found and over 30,000 were injured. Nearly 120,000 buildings were destroyed or damaged, making more than half a million people homeless, but the symbol of Nagoya, two ten-foot-tall dolphin-like sculptures that adorned its ancient castle, escaped undamaged.

It emerged that a survey carried out earlier in the year had concluded that flood control plans were inadequate. *The Times'* correspondent went to visit the Mayor of Nagoya and found him in a room full of quarrelling officials. The mayor explained: 'People in their present extremity cannot criticise heaven, so they criticise the mayor and city officials as responsible for the acts of heaven.'

Still, the city recovered quickly, and Edwin Reischauer paid tribute to the Japanese people and their 'great capacity to dig themselves out . . . after such catastrophes to start afresh'. The restored Nagoya had stronger breakwaters by the port, and higher, tougher embankments along its rivers.

## · THE DEADLIEST STORM IN HISTORY ·

Bangladesh is the world's seventh most populous country, home to about 150 million people, but it is also one of the poorest and most crowded, where subsistence fishermen and rice farmers eke out a precarious existence. Three-quarters of the nation lies less than ten feet above sea level, and many of the population live on the deltas of the Brahmaputra, the Meghna and the Ganges as these great rivers drain into the Bay of Bengal. People often build their houses on embankments to try to escape flooding, but it does not always work, especially when Bangladesh is hit by a cyclone.

During the night of 12–13 November 1970, as most people slept, a 115-mile-an-hour wind funnelled a terrifying forty-foot wave on to what was then East Pakistan. Kamaluddin Chodhury, a farmer on Manpura Island in the Ganges Delta, heard a great roar: 'It was pitch black, but in the distance I could see a glow. The glow got nearer and nearer and then I realised it was the crest of a huge wave.' He rushed his family to the top of the house just in time, as the island disappeared under an avalanche of water. It kept surging just below them as they huddled together, lashed by wind and rain, but fortunately their home was more solidly built than the island's usual thatch and bamboo huts. Towards dawn, the waters receded, and the Chodhury family were left to contemplate a scene of utter devastation. Of 4,500 huts on the island, only four were still standing. Nearly every landmark had been obliterated, and anything spared by the fearful flood was covered in mud. There had been 30,000 people living on Manpura; 25,000 were now dead. Corpses hung from trees or lay in heaps on the beaches.

On Bhola, the biggest island in the Bay of Bengal, about 200,000 people drowned, a fifth of the population. Nurul Huq, a rice farmer, watched his seventy-five-year-old mother being washed away. 'We have been through many storms,' he said, 'but there has never been anything like this. Only Allah knows why this has happened to us.' Ninety relatives of Ali Husain, a soldier in the Pakistan Army, lived together in a compound. Ali managed to climb a palm tree and hung on until the waters subsided, but seventy members of his family were killed. On one of the smaller islands, a rice farmer named Munshi Mustander Billa also survived by clinging to a tree. He saw five of his children picked off by the waters, then had his one-year-old baby wrenched from his arms. When his wife was also swept away Munshi was overcome with grief and let go of the tree, but he managed to grab hold of another and then caught hold of his wife. The waters tore the clothes off their backs, so the next morning they had to pick their way through floating corpses and animal carcasses to a neighbour's house, hoping to find something to wear. The neighbours were dead, but a boy who had survived collected some rags and gave them to the couple.

On the small islands off Chittagong no one was left alive, and the city itself was devastated. In most places the heaviest death toll was among children who were not strong enough to hold on to trees, but one group had an extraordinary escape. Three days after the cyclone a wooden chest was washed ashore with six youngsters, all under thirteen, clinging to it. They had been put on it by their grandfather, who had then crawled inside. He was dead from exposure.

After the waters receded, survivors wandered around searching desperately for loved ones, or burying the dead, with scarves wrapped around their mouths and noses to try to combat the dreadful smell. One old man piled the remains of fifty-two relatives into a single grave, but there were so many corpses that it was impossible to bury them all, so some were put on makeshift rafts and floated out to sea. All too often it just washed them back to shore. A million cattle were drowned, nearly every fishing boat was lost, and three-quarters of the rice crop was destroyed. Villagers would search in the mud for single grains. There was no clean water, either. In the towns the mains were fractured; in the country springs were fouled by seawater and rotting carcasses.

Within four days Red Cross shipments began to arrive at Dacca's airport and an international fleet of helicopters ferried supplies to the stricken region, but not fast enough to prevent more deaths from starvation, exposure and disease. Four days after the cyclone, a *Times* correspondent flew over the island of Bhola and saw survivors dragging bloated corpses of cattle into burial pits. Other cows were still alive but 'without a blade of grass to eat', and human bodies were still sprawled in the sodden fields: 'Even from the aircraft it was possible to smell the odour of death.' The inhabitants had never had a chance. The land was completely flat, with nothing that offered shelter from the great waves. Whole villages had disappeared 'as if sucked up by a huge vacuum cleaner'. On one island the journalist saw a cargo ship dumped fifty yards inland by the storm. But in some places, astonishingly, rudimentary new homes were already springing up, a vision of 'curious tranquil domesticity with bright clothes hanging on lines and draped over fodder mounds to dry'.

Officially, the death toll was estimated at half a million people, with another 100,000 missing, making this the deadliest tropical storm in history. Other estimates put the figure even higher – up to one million dead – and millions were left homeless. There was widespread resentment at what was seen as the dilatory response of the government in faraway West Pakistan, with complaints that forty army helicopters had stood idle when they could have helped with the relief effort, and that there had been unreasonable delay in releasing half a million tons of grain from government stores. Angry demonstrations ensued, and by March 1971 a full-scale civil war was raging. Pakistan's president, Yahya Khan, launched a bloody assault on the East that led to perhaps one and a half million civilian deaths. About ten million more fled from East Pakistan to India, and Indian troops joined anti-government forces to defeat Pakistan's army decisively in December 1971, allowing East Pakistan to become the independent country of Bangladesh.

In addition to spawning a new nation, the cyclone inspired the first great charity rock concert, a forerunner of events such as Live Aid. The Bengali musician Ravi Shankar asked his friend, former Beatle George Harrison, for help, and the result was the Concert for Bangladesh in New York, attended by 40,000 people. Bob Dylan, Eric Clapton and Ringo Starr joined Shankar and Harrison on stage to raise more than £120,000.

The new Bangladeshi government tried to provide better storm shelters, but when another major cyclone struck in 1991 the death toll still reached 140,000, and ten million homes were destroyed.

## · HURRICANE MITCH ·

On 29 October 1998 Hurricane Mitch carved a trail of devastation through Central America, with winds reaching 180 miles an hour. It made landfall at Choluteca in Honduras, dropping thirty-six inches of rain and bloating the Choluteca River to six times its normal size. The coastal city of Puerto Cortes was flooded and wooden homes were smashed to pieces.

Even before the disaster, Honduras was one of the poorest countries in Latin America, with 82 per cent of the population living below the poverty line. Now people were desperate. One man who had lost the wooden house in which he lived with seventeen relatives, said: 'I do not know how we will rebuild our lives. We are very poor and need help from someone because we have nothing left.' After two days with nothing to eat, another local man had to leave an emergency shelter with his wife and eight children and walk for miles on a flooded road through the driving wind and rain back to their home to salvage what little food they could. 'The shelter has no food, nothing,' he complained. 'It's just a roof.'

President Carlos Flores declared defiantly: 'Honduras is mortally wounded, but not about to expire. We will get back on our feet.' But after examining the damage from a helicopter, Vice-President William Handal said it might take forty years for the country to recover. They had tried to pick up four people who were stranded, only to see them disappear in a torrent. Seven out of ten Hondurans had no electricity or water. Most roads were blocked, eighty-nine bridges were down, and many parts of the capital Tegucigalpa had been washed away. An eyewitness stood on the city's only surviving bridge and 'counted 18 buses floating down the river'. She met a man carrying his dead three-year-old daughter wrapped in a plastic tablecloth. He had been turned back from the morgue because it had no electricity and was already stuffed to the ceiling with dead bodies. Then she watched as the walls of the central prison collapsed and 2,000 inmates tried to jump into the river below. The police opened fire and it was 'like a set from a horror movie' as the prisoners' dead bodies rushed along in the water alongside fridges, televisions, pick-up trucks and bits of houses.

It was estimated that before the disaster up to 7,000 children were living rough by the river in Tegucigalpa. One homeless fourteen-year-old said: 'The water was up to our necks when the police came and told us to get out.' Over the whole of Honduras there were perhaps 20,000 'street children'. A charity worker said that no one could know how many of them died: 'When they disappear, nobody looks for them. For the authorities, they don't exist.' In the mountains, up to seventy-five inches of rain fell, causing widespread mudslides, which destroyed about twenty-five villages. Throughout the country more than 6,500 people were killed, and several thousand more were never found or had been buried in mass graves before they were identified. Up to one and a half million people, more than a fifth of the population, were left homeless. Mitch also destroyed nearly three-quarters of Honduras's crops, and killed more than 50,000 cattle and 60 per cent of the country's poultry. The food shortages that came in its wake left many villages on the brink of starvation, while diseases like malaria, dengue fever and cholera broke out.

Mitch also caused destruction in Nicaragua, El Salvador and Guatemala. Across Central America the death toll was put at 11,000, with up to 8,000 others officially 'missing'.


## · MYANMAR ·

Just as in Bangladesh (see above), many people in Myanmar lived on the delta of a great river. Three and a half million crowded on to the rich soil where the Irrawaddy fans out and enters the Andaman Sea. A sullen calm had lain over the country since the military junta brutally suppressed pro-democracy protests in September 2007, but on the night of 2 May 2008 it was rudely shattered. Cyclone Nargis struck, sending a twenty-foot surge of sea water through the low-lying villages of the delta, sweeping away whole communities. Further inland, winds of up to 120 miles an hour flattened buildings and killed thousands more. Tangled bodies lay crushed in the ruins of homes, rice paddies were strewn with corpses, wells were poisoned and livestock was wiped out.

In the town of Labutta at least half the houses were destroyed, while in Bogale only one building in twenty remained standing and at least 10,000 people were killed. At Kyaiklat, which had been home to 50,000 people, every house was damaged. Some were crushed by huge trees, others just collapsed. A few details seeped out, but Myanmar was a closed society, and anyone talking to a foreigner took a grave risk. It soon became clear, though, that the rescue effort was going badly wrong. Myanmar's leaders seemed overwhelmed by the disaster, yet were so paranoid about being overthrown they remained deeply obstructive towards aid teams from overseas. It took weeks for relief workers' visas to be issued, and supply planes were refused permission to fly over the country. Four days after the disaster, the inhabitants of one town thought that help was at hand when some soldiers arrived, but once the troops had dispensed a few meagre rations they just hung around by the road-side. A BBC team trying to reach the delta area found itself confronted by a barbed-wire barrier at a military checkpoint and was turned back. Astonishingly, the regime went ahead with a referendum on a new constitution that was designed to entrench the junta even more securely just eight days after the cyclone, although it agreed to post-pone the vote for two weeks in the worst-hit areas. By then, it was reckoned that two and a half million people were in desperate straits. In what was left of the fishing village of Uomiou a seventy-seven-year-old woman who had lost all her children and grandchildren cried: 'We are starving.' She and twenty others were sheltering in the only build-ing still standing.

American ships laden with supplies waited in vain off the coast for permission to land before reluctantly deciding to leave, while the United States' defence secretary, Robert Gates, accused the regime of 'criminal neglect'. Meanwhile, three weeks after the disaster, Médecins sans Frontières was still finding villages where people had received virtually no help. ShelterBox, a charity that had flown in tents, water-purification kits and mosquito nets, was not allowed to send its experts to the delta with them. The biggest provider of emergency relief, the United Nations' World Food Programme, complained that it was able to deliver only about a fifth of the aid that was needed, and it was not allowed to fly its helicopters until a month after the cyclone. Throughout this time, torrential rain continued to fall on survivors huddling in roofless buildings, while hundreds of bodies still floated in the floodwaters. Junta propaganda remained in full swing, though: Myanmar's army stuck its own labels on food packages donated by Thailand, while the government-controlled press peddled the fantasy that relief was reaching all those in need.

As the official response failed, individuals tried to help by driving out to the stricken areas, but the generals frowned on this freelance activity. Myanmar's most famous comedian, Zarganar, was arrested for his efforts. At the same time, human rights groups accused the authorities of evicting survivors from temporary shelters and sending them back to their devastated villages. One young girl who tried to enter a camp was told that she was not on the list of survivors and was turned away. 'I don't know where to go,' she said. Some took refuge with the Buddhist monks who had been viciously attacked by the regime the previous year. Many had been killed in the storm, but those who survived ran makeshift clinics. One forty-five-year-old woman who had lost all eight members of her family, and had no money for food, thought about killing herself. Then she heard of a clinic six miles upriver and managed to reach it by boat. 'I don't know where the government office is,' she said, 'so I came to the monks.'

India's meteorological agency claimed it had given the Burmese authorities a clear warning about the storm 48 hours before it struck. The generals insisted that 'timely weather reports' were issued, but people complained the bulletins did not spell out how deadly the storm would be, nor did they offer any advice on what to do.

According to official figures, issued a month after the disaster, the cyclone had killed at least 78,000 people, and another 56,000 were missing. Still, one thing had gone to plan. The junta got a 93 per cent vote in favour of its new constitution.

# 6

## OTHER EXTREME WEATHER & A MYSTERIOUS POISONING

### · HAILSTORMS ·

The deadliest hailstorm on record killed 246 people in northern India on 20 April 1888. *The Times* reported that the hail fell for only two minutes, but that it was 'virtually a shower of lumps of ice'. Most of the deaths were at Moradabad in Uttar Pradesh, although sixteen perished at Bareilly, and twenty in Lower Bengal, where 2,000 huts were destroyed. Most of the victims were knocked out, then suffocated or froze under drifts of ice. One hailstone found near Moradabad's telegraph office was said to be the size of a melon and weighed two pounds.

It is possible, though, that India has experienced something even worse. In 1942 a ranger found 600 skeletons in a mass grave on the edge of a remote lake at Roopkund, 16,000 feet up in the Himalayas. Radiocarbon dating suggested the bodies were from the ninth century. After studying fractures to the skulls, scientists concluded that they had been killed by hailstones as big as cricket balls. The area around the lake was completely open, so if huge lumps of hail had started raining down there would have been nowhere to shelter.

## · AMERICAN TORNADOES ·

Tornadoes generate the strongest winds on earth, violently rotating columns of air that whirl along the ground spinning at up to 300 miles an hour. Bizarrely, the UK has the most tornadoes per square mile, but they are usually weak and go unnoticed. The United States has by far the largest number, averaging more than 1,000 a year, and some of the most violent. One of the worst hit the city of Natchez on the Mississippi River on 7 May 1840.

At two o'clock in the afternoon it started knocking down houses. 'The air was filled with bricks and large pieces of timber,' said one eye-witness, 'and even ox carts were uplifted and thrown hundreds of yards.' Those who saw it and lived to tell the tale said the tornado looked like a rolling fog or boiling clouds on the ground. Within five minutes it had destroyed much of the city's residential area, and had killed forty-eight people. On the river the toll was much higher. About sixty boats sunk; and a ferry went down, drowning everyone on board. After Natchez, the tornado continued along the Mississippi and levelled the courthouse in Vidalia, Louisiana, killing the judge. The total death toll was put at 317, though it may well have been much higher, as slaves killed on nearby plantations were probably not counted.

The most lethal American twister of all was the Great Tri-State Tornado of 18 March 1925, which first struck Ellington, Missouri. It cut a swath up to a mile wide flattening anything in its path. At least eleven people died in Missouri before the wind crossed the Mississippi and blew into Illinois, virtually obliterating the town of Gorham and killing thirty-four. Travelling at up to 73 miles an hour, it wrought its worst devastation in Murphysboro, where 234 people were killed – the greatest loss of life from a tornado in a single city in US history. Half the population was made homeless, as 1,200 houses were felled. At De Soto, whole blocks were torn down and 100 people died. The president of a bank sheltered in his vault and survived even though the building above him was destroyed, but in the schoolhouse thirty-three chil-dren perished. Fires broke out in both towns, causing even more damage. Hurst-Bush was shattered and West Frankfort virtually wiped out. Rural areas were also devastated, and at South Greenfield the wind overturned a passenger train, killing a number of passengers. In all, Illinois lost at least 613 people, the most in a single state in US history.

Next in line was Indiana, as the tornado crossed the Wabash River. It nearly demolished Griffin, then destroyed half of Princeton, before it finally dissipated, having killed seventy-one people in the state. In a 219-mile rampage, the Great Tri-State Tornado had devastated nineteen communities, knocked down 15,000 homes, and claimed over 700 lives. Some of the places it tore apart never recovered. One survivor said: 'We didn't even know the word "tornado". To us, it was just a storm.' The disaster made America realise it had to develop a proper warning system, but that proved difficult, and it was only in 1952 that forecasters began issuing regular warnings.

## ·  AMERICAN HEATWAVES  ·

While America's economy slumped during the Great Depression of the 1930s, thermometers were soaring to unprecedented heights as the longest drought of the twentieth century parched the country. In June 1936 temperatures of more than thirty-eight degrees were common. July was even hotter, and many temperature records were set. In Steele, North Dakota, the thermometer reached forty-nine degrees, the highest reading ever in the state, and records were set in fourteen other states. By 18 July, it was reported that 3,715 people had died from the heat in the previous two weeks.

August blazed too, setting temperature records for the month in five states. Many a farmer saw his harvest destroyed, and by October one observer said the 'wide Missouri' at Kansas City was reduced to 'a mere skeleton of a river, a languid thread of water in a great bed of baked mud'. The same was true of the Mississippi at St Louis, where more than 420 people had died from the heat. Altogether, the heatwave killed perhaps 15,000 in the three years from 1934 to 1936.

It was nearly half a century before America suffered anything like it again. Then, in 1980, the Midwest and South saw temperatures reach thirty-two degrees nearly every day from June to September. In Kansas

City, for seventeen days without a break, the thermometer went over thirty-eight degrees, while in Memphis it climbed to an all-time high of forty-two degrees on 13 July, and temperatures never dipped below thirty-eight for fifteen consecutive days. In Wichita Falls it was even hotter – forty-eight degrees – the second-highest temperature ever recorded in Texas. A local joke ran: 'I've got to go and boil some water so I can have a cool drink.' Everywhere there were reports of old people collapsing in the streets, and of crime rates and child abuse soaring as the heat dramatically shortened tempers. In Missouri a two-year-old boy died after being locked in a van parked in the street for two hours. His mother had not been able to find a babysitter.

Raging bush fires swept through Arizona, while at Okemah, Oklahoma, a road blew up, 'scattering chunks of concrete as effectively as if it had been dynamited', according to the highway patrol. In many places people suffered heatstroke in their homes, and in Atlanta a man was taken to hospital with a body temperature of forty-seven degrees. They packed him in cold, wet sheets and ice, and he recovered. He also won a place in the *Guinness Book of Records* for having the highest body temperature ever recorded.

From the air, a *Guardian* correspondent saw 'parched, brown fields shorn of grass or dotted with stunted crops. Each morning at dawn, the sun comes up as a bright red ball over the flat plain, signalling another day of unremitting heat.' Crops were again devastated, with 80 per cent lost in some areas, while many pigs simply dropped dead. Eight million broiler chickens suffocated in a week in Arkansas. Even at night temperatures stayed in the high twenties. In the 1930s people had slept on benches in public parks to keep cool, but now that was considered too dangerous. Indeed, Americans were even reluctant to open their windows or go to the relative cool of an emergency centre in case their homes were robbed. Although many houses now had air-conditioning, poorer ones did not, so the Red Cross went from door to door, handing out electric fans.

Before most Americans had realised what was happening, up to 10,000 people had died. As Don Eisenberg of the Kansas City Red Cross put it: 'With a tornado or a flood or a fire, it's not too hard to tell what's happened. This heat just crept on.' Among the few people not fazed by the weather were British tourists in Florida. While it is not clear what mad dogs did, visiting Englishmen and women caused astonishment among the locals by going out in the midday sun to the beach.

## · THE MONSOON FLOOD OF 1978 ·

One of the deadliest monsoon floods of all time struck India in the first few days of September 1978. The army put up earthworks to try to protect people's homes, but an estimated one million people fled from Haryana to Delhi, where there were at least fifty deaths. In Uttar Pradesh, wide areas around Allahabad and Agra were flooded, and the 2,500-year-old holy city of Varanasi was completely cut off.

On 12 September the Ganges and Yamuna rivers burst their banks, flooding hundreds of towns and villages. Cholera broke out as drinking water was contaminated, and seventeen people died from an especially virulent form of the illness in Bihar. But it was in West Bengal where the worst flooding occurred. Nearly nine inches of rain fell in Calcutta on 26 September alone, and thousands had to climb on to roofs. Twenty miles out of the city, seventy-four passengers were drowned when their bus skidded off the road into deep flood water.

In the first week of October the floods were exacerbated by a cyclone. Altogether, they are estimated to have killed 15,000 in the region, and over the whole of India no fewer than 43 million people were driven from their homes. Across the border in Bangladesh, 50,000 inhabitants of Dacca were forced to flee as the Mahananda River burst its banks. Floods also killed 195 people at Kathmandu, Nepal.

## · THE DEADLIEST TORNADO ·

The USA may suffer the greatest number of tornadoes, but those that strike Bangladesh are more lethal. In 1964 a twister accounted for up to 500 people, but the most deadly struck at about half past six on the evening of 26 April 1989. It devastated at least fifty villages. Survivors reported huge trees flying through the air and winds that grabbed hold of cattle and smashed them to the ground hundreds of yards away. 'It looked as though the whole village was being uprooted,' said one eyewitness. Not a single house was left standing at Hargoz, where nearly 700 people died. Bodies were said to have been found up to two miles away. A Reuters correspondent reported that survivors had fled in search of food and shelter, so the village was almost completely deserted, but 'Toys and household goods lie scattered amid heaps of debris, reminders that this was once a thriving community.' A local councillor said: 'The village has turned into a mass grave. We had no time to mourn the dead or perform funeral rites for them.' In the graveyard a solitary man wept as he waved a bamboo pole to scare off the vultures who were trying to eat the bodies of his child and his neighbours.

A week after the disaster people fought for meagre supplies of food, water and medicine as hunger and disease closed in, and many fell ill after eating rotten food or drinking contaminated water. When government relief workers arrived at the remote villages of Dhamsara and Kalia, they were besieged by hungry people; more than 100 perished in the resulting stampede.

In addition to an estimated 1,300 people killed by the twister, 12,000 were injured and 80,000 lost their homes, making this the most lethal tornado in history. Another, in 1996, killed up to 1,000 people in the same region.

## · GREAT AMERICAN BLIZZARDS ·

The 'Schoolhouse Blizzard' hit the Great Plains of the United States on 12 January 1888. It got its name because many of its victims were children being taught in the one-room schoolhouses that were then common in rural America. A Nebraskan schoolteacher named Minnie Freeman is said to have tied her pupils together with a clothes line and led them through the storm to safety – an achievement commemorated today in a mural in the state's Capitol Building. Another Nebraskan teacher was less fortunate. When her schoolhouse ran out of fuel at three o'clock in the afternoon she decided to take the three pupils trapped with her to her boarding house, which was just eighty yards away. But they were barely out of the door before they were blinded by the snowstorm. They lost their way and the three children froze to death. The teacher survived but lost both her feet through frostbite. The blizzard raged from noon until early evening, killing an estimated 236 people.

A couple of months later, New York was enjoying its mildest winter for seventeen years, but on 11 March, snow started to fall. Soon it had turned into a fierce blizzard – according to *The Times*: 'the worst ever known in the city'. What would be dubbed the 'Great White Hurricane' paralysed the east coast of the United States from Chesapeake Bay to Maine, as well as affecting parts of eastern Canada. It raged for three days, with nearly sixty inches of snow estimated to have fallen on Saratoga Springs, New York, fifty inches on Connecticut and Massachusetts, and forty inches on New Jersey. Winds of nearly fifty miles an hour created drifts up to fifty feet deep. Major cities such as New York, Boston, Philadelphia and Washington, D.C., were cut off as telegraph wires snapped. 'Each city was as much deprived of communication with the world as if it had been in the centre of the ocean' was the verdict of *The Times*. Two hundred ships were driven aground and at least 100 seamen perished. On land, an estimated 400 people died, including 100 in New York City, and the disruption helped persuade the authorities they needed a subway system, which was approved in 1894.

What became known as 'the Storm of the Century' struck America in March 1993. One meteorologist described it as having 'the heart of a blizzard and the soul of a hurricane'. It triggered tornadoes in Florida, floods in the Carolinas, and high winds and surging tides along the entire east coast. On Monday, 8 March, a number of weather forecasters were warning of a significant snowstorm by the end of the week. It was the first time such an event had been predicted so far in advance, and several north-eastern states declared a state of emergency before the first flake had fallen. In the south-east, temperatures had been fairly normal for the time of year, and with heavy snow being such a rare occurrence some television stations were too sceptical to transmit the forecasts. Even when they did, many people disregarded them.

On 12 March, though, snow began to fall as far south as Georgia and Alabama, with Birmingham recording twelve inches. Hartford, Connecticut, received two feet, while Syracuse, New York, and Chattanooga, Tennessee, both reported nearly four feet. Ten million people lost their electricity, and every airport from Halifax, Nova Scotia, to Atlanta, Georgia, closed for a time. The south-eastern states did not have the infrastructure to cope, and much of the region was completely shut down for three days. The coastguard mounted a record number of rescue missions, scrambling hundreds of aircraft and ships, but at least nine vessels still sank as seventy-mile-an-hour winds conjured up forty-foot waves. Altogether, 500 people died, many from heart attacks as they shovelled snow.

## · A EUROPEAN HEATWAVE ·

In 2003 Europe endured one of its hottest summers. The United Kingdom's highest temperature ever was recorded near Faversham in Kent as the thermometer climbed to thirty-eight degrees on 10 August. Germany also saw a record temperature – nearly forty-one degrees in Bavaria. In Portugal fires destroyed up to 10 per cent of the country's forests. Italy and Spain hovered around thirty-eight degrees for weeks.

France, though, was worst hit. Especially in the north, its summers are not normally very hot, and few houses or old people's homes had air-conditioning. The whole country tends to shut down in August, so when the thermometers soared many doctors and government ministers were away on holiday. By the second week, up to 180 people a day were dying in Paris in what was the country's hottest summer on record. Most of the victims were elderly. Some collapsed while walking up stairs; others died alone in their apartments, their demise only coming to light when the smell alerted neighbours. Morgues filled to overflowing, so bodies had to be stored in refrigerated lorries.

On 12 August Health Minister Jean-François Mattei announced that an estimated 3,000 people had already died across France. He called it 'a true epidemic'. The situation was so serious that some health workers were called back from their holidays. Patrick Pelloux, head of the Emergency Physicians' Association, claimed doctors had been issuing warnings about the impending disaster since late July, 'but no one listened'. He claimed France faced 'a nationwide catastrophe the likes of which we've never seen'. The authorities in Paris even ordered municipal funeral parlours to stay open on a public holiday.

A week later the heatwave claimed its first political victim when the director-general for health, Dr Lucien Abenhaim, resigned, though he denied any mistakes had been made, saying: 'It is necessary the French understand that this type of situation cannot always be anticipated.' Mattei lost his job in a cabinet reshuffle the following year.

The prime minister, Jean-Pierre Raffarin, who had to abandon his own holiday, chastised the French people for neglecting their elderly and infirm relatives and leaving them at home alone for weeks on end while they enjoyed their vacations. As the death toll mounted to 15,000, his opinion seemed to be confirmed by the length of time it took for some of the bodies to be claimed. Estimates for the number of people who died from the heat throughout Europe range as high as 50,000. When figures for Britain were analysed, it was concluded that the soaring temperatures had caused 2,139 deaths between 4 and 13 August alone, and that more than 85 per cent of the victims were aged seventy-five or over. The following year the French government cancelled the public holiday on the day of Pentecost to raise money to improve healthcare for the elderly, but half the country's workers took the day off anyway.

## · THE MYSTERY OF LAKE NYOS ·

One of the world's strangest disasters happened at a beautiful lake in the highlands of western Cameroon. Surrounded by green mountains and rich, fertile land, Lake Nyos lies high on the flank of an inactive volcano. It is a mile wide and 600 feet deep, and carbon dioxide leaks into it from the layer of molten rock beneath, making it one of only three lakes in the world known to be saturated with the gas in this way. Another is Lake Monoun, just sixty miles away. There, in 1984, thirty-seven local people died suddenly and mysteriously. There had been rumours that chemical weapons were being secretly tested or of a bizarre terrorist massacre, but no one knew for sure what had happened.

When there was a strange distant rumble near Lake Nyos at around nine o'clock on the evening of 21 August 1986 many local people were already asleep in their beds. Those still awake probably put the noise down to thunder. In no time, though, 1,700 people would be dead. Few lived to tell what happened, but one man said he heard what sounded like an explosion, then went outside and saw all his cows lying on the ground. When he returned indoors he found his wife and daughter dead. Another saw a kind of cloud, 'white like cloth. It didn't go up in the air; it mostly went down near the ground.' A woman told how she found herself 'just sitting among the dead . . . some of them were outside, some of them behind the houses and there were animals lying everywhere, cows, dogs, everything'. Of the fifty-six people in her extended family, fifty-three died. Francis Fang was one of the many farmers who had been attracted to the area by its fertile soil. His wife dropped to the ground, vomiting blood, and died: 'The children were burned and screaming . . . I picked up my girls and started walking to the hospital. There were dead people everywhere on the road – so many I started stepping on them.'

Three villages by the lake were overwhelmed, with just four out of 1,300 people surviving in Nyos itself, but deaths were also recorded up to sixteen miles away. A government employee riding along on his motorcycle was one of the first outsiders to learn of the disaster. He found a dead antelope on the road and picked it up. Its meat would make a magnificent gift for the family he was on his way to visit. But as he went on he began to feel dizzy. Then, to his horror, he started finding dead humans. He turned his bike around and fled. When his story reached the provincial capital a government official was sent to investigate. He could not believe his eyes: there were bodies everywhere, while the few survivors were coughing up blood. A Dutch priest named Fred Tenhorn also went to the stricken area. He said it looked 'as if a neutron bomb had exploded. The foliage was green and healthy, but every human being had been killed.' Soon hospitals were inundated with people coughing and suffering from burning pains in their eyes and noses. Doctors said they looked as if they had been gassed by a kitchen stove. Rescue teams wearing gas masks now began rushing oxygen cylinders to the area for anyone who might have survived. They found thousands of dead animals around the lake, but no vultures fed on them because they were dead too.

For some local people, the explanation was obvious. Three years earlier, the tribal chief had ordered on his deathbed that his finest cattle should be drowned in the lake, where the living spirits of the dead rested, but his family had ignored his wishes. This was his terrible revenge.

Government officials, on the other hand, suggested the volcano under the lake must have erupted. But scientists insisted that it was extinct. Eyewitnesses told investigators how the waters of the lake, usually so clear, had turned a reddish brown, while a wind had suddenly arisen and whipped up huge waves.

They concluded that, over time, huge quantities of gas had been absorbed by the water. Then a disturbance – perhaps a landslide or even just a heavy fall of rain – had caused a great bubble of colourless, odourless, poisonous carbon dioxide to be released. The gas had churned up the lake, bringing iron-rich water from the bottom and turning the surface red. Being heavier than air, it had then slid down the mountain into the two adjoining valleys, suffocating every living thing in its path. It soon became clear that two years earlier the people at Lake Monoun had also been killed by carbon dioxide.

Disturbingly, scientists said that another mass poisoning at Lake Nyos was likely. To prevent it, they recommended a system of pipes in the lake's lower depths to siphon off the gas in small amounts and release it high into the air, where it would disperse harmlessly. The first pipe – 690 feet long – was installed in 2001. A similar one was installed at Lake Monoun in 2003. But after American scientists had tested both lakes for carbon dioxide levels, they said the single pipes were insufficient. They recommended siting another four in each lake, especially as people were resettling around Nyos, attracted once again by the fertile soil.

# 7

## PLAGUES

### · ANCIENT ATHENS ·

In 431 BC Athens was at the height of its power, with a mighty empire founded by Pericles, builder of the Parthenon. Now it embarked on a titanic struggle with Sparta in what became known as the Peloponnesian War. Athens had a vastly superior navy, but the Spartans could muster huge armies which the Athenians regarded as unbeatable, so they decided to withdraw behind their city walls, allowing the enemy to take over the surrounding land of Attica, while they harassed Spartan troop transports and tried to cut their supply lines.

For a time, these tactics seemed to be working: there was little fighting and Athens sustained few casualties. As the second campaigning season began in the spring of 430, the people of Attica again withdrew behind the city walls. Soon every house was crowded, and the refugees were having to erect squalid little shacks everywhere. Right on cue, the Spartan armies attacked again and began devastating the countryside.

Within days, though, strange things were happening in the city. The great historian Thucydides recorded: 'those who enjoyed the most perfect health were suddenly, without any apparent cause, seized with extremely violent headaches, with inflammations, and fiery redness in the eyes'. Their throats and tongues began to bleed, and 'breath was drawn with difficulty, and had an unpleasant smell'. Then came a violent cough and painful vomiting. Their bodies turned 'livid, marked all over with little pustules and sores', and they 'could not bear the lightest covering or the finest linen, but must be left quite naked'. They did not feel hot if you touched them, but they had a desperate thirst, and 'longed for nothing so much as to be plunging into cold water; and many of those who were not properly attended threw themselves into wells'. No matter how much they drank, though, 'their torment still continued the same'.

According to Thucydides, the pestilence had first appeared in Ethiopia, then spread into Egypt and Libya, before cases began to be reported in Athens's port, Piraeus, which had become its sole source of food and supplies. It then spread through the overcrowded city like wild-fire. Thucydides himself caught the disease. He recovered, but said that most victims died within nine days. Some who survived lost their fingers, toes or genitals. Others went blind or 'totally lost all memory, and quite forgot not only their most intimate friends, but even their own selves'. Many dead bodies lay unburied, but 'the birds and beasts that prey on human flesh' avoided them. Any that did dare to eat the infected flesh died too.

Doctors and those who cared for the sick often perished, so many victims were abandoned. The medical profession could not help much anyway, because they could not agree on the best treatment: 'Some died merely for want of care; and some with all the care that could possibly be taken; nor was any one medicine discovered, from whence could be promised any certain relief, since that which gave ease to one was prejudicial to another.' The refugees from the country 'died like flies'. In their hovels 'there was scarce room to breathe' and everywhere 'they lay together in heaps, the dying on the dead, and the dead on the dying'.

The Athenians knew that before the war the Spartans had consulted the oracle of Apollo, god of medicine, at Delphi, and had been promised help. As the plague raged, Athenian values began to crumble. Many refugees had put up tents in the city's temples, which were now full of bodies: 'things sacred and holy had quite lost their distinction'. If people ran out of space in their own family sepulchre, they just commandeered someone else's. If they saw a body burning on a funeral pyre, they 'tossed on another body they had dragged hither, and went their way'. Athens was caught up in a mood of live now, pay later – if ever. 'They thought it prudent to catch hold of speedy enjoyments and quick gusts of pleasure . . . No one continued resolute enough to form any honest or generous design, when uncertain whether he should live to effect it.' Religion 'laid no restraint on them; judging that piety and impiety were things quite indifferent, since they saw that all men perished alike'. Nor did the law, 'since justice might be prevented by death'. The new liberated behaviour of some women was seen as particularly alarming, so a special magistrate was appointed to try to control them.

When the plague died down a little, Pericles sent out the Athenian fleet to resume the attack on the Spartans, but the sailors had scarcely left port before the disease broke out among them with such violence that they had to return. The Athenian leader himself fell victim and died in 429.

Thucydides says that, of 15,500 infantrymen in the army, 4,000 died, as did 300 cavalrymen out of 1,000. On that basis, most historians have assumed that about a third of the total population perished, which would mean something in the region of 100,000 deaths. 'A plague so great as this, and so dreadful a calamity, in human memory could not be paralleled,' Thucydides wrote. It was a blow from which Athens never fully recovered. The city's population did not return to its earlier level for many years, and they never found another leader like Pericles. The war dragged on for another twenty-five years, and Athens lost. The high water mark of its power had passed.

So what exactly was this deadly disease? The physicians of the time blamed it on a *miasma* – poisonous air. Later historians thought it was the first appearance in the West of bubonic plague. But nowadays other candidates are more favoured, such as typhus, typhoid, smallpox, influenza, scarlet fever, ebola, or even anthrax, brought by the livestock cooped up inside the city during the siege. It could equally have been a disease that has since mutated into something less lethal, such as measles; or one that has disappeared altogether; or, given the dreadful overcrowding and squalor in Athens, a combination of several diseases. Perhaps we will never know what hit the ancient Athenians any more than they did.

## · PLAGUES OF ROME ·

The word 'plague' has become synonymous with bubonic plague – the most fearsome disease in history. Some scientists believe it first appeared around 1320 BC. Others say it arrived much later, in the first century AD, when a pestilence swept through Libya, Egypt and Syria, with symptoms including buboes – big, hard swellings – on various parts of the body, such as behind the knees and around the elbows. The death rate was very high.

The Roman Empire was devastated by a number of fearsome epidemics. It was once believed that bubonic plague scythed through a Roman army campaigning in the Near East in AD 164, though some modern scholars now think it was smallpox. Whichever disease it was, when the soldiers returned they spread it through the empire until it reached the capital in 166. At that point Rome probably had around a million inhabitants, making it by far the biggest city on earth, and it was terribly overcrowded, with the poor living in grotesque squalor. The Roman historian Tacitus dubbed it 'that great reservoir and collecting ground for every kind of depravity'. Wealthy people believed it was healthier to stay on their rural manors.

The disease raged for fifteen years and became known as the Antonine Plague. It claimed the life of Emperor Lucius Verus in 169, and that of Emperor Marcus Aurelius Antoninus eleven years later. Portrayed in the early part of the film *Gladiator*, the latter was regarded by Edward Gibbon as the last great ruler of Rome in its golden age, before the rot described in his classic *Decline and Fall of the Roman Empire* set in. In his *Meditations* Marcus Aurelius writes that the pestilence raging in Rome is less deadly than falsehood and evil conduct. He died on the seventh day of his illness, refusing to see his son in case he too should become infected. His last words were: 'Weep not for me; think rather of the pestilence and the deaths of so many others.'

The plague killed perhaps a third of the population of Asia Minor, Egypt, Greece and Italy. At its height, 2,000 bodies a day were being carted off in Rome, while many towns and villages lost all their inhabitants. It also infected Germany, Gaul and perhaps even Britain. The epidemic also goes by the name of the Plague of Galen, after the Greek physician who provided a description of its symptoms, mentioning fever, diarrhoea, a parching thirst and skin pustules.

Whatever it was, some believe it played a crucial role in Rome's decline. Until its appearance, the empire had managed to expand and keep its frontiers secure, but now, with troops in short supply, a Germanic horde was able to take control of part of north-eastern Italy. The loss of manpower also meant that in future Rome had to rely increasingly on mercenaries to defend its borders.

The year 251 saw the Plague of Cyprian, named after the Bishop of Carthage, who described the illness as starting with violent vomiting and diarrhoea. Other torments included a burning fever, eyes 'on fire', blindness, deafness and gangrene – 'in some cases the feet or some parts of the limbs are taken off by the contagion of diseased putrefaction'. The disease was said to have originated in Ethiopia and advanced at great speed to Egypt and Rome's colonies in North Africa, then through the rest of the empire.

Cyprian's biographer Pontius wrote about its impact on Carthage: 'a hateful disease invaded every house in succession of the trembling populace, carrying off day by day with abrupt attack numberless people . . . All were shuddering, fleeing, shunning the contagion.' As the bodies mounted in the streets Pontius said the plague brought the same selfishness seen in Athens nearly 700 years before: 'No one regarded anything besides his own cruel gains.' Christians proved convenient scapegoats, and the authorities launched an energetic persecution. Cyprian himself was executed in 258. The nature of this disease is also debated – it could have been smallpox, measles, typhus, or epidemic ergotism, caused by a fungus that attacks rye. It is said to have raged for up to twenty years, claiming 5,000 lives a day at its height, including perhaps the emperor Claudius Gothicus. Some at the time believed that the human race would not survive. Like the Antonine Plague, it severely depleted the army and caused further major labour shortages, constituting perhaps another crucial step in Rome's decline and subsequent destruction.

## · THE PLAGUE OF JUSTINIAN ·

By 542, the Roman Empire in the West had completed its decline and fall, but there remained a Roman Empire in the East, Byzantium, with its capital at Constantinople (now Istanbul), which was then perhaps the greatest city on earth. Emperor Justinian the Great was fighting wars to try to restore the Roman Empire in the West, but his plans would be sent haywire by bubonic plague. According to the contemporary scholar Procopius, the disease was first seen in Egypt, then in Palestine, 'and from there it spread over the whole world . . . as if fearing lest some corner of the earth might escape it. For it left neither island nor cave nor mountain ridge which had human inhabitants; and if it had passed by any land, either not affecting the men there or touching them in indifferent fashion, still at a later time it came back.' As would often happen, caravans or ships carried the disease along trade routes. Constantinople imported huge amounts of grain, mostly from Egypt, and the ships may have carried the rats that brought the contagion to the city in the spring of 542, while Procopius was staying there.

According to the scholar, its arrival was preceded by 'apparitions of supernatural beings in human guise', who seemed to strike all those they encountered, making them fall ill. Even uttering 'the holiest of names' offered no protection. Those not yet smitten shunned appeals for help from friends or loved ones who had fallen ill. Instead, 'they shut themselves up in their rooms and pretended that they did not hear, although their doors were being beaten down, fearing, obviously, that he who was calling was one of those demons'. But not all of those struck down encountered one of the wandering spirits. Others 'saw a vision in a dream' or heard a voice 'foretelling to them that they were written down in the number of those who were to die'.

Victims suffered 'a sudden fever', but at first it was rather 'languid', so neither doctor nor patient usually thought it was anything much to worry about. Within a day or so, though, the dreaded buboes appeared, in the groin or the armpits. Some victims went into a deep coma. If they had someone looking after them, 'they would eat without waking', but those abandoned 'would die directly through lack of sustenance'. Others became wildly delirious, and might run screaming out of their houses because they thought someone was coming to kill them. For those who suffered neither coma nor delirium, the buboes caused excruciating agony, and they would die when 'no longer able to endure the pain'. Sometimes the buboes burst and the patient survived, though their tongue might be damaged and 'they lived on either lisping or speaking incoherently'.

Being close to victims did not seem to increase the chance of catching the illness. Indeed, wrote Procopius, some people 'positively embraced death on account of the total loss of their children and family, and for this reason went cheek-by-jowl with the sick, but still were not struck down'. Doctors' prognoses proved woefully inaccurate: 'the most illustrious physicians predicted that many would die, who unexpectedly escaped entirely from suffering shortly afterwards, and . . . they declared that many would be saved, who were destined to be carried off almost immediately'. Nor did they know what treatments to offer, because what helped some harmed others. In short, 'no device was discovered by man to save himself'.

Though no one knew it at the time, bubonic plague is carried by the flea of the black rat, which can also live on other rodents. Sometimes the flea falls ill, and its gut becomes blocked with multiplying plague bacteria and clotted blood. As it begins to starve, it will jump on any potential host to try to satisfy its hunger, but because of its blocked gut nothing works, so it keeps leaping from host to host, spreading the bacilli as it goes. The disease comes in three versions: bubonic, which killed about seven cases in ten; pneumonic, where the plague bacilli settle in the lungs, which carried off nine in ten; and septicaemic, where they attack the blood, which killed virtually everyone. While bubonic plague has to be transmitted by the black rat flea, pneumonic can spread through the air directly from person to person, and with septicaemic there are so many bacilli in the blood that the human flea may be able to pass it on. All three forms were probably present in Constantinople, with bubonic the most common.

According to Procopius, the disease ravaged the city for four months, with up to 10,000 dying each day, while 'confusion and disorder everywhere became complete'. The dead, rich or poor, might lie for days without being buried. Another eyewitness, the historian John of Ephesus, wrote: 'God's wrath ... piteously trampled and squeezed the inhabitants like fine grapes.' Justinian himself fell ill, with 'a swelling of the groin', but he recovered. When all the tombs were full the survivors dug trenches, but even this could not keep pace with the numbers dying, so they climbed the fortified towers by the Golden Horn 'and tearing off the roofs threw the bodies there in complete disorder', then covered them over. With so many dying, funeral rites were forgotten, and 'it was sufficient if one carried on his shoulders the body of one of the dead to the parts of the city which bordered on the sea and flung him down'. John said thousands of bodies awaiting disposal piled up on the shore 'like flotsam on great rivers'. The authorities tried to keep count of the dead until they reached 230,000, when, 'seeing they were innumerable, they gave up'. They also tried to preserve some kind of normality, with church services and public entertainments continuing, and overseas dignitaries received with due ceremony, but victims were dropping dead in the street: 'In some places, as people were looking at each other and talking, they tottered and fell.' In the market, while they 'were standing and talking or counting change, suddenly the end would overcome the buyer here and the seller there'. The normally bustling city was deserted 'as if it had perished', and the dead and dying could look fearful with 'their bellies swollen and their mouths wide open, throwing up pus like torrents'. Procopius wrote: 'work of every description ceased, and all the trades were abandoned by the artisans ... Indeed in a city which was simply abounding in all good things starvation almost absolute was running riot.'

In some the crisis engendered solidarity, as people 'carried with their own hands the bodies of those who were no connections of theirs and buried them'. In contrast with some other pestilences, this one promoted religious observance even among many 'who in times past used to take delight in devoting themselves to pursuits both shameful and base', but as soon as they felt safe again, they reverted to type – 'surpassing themselves in villainy and in lawlessness of every sort'. Perhaps they need not have worried because, claimed Procopius, 'this disease, whether by chance or by some providence, chose out with exactitude the worst men and let them go free'.

The plague is estimated to have killed a third of the population of the empire, and perhaps 40 per cent of Constantinople's inhabitants. Justinian would survive another twenty-three years, but the epidemic put paid to his hope of reviving the Western Roman Empire. The disease attacked Persia, Arabia, Africa, and Central and South Asia. In Europe it ravaged as far north as Denmark and as far west as Ireland. In 547 the Welsh king Maelgwn of Gwynedd was said to have died of plague, and the Annals of Ulster record a 'great death' stalking the land. John of Ephesus wrote that there were 'ships in the midst of the sea whose sailors were suddenly attacked . . . and became tombs adrift on the waves'. Across the world, the Plague of Justinian would kill perhaps twenty-five million people. John himself tried to flee, but wherever he went it seemed to pursue him. He saw fields of wheat with no one to harvest it, 'desolate villages and corpses spread out on the earth . . . cattle abandoned and roaming scattered over the mountains with nobody to gather them'. At first, the historian was reluctant to write the story of the epidemic – 'What use would it be, when the entire world was tottering and reaching its dissolution . . . for whom would he who wrote be writing?' Then he changed his mind in the hope that any who did come after would 'fear and shake because of the terrible scourge with which we were lashed through our transgressions and become wiser through the chastisement of us wretches'.

Procopius considered 'the whole human race came near to being annihilated'. Clever men, he said, love to dream up explanations for such 'scourges', but no theories could be offered for this plague because 'it embraced the entire world, and blighted the lives of all men . . . and it attacked some in the summer season, others in the winter, and still others at other times of the year'.

For the next two centuries, plague was a regular visitor, with eighteen major outbreaks between 541 and 717 in the Mediterranean region alone.

## · THE BLACK DEATH ·

It was probably the greatest disaster in recorded human history, killing perhaps seventy-five million people, and many caught up in it believed they were witnessing the end of humanity. Its chilling name – 'Black

Death' – came from the dark blotches that appeared on victims' bodies, caused by haemorrhages under the skin. It is now generally accepted that the epidemic was a fearful cocktail of bubonic, pneumonic and septicaemic plague, though some experts have suggested it was actually a completely different, viral infection.

The plagues that ravaged Europe after Justinian's time died away in the eighth century, and at the beginning of the fourteenth the continent was nearing the end of a long period of prosperity. The Great Famine of 1315–19 (see Chapter 9) was followed by more hunger in 1345 as six months of virtually continuous rain made it impossible to sow crops in some areas. Over the next two years many people died, and many who survived were left weak and sickly. For those who claimed to understand such things, there were portents of disaster – falling stars, a column of fire that settled above the pope's palace at Avignon, and a violent earth tremor that set the bells pealing at St Mark's in Venice.

Though people did not know it at the time, more significant was the fact that squirrel-like rodents named marmots had begun to desert their remote home near Lake Issyk Kul in Central Asia, carrying with them fleas that harboured the plague bacillus, and as they came into contact with black rats the fleas migrated to these new hosts. The rats were great travellers, usually in the holds of ships carrying grain, and a flea could survive for weeks in cargoes of wool or cloth even if the rats had gone. On shore, the rodents lived cheek-by-jowl with humans. By the 1330s, cases of plague were beginning to surface. In 1334 it struck China, where it may have killed up to five million people. Then, as it worked its way slowly westwards along the trade routes, news began to reach Europe of a plague of unparalleled fury. India, Tartary, Mesopotamia, Syria and Armenia were all hit, and by 1346 the disease was in Anatolia. In the Crimea alone 85,000 people were said to have died, and the Tartars found a convenient scapegoat – the Christian merchants who were dominating the east–west trade the Tartars coveted. In 1346 they chased the Genoese to their fortified trading centre at Caffa (now Feodosia) on the Black Sea and camped outside, but as they prepared to bombard the city into submission plague swept through their ranks and they were forced to call off the siege. Before they left, though, they catapulted some of their dead into the city. The Genoese dumped the bodies in the sea but soon plague was raging in Caffa, and the defenders' forces became so depleted that the following year they had to take to their galleys and set sail for Italy. They have traditionally been seen as the people who carried the plague to Europe, but it undoubtedly arrived by other routes, too.

In October 1347 a dozen Genoese galleys put into Messina on Sicily with silks and spices from the East. We do not know whether they were from the Crimea or somewhere else but, according to one chronicler, the sailors had 'sickness clinging to their very bones'. As the port's inhabitants began to fall ill and die, those still well drove the plague ships back out to sea, but it was too late. The pestilence had taken hold. The Messinese begged their Catanian neighbours to let them borrow the holy relics of St Agatha from the cathedral. The archbishop agreed, but the Catanians 'tore the keys from the sacristan and stoutly rebuked the patriarch, saying they would rather die than allow the relics to be taken to Messina'. So he had to be content with dipping them in holy water and taking that to the stricken city instead. A few days after returning to Catania, he died from the Black Death. In January 1348 a chronicler reported that three galleys from the East had landed at Genoa 'horribly infected'. The locals drove them away with 'burning arrows and divers engines of war', so they sailed west, seeking refuge along the coast of the Mediterranean, carrying the plague to the ports of France and Spain. The disease was also spreading on land, and by the spring it had a firm grip on mainland Italy.

One of the most striking accounts of the epidemic comes from the great writer Boccaccio, who was in Florence when it struck the city. His *Decameron* is a collection of stories supposedly told by a group of young aristocrats who take refuge in a secluded villa. In the preamble the author gives a vivid description of the disease – how it began 'with swellings in the groin or under the armpit. They grew to the size of a small apple or egg.' Soon they spread all over the body, then black and purple spots appeared on arms, thighs and elsewhere. 'These spots', wrote Boccaccio, 'were a certain sign of death.' The victim would not have long to wait: the disease might run its whole course from first appearance to death in just three days. Boccaccio wrote that 'such terror was struck into the hearts of men and women by this calamity that brother abandoned brother, and the uncle his nephew, and the sister her brother, and very often the wife her husband. What is even worse and nearly incredible is that fathers and mothers refused to see and tend their children.' Dead bodies 'filled every corner', and instead of being accompanied on its last journey by grieving loved ones, the victim's body would have only 'a sort of corpse-carrier drawn from the baser ranks, who called themselves *becchini* and performed such offices for hire'. Priests did not linger over the interment either. They avoided 'too long and solemn an office, but with the aid of the *becchini* hastily consigned the corpse to the first tomb which they found untenanted'. There would be no ceremony, no tears, no mourners: 'a dead man was then of no more account than a dead goat would be today'. There were stories of the *becchini* forcing their way into the houses of the living and threatening to dispose of them with the dead unless men bribed them with money or women with their virtue. Many victims died at home without anyone knowing 'until the stench of their putrefying bodies carried the tidings'. Neighbours would then drag out their bodies and leave them lying in the street.

The churchyards of Italy were soon overwhelmed, so huge trenches were dug in which hundreds of corpses were piled up 'as merchandise is stowed in the hold of a ship, tier upon tier, each covered with a little earth until the trench would hold no more'. A citizen of Siena named Agnolo the Fat buried his five children with his own hands, lamenting: 'None could be found to bury the dead for money or for friendship . . . And there were also those who were so sparsely covered with earth that the dogs dragged them forth.' According to a chronicler in the city: 'people said and believed: "This is the end of the world."' Half of Siena's population perished, with a similar proportion dying in Orvieto, while in the city of San Gimignano, with its famous towers, the death rate reached 58 per cent. In some places the disease was said to be so virulent that doctors might catch it at a bedside and succumb 'even before the sick person they had come to assist'.

Italy at the time had three of Europe's four greatest cities – Genoa, Venice and Florence. In the last of these the epidemic raged for four months and may have killed 65,000, well over half the population. Boccaccio says some thought the best way to survive was to 'live temperately and avoid all excess'. They formed isolated communities 'avoiding every kind of luxury, but eating and drinking very moderately of the most delicate viands and the finest wines . . . and diverting their minds with music and such other delights as they could devise'. Others took the opposite view, and 'maintained that to drink freely, to frequent places of public resort, and to take their pleasure with song and revel, sparing to satisfy no appetite', was the best course. Riotous living was also advocated by those who did not expect to survive, and they became 'as reckless of their property as of their lives'. Respect for 'laws, human and divine, was abused and all but totally dissolved'. With those charged with trying to maintain law, order and decorum themselves dropping dead, many a citizen felt 'free to do what was right in his own eyes'.

In Venice precautions by the doge and council gave us the word 'quarantine', from the Italian *quarantena* – meaning forty days. That was how long travellers from the Orient had to wait before being allowed into the city, but it did not stop the epidemic, which carried off 600 citizens each day at its height. The city fathers decreed they should be buried on an island in the lagoon, which is now the Lido. Milan took no-nonsense measures: all occupants of an infected house, whether sick or well, were walled up inside and left to die. This ruthlessness meant Milan suffered a lower death rate than any of Italy's other great cities.

For many, flight seemed the best protection, 'as if God, in visiting men with this pestilence in requital of their iniquities, would not pursue them with His wrath wherever they might be'. But the countryside offered little refuge, with the death rate probably approaching one in three. 'How many grand palaces, how many stately homes, how many splendid residences, once full of retainers, of lords, of ladies, were now desolate of all, even to the meanest servant!' wrote Boccaccio. 'How many families of historic fame, of vast ancestral domains and wealth proverbial, found now no scion to continue the succession! How many brave men, how many fair ladies . . . broke fast with their kinfolk, comrades and friends in the morning, and when evening came, supped with their forefathers in the other world!'

According to one contemporary, plague came into France through the port of Marseille, brought by one of the galleys expelled from Italy. Paris had more doctors than any other city in Europe, but that did not prevent the deaths of about 50,000 people, a quarter of the population. In

Avignon, the pope's doctor, Gui de Chauliac, said: 'The plague was shameful for the physicians who could give no help at all, especially as, out of fear of infection, they hesitated to visit the sick. Even if they did, they achieved nothing.' The Black Death did not provide a dignified end for its victims. In the words of a French chronicler: 'all the matter which exuded from their bodies let off an unbearable stench: sweat, excrement, spittle, breath, so fetid as to be overpowering; urine turbid, thick, black or red'. In Avignon perhaps half of the inhabitants died, and the pontiff had to consecrate the waters of the Rhône so dead bodies could be thrown into it. It was said that many Parisian priests 'retired through fear' and left their flocks to fend as best they could. On the other hand, the nuns of Paris's Hôtel Dieu courageously tended the sick, often paying for their devotion with their lives. Everywhere, travellers would find fields uncultivated, cattle wandering, houses empty and wine cellars open. When the disease struck Tournai the town council banned extramarital sex, swearing, playing dice and working on the Sabbath. Whether this halted the disease is not clear, but it persuaded the dice-makers to diversify into producing religious objects.

The epidemic is often said to have been brought to England by an infected German sailor who came ashore at Melcombe Regis in Dorset, but it may also have arrived in Bristol or Southampton. Bristol is said to have lost 4,000 of its 10,000 inhabitants, while half the people in Winchester died. About 70,000 – a third of the population – perished in London. East Anglia suffered particularly badly, with perhaps half of its inhabitants dying; Norwich's population did not return to pre-Black Death levels until about 1700. In Kent the old and decrepit Bishop of Rochester survived, but he had almost no one left to serve him, as four priests, five esquires, ten attendants, seven young clerics and six pages all died. In the town no one could be found to bury the dead, so 'men and women carried their own children on their shoulders to the church and threw them into a common pit'. A Rochester monk complained that most people had become 'even more depraved, more prone to every kind of vice, more ready to indulge in evil and sinfulness'. The Welsh poet Jeuan Gethin wrote: 'We see death coming into our midst like black smoke, a plague which cuts off the young, a rootless phantom which has no mercy for fair countenance.'

Before the arrival of the Black Death, Britain's population had been about four million. The disease probably killed nearly one and a half million. Whole villages disappeared, like Tilgarsley in Oxfordshire and Ambion in Leicestershire, while fifteen in Lincolnshire were said to have ceased to exist either at the time of the outbreak or in the two decades that followed. The lord of the manor of Noseley in Leicestershire burned down the village when the Black Death first appeared, an action which seems to have stopped it reaching the manor house.

The plague spread as far as Moscow, and was said to have been brought to Norway by a ghost ship that drifted ashore near Bergen with a cargo of wool and a crew of dead men. Some places managed to escape its worst ravages, such as Poland, which established a quarantine system at the border, while almost everywhere the rich and powerful were most likely to escape. The only reigning European monarch to die was Alfonso XI of Spain, on Good Friday 1350, while he was besieging Gibraltar. King Edward III of England lost his daughter Princess Joan; King Pedro of Aragon's wife, youngest daughter and niece all perished; the Emperor of Byzantium lost a son; the King of France his wife and daughter-in-law; and the King of Sweden two brothers.

As ever, the plague was blamed on man's wickedness: 'these pestilences were for pure sin', wrote the contemporary poet William Langland in *Piers Plowman*. While the Bishop of Winchester commented that humankind's misdemeanours had 'justly provoked the Divine wrath'. Placating God in some way therefore seemed a good idea. King Magnus II of Sweden ordered people to eat only bread and water on Fridays and to walk barefoot to church. Pope Clement VI ordered the devout to hold a procession every week, but in the apocalyptic atmosphere, things soon got out of hand: 'many of both sexes were barefooted, some were in sack cloth, some covered with ashes, wailing as they walked, tearing their hair, and lashing themselves with scourges even to the point where blood was drawn'. These hysterical displays spawned the Brotherhood of the Flagellants, which won widespread support, especially in Germany. The brothers were not allowed to wash, change their clothes, sleep in a bed, or have any contact with the opposite sex. They would march in groups of up to a thousand, with bell-ringers going ahead to announce them. Each man beat himself with a scourge as he walked. The chronicler

Henry of Herford said, 'the blood ran down to the ground and bespattered the walls of the churches'. As the flagellants marched, the spectators chanted. The whipping grew more frenetic, then the townspeople began sobbing and groaning, urging the brothers to ever-greater excesses. At first, the brotherhood was run very strictly, with new recruits having to make a full confession of their sins, and provide enough money to pay their way on the pilgrimage. In some of the places they visited adulterers repented and robbers returned stolen goods, but the authorities began to take fright as the flagellants claimed that they could drive out devils, heal the sick, or even raise the dead. Some said they had eaten and drunk with Christ, and spectators treated rags dipped in their blood as sacred relics. Most alarmingly, the flagellants started to denounce a religious hierarchy which seemed helpless in the face of this fearful disease, interrupting services and driving priests from their churches. In October 1349 the pope called for the brotherhood to be suppressed. The Bishop of Breslaw responded by burning a master at the stake, and hundreds of brothers were incarcerated, tortured and executed.

It is not clear how much of the credit should go to the flagellants, but Germany escaped more lightly from the plague than either France or Italy. Other German holy men, though, tried a different approach, as a group of monks deserted their monastery to move *en bloc* to Ulm, where they spent their way through its wealth enjoying the high life.

The flagellants were among those who responded to the plague by massacring Jews. As soon as they arrived at Frankfurt am Main in July 1349 they rushed straight to the Jewish quarter and led the slaughter, while in Brussels just the news that they were on their way was enough to spark a massacre of 600. Some claimed the Jews had caused the plague by poisoning wells, and in Narbonne and Carcassonne they were dragged from their homes and flung on to bonfires until the whole community was virtually exterminated. At Basel, the townspeople penned all the Jews in a wooden building specially erected on an island in the Rhine, then burned them alive. Jews were also burned in many other cities including Stuttgart, Dresden, Cologne and Mainz, which had the biggest Jewish community in Europe, and where 6,000 are said to have been murdered. The pope condemned the killings, and threatened to excommunicate anyone taking part, but by the time the Black Death had passed, there were few Jews left in Germany or the Low Countries. When the plague hit Cyprus the islanders massacred their Arab slaves.

The role of the flea in transmitting the disease was still unknown, and the most popular theory, just as in Athens 1,700 years earlier, was that it was spread by a *miasma*. Another idea was that an 'aerial spirit' escaped from the eyes of the victim – looks could literally kill. In Vienna the plague was seen flying through the air as a blue flame, while in Lithuania it appeared when a mysterious maiden waved a red scarf at a window. Philip VI of France asked the medical faculty of the University of Paris to come up with an answer. The academics blamed the Black Death on a triple conjunction of Saturn, Jupiter and Mars in the 40th degree of Aquarius on 20 March 1345, but they were humble enough to acknowledge that some things were 'hidden from even the most highly trained intellects'. Ignorance did not stop doctors offering all sorts of suggestions for prevention. Some advised keeping the *miasma* at bay by burning richly scented wood, such as juniper, filling the house with sweet-smelling plants, and sprinkling the floor with vinegar and rose water. Hot baths were to be avoided because they opened the pores to infection. If you really had to go out, the best plan was to carry a concoction of pepper, sandalwood, roses and camphor, to be moulded into apple shapes with a paste of gum Arabic. Bad smells were thought to have power against infection, so people crouched over latrines to smell the odours. As for diet, some physicians approved of fresh fruit and vegetables, others were against. Some were pro-lettuce, some anti-. Some urged aubergine, others forbade it. When it came to treatment, some medical opinion advocated applying a poultice made from gum resin, roots of white lilies and dried human excrement to buboes; other doctors swore by bleeding.

The terrible epidemic did not die out in Europe until 1351, by which time it had carried off perhaps a third of the population. The Italian poet Petrarch wrote of 'a vast and dreadful solitude' everywhere. As he was dying, an Irish priest, Brother John Clyn, compiled an account of what he had seen, prefacing it, 'if perchance any man survive and any of the race of Adam escape this pestilence . . .' The Florentine chronicler Matteo Villani believed he was recounting 'the extermination of mankind'. He was wrong, but the Black Death shook society to its foundations. The

Church was dreadfully damaged. Some priests had shown brave dedication, but many others had abandoned their flocks, and if the plague was God's judgement, congregations asked why their priests had not warned them that the Almighty was so angry and was preparing this terrible punishment. When the Bishop of Bath and Wells tried to hold a service of thanksgiving at Yeovil, where the disease had killed about half the population, an angry crowd attacked the church. The mystique of the priest had also been compromised, because the Church had had to provide alternative arrangements for the dying to make their confessions. The Bishop of Bath and Wells told people: 'if they are on the point of death and cannot secure the services of a priest, then they should make confession to each other', adding that *in extremis* they could confess 'even to a woman'.

The standing of the rich and powerful was also damaged because they had fled, and the disease shifted the balance of economic power in favour of the labourer, who was often able to use his scarcity value to exact better pay and conditions. The kings of France and England tried to prevent this unwelcome effect of the free market by bringing in a wage freeze. Still, poor survivors took over wine presses or mills that had been left empty, looted deserted houses, or even moved into them and enjoyed for the first time the comforts of sleeping in beds or eating off silver plates.

## · LATER PLAGUES ·

After the Black Death, bubonic plague would return to Europe six times in the next six decades, reducing the continent's population by nearly half. In the first half of the seventeenth century there were a number of further outbreaks. One in 1603, the first year of James I's reign, killed 34,000 people in London – more than a seventh of the population – while York lost nearly a third of its inhabitants. Then, when James's son Charles I succeeded in 1625, another outbreak carried off 40,000 in London. It was a disastrous start to a disastrous reign that would end with the king becoming the only monarch in English history to be publicly beheaded. Four years later Milan again tried to fight off the plague, but this time it failed and 60,000 died – nearly half the city's population.

Another 220,000 perished across northern Italy. This plague provided the backdrop for Alessandro Manzoni's great novel *The Betrothed*. Then came the last major epidemic in Britain. Just as Boccaccio had been the chronicler of the Black Death in Florence, so the diarist Samuel Pepys left an unforgettable account of the Great Plague in London.

The disease had struck the Netherlands in 1663, and the government in London had tried strenuously to keep it at bay, but on 7 June 1665, 'the hottest day that ever I felt in my life', Pepys saw houses marked with red crosses and the plea: 'Lord have mercy upon us.' King Charles II and his court soon moved out, but the lord mayor stayed, having a glass cage made from which he could receive visitors and run the city. Pepys decided it was time 'to put my things and estate in order, in case it should please God to call me away'. He packed off his wife and maids, and sorted out his will, mindful that 'a man cannot depend on living two days'. By July, corpse bearers were constantly passing through the streets. At one point, the authorities opened all the cesspits in the hope that the stench might drive away the disease, but through August it advanced remorselessly. London was becoming a ghost town. Another famous diarist, John Evelyn, bemoaned its 'mournful silence', while Pepys commented how sad it was 'to see the streets empty of people . . . and about us, two shops in three, if not more, generally shut up'. The nonconformist minister Thomas Vincent recorded that people fell 'as thick as the leaves in autumn'. Death's arrows, it was said, struck the spotted whore and the sainted wife, and he rode his pale horse to every house.

September was the worst month of all. Now Pepys noted that only 'poor wretches' were to be seen out and about, and that if he walked the whole length of Lombard Street, once one of the busiest in the city, he would meet only twenty people. Grass was growing in the streets, and all conversation was 'of this dead, and that man sick, and so many in this place, and so many in that'. As coffin-makers found themselves unable to keep up with demand, ever more people had to be buried in shrouds. When they ran out, victims were dumped naked into pits, often lined with quicklime. Nurses robbed or left to starve the victims they were supposed to be tending, while apothecaries were accused of strangling patients so they could ransack their homes. 'The plague', wrote Pepys, 'made us as cruel as dogs one to another.' The authorities' attempts to quarantine houses faced growing, sometimes violent resistance, and had to be abandoned, while London's cornucopia of sounds and cries now seemed to have been reduced to the endless tolling of church bells, the rolling wheels of carts collecting corpses, and the shouts of 'bring out your dead' interspersed with the oaths and curses of the ruffians who manned them. The dead, or sometimes nearly dead, were flung aboard to be robbed of anything of value or, it was whispered, sexually assaulted.

By November, mercifully, the epidemic was subsiding. On the 24th Pepys visited his old oyster-seller and 'bought two barrels of my fine woman of the shop, who is alive after all the plague – which now is the first observation or enquiry we make at London concerning everybody we knew before it'. On Christmas Day the diarist's heart was gladdened when he came across a wedding, 'which I have not seen many a day, and the young people so merry with one another'. In the first week of January his wife returned home as he noted, 'the town fills apace', and by February the king and court were back. The death toll in London was estimated to be up to 100,000 out of a population of about 500,000. In the rest of the country the Great Plague, as it became known, was not as widespread as the Black Death, but some places suffered severely, with Dover and Newark losing up to a third of their inhabitants, and Norwich a quarter.

While this was the last major outbreak in Britain the last in Western Europe did not come until 1720, when a ship arrived at Marseille from Syria with a number of sick men on board. It was carrying an important cargo of silk and cotton, and powerful merchants persuaded the authorities to waive the usual quarantine regulations. Soon the plague was ravaging the city, and it is estimated that 50,000 people died there, perhaps half the population, and another 50,000 in the surrounding area.

Since then, plague has been seen in devastating epidemics only further east. Two hundred thousand died in Moscow in 1771, while what historians regard as the third pandemic (the Plague of Justinian being the first, the Black Death and its successors the second) began in China's Yunnan province in 1855. Initially it spread slowly, but once it reached Canton in March 1894 it killed 60,000 people in a few weeks. When it spread to Hong Kong 100,000 perished, mainly native Chinese. Medical treatment had moved on surprisingly little since the Middle Ages, and between 60 and 90 per cent of those who contracted the disease were still expected to die, while recovery from the pneumonic variety was virtually unknown. But as the disease raged scientists identified the plague bacillus, and in 1898 a French researcher was able to establish that it was spread by the black rat's flea.

India's poverty meant public health officials there lived in constant fear of epidemics, so when the plague attacked Bombay and Calcutta in 1896 many predicted disaster. The British authorities tried isolating those who had been in contact with the sick, disinfecting houses, fumigating or burning possessions, and flushing out drains and sewers every day with carbolic acid. The pestilence spread regardless, killing 853,000 people in 1903, then over a million the following year. *The Times* considered the extent of the disaster 'incredible'. Once again it was the native population that suffered: of more than a million people who died of plague in 1904, only five were Europeans. In 1906 there was a determined effort to exterminate rats, and the death toll fell below 300,000; but the following year was the worst of all, with more than 1.3 million victims. By the end of 1910, the toll from the epidemic was put at nearly seven million.

With trade ever more globalised, plague was able to penetrate Africa from Egypt to South Africa, the Middle East, most of South America, the Caribbean, South-East Asia and Australia, and the pandemic would go on for another half century. The last major outbreak was in Peru and Argentina in 1945, but the World Health Organisation did not consider the third pandemic over until 1959. As recently as 2006, 100 plague deaths were reported in the Democratic Republic of Congo, where war had made it harder to control the disease.

# 8

———

# OTHER DISEASES

## · A PRESENT FROM THE CONQUISTADORES ·

In the second decade of the sixteenth century the Aztecs saw strange omens: a mysterious tongue of fire lit the heavens; a holy shrine burst into flames; a comet raced across the sky; and on a calm day Lake Texoco, which surrounded their fabled island capital, Tenochtitlan, started boiling up. Inside Tenochtitlan itself, which stood on the site of modern-day Mexico City, the superstitious emperor, Montezuma, was deeply disturbed. He had heard reports from the Mayans' territory in the Yucatan that a race of white men had appeared from across the sea, sailing on 'winged towers' with weapons that spewed out deadly fire. Like many Aztecs, Montezuma believed that long ago the plumed serpent god Quetzalcoatl had appeared on earth in the guise of a prophet king, bearded and pale-skinned, and that one day he would return. What the emperor did not know was that the white men had brought with them an invisible weapon far more deadly than their fire-spitting guns – smallpox. In 1507 it had already caused a terrible epidemic among the Indians of Hispaniola, the island that nowadays comprises Haiti and the Dominican Republic, and in 1519 another had broken out there, killing up to a third of its inhabitants before spreading to Puerto Rico, Jamaica and Cuba.

That was about the time the Spaniard Hernán Cortés landed near what is now Vera Cruz with a force of 550. He literally burned his boats to dispel any thoughts his followers might have about cutting and running. Then, on 16 August, with 350 soldiers, he set off into the interior. Montezuma kept sending Cortés gifts of gold and jewels, with promises of more if he would stay away, but they only stoked the Spaniards' greed and on 8 November Cortés arrived at Tenochtitlan. Montezuma came down one of the causeways linking the island with the mainland, and, in front of his subjects, greeted the Spaniard as the long-awaited god returned once more to rule. He put up his visitors in a palace filled with treasure, then gave them a tour of one of the world's most spectacular cities, home to about 300,000 people, its markets crammed with goods, but its temples dripping with the blood of human sacrifices. Mutual suspicion quickly grew. For all Montezuma's hospitality, Cortés could see how much his people hated the new arrivals, while the Spaniards' lust for gold and their revulsion at human sacrifice began to convince the emperor that Cortés was not Quetzalcoatl after all. The conquistador took Montezuma hostage and made him hand over the treasures of his father's palace, angering the Aztecs even more.

Cortés had gone far beyond his orders, and another Spanish army was sent out to Vera Cruz to cut him down to size, bringing with it fresh supplies of the smallpox virus. But the wily Cortés left Pedro de Alvarado in charge in Tenochtitlan and hurried back to Vera Cruz, where he soon assumed command of the new army. By the time he got back to the Aztec capital, he found Alvarado had ordered a senseless massacre of hundreds of unarmed Aztec noblemen. Montezuma's more forceful brother Cuitlahuac was laying siege to the Spaniards in their palace, and they were in danger of being overwhelmed. The emperor climbed on to the roof and appealed for peace, but he was injured as his people responded with stones and arrows. Three days later he died, perhaps from his wounds, or maybe murdered by the Spaniards. On 30 June 1520 the conquistadores tried to break out, but their booty slowed them down so much that many drowned in Lake Texoco, while others were cut down by the Aztecs or dragged off to be sacrificed. As the Aztecs looted the corpses they came upon at least one man with smallpox.

Smallpox is one of the easiest diseases to pass on in a crowded city, and within two weeks the locals were beginning to fall ill. They called it 'the great rash', and were dismayed at the symptoms: pustules 'erupted on our faces, our breasts, our bellies, we were covered with agonising sores from head to foot . . . The sick were so utterly helpless they could only lie on their beds like corpses, unable to move.' The disease cut through them like a forest fire. Among the many who died were Cuitlahuac and his son. Twenty years later the missionary Fray Toribio wrote in his history of the Indians that smallpox victims 'died in heaps, like bedbugs. Many others died of starvation, because, as they were all taken sick at once, they could not care for each other.' It was impossible to bury all the dead, so when households were wiped out, 'they pulled down the houses over them so their homes became their tombs'.

In 1521 Cortés returned to Tenochtitlan with a great army of a few hundred Spaniards and tens of thousands of Indians, enemies of the tyrannical Aztecs. Although desperately weakened by smallpox, the Aztecs mounted a heroic defence for three months before the city fell. As they entered the Spaniards found they could not walk through the streets without stepping on the bodies of those who had died of the disease. It seemed to have killed at least half the population, and outside hardly a village was spared a similar toll. After taking Tenochtitlan, the Spaniards destroyed it and the Aztec Empire disintegrated.

While this disaster was unfolding in Mexico, further south the Incas had been extending their empire under their very powerful king, Huayna Capac Inca. Eighty years later the Peruvian native chronicler Guaman Poma would write: 'Having read accounts of the various kings and emperors of the world, I am sure none of them had the majesty or power of Inca . . . none of them enjoyed such esteem or wore so lofty a crown.' In 1527, Huayna Capac's armies were bringing ten years of war in Ecuador to a triumphant conclusion, but at the same time smallpox was extending its reach along the Caribbean coast and through the valleys of Colombia and Venezuela, helped by the excellent Inca road system. When the mysterious disease struck the Inca capital of Cuzco, messengers ran the 1,000 miles to Quito to tell the king.

Early in 1528 he learned that members of his family, his favourite general and the governor of Cuzco were all dead, and that traditional healers were saying their medicine was no use. Huayna Capac began the long journey home, but after 150 miles the disease struck. In no time it had swept through the army, killing many more trusted generals, 'their faces all covered with burning scabs'. The distraught king, according to a seventeenth-century Peruvian chronicler, 'ordered a stone house to be prepared for him in which to isolate himself. And there he died.' Unfortunately, he had left no clear word as to who was to be his successor, so a civil war broke out between two of his sons. At that point, another conquistador, Francisco Pizzaro, arrived. He quickly captured the young king Atahualpa, who had emerged victorious from the internal power struggle, and made him hand over a room full of gold plus double the amount in silver as the price of his release.

Once he had the treasure, though, Pizzaro set up a kangaroo court to convict his captive on various counts, such as idolatry, and get him sentenced to death by burning. Atahualpa was horrified, believing his soul would not be able to go to the afterlife if his body was burned. A Dominican friar named Vicente de Valverde came up with an offer Atahualpa could not refuse – if he would convert to Christianity, he could be garrotted instead. The king agreed. He was succeeded by a series of puppet rulers, the last of whom was beheaded in 1571. By then, the Incas had been overwhelmed by three more smallpox epidemics and devastated by other new illnesses, like mumps and measles. By 1576, their number in Peru had fallen from seven million to just half a million.

Measles killed a further two million Mexican natives in the 1600s, and the North American Indians were also devastated by the virus. In total it is estimated that newly introduced diseases killed about forty-five million people in the Americas between 1500 and 1650, perhaps 90 per cent of the native population.

## · TYPHUS ·

Typhus is spread by infected lice, and prospers in crowded places with poor hygiene, like prisons, refugee camps or among armies in the field. Symptoms include fever, excruciating headaches, severe muscle pains, stupor and delirium. It is sometimes blamed for the plague that swept through Athens in 430 BC (see Chapter 7) but the first definite outbreak in Europe was among Spanish soldiers besieging the Moorish city of Granada in 1489. Major epidemics came in times of famine, extreme poverty or war, and it went by names like 'famine fever' and 'jail fever'. In

1759 it was estimated that a quarter of those incarcerated in England's prisons died from it.

The disease raged through Ireland at the time of the Great Potato Famine (see Chapter 9), and conditions during the First World War also assisted it. On the Western Front de-lousing stations helped keep typhus under control, but in 1914 it broke out in a Serbian prisoner-of-war camp, and then spread to the civilian population. In May 1915 the tea magnate Sir Thomas Lipton, returning from a humanitarian mission, reported that typhus was 'raging everywhere . . . Neither man, woman, nor child, of whatever station in life, is immune from it.' Of twelve American nurses in one hospital, nine were ill, and an American doctor who had met Lipton on his arrival was dead when Sir Thomas returned a few days later. Men were shivering on the roadside 'too feeble to walk', while hospitals were overcrowded and victims were being left outside to die because there was not even room for them to lie on the floor. Of those who caught the disease, about three-quarters would die, and although centres were opened to disinfect victims and their clothes, more than 150,000 perished in six months.

By 1916, scientists had discovered the organism that causes typhus, but that did not prevent it continuing to wreak havoc the following year as the chaos of the Russian Revolution compounded that of the Great War. For a long time, the outside world did not know what was happening, but on 29 January 1918 *The Times* reported that the Russians had finally admitted that typhus was raging 'with unprecedented severity'. Food was short and doctors were scarce. Grozny had only seven physicians for 11,000 patients: 'Buildings were hospitals in name only, the sick were packed in bare rooms, and lay in blankets on the floor, with no one to nurse them and nothing to support life beyond a ration of brown bread thrust every morning into their hands,' wrote *The Times*' reporter. 'The little white lice that swarm and pullulate everywhere, pensioners of the starved, unwashed, exhausted and war-weary, communicate the germ.'

By the end of the First World War, a pandemic was also raging in Serbia, Macedonia, the Ukraine, Austria and eastern Poland. Serbia's cities were swollen with refugees, and measures like spraying people with petrol were not enough to prevent 120,000 cases in the last nine months of 1919. The Bolsheviks admitted to 1.3 million cases in Russia from

September 1918 to March 1919, and bodies were piled up in heaps. More than a million people fleeing the internal conflict overwhelmed quarantine stations at the borders, and they were constantly transporting the disease into neighbouring countries. A report from Dorohusk in Poland said of one trainload of refugees, 'All were verminous, and among them were 15 advanced cases of typhus.'

Mobile sanitary units had disinfected more than 300,000 people and 72,000 houses in Poland in 1919, but in June 1920, *The Times* reported that typhus had wrought such havoc that it was like 'the days when the Black Death ravaged medieval Europe'. In Galicia the schools were closed and business was at a standstill. There was no clean clothing, no medicine and little food. In the smaller towns and villages there was no water either, and sewage ran freely in open gullies. 'In almost every hut,' reported *The Times*' correspondent, 'there are several cases of typhus and in many instances whole families are stricken with the disease, and are perforce left to die unattended.' Nearly fifty doctors had died in the region, and now there was only one for every 150,000 inhabitants, so the peasants had to perform the roles of doctor, nurse and undertaker themselves: 'when a patient who has no relative dies, his penniless and starving neighbours strip the filthy and infected clothing from his corpse and sell it for a few pence, thus spreading the disease'. In July 1920 Dr Norman White of the League of Nations' Typhus Commission on Galicia said: 'the poorer classes were almost universally infested with lice', while *The Times* identified the louse as 'a menace more deadly than the armed man'. The following year a *Times* correspondent went to Suizran in Russia and learned that the situation was still just as grim. People were 'cadaverous, verminous, and exhausted', living in 'indescribably unhygienic' conditions in crowded camps, 'covered with buzzing flies, clad in rags and tatters. I wondered how many of them would survive the winter.' The League of Nations estimated that by the time the epidemic died down, up to three million people had died in Russia. Typhus had once again proved itself 'one of the immemorial plagues which in all ages have brought ruin and death to mankind'.

By the time of the Second World War, DDT's insecticide properties had been discovered and it proved extremely effective against lice. This combined with improvements in hygiene, and the development of a vaccine, ensured that no US serviceman died from typhus during the war. The disease did, however, strike the German army that invaded Russia in 1941, and 50,000 died from it in Egypt, Algeria and Morocco. In concentration camps the Nazis created conditions in which the illness could flourish, and typhus cut a swathe through camps like Theresienstadt and Bergen–Belsen.

Nowadays, treatment with antibiotics is very effective, but outbreaks still occur in remote areas like the Andes, the Himalayas and parts of Africa.


## · CHOLERA ·

Cholera attacks the intestines, causing diarrhoea and vomiting. A victim suffers acute pains in the limbs and stomach, and can lose pints of fluid in a few minutes, becoming shrunken and shrivelled. The skin turns black or blue, and breathing becomes a terrible effort. Sometimes the pain is so severe that the body convulses almost into a ball and can be returned to its normal shape only after death, which can arrive in less than twenty-four hours. An English doctor described finding a thirty-year-old victim 'shattered by six hours cholera into a torpid skeleton of 70 years'.

The disease may have struck India as early as the fourth century BC, when a temple inscription lamented: 'The lips blue, the face haggard, the eyes hollow, the stomach sunk in, the limbs contracted and crumpled as if by fire, those are the signs of the great illness which . . . comes down to slay the brave.' But the first pandemic is reckoned to have begun in 1817 at Jessore, and then spread through the rest of India. Next, it moved into Myanmar and Ceylon, and by 1820 it had been reported in China, Thailand, the Philippines and Indonesia, where 100,000 died on Java alone. At Basra in Iraq, 18,000 perished during a three-week period in 1821. The disease also infected Turkey, Russia, Arabia and East Africa, before petering out in 1823. It may be that an exceptionally cold winter prevented it reaching Western Europe.

The second pandemic started in Russia in 1830, then spread to Finland, Poland and Germany. In Britain's churches a new prayer was heard: 'Spare, we beseech Thee, this Thy favoured land, the wrath which to our sins is justly due.' The government quarantined ships arriving from Russia, but in 1831 the disease appeared in Sunderland, where gutters into which 'all the filth of human habitations is heedlessly thrown' flowed down the middle of crowded streets. Soon cholera was rampaging through north-east England. A surgeon from Northumberland was horrified: 'Oh what a frightful disease it is: how different from anything I ever saw before! The sunken eyes and ghastly countenance, cold blue skin, no pulse, violent and excruciating spasms, voice weak and almost inaudible, constant moaning.' Government advisers dispatched to the stricken region were handicapped by the fact that no one knew what caused cholera. Some doctors believed it was contagious, while others maintained it was transmitted by a *miasma* – bad air infected with refuse or sewage. The *Lancet* mused: 'Is it a fungus, a *miasma*, an electrical disturbance, a deficiency of ozone, a morbid off-scouring of the intestinal canal? We know nothing; we are at sea in a whirlpool of conjecture.' For those who thought cleanliness and hygiene were in any way relevant to halting its spread, the signs were not encouraging. One group of 100 houses in Tynemouth did not have a single lavatory between them, while hardly anyone had access to running water. Early in 1832 the government urged people to fast to placate the Almighty, but cholera marched on regardless. A number of towns introduced public health measures, like closing theatres, restricting church services, or cleaning up the worst slums, but one Manchester doctor described them as being like the practice of 'the country gentleman . . . who thought to keep out the crows by nailing up his park gate'. The suddenness with which the disease could strike caused great terror. In Exeter a man is said to have set off for work one morning, leaving his wife and daughter in good health, only to find them both dead on his return. The epidemic reached every corner of Britain and killed an estimated 60,000 people.

France suffered even more, losing 100,000, including 20,000 in Paris alone. The German poet Heinrich Heine described how at a masked ball in the city the guests 'mocked the fear of cholera'. Suddenly, amid the music and laughter, 'the most light-hearted of the harlequins felt his legs growing cold, took off his mask; to the astonishment of everyone present, he revealed a face turned violet-blue'. The bustle of the ball was silenced in a flash, and the revellers dashed for their carriages. It was a microcosm of what was happening all over the French capital, as those who could afford to fled. Some of the people left behind decided they were being poisoned, and six unfortunate suspects were hanged from lamp-posts.

By the end of 1835, cholera was present in most of Europe. It was estimated to have claimed 200,000 lives in Hungary and at least that number in Russia, where more rumours of poisoning led to a series of riots that were brutally suppressed. The disease had reached North America in 1832, killing 1,000 in Quebec, before travelling down the eastern seaboard of the United States. New Yorkers who tried to flee across Long Island Sound ran into volleys of gunfire from Rhode Islanders, but the disease spread along the Erie Canal to the Midwest. At Ypsilanti in Michigan the local militia opened fire on a stagecoach arriving from Detroit because cholera had been reported there. Still it moved on, reaching New Orleans, where it killed 5,000, before infecting Mexico and Cuba in 1833.

Treatments for the mysterious disease included the drastic, such as mercury, ammonia, arsenic and the application of red-hot irons, as well as castor oil, rhubarb, opium and electric shocks. A Scottish doctor who saw more than 1,000 victims in the second pandemic was tortured by 'withering disappointment' as all his remedies failed. He tried 'leeches, blood-letting, blisters, warm baths, stimulants, in a word everything that empiricism could suggest without avail'. As for prevention, there was a general feeling that the sordid living conditions brought to so many places by the industrial revolution were somehow to blame, so Britain and parts of Germany set up public health authorities to try to improve the environment. The *Lancet* published a vitriolic attack on these new-fangled ideas, but after Britain's first epidemic a Royal Commission inquiry into the fifty towns that had been worst hit found only six had an adequate water supply, and only one a proper sewerage system. Social reformers complained that black slaves in America had a better life than the British working classes.

Cholera returned to Britain in 1848. As forty people fell ill in the Scottish village of Carnbroe, one man, convinced he was going to die, cut his throat rather than wait for the agonies of the disease. Mevagissey in Cornwall had no proper drainage, so when cholera came local doctors borrowed tents from the government, and evacuated 1,300 people to a camp half a mile away with a good supply of fresh water. None of them caught cholera, while nearly all those who stayed in the village contracted the disease. Again, more than 60,000 Britons died, but by now Queen Victoria's anaesthetist, John Snow, was hot on the trail of the cholera bug. When this was a disease of the intestines, he wondered, why should it be spread in the air as the *miasmatists* maintained? Snow argued that it was far more likely to be transmitted through contaminated water, but his theory failed to win general acceptance.

While the debate continued, a third pandemic, generally regarded as the most deadly, began. It is thought to have erupted in India in 1852, and then spread to Iran, Europe, the United States and the rest of the world. Africa was particularly badly hit, and there were more than a million deaths in Russia. In Chicago it was said to have claimed one person in twenty. Although it reached Britain late in 1853, the following year Parliament went ahead with its plan to abolish the Board of Health. *The Times* rejoiced, declaring: 'We prefer to take our chance of cholera and the rest than be bullied into health.' However, MPs soon reconsidered and created a similar body.

There were 500 deaths around Snow's surgery in London's Soho, but virtually none in the surrounding area. He managed to persuade the authorities to remove the handle from the local water pump, and the deaths stopped. But when Snow died from a stroke in 1858 his theory was still being disputed. Indeed, during the fourth pandemic in 1865 a *miasmatist* maintained that areas affected by cholera were marked out by a 'thin transparent bluish haze'. In 1875, though, Disraeli's government compelled all local authorities to provide drainage, sewerage and an adequate water supply. By 1896, cholera was rare enough in Britain to be classified as an 'exotic disease', but it remained a menace in other parts of the world.

The fifth pandemic, beginning in 1881, hit Spain badly, killing at least 60,000, and Russia, where as many as 200,000 died in 1893–4. By then, the German bacteriologist Robert Koch had managed to isolate the comma-shaped bacterium that causes cholera, and to confirm Snow's theory that it was transmitted in contaminated water. Improved sanitation stopped it taking hold in many European cities, and it was unable to re-enter the United States because the authorities established more effective quarantine measures. Among the famous victims of cholera in the nineteenth century was Tchaikovsky who insisted on drinking tap water while the illness was rampaging through St Petersburg in 1893. Others included the philosopher Hegel and the great military theorist Carl von Clausewitz. The French novelist Alexandre Dumas caught cholera in 1832 but survived to write books like *The Three Musketeers* and *The Count of Monte Cristo*.

The sixth pandemic ran from 1899 to 1923 and again hit Russia hard, claiming about half a million lives. The chaos of the civil war that followed the Bolshevik Revolution made it more devastating. This outbreak was especially lethal in India and Arabia, where more than 20,000 pilgrims died on the hajj to Mecca in 1907–8. It also hit North Africa, with about 34,000 dying in Egypt in just three months. The British authorities tried putting disinfectant into Cairo's water supply, whereupon they were accused of mass poisoning by the local people.

The seventh pandemic lasted from 1961 to 2005 and afflicted nearly 120 countries, but most of the industrialised world escaped. Nowadays, treatments that replace lost fluids and salts, combined with the use of antibiotics, can reduce death rates to below 1 per cent.

## · SLEEPING SICKNESS ·

One of the new pests encountered by European explorers in Africa was the tsetse fly, whose bite feels like the insertion of a red-hot needle. In 1857 David Livingstone reported that it could kill horses and cattle, though he did not make the connection with sleeping sickness which afflicted humans. The symptoms build up gradually, with joint pains, headaches, insomnia and lethargy that can blight the victim's life for years. Then the central nervous system is affected. Sufferers develop a weary, shuffling walk and daytime drowsiness so extreme that they can fall asleep even while eating. In the final stage come tremors and paralysis of the limbs, and extreme loss of appetite, so the victim wastes away to little more than a skin-covered skeleton, then sinks into a coma that deepens into death. It would emerge that this too was spread by a parasite carried by tsetse flies.

Sleeping sickness has probably been present in Africa in relatively isolated pockets for centuries. Tsetse flies tend to colonise belts of countryside rather than spreading haphazardly, and before the nineteenth century infected people rarely travelled beyond their home areas. But when Western traders and explorers started criss-crossing the continent with teams of native porters the parasite travelled great distances with them. By the middle of the century, non-African visitors were arriving at the north and west of Lake Victoria (modern-day Uganda), where the tsetse fly thrived. In 1900 the British authorities began to see the first cases of sleeping sickness. Two years later the government sent a Dr Low from the London School of Tropical Medicine to investigate. He reported that the disease had already killed between 20,000 and 30,000 people, and added ominously that it was still spreading and 'its virulence was apparently on the increase'. He concluded, 'The disease is practically invariably fatal,' so the outlook was 'very gloomy'. There was no known cure, and although missionaries set up camps for sufferers, all they could do was try to make death a little less unpleasant.

Back in 1894, a British Army doctor named David Bruce had identified the parasite that caused the illness in the blood of horses and cattle. Seven years later another British doctor working in the Gambia isolated it in humans with sleeping sickness. Bruce advocated killing the flies and restricting the movement of infected humans and cattle. In 1903 he reported the native population of Buvuma Island in Lake Victoria had fallen from 22,000 to just 8,000, while the southern part of Bugosa province on its shore had lost nearly all its inhabitants. By 1907, according to some estimates, up to 200,000 Africans had died in the region, perhaps two-thirds of the population.

The disease was eventually defeated by political action. Sir Hesketh Bell, the British commissioner in Uganda, had repeatedly asked the Colonial Office in London for permission to move the entire population out of the infested areas, but it always refused because of fears that the natives would rebel, resentful at having to leave such fertile land. In the end, in despair, Bell broached the idea with the local chiefs himself, and they agreed. The evacuation passed off peacefully, and the epidemic waned. Bell hoped that once the people had been removed, the flies would become disease-free, and the inhabitants would be able to return. Unfortunately, the parasite found a permanent home in wild animals, which did not show any symptoms but acted as carriers, continually infecting the flies that bit them.

Nowadays there are effective treatments for sleeping sickness, provided it is diagnosed before it reaches the central nervous system. Even so, the World Health Organisation estimates that 66,000 people still die of it every year.

## · FLU ·

Influenza is one of the most difficult illnesses to combat because of the speed with which the virus mutates and its thousands of different strains. Some believe it may have appeared as 'the sweat' in England in 1485. The symptoms included fever, a burning thirst, a headache and painful joints, sometimes accompanied by abdominal pain and vomiting. It could kill in a matter of hours, or the victim might lie ill for several days then recover. There were half a dozen epidemics in the sixteenth century, one of which nearly killed Anne Boleyn.

Perhaps the first flu pandemic came in 1580, when the bug travelled through Asia and Africa, and killed many people in Italy, Spain and Germany. That was when it acquired its name, which comes from the Italian for 'influence', because it was put down to unfavourable astrological influences. In the eighteenth century there was a series of European pandemics, and the disease spread to the Americas. Then it seemed to recede, until 'Russian flu' appeared in St Petersburg in December 1889. By March of the following year it had killed at least 250,000 Europeans, and perhaps another 750,000 across the rest of the world.

The worst outbreak of all, though, began in the final months of the First World War. It would eventually kill more people than that dreadful conflict. In February 1918 'three-day fever' afflicted eight million Spaniards, including King Alfonso XIII. In Madrid, it hit a third of the population. Victims had a temperature of forty degrees, pain behind the eyes, in the ears, in the lumbar region, until every fibre seemed to ache. Then, after three days, most recovered. It became known as 'Spanish flu', though many believe it had already appeared among the warring armies, perhaps in the American camps where soldiers gathered before being sent to Europe, but the news had been suppressed because it would have been useful to the enemy. In neutral Spain there were no such considerations. Certainly, in the spring of 1918 a flu epidemic at Fort Riley in Kansas killed forty-six men and made another thousand ill, and soon it was spreading on too grand a scale to be kept hidden. For twelve days in May the British Grand Fleet had more than 10,000 men sick and could not put to sea. *The Times* wrote of 'persons who feel perfectly well and are able to go about their business at ten o'clock in the morning being prostrate at noon'. Whatever the disease's origins, it was soon active in Britain, France, Germany, Italy, Egypt, Austria and Norway, then India, China, Peru and Costa Rica. All the armies on the Western Front suffered, and General Pershing was warned that a consignment of fresh men from America would not be coming because of the epidemic back home.

This strain of the disease was fairly mild: it incapacitated many but killed relatively few. By the autumn, though, it had become more lethal, and often turned to deadly pneumonia. One physician said patients simply suffocated after a desperate battle for breath. Another described unfortunates who 'died struggling to clear their airways of a blood-tinged froth that sometimes gushed from their nose and mouth'. Manchester's medical officer of health visited schools and found children collapsing 'like poisoned flowers' across their desks. Across the Atlantic, at a military camp in Massachusetts, the first case was diagnosed on 12 September. Less than two weeks later 12,604 soldiers had been taken ill. Altogether, 11,000 US soldiers would die of flu on the Western Front, and another 22,000 would perish without ever leaving America. At one point, the public health guru Dr Victor Heiser (who had survived the Johnstown flood – see Chapter 4) commented: 'It is more dangerous to be a soldier in the peaceful United States than to have been on the firing-line in France.' At one camp special trains were provided to take away the dead, and the bodies were laid out in long rows. A doctor said: 'It beats any sight they ever had in France after a battle.' A peculiarity of this outbreak was that, unlike most flu epidemics where the very young and the very old are most at risk, this one seemed to carry off those in the prime of life.

In Washington, D.C., a distraught young woman rang the phone company to say two of her roommates were dead and the third was ill. When the police came to investigate, though, they found four bodies. It was estimated that one person in ten in Boston caught flu, and two-thirds of them died. The *New York Times* advised any man kissing a girl to do so through his handkerchief. In Rio de Janeiro a medical student said a man asked him where the tram stop was, then promptly dropped dead. In Cape Town six people died on a single short tram journey. At the other end of the country, forty miners were being hoisted the 3,000 feet to the surface of a gold mine in the Witwatersrand when the winding-gear operator suddenly found his body drenched in cold sweat and his arms without any strength. He was unable to apply the brake and the cage ploughed into the gear at the top of the shaft, killing twenty-four. An inquiry cleared the operator of any blame. In Bombay 700 people died in a single day. 'Untouchables' had the lowest death toll since everyone shunned them. In Britain an army officer campaigning for the November 1918 general election reached a small village and found everyone dead. At Dover a stoker married a Woolworth's shop girl, then twenty-four hours later found himself standing in his wedding suit by her grave.

Sometimes the public health response was inadequate. Flu arrived in Cape Town on a ship from Sierra Leone, where 500 stevedores had been struck down. Even though ninety people had died on the voyage, the South African government did not impose quarantine restrictions until a month after the vessel had docked, by which time the disease was well entrenched on shore. In many places victims became as isolated as those struck down by bubonic plague centuries before. They would post a sticker in their window, and tradesmen would leave provisions at the door. Nor were normal prejudices suspended. Warsaw's anti-flu hygiene drive concentrated on the Jewish ghetto, because, said a proclamation, the Jewish race is 'a particular enemy of order and cleanliness'. South-West African hospitals would not admit blacks, and a *Montreal Gazette* headline ran: 'No Panic Except Amongst Orientals'.

But there were many acts of generosity and courage. A girls' school outside Cape Town was turned into a makeshift hospital, and business-men and company directors came in to do laundry for the sick. A

Uruguayan doctor in Paris for a medical conference went off to tend the sick in the city's poorest districts instead, then caught flu himself and died. For all doctors, the workload was ferocious. In Quebec City they were so overwhelmed that at least 10,000 victims received no medical attention. In a hospital in Adelaide patients had to share beds. Even when doctors got to a victim they often had no idea what to do. One American physician admitted they 'knew no more about the flu than fourteenth-century Florentines had known about the Black Death'. Understandably, therefore, treatment was hit and miss. A colleague in Amsterdam agonised: 'Why did I become a doctor? I can do nothing to help, and soon there won't be any more people.' Many remedies were tried – morphine, phenacetin (though it could damage the kidneys) and a compound of mercury. Some doctors had good results with vaccinations: of 16,000 British Tommies inoculated, only two died. There was a fierce debate on whether alcohol offered protection or made people more susceptible. In Canada you could get it on prescription, and long queues formed; but the Danish government banned it. Some people swore by tobacco, and a grocer at Delft made all his staff smoke cigars; all became infected except for a single employee who had refused to comply. The Mayor of Santiago in Chile banned the consumption of uncooked vegetables. On the other hand, a four-year-old girl at death's door in Portland, Oregon, was allegedly saved by taking onion spirit and being buried from head to foot for three days in raw, sliced onions. Some experts favoured plunging feet into scalding-hot water; others recommended icy sheets. Among the many quack 'cures' on the market were sacred pebbles from a Japanese shrine and Swedish surgical vests that allegedly 'sucked out' the disease. There was also profiteering: in Philadelphia some undertakers were said to have raised their prices by 500 per cent.

Methods of prevention tried were just as varied. A cinema in Liverpool put a block of camphor under every seat; in Nottingham they sluiced the streets with disinfectant; and Christchurch, New Zealand, launched a hunt for rats. In Prescott, Arizona, the authorities banned shaking hands. Many churches, schools and theatres were shut down. Sing Sing Prison in New York State demonstrated the benefits of quarantine by isolating any man who showed the slightest sign of flu, and putting him on a diet of milk, whisky and four raw eggs a day. Not a single inmate was lost. Australia quarantined new arrivals for a week, and managed to keep the number of deaths down to 13,000 out of a population of five million. If you coughed or sneezed in the street in New York, you could be fined $500 or jailed for a year; within days of the legislation being passed, hundreds had appeared before the courts. Just one sneeze could leave eighty-five million bacteria suspended in the air for half an hour, so the surgical mask became a favourite precaution. In Calgary all workers who came into contact with the public – whether in banks, shops, restaurants or lifts – had to wear them, while in Edmonton the measure was extended to everyone riding in a tram. The masks did seem to have some effect: the infection rate was much lower in Sydney, where they were mandatory, than in Melbourne, where they were not. The mayor of San Francisco boldly declared, 'Wear a mask and save your life! A mask is 99 per cent proof against influenza,' and 'mask slackers' were given a hard time.

One American statistician calculated that if ten people contracted the disease, in a week they could have passed it on to a million others. He concluded: 'If the epidemic continues its mathematical rate of acceleration, civilisation could easily have disappeared from the face of the earth within a matter of a few more weeks.' Many felt this was going a bit far, but the complex infrastructure of modern society did indeed seem under threat. A South African reader wrote to *The Times*: 'within a few days, doctors, chemists, nurses, butchers, bakers, and railway staffs were struck down, and the complete paralysis of communities resulted'. In San Francisco there were so few rubbish collectors at work that huge mountains of refuse accumulated. Parts of Britain had no firemen. The signing of the armistice that ended the First World War on 11 November 1918 produced scenes of unprecedented public celebration, which in many parts of the world must have provided wonderful opportunities for the virus. In the week that followed 19,000 people died of flu in Britain. One German newspaper detected some sort of international brotherhood in the dire situation: 'Today,' it said, 'all nations sneeze as one.'

By the end of 1918, the worst of the pandemic was over, though in May of the following year 15,000 people died on Mauritius. Over the globe, more than a billion people had caught the disease, and perhaps seventy million died, compared with ten million military deaths during the war. India suffered the greatest number of deaths of any country – up to seventeen million, one in twenty of the population. The Dutch East Indies, now Indonesia, lost 800,000 people; the United States 540,000; Russia and Italy 375,000 each; Britain and Germany more than 220,000 each; and Spain 170,000. More than a quarter of a million died in Japan. South Pacific islands were especially hard hit, with one in five Western Samoans (7,500 in total) perishing, while one in seven of the population of Papeete, the capital of Tahiti, also died. But one of the highest death rates of all occurred on the coast of Labrador: out of 3,000 local Inuit, 2,000 died. Famous victims included General Louis Botha, the first premier of the Union of South Africa; the Austrian painter Egon Schiele; Edmond Rostand, author of *Cyrano de Bergerac;* and Sir Hubert Parry, who composed the music to *Jerusalem.* As if to prove that fitness was no guarantee of survival, Harry Elionsky, an American champion swimmer who had once covered ninety miles non-stop, died from the disease. A number of wartime heroes also succumbed, including Canada's youngest VC, Alan McLeod, who had once had to leap on to the wing of his aircraft after it had been set on fire, and then crash-land it. Among those who caught the disease but survived were King George V and Kaiser Wilhelm, British Prime Minister David Lloyd George, American President Woodrow Wilson, General Pershing, Walt Disney, and Mary Pickford, America's sweet-heart and the richest woman in the world.

It is not clear how much the privations of the war lowered people's resistance and so made the 1918 flu outbreak so deadly. It was not just the dreadful conditions in the trenches, many millions of civilians had been driven from their homes, and countless others had little or no food. The war also hampered the public health response. France, for example, had 19,000 doctors in military service, and at home the minister of the interior could not call on a single one under the age of sixty-five. The disease struck far beyond the theatres of battle, though, and many doctors saw for the first time the unsanitary conditions in which so much of humanity lived, whether it was the 10,000 houses in Melbourne that were not connected to the sewerage system or the stable in Cape Town that housed twenty families. A newspaper in Copenhagen proclaimed, 'The lesson of the pandemic is to fight poverty,' and it did indeed precipitate some improvements in public health. Italy introduced compulsory medical examinations for schoolchildren; Cape Town and Berlin launched big slum clearance programmes; while in America more stringent hygiene regulations were introduced for shops, hotels and restaurants.

There would be further serious outbreaks. In 1957 'Asian flu' killed up to four million people worldwide, while 'Mao flu' was responsible for an estimated 33,000 deaths in the USA and 9,000 in Britain in 1968. As the twentieth century drew to a close, interest in the 1918 outbreak grew with people getting alarmed at the spread of diseases like SARS and 'bird flu', and there were dire warnings that the world was due for another pandemic. In 1998, using the corpse of an Inuit woman buried for eighty years in the ice of Alaska, American scientists were able for the first time to extract and examine the virus that caused the 1918 pandemic.

## · MALARIA ·

Malaria has been infecting human beings for at least 50,000 years. The disease is spread by the female mosquito's bite, which passes on parasites that make a home in human red blood cells. It causes fever, chills, nausea and, in severe cases, coma and death. It is known to have struck China in 2700 BC, and also seems to have played a part in the decline and fall of the Roman Empire. Italy suffered a major outbreak in AD 79, which may have lowered the birth rate, gradually undermining Rome's ability to hang on to its territory. The name 'malaria' comes from the Medieval Italian for 'bad air'.

It was only in the twentieth century, though, that a British Army medical officer, Major Ronald Ross, proved that the disease was transmitted by mosquito bites. He won the Nobel prize in 1902 for his research. This new knowledge did not save eighteen million Russians from catching malaria in 1923 during the post-revolutionary chaos. In some places 40 per cent died. The disease also profited from the disorder in India following partition in 1947 (see Chapter 12), when seventy-five million people contracted it and an estimated one million died. DDT was used against mosquitoes with some success, but it was banned in many countries in the 1970s. By then, the insects had already developed resistance anyway. Today hundreds of millions of people still fall ill from malaria each year, and it kills between one and three million, mostly young children in sub-Saharan Africa.


· AIDS ·

By the 1980s, in much of the world, the curse of infectious diseases – smallpox, polio, diphtheria, measles and others – seemed to have been tamed by vaccines or treatment. Then, on 5 June 1981, the US Centers for Disease Control and Prevention received reports that five homosexual men from Los Angeles all had a rare form of fungus-borne pneumonia known as PCP. They also had a reduced resistance to all infections, something that had already been observed in gay men in San Francisco and New York. Before long, European cities were recording similar cases. Popular newspapers called it the 'gay plague'. By 1983, about 3,000 people in the United States had been infected, and nearly 1,300 had died. The condition became known as AIDS – Acquired Immune Deficiency Syndrome.

In January 1985 the Ugandan government dispatched a team of doctors to investigate a series of unexplained deaths at the village of Kasensero on Lake Victoria, near the border with Tanzania, a haunt for bar-girls and smugglers. Over the previous four years more than 100 people there had succumbed to a mysterious wasting condition, dubbed the 'slim disease' by locals. Some believed it was caused by witchcraft; others that it was a punishment from God for loose living. Blood samples revealed the human immunodeficiency virus (HIV), which causes AIDS.

One of the peculiarities of HIV is that it acts very slowly, so people can be living with it, and infecting others, for up to ten years before they show any signs of illness. It is now thought the infection originated among chimpanzees and monkeys, probably passing to humans through blood-to-blood contact during hunting or butchering, and that it was active in Africa for at least twenty years before its appearance in the United States. Indeed, an examination of blood samples taken in Kinshasa in 1959 showed one to be HIV positive. The victims in Africa, though, were usually not homosexual. European doctors who went to investigate concluded that the disease was being spread there through promiscuity and sex with prostitutes. At Lyantonde, a Ugandan truck stop on a major route to Rwanda, Burundi and Zaire, blood tests revealed that two-thirds of the bar-girls and one in six of all pregnant women were infected. By the end of the 1980s, nearly one person in five in Rwandan cities was HIV positive.

Soon AIDS was spreading across the continent, usually infecting people between fifteen and fifty, the most economically productive members of the population. Most were dead within ten years. By now, the main routes of transmission had been established – sex or blood (putting intravenous drug users and those given contaminated transfusions or blood products at great risk) and from mother to child. Health services in some African countries were overwhelmed, and AIDS seemed a death sentence. There was no vaccine and no cure. Many African governments denied the existence of the disease, saying it was racist Western propaganda. Some anti-apartheid campaigners in South Africa considered it an attempt by the white government to stop black people reproducing, saying AIDS stood for 'Afrikaner Invention to Deprive us of Sex'. At first, Kenya tried to keep its outbreak secret to protect the tourist industry, while Zimbabwe's minister of health ordered doctors not to identify it as a cause of death. Many richer countries mounted ambitious public health campaigns, promoting 'safe sex', but in Africa only Senegal and Uganda launched effective anti-AIDS initiatives in the 1980s, with the latter's President Museveni touring the country urging people to 'love carefully'. In Senegal President Diouf decreed that sex workers must have regular checks, which kept the infection rate below 2 per cent.

Medical science came up with a treatment remarkably quickly: the first anti-AIDS drug, AZT, was approved in America in 1987 and a number of others followed. They did not cure the disease, but they slowed its progress so dramatically that many doctors in the advanced world considered that AIDS had been converted from a death sentence to a chronic condition. These drugs were expensive, however, so, although they saved thousands of lives in the industrialised world, many sufferers in poorer countries could not afford them. After black majority rule came to South Africa the government refused to provide AZT even though it had been shown to reduce transmission from mother to child by half. By the time Nelson Mandela stood down in 1999, about half a million South Africans had died of AIDS, and four million were infected. Mandela's successor Thabo Mbeki said those who linked the disease to promiscuity were propagating racist sexual stereotypes of Africans, and he seized on the views of a small group of maverick scientists who maintained there was no such thing as AIDS, claiming South Africans were being turned into 'guinea pigs and conned into using dangerous and toxic drugs'. Unsurprisingly, the infection continued to spread, and it is estimated that one South African adult in every nine is HIV positive, while the South African Paediatric Association said 70,000 babies had been born with the virus in the year 2000 alone.

By 2004, sub-Saharan Africa, with just 10 per cent of the world's population, had 70 per cent of its AIDS cases. There were also about twelve million AIDS orphans living in the region. Botswana had the highest rate of infection in the world at 37 per cent. Across the globe, about twenty million people had died of the disease, and in 2005 alone AIDS claimed the lives of 570,000 children. That year, the total number of infected people passed forty million, but it was not only in Africa that drawing attention to the epidemic was discouraged. In China a human rights activist was put under house arrest after exposing the failure of the authorities in Henan to carry out HIV tests on blood donations in the 1990s, resulting in an estimated 55,000 people being infected.

# 9

## FAMINE

### · EGYPT ·

According to the Greek historian Herodotus, Egypt was 'the gift of the Nile'. Without the river, he wrote, the country would be an arid desert. In a typical year the Nile would start to rise in late June and continue to swell until September, when the waters would recede, leaving a thick layer of silt for the locals to cultivate. The problem was that if it went over thirty-five feet, the resulting flood would destroy villages and drown people, while if it rose less than twenty-eight feet, the silt would be too shallow, the crop would be poor and food would be short; and if this happened two years on the run, it could be disastrous. One flood in five was either too high or too low.

An ancient stone tells the story of a famine 2,500 years before Christ. Grain was scarce for seven years and 'everyone was in distress'. In AD 967 the waters again failed to rise sufficiently, and a two-year famine left 600,000 people dead. From 1064 to 1071 there was another devastating dearth. Women tried to use their precious pearls and emeralds to buy food, but when they could find no takers they simply threw them away in the street.

One of the worst Nile famines of all, though, came at the beginning of the thirteenth century. Writing in 1204, the Baghdad-born scientist and historian Abd al-Latif said that only six times in the previous six centuries had the river failed to reach twenty-four feet, but in 1200 it had not even struggled to twenty-three. The first hint of disaster had come in

April, when the Nile turned green and smelled 'fetid and corrupt'. Latif carried out a series of experiments and found it was choked with vegetable matter, something he correctly attributed to a shortage of rain at its source. The colour disappeared, but the water still did not rise enough. As the harvest failed food prices increased, and people began deserting the parched countryside and heading for cities like Cairo and nearby Misr, finding only 'an appalling famine and a frightful mortality'. By March 1201, disease was stalking the land and the poor 'ate carrion, corpses, dogs . . . and the filth of animals'. As they grew more desperate cannibalism became widespread, and 'it was not rare to surprise people with little children roasted or boiled', wrote Latif: 'I myself saw a roasted child in a basket.' The mother and father who had cooked it were condemned to be burned alive, but the writer says even punishment of this severity was no deterrent, and there were reports of storerooms full of human bones that had been picked clean, and cauldrons in which children's heads bobbed. Bands of marauders would roam the countryside eating anyone they could grab, graves were ransacked, while young girls were often sold into slavery for a pittance by their parents in the hope that the buyers would keep them alive; even noblewomen sometimes implored people to buy them.

'God alone knows' how many died, wrote Latif. 'In the streets where I trod, there was no single one where the feet or the eyes did not meet with a corpse or a man in the throes of mortal agony.' Five hundred bodies a day were being removed from Cairo, while at Misr 'the number of the dead was incalculable; they could not inter them, but contented themselves with throwing them outside the town'. Travellers could pass through towns without seeing a living soul. Inside the houses were piles of bodies, and the roads 'had become like a banqueting room for birds and wild beasts, who gorged themselves on the flesh of the corpses'. Imagine the horror in April, then, when the Nile again turned green and smelly. In September it started to subside before it had reached twenty-eight feet. The price of beans, barley and wheat rocketed, and famine returned. This time there was said to be less cannibalism, but perhaps only because there were fewer potential victims. Plague followed hunger, and many peasants fell dead at their ploughs. The Nile ran so low that it could be forded on foot in parts, and in February 1202 it yet again turned green. In June and early July it rose only very slowly, and 'despair was general'. People began to think that something terrible had happened to the source of the river, then suddenly 'mountains of water precipitated themselves one on the other', and the crisis was over, as the flood reached the required twenty-eight feet. The authorities estimated that 111,000 people died between July 1200 and April 1202, although Latif believed it was many times that figure. And Egypt's suffering was not yet over: in July 1202 it was one of several countries rocked by a huge earthquake that devastated the region (see Chapter 2).

## · THE GREAT FAMINE ·

From the eleventh to the thirteenth century Europe prospered. In many areas the proportion of land being cultivated in 1300 would not be reached again for another 500 years. The population had grown, too. At the end of the eleventh century England had about 1.4 million people; by 1300, it had 5 million. During the same period, France's population increased from 6.2 million to more than 17 million. But by the beginning of the fourteenth century, food production in some places was beginning to fall as a result of erosion or exhaustion of the overworked soil, and the problem was exacerbated by global cooling. The Arctic glaciers were advancing, and the Baltic froze in 1303 and 1306–7. This 'Little Ice Age' virtually ended wine-making in England, while it became impossible to grow wheat in parts of Denmark and the uplands of Provence. Everywhere the agricultural growing season was cut by up to two months, and more fungi attacked crops in the cooler, wetter summers.

In the spring of 1315 it rained unusually heavily over much of Europe – 'most marvellously and for so long', as one contemporary put it – and summer brought no respite, with the wet weather continuing. Crops were beaten to the ground, and there was no fodder for livestock. The rains were soon being compared to Noah's flood, and in England the *Chronicle of Malmesbury* noted: 'the anger of the Lord kindled against his people, and he hath stretched forth his hand against them, and hath smitten them'. In parts of Central Europe floods swept away whole villages at the cost of hundreds of lives, while Normandy was devastated by vicious wind storms. Wheat prices more than quadrupled in some regions, and many people faced starvation. In desperation, they started to eat roots, grass and the bark of trees. Even the apparently well-to-do were beginning to suffer. A German chronicler recorded that knights sitting on 'magnificently outfitted' horses would swap their mounts and their weapons for 'cheap wine . . . because they were so terribly hungry'. On 10 August, when King Edward II of England rolled up at St Albans with his entourage, they could not find bread for love nor money. The king tried to bring in price controls, but that just made dealers withdraw their produce, and the ordinance had to be repealed. As people grew desperate, the number of robberies in Kent rose by a third, and in the countryside it was said that men were murdered for food.

Through the spring of 1316 the rain still fell. Peasants were now having to eat their seed corn, and had started to slaughter their working animals. Some abandoned their children, while many of the old refused food to try to help the young survive. The streets and alleys of Bruges were full of the bodies of peasants who had fled there to try to escape the famine in the countryside. One chronicler reported that the poor ate dogs, cats, the dung of doves, and even their children. In Baltic towns it was said that 'mothers fed upon their sons'. From Poland, there were reports of people harvesting hanged bodies from gibbets, while being put in jail became particularly hazardous, as the existing inmates would overpower and devour newcomers.

It seemed beyond belief when the wet weather continued into 1317. Diseases like pneumonia, bronchitis and tuberculosis had appeared in the wake of famine, so, although the summer finally brought better weather, it was too late for many. Fodder for animals remained very short, and the 'great dying of beasts' continued into the early 1320s. Because so much seed corn had been consumed, food production did not return to anything like normal until 1325. Historians believe that by the end of the famine, up to a quarter of the population of Europe had died.

## · INDIA ·

It is estimated that India suffered fourteen major famines between the eleventh and the sixteenth century. Later, in 1630, a drought brought nine years of hunger in which four million people died; while in 1769 a terrible famine broke out in Bengal, which was then ruled by the British East India Company. The harvest of 1768 had been poor, and native field officers had expressed their concerns, but there was a belief that they would exaggerate even the smallest shortfall in the harvest in order to underline their own efficiency in managing to collect taxes. The spring rains came in 1769, but soon there was a severe drought, and, according to a native superintendent at Bishenpore in West Bengal, the rice paddies 'became like fields of dried straw'. Still, the government in Calcutta found it hard to believe that the situation was as bad as the local officials claimed.

In fact, during the stifling summer of 1769 people were already dying of hunger. They sold their livestock and their tools; they ate their seed corn. Then, in the words of a history of the famine written a hundred years later: 'they sold their sons and daughters, till at length no buyer of children could be found; they ate the leaves of trees and the grass of the field'. Reports of cannibalism began to emerge, and disease took hold as people migrated in a desperate search for food, spreading infection as they went. Smallpox attacked Murshidabad. It killed the prince in his palace, while corpses in the streets were eaten by dogs and jackals.

The rains returned in 1770, and the province had an abundant harvest, but not quite in time. Millions died 'in the struggle to live through the few intervening weeks that separated them from the harvest, their last gaze being probably fixed on the densely covered fields that would ripen only a little too late for them'. On Christmas Eve Calcutta was able to report back to London that the famine was over, and that the harvest had been so plentiful that it anticipated being able to buy its supplies for the coming year very cheaply. According to official figures, ten million people had died in Bengal, nearly a third of the population.

During the nineteenth century there were more famines, with some historians arguing they were exacerbated by British policies, such as converting land farmed by locals into foreign-owned plantations, and imposing heavy taxes to fund the wars in Afghanistan. One in 1865–6 followed a severe drought in Orissa state on India's east coast. The government espoused the laissez-faire economic principles fashionable at the time, which held that if grain was short in one region, prices would rise, so supplies from other regions would automatically find their way there, and any attempt by the government to 'buck' the market could only make matters worse. The commissioner in Cuttack therefore said there must be no interference with 'local trade'. As more than a million Orissans died, Secretary of State for India Lord Salisbury (who went on to become prime minister three times) wondered 'why in spite of the applications of the principle of political economy, people were dying in their thousands'. He later regretted his inaction, acknowledging: 'The governments of India and Bengal had taken in effect no precautions whatever.'

A decade later India was struck by another drought. In 1875–6 the monsoon rains failed in the south. Millions of acres went unplanted, food prices soared and the poor began to starve. Again the government was reluctant to interfere with the market, and by the time relief programmes started it was too late for millions. Awful sights once more became familiar. The *Madras Times* reported: 'A coffee planter seeking shelter from the rain in a hut found six decomposing corpses. On any day and every day mothers may be seen in the streets of Madras offering their children for sale.' In the autumn the famine began to spread north. By the end of 1876, the government was employing more than a million people on public works to save them from starvation. Charities also did their bit, but *The Times'* correspondent reported that the streets were full of starving people. Outside a house where free food was sometimes distributed, the reporter saw 800 people queuing: 'They had been waiting patiently for two or three hours . . . They were unsuccessful in their quest.' Among them were 'more than 50 young children who, judging from their appearance, had not long to live'.

By January 1877, the price of grain had trebled in places, with perhaps five million people hit by the shortages. Cholera was also widespread. The government reprimanded the authorities in Madras for buying grain to relieve the hunger, but when *The Times'* Madras correspondent visited a relief camp that had just opened in the Chingleput district, he found 'nearly 2,000 miserable scarecrows, not one of whom was in a state to earn a day's pay, and of whom it was easy to prophesy that 25 per cent would not survive'. An extra 100,000 people had crowded into Madras, and in Bellary 'every hospital in the town and every relief camp is full to overflowing'. All this time, Indian grain continued to be exported to Europe.

Some voices were raised for more energetic famine relief, but the viceroy, Lord Lytton, believed this might encourage shirking. He declared: 'Let the British public foot the bill for its "cheap sentiment", if it wished to save life at a cost that would bankrupt India,' and ordered there should be 'no interference of any kind on the part of government with the object of reducing the price of food'. He even instructed district officers to 'discourage relief works in every possible way . . . Mere distress is not a sufficient reason for opening a relief work.' By the time the famine ended in late 1878, at least five million people had died of starvation and disease. The government set up an early warning system for shortages, and started a programme to improve irrigation. These measures helped, as did an Indian famine fund which fed three million people between 1899 and 1901. Six years later the harvest was again poor but grain was imported promptly and famine was avoided.

The last great Indian famine came during the Second World War. As the Japanese overran Burma in 1942 India lost 15 per cent of its rice supplies, while at the same time Calcutta was swamped with tens of thousands of refugees. The shortage was worsened because Britain was stockpiling grain for its soldiers, while in the Chittagong area, by the Burmese border, it adopted a scorched-earth policy in case the Japanese invaded. In October Bengal and Orissa were hit by a cyclone that made the crop fail over a wide area, so seed that should have been planted in the winter of 1942–3 was eaten instead. Some suggest that the shortage was not as bad as it seemed, and that hoarding was the real problem. Certainly, for those who could afford to amass rice, there were potential fortunes as its price escalated. As famine spread through Bengal, Orissa and Malabar in 1943, the official response was sluggish. The Bengal government failed to prevent rice being exported, and made little attempt to pull in supplies from other parts of India or buy up stocks from speculators. Cholera and malaria also claimed many lives, and up to five million died.

An official British inquiry acknowledged that 'bold, resolute and well-conceived measures' could have 'largely prevented' the famine, and that Britain had failed to protect the 'weaker members' of society. Nehru, who was in jail during the disaster, said many Indians had tried to work together to help victims, but some 'were too full of their petty rivalries and jealousies to cooperate'. He considered the famine 'the final judgement on British rule in India . . . What will they leave when they have to go, what human degradation and accumulated sorrow?'

## · THE IRISH POTATO FAMINE ·

By the nineteenth century, Ireland had become dangerously reliant on the potato. Most farmers had only about five acres of land, and only potatoes could produce a sufficient crop to feed a whole family, so they became the staple diet for about half of the island's eight million people, who planted them in every nook and cranny. In larger fields crops like wheat and oats were grown, and sold to pay the rent. In 1741 two years of cold, rainy weather had caused poor potato harvests, and up to a quarter of a million had died. In 1816 the harvest failed again, and, with typhus putting in an appearance too, about 50,000 people died over the next two years.

Much worse was to come, though. In the summer of 1845 reports began to emerge from the Isle of Wight that potatoes in the fields were decaying. This was because of a microscopic fungus, *phytophthora infestans*, that had appeared in the United States three years before and probably crossed the ocean in the hold of a ship. Once ashore, its spores could spread on the wind or be carried by insects. Soon there were stories of crops rotting in other parts of Britain, as well as in Holland and France. At first, this did not cause too much alarm in Ireland: the potato was routinely attacked by a variety of pests and was regarded as a hardy plant. The summer was warm and the countryside thick with bright potato flowers, but by September leaves began to curl at the edges in the fields around Waterford and Wexford. A plant might look fine in the morning, but by the evening it would be turning black, soft and slimy. By October, blight was being reported in sixteen counties, but even then the government thought that overall the crop would be good. Experts in Britain decided the decay was being caused by damp, so Sir Robert Peel's government sent out thousands of sets of instructions on how to build a well-ventilated store. It was a waste of paper. Potatoes that had looked fine when they were pitted had turned to a stinking mess by the time they were uncovered. Even some tubers that looked healthy might be contaminated, and if they were used as seeds for the next crop, it would be blighted. A disaster was in the making.

Britain's Corn Laws kept grain prices artificially high by restricting imports, so Peel now took on many of his own party and insisted they be repealed. He won, but it cost him his job. Before he fell, though, he had begun secretly importing maize, 'Indian corn', from America into Ireland. Unfortunately, there were not enough mills to grind it into corn meal, and when people received the maize they did not know how to prepare it. A doctor at Ballinrobe, County Mayo, said he had even seen people 'devouring it raw, from hunger'. Eating inadequately cooked maize brought an increase in deaths from dysentery, and the emergency food became known as 'Peel's brimstone'. During that first year of blight many peasants kept themselves alive by selling livestock, pawning their belongings, or borrowing from money-lenders. After all, the crop could surely not fail again; and indeed, during the damp, hot summer of 1846, luxuriant growth began to cover the potato fields. Within a few days, though, the stalks again turned black and died. On 27 July a priest travelling from Cork to Dublin saw blooming flowers that promised 'an abundant harvest', but on the journey back, just six days later, he 'beheld with sorrow one wide waste of putrefying vegetation. In many places the wretched people were seated on the fences of their decaying gardens, wringing their hands and wailing bitterly of the destruction that had left them foodless.' The Reverend Samuel Montgomery, from Ballinascreen, County Londonderry, wrote: 'The whole atmosphere in the month of September was tainted with the odour of the decaying potatoes.' This time the crop seemed to fail all over the island, and the price of potatoes rose from two shillings a hundredweight to seven shillings; then to twelve, if they could be found at all. Unfortunately for Ireland, Peel's Tories had by then been succeeded by the Whig government of Lord John Russell, who felt that interfering with the market was not only unwise but wicked. He fervently believed that if food was just handed out to the Irish it would make them lazy and dependent, so the government stopped importing maize. That could safely be left to private enterprise.

The blight in 1846 was much more widespread, and the winter that followed was unusually severe. Famine began devastating the land. As ever, it also brought a number of diseases. The most common was oedema: 'first the limbs, and then the body swell most frightfully, and finally burst'. Many victims were children: 'too weak to stand, their little limbs attenuated, except where the frightful swellings had taken the place of previous emaciation'. Then there was scurvy, which made people's teeth drop out and their legs turn black as blood vessels ruptured, and, as ever, typhus. The fear of disease made parents abandon their children, and children their parents. The *Belfast Newsletter* reported 'haggard, sallow and emaciated beings . . . stretched prostrate upon the footways of our streets and bridges'. County Cork was hit particularly badly, and local magistrate Nicholas Cummins warned the government that unless 'great amounts' of food were supplied immediately, 'the prospect is appalling . . . the people must die'.

Cummins told *The Times* in December 1846 that he and four others had gone to a 'wretched hamlet' with as much bread as they could carry. He was surprised to find it apparently deserted. Then he went into one of the hovels: 'six famished and ghastly skeletons, to all appearances dead, were huddled in a corner on some filthy straw, their sole covering what seemed a ragged horsecloth . . . I approached with horror, and found by low moaning that they were still alive – they were in fever, four children, a woman and what had once been a man.' When he left, he was 'surrounded by at least 200 such phantoms, such fearful spectres as no words can describe, suffering either from famine or from fever. Their demoniac yells are still ringing in my ears . . . I found myself grasped by a woman with an infant just born in her arms and the remains of a filthy sack across her loins – the sole covering of herself and her baby . . . A mother, herself in a fever, was seen the same day to drag out the corpse of her child, a girl about 12, perfectly naked, and leave it half covered with stones.' At a house in Skibbereen, 'the dispensary doctor found seven wretches lying unable to move, under the same cloak. One had been dead many hours, but the others were unable to move either themselves or the corpse.' He related another episode in which police opened up a house after reports that there had been no signs of life for days, and found two corpses lying on the mud floor, 'half devoured by rats'.

At about the same time a local official wrote to his superiors: 'Although a man not easily moved, I confess myself unmanned by the extent and intensity of the suffering I witnessed.' In the turnip fields he saw people scattered 'like a flock of famishing crows, devouring the raw turnips and mostly half-naked, shivering in the snow and sleet, uttering exclamations of despair, whilst their children were screaming with hunger'. Many were reduced to eating nettles, roots and grass, but throughout the famine grain and livestock were constantly shipped out of Ireland. One Irish writer watched 'immense herds of cattle, sheep, and hogs . . . floating off on every tide, out of every one of our thirteen sea-ports, bound for England'. For the government, this might be nothing more than the normal workings of the market, but in Ireland it caused riots. At Youghal, near Cork, peasants tried unsuccessfully to seize a cargo of oats, while at Dungarvan British troops opened fire on a crowd, killing two and wounding several more. Overwhelmed by the suffering in the west of Ireland, the coastguard's inspector-general, Sir James Dombrain, ordered food to be handed out, and was publicly rebuked by the senior British civil servant in charge of relief, Sir Charles Trevelyan. The government had had to resume imports of maize in December 1846, but it still tried to limit relief operations. It wanted anyone needing help to be sent to the workhouse, as happened in England, but those in Ireland could accommodate only about 100,000 and it was clear they would soon be overwhelmed, so the Whigs also set up a programme of emergency 'outdoor' relief, though under very restrictive terms. No man who was renting more than a quarter of an acre, for example, was enti-tled to help, even if his land was producing nothing; and no government depot was supposed to open while there was any food in the district. The one in Skibbereen was kept closed until 7 December, even though many people had died in November, and there were strict regulations on the prices to be charged because the government did not want to undercut local retailers. So maize that had cost the government thirteen pounds a ton was being sold in the depots at nineteen pounds a ton. Free food was to be distributed only to the infirm and only when there was no room in the local workhouse.

A senior army official, Sir Ronald Routh, was in charge of organising the relief effort, but obviously he was not completely up to speed with the free market ideology. He complained about wheat and oats being exported from Ireland while people starved, and he encouraged local committees to set up soup kitchens. By March 1847, despite the government's reluctance, nearly three-quarters of a million people were receiving 'outdoor relief'. These were often literally job creation schemes – with starving people ordered to build fine roads leading from nowhere to nowhere. Another eccentricity of the scheme was that people were paid by results, so presumably the weakest, and most in need of help, received least. At Cong, County Mayo, it was reported that families ran out of money and could not afford to eat for up to thirty-six hours before each pay day, which of course further limited their ability to earn enough. Eventually, the government was forced to abandon piece work. Another problem was that payment was often late. Denis McKennedy of Caharagh, County Cork, died on the roadside while he was employed by the Board of Works. He was owed two weeks' wages, and the inquest jury declared he 'died of starvation due to the gross negligence of the Board'. 'Death by starvation' verdicts became increasingly common, even though the Board of Works tried to stop them, but often juries went even further. One at Lismore, County Waterford, blamed 'the negligence of the government in not sending food to our country', while another at Galway delivered a verdict of wilful murder by Russell and Routh.

Another problem with making starving people build unnecessary roads before giving them food was that they had no energy to work in their fields, so production fell even further. Finally, the government closed down the public works schemes and opened soup kitchens to simply give food to the starving, but there was so much red tape – the commissioners in charge handed out fourteen tons of paperwork – that the start was delayed. As a result there was an interval between the two schemes during which many people received no state help, so it was left to private charity, such as that offered by the Quakers, to fill the gap. Even when the new scheme finally got going applicants were sometimes refused because they owned a horse or a cow or an acre of land, and much of the soup was of such poor quality that it made people ill. By mid-August 1847, though, the soup kitchens were providing food for more than three million people every day.

Meanwhile, the workhouses were being overwhelmed. One Quaker visitor said there were no mattresses: 'the floors were strewed with a little dirty straw, and the poor creatures were thus *littered* down as close together as might be, in order to get the largest possible number under one miserable rug'. An inspector at Lurgan workhouse in February 1847 said a shortage of clothes meant linen from some of those who had died of fever or dysentery had to be given to other inmates 'without time having been afforded to have it washed and dried'. Workhouse officials often let in people who clamoured for admittance even if they had no room, because the alternative was to leave them outside to die. Skibbereen's workhouse, designed to hold 500, had 889 inmates, of whom 869 were sick, when 90 'miserable creatures', most of whom barely had the strength to crawl, begged to be let in. The authorities decided to give them dinner, then send them away, but when it came to it they could not – 'such were the heartrending shrieks of the poor wretches, saying they would lie down and die around the walls of the house. They could not drive them out into the heavy rain.'

Disease was a major risk. Ballinrobe's workhouse, though over-crowded, had been free of infection until the end of February 1847. Then it admitted a wandering beggar who died of typhus. The illness swept through the establishment and killed many inmates and staff.

The peak of workhouse overcrowding came in 1849 when more than 930,000 were in establishments for at least some of the time. At Lurgan, there were ninety-five deaths in the first week of February. The chaplain blamed this on stew made from putrid beef, while the medical officer said most new arrivals were already at the point of death: some died on the way, 'others on being raised from their beds to come to the work-house have died before they could be put into the cart, and numbers have died in less than 24 hours subsequent to their admission'. Workhouse food was generally worse than what was served up in jail, so some inmates deliberately committed petty crimes, though this in turn led to overcrowding in the prisons, and in Castlebar two out of every five inmates and staff died of fever. Even transportation to Australia seemed preferable to staying in Ireland. One teenage convict declared: 'Even if I had chains on my legs, I would still have something to eat.'

Many landlords were absentees who hardly ever saw their tenants; hundreds of thousands of whom were evicted and had their cottages 'tumbled' to make way for cash crops or pasturage. Sometimes the evictions came when the Poor Law guardians insisted that a family must enter the workhouse before they could qualify for outdoor relief, so many of the poor preferred to stay in their hovels and risk starvation. Many landlords themselves were ruined, though, because their tenants had no money for rent. And some did all they could to help. The Marquess of Waterford sent £300 to provide soup and bread for his starving tenants, and told his agent to 'set the pot a-boiling as soon as you can'. Many relief workers also toiled selflessly. A Quaker visitor saw them 'labour from morning to night' serving soup 'to crowds of half-clad, hungry people sinking with weakness and fever'. Doctors, priests and nuns cared for the sick in spite of the risk from typhus: thirty-six doctors appointed by the Board of Health died. But medical provision was often hopelessly inadequate: at Frenchpark in Roscommon there was none at all for 30,000 people.

Some people left Ireland for ever – bound for Liverpool, Glasgow, south Wales or more distant places – but many emigrants were destined never to arrive at their new homes. Of 100,000 sailing to North America in 1847, a fifth died of disease or malnutrition. Those who survived often faced hostility and discrimination when they arrived, but a 'greater Ireland across the sea' was created by the likes of John F. Kennedy's great-grandfather, who fled County Wexford in 1849.

By the time the blight ended in that year, one and a half million out of Ireland's population of eight million had perished, and another million had fled or died trying. The British government had spent eight million pounds on relief, but in Ireland its response was seen as grudging and ineffective, and there was a burning anger at the way food had been exported throughout the famine. At the general election of 1847 the Irish had overwhelmingly returned MPs who wanted to repeal the Act of Union with England. Russell regarded this as an act of breathtaking and incomprehensible ingratitude, muttering in exasperation: 'How can such a people be assisted?' Trevelyan thought the problem was simply that Ireland had become overpopulated, and now 'the cure had been applied by the direct stroke of an all-wise Providence'.

The famine would be followed by a long struggle for independence, ending with twenty-six of Ireland's thirty-two counties leaving the United Kingdom.

## · CHINA ·

Between 108 BC and AD 1911, famine struck some parts of China more than 1,800 times. The year 537 brought snow in August in Qingzhou, and a 'great famine' devastated four provinces. It is said that up to 80 per cent of the population died in places. In the 1320s drought and famine devastated central and northern China, and more than seven million people starved to death. To try to get through the lean years, China had traditionally relied on a network of surplus grain stores, but by the nineteenth century this had virtually collapsed due to neglect and corruption, so food supplies were often on a knife-edge even in the best of times.

During the mid-1870s, five provinces had virtually no rain. In the winter of 1875 the child Emperor Kuang-hsu implored the gods for help, but it remained as dry as ever. The following spring the city magistrate of Ch'ing-chou tried the traditional method of ending a drought: he issued a decree banning the eating of meat, got his attendants to bind his neck, wrists and feet in chains, and hobbled through the city to the main temple to pray. Behind him walked a procession of worshippers decked out in the time-honoured regalia of willow leaves and twigs. They had no more success than the emperor, and the earth grew even more parched and barren. Food prices soared, and by the autumn of 1876 people were starving to death in Shantung. A Welsh Baptist missionary preaching in the area, Timothy Richard, advocated turning away from idolatry and praying to the one true God. He posted notices to this effect in the towns he visited, where he witnessed dreadful sights – people eating grain husks, stalks, bark, turnip leaves and grass seeds. 'When these are exhausted they pull down their houses and sell the timber, and it is reported everywhere that many eat the rotten sorghum stalks from the roof . . . thousands die because they cannot get even that.' When winter came those peasants who had demolished their houses had to take refuge with hundreds of others in great underground holes. Many would never emerge alive, but no sooner was a corpse carried out than others were fighting for its place. Children were sold; women were forced into slavery or prostitution; starving men turned to robbery and murder. The government tried in vain to halt the crime wave by summary beheadings or putting criminals in a 'sorrow cage', in which they were left to starve to death. Richard reported that nine out of every ten people had died in some villages. Disposing of the corpses became a nightmare, and many had to be buried in huge communal pits known as 'ten-thousand-men holes'.

The imperial court decreed that 'not a single subject be left in a state of destitution', and the government tried its best to help. It suspended land taxes, distributed what grain it could find in its granaries, and encouraged the better off to assist the starving, but the primitive trans-port system thwarted most of its efforts. Roads were poor, and the Grand Canal that could have taken supplies to Shantung was almost unusable because of the drought and the decades of neglect that had preceded it. *The Times'* correspondent reported: 'men of 20 have become so weak that they cannot walk three miles' to where there was food, so they died where they were. Up to 25,000 refugees went to Tientsin, where more than 100 a day died. Some were sent away again with just a few days' rations, but they left 'quietly, manifesting no unwillingness'. One day Richard met a father and son carrying a beam ten miles in the hope of selling it for food: 'The son had not recovered from smallpox, but was obliged to get up or starve.'

The missionary launched a relief fund, which eventually saw money pouring in from all over the world. When the worst appeared to be over in Shantung he moved to Shansi, which seemed even more vulnerable because of its poor soil and mountainous terrain. The 1877 spring wheat crop had largely failed, and the few shoots that had appeared above ground had been eaten by locusts. The winter that followed was bitterly cold, and as coal prices rose people tore down their houses and burned the wood to try to keep warm. They were living on roots, twigs, sawdust and mud cakes. Some of these recipes proved fatal. Then, to make mat-ters worse, typhoid broke out.

Getting relief to the province meant negotiating tortuous roads and running the gauntlet of gangs of bandits. Richard saw wolves and foxes grown fat on human corpses. One man on the road was walking 'with unsteady steps', then 'A puff of wind blew him over to rise no more.' Approaching the gate of a city, the missionary found 'a pile of naked dead men, heaped on top of each other as though they were pigs in a slaughter-house. On the other side of the gate was a similar heap of dead women, their clothing having been taken away to pawn for food.' There were many stories of people throwing themselves into rivers or hanging themselves from roof beams. Women and children were sold for pennies in markets, while human flesh was being traded and devoured everywhere. Richard heard stories of parents exchanging children to eat, as they could not bear to devour their own, while men did not dare to try and collect coal 'as mules, donkeys, and their owners were liable to be killed and eaten'. The special commissioner for famine relief in Shansi, dispatched to file a report for the emperor, found himself surrounded everywhere by crowds of starving people, begging for help. When the rains finally came in August 1879, up to 13 million had died of starvation or famine-related diseases in northern China, including 5.5 million in Shansi.

China would have many more famines. In 1901 food shortages following a drought in Shaanxi province led to an estimated 2.5 million deaths, while in 1920 the harvest failed in Hebei, Henan and Shantung, and perhaps 15 million people died. In 1924 a Westerner travelling from Sichuan to Guizhou reported dogs eating human flesh, and skeletons by the thousand. Three years later the American journalist Edgar Snow was haunted by the starving people he saw – their flesh hanging 'in wrinkled folds', with every bone visible, eyes 'unseeing', and even if he is a youth of 20 he moves like an ancient crone'. The children were 'bent over and misshapen, their crooked bones, their little arms like twigs, and their purpling bellies, filled with bark and sawdust'. Women lay 'slumped in corners, waiting for death . . . But there are, after all, not many women and girls. Most of them have died or have been sold.' China still had few railways, and there were fewer than 2,000 miles of good roads, so a man's back remained the only viable transport for grain in many places, and famine could exist happily alongside plenty. The socialist writer R.H. Tawney noted that in some parts of the country 'the position of the rural population is that of a man standing permanently up to his neck in water, so that even a ripple is sufficient to drown him'. The land was exhausted in many places because there was not enough fertiliser, and taxes were so high that peasants could not afford to let it lie fallow, but Edgar Snow complained there was plenty of food for those with money and that hoarders were making fortunes.

By January 1928, in parts of Shantung two-thirds of the people were said to have left, and of those remaining many were ill from living on bark and leaves. Again, peasants were demolishing their houses and selling the raw materials to buy food, while once law-abiding citizens were turning to robbery. A Church of England missionary, the Reverend F.J. Griffith, reported from Suiyuan that the 1928 harvest had failed almost everywhere, that scores of refugees were dying of starvation every day, and pneumonic plague was killing those whom hunger had spared. When the mission doctor shot a rabid dog, Griffith reported that he was besieged by well-to-do Chinese desperate to buy the carcass. An estimated 22,000 women and girls had been sold (in some places the going rate was just over one pound), while other parents would give their children away to anyone who would feed them. Even the bandits had given up as there was nothing left to steal. By July 1929, the wheat-growing area of central Gansu had had no rain for four years and was looking like a desert. A magistrate wanted to punish people for eating the corpses of famine victims, but they argued that if they did not, the bodies would only be devoured by dogs. The crisis was exacerbated by the struggle between nationalists, communists and warlords, as millions of armed men seized food, animals or sons from the peasantry. Altogether, perhaps three million died. The warring factions would make life in China a misery for many years to come, with the invading Japanese joining in enthusiastically. In 1943 famine struck again, with at least five million perishing.

## · POST-REVOLUTIONARY RUSSIA ·

Hunger is one of the evils from which the communist anthem 'The Internationale' promises to liberate the working man:

> Arise, ye prisoners of starvation,
> Arise, ye wretched of the earth'

The Bolsheviks never seemed quite sure, though, whether the brotherhood of man extended to the peasantry. The founder of Russian Marxism, Georgi Plekhanov, thought Russian peasants were 'barbarian tillers of the soil, cruel and merciless', while Maxim Gorky, a writer much favoured by the communists, referred to their 'animal-like individualism' and 'almost total lack of social consciousness'. In May 1918 the Soviet Central Executive Committee said that it was essential to foment class war in the countryside in order to establish communism, 'setting the poorest layers of the population against the kulak [more prosperous] elements'. At the same time, a new law allowed the state authorities to enter villages and confiscate any grain they considered surplus. Many peasants resisted, and were bloodily suppressed. *The Times* dryly commented that production plummeted 'because the peasants had no impulse to sow corn for the benefit of the armed requisition detachments'. By 1921, the harvest was down by nearly two-thirds compared with the pre-Bolshevik era.

To be fair, Tsarist Russia had not been very good at feeding its people either – in 1907 widespread harvest failures had led to more than a million deaths – while the Bolsheviks had been hamstrung by a complicated and brutal civil war in which a number of foreign armies had intervened. Still, Lenin admitted his government's failings, and in March 1921 much dogma went out of the window as he brought back a degree of capitalism and allowed peasants to sell surplus food. Compulsory requisitioning of grain was abolished; instead there was a tax in kind, which amounted to just over half of what the state had previously been seizing. Indeed, the situation was so desperate that leading Bolshevik Nikolai Bukharin was having to urge the peasants, 'Enrich yourselves!' while Lenin begged for foreign aid. The U-turn, though, came too late to prevent widespread starvation that summer through most of central Russia. The Communists hoped the Caucasus, which they had just taken over, would provide enough food to fill the gap, but peasants there still did not feel they had enough incentive to increase production. To make matters worse, some areas were devastated by drought and swarms of locusts, and instead of sowing their fields many peasants were taking to the road.

By July, *Pravda* said the 'food crisis' was so severe that it was 'necessary to forget everything else'. On 5 August *The Times* painted an equally bleak picture: 'Russia was the granary of Europe, and Russia is now starving.' The newspaper's correspondent said that in the south of the country there had once been 'little to break the rich monotony of the expanse of corn'. Now fields were burned dry with just a few stalks of corn poking above the surface and people were 'making desperate attempts to support life like the beasts of the field, eating grass, dry leaves, and weeds'. They were fleeing in hundreds, 'sometimes in a fit of wild despair setting their deserted dwellings on fire'. Every town seemed to be crammed with peasants begging for bread, and cholera had broken out. Dr Semashko, the people's commissar for health, wrote that conditions were 'alarming'. Sewerage and drainage systems had collapsed, leaving the streets full of filth, and the 'starving population of the Volga' was moving 'like an avalanche, sowing contagion and death on the way'. Revolts in the Ukraine and Siberia were deepening the chaos.

The following year the misery went on. The acreage of land under cultivation had fallen every year since 1917. Now even some of the peasants who had remianed on the land could not sow their fields because they had eaten the seed corn, particularly in the Ukraine, where the produce tax was collected twice. Locusts and grasshoppers were again causing devastation, too.

Foreign countries, including the USA, sent generous help, and the Red Cross dispatched the great Arctic explorer Dr Fridtjof Nansen to run the relief effort, helped by an army officer named Vidkun Quisling, who would later be executed for leading Norway's Nazi puppet government during the Second World War. Nansen told the *Manchester Guardian*: 'Words cannot possibly describe the misery and horrors I have seen. People are dying in their houses and in the village streets in the pitiless cold of a Russian winter without food or fuel to feed them.'

Foreign relief organisations saved millions of lives, but the famine is still estimated to have carried off five million people. An even worse one would come at the end of the decade, but this time it would be created by Stalin's government (see Chapter 11).

## · ETHIOPIA ·

Africa has often suffered famine. Ethiopia had at least one per decade from the fifteenth to the nineteenth century, and they did not end in the colonial era. In 1888 the cattle disease rinderpest arrived from Europe and ran through the continent, killing 90 per cent of all herds in some places. The cattle epidemic coincided with drought, smallpox and war, and across the Horn of Africa perhaps a million people died. Liberation and independence would not bring an end to hunger either, as Africa's food supply remained on a knife edge. Political leaders concentrated on holding food prices down to keep people in the cities happy, even though four Africans in five worked on the land. Sometimes they were so low that farmers could not even cover their costs, and Africa became the only continent where output per head fell in the 1960s and 1970s. Production was also hit by soil erosion as a growing population ploughed up grassland to plant grain or felled trees for firewood. Any disruption, such as the Nigerian civil war of the 1960s, could bring famine. Then, as Biafra tried to secede, nearly a million people starved to death.

Ethiopia's Emperor Haile Selassie had become a national hero in the 1930s for leading the resistance against Mussolini's brutal invasion, and he had been widely revered when he was restored to power in the 1940s. In his early years he had abolished slavery, and built roads, railways, schools and hospitals. But by the 1970s three-quarters of the population were still trying to eke out an existence as tenant farmers who had to give three-quarters of their produce to their landlords. Now in his eighties, Selassie still ruled as an autocrat, but he was drifting into senility. In 1973 drought and famine hit the province of Wollo. The emperor talked about 'natural disasters beyond human control', and the government would not seek help from international agencies. The Ethiopian people saw it differently, and the famine, which killed 200,000, proved the catalyst for widespread revolt in 1974. That September, a British television documentary, *The Hidden Famine*, contrasted the people starving in Wollo with Selassie and his entourage drinking champagne, eating caviar and feeding meat to the emperor's dogs. The next day a group of army officers deposed him, and he spent his last months imprisoned in a few rooms of his palace until he died, or was killed, in August 1975.

Two years later Lt.-Col. Mengistu Haile Mariam began a reign of terror in which thousands were tortured and killed. He ran Ethiopia according to Marxist principles, but the change of ideology did not see the end of hunger or the government's wish to hide it from the outside world. In 1984 Mengistu spent months planning a spectacular tenth-anniversary celebration of the revolution. North Koreans advised him on the most impressive revolutionary slogans and on where to hang the huge posters of Marx, Lenin and, of course, himself. While he was engaged in this important work, maddeningly, there came warnings of famine. For months, Mengistu tried to impose a news blackout. His land reforms had freed peasants from debt and the need to pay rents to land-lords, but they now had to accept prices set by the state, designed to supply the towns and the army with cheap food. If peasants failed to supply the amount the state demanded, they could be imprisoned, so some had to sell livestock in order to buy grain. They also faced heavy taxation, and were forced to work for nothing on government projects. Some were drafted into state and collective farms – one of Mengistu's pet projects. These were hopelessly inefficient, and produced less grain, so Ethiopia became increasingly dependent on food imports.

Also threatening to spoil the president's party was a revolt in Tigray and north Wollo by the Tigrayan People's Liberation Front. In August 1980 Mengistu had launched a seven-month scorched-earth campaign, destroying houses, crops and livestock. About 80,000 farmers had fled, but even that had not quelled the opposition, and the government had launched a similar campaign in February 1983, driving nearly half a million people from their homes. It had also seized food and pinned people in their villages, trying to starve them into submission. At this point, the rains had failed, but when the organisation in charge of relief asked for more money, Mengistu was dismissive. Its head, Dawit Wolde Giorgis, a close associate of the president, said he 'listened impatiently and told me not to be so panicky', arguing this was one of those 'petty human problems that always exist in transitional periods . . . There was famine in Ethiopia for years before we took power – it was the way nature kept the balance . . . Let nature take its toll – just don't let it out in the open.'

Except for a few isolated showers, no rain fell in the stricken provinces from October 1983 to May 1984, and the spring harvests failed. All over Tigray and north Wollo, farmers sold livestock, agricultural equipment and anything they could lay their hands on, then abandoned their farms and took their families to the relief centres. These were soon over-whelmed. By March 1984, 16,000 people a week were dying in the shelters. As he journeyed around the country, Dawit saw 'miles of starv-ing, ragged people, begging for a bowl of grain'. In every village he found 'people carrying corpses, digging graves, grieving, wailing and praying'. Desperately weak people who had not eaten for days were on the road 'in an endless, winding stream of suffering'. As Dawit passed in his car, some would collapse and die before his eyes. Those who were stronger carried children or the sick or the old. Others faced 'the terrible agony of people forced to choose between leaving their dying wives, husbands or children behind, or staying to die with them'. The hill station of Korem usually had a population of 7,000. That had swollen to 100,000, but Save the Children's relief centre could look after only 10,000. The rest had to fend for themselves. Most had only rags to wear in the cold highland nights. 'The exhausted relief workers held the power of life and death,' wrote Dawit, 'as they walked through the crowds selecting only the most needy to receive what food there was, while the unlucky thousands watched grimly and waited another day.' The children had 'the faces of old men and women, listless faces crawling with flies, faces without hope'. Everywhere, there were corpses.

Many governments who might have helped had been alienated by Mengistu's anti-Western rhetoric and by what seemed the warped priorities of his regime. While his people starved, it was alleged that he had ordered half a million bottles of Scotch whisky to lubricate his £75-million anniversary celebrations. They were also worried that any aid they gave might be diverted into financing his wars. Even the aid agencies were suspicious. Meanwhile, the Ethiopian press was silent on the famine, and foreign journalists were banned from the stricken areas. When Mengistu's celebrations kicked off in September, any destitute peasants who had made it to Addis Ababa were rounded up and removed from view. An Organisation of African Unity summit followed in November. The hundreds of delegates were well fed and watered, and Mengistu had cleared out the bread queues for the duration of the meet-ing, but then, as *The Times* noted, while tribespeople were dying of hunger, in the capital there was 'plenty of food for those who can afford it'.

Once the celebrations were out of the way, the president admitted there was a 'drought problem' and let in foreign journalists. Once again it was a documentary, this time made by the BBC's Michael Buerk at Korem, that opened the world's eyes; it was shown by more than 400 television stations across the world. Buerk reported 'a biblical famine, now, in the twentieth century'. There were now 15,000 children in the camp, and every twenty minutes someone died. Many perished in the night as they lay uncovered in the cold air. Some starving people walked for eighteen days to get to Addis Ababa, but the government was constantly picking up others on the road and dumping them hundreds of miles away. *The Times'* correspondent said that as lorries approached, children would throw themselves down: 'Occasionally, truckers throw small bags of grain to them. Suddenly there are scores of children running from the road's edge to grapple for the few grains.' Most of the country-side had been forsaken: 'as far as the eye can see the land is empty. River beds lie baked dry, and terraced fields which have supported genera-tions of people are deserted.' Mengistu made just one visit to the stricken area, lasting half an hour. The horrific reports inspired Bob Geldof to organise a star-studded record and then the Live Aid concert to raise money.

In an effort to undermine the rebels, Mengistu planned to resettle 1.5 million able-bodied people from Tigray and Wollo on collective farms far away. The very young and the old would be left behind. The president declared: 'The people are like the sea and the guerrillas are like fish swim-ming in that sea. Without the sea there will be no fish.' Most Western governments refused to help him, but the USSR provided aircraft, trucks and soldiers. As people were packed into the Soviet lorries, some were crushed or suffocated to death, pregnant women miscarried, while to escape the deportation hundreds of thousands of starving refugees fled into neighbouring Sudan. Dawit was in charge of this programme, which was, he later conceded, 'perhaps the cruellest chapter of the entire famine'. By the time it ended in February 1986, 600,000 had been resettled, and 50,000 killed in the process. Mengistu also prevented any food being given to the three million civilians in Tigray. One of his min-isters explained: 'Food is a major element in our strategy against the secessionists.'

Altogether, perhaps a million people died in the famine. Finally, in 1991, Mengistu was driven out by a joint army of Eritrean and Tigray rebels. He found refuge with Robert Mugabe in Zimbabwe. In 2008, in his absence, the Ethiopian Supreme Court sentenced him to death for genocide and crimes against humanity. The drought played havoc right across the Sahel. Many rivers dried up completely, and Lake Chad had lost nearly 90 per cent of its area by 1985. The West may not have cared for Mengistu, but the United States supported his rival, Gaafar Numeiri, in the Sudan. He invested heavily in mechanising agriculture, but output fell, and when the drought struck, like Mengistu, he tried to sweep the problem under the carpet. Many of his people – perhaps a quarter of a million – starved to death. He fell from power in 1985. Across the region, a million people are thought to have died.

## · NORTH KOREA ·

By the 1990s, the fundamentalist communists of North Korea had fallen out with the turncoats in Russia and what must have seemed like the increasingly communist-lite regime in China. As a result, they lost heavily subsidised food, fertilisers, oil and other imports, which sent their fragile economy into meltdown. North Korea is short of arable land, its collective farming is inefficient, and much of what it does manage to produce rots or is eaten by rats and insects. As famine loomed, the government launched a campaign to get people to cut down to two meals a day, but by 1994 defectors reported old people going out to the fields to die so their families would not have to feed them.

To make matters worse, 1995 and 1996 saw record-breaking floods, covering nearly a million acres, while 1997 brought a severe drought. The country ended up a million tons of grain short of what it needed to provide even the most basic diet, and the government appealed for international help. The authorities appeared to have been giving priority to people in the capital, Pyongyang, workers in critical industries, party activists, and the army of more than one million, leaving everyone else to fend for themselves. In 1998 a visiting research team from the United States Congress estimated at least 900,000 people had died of starvation over the previous three years, though the figure might be as high as 2.4

million. They said there was no medical care in most areas, and that many children and teenagers were stunted by malnutrition. The United Nations' World Food Programme mounted the biggest emergency operation in its history. North Korea's 'Dear Leader', Kim Jong-il, on the other hand, was said to dine on fine dishes and drink good wine.

By 1999, foreign aid had reduced the number of deaths, but in 2000 there were still reports of famine in most parts of the country outside Pyongyang, and it was estimated that about ten million people were malnourished. Two years later the government said it no longer needed food supplies from abroad, but in 2005 the World Food Programme reported there was a danger of famine returning. Tens of thousands fled into China, often living in holes in the ground to hide from the police. Women were sold as brides to lonely Chinese bachelors or forced into brothels or illegal sweatshops. Estimates of the total number of deaths in North Korea's famine range up to 3.5 million.

# 10

## WAR AND INVASION

All wars are disasters for those caught up in them, but risking life and limb is part of the soldier's trade. This chapter concentrates on those conflicts in which civilians suffered most.

### · THE ROMANS ·

Rome was a civilisation of extraordinary sophistication, but a brutal foe to any who dared defy it. The Roman historian Tacitus quoted a Scottish tribal leader complaining that they 'rob, kill and rape and this they call Roman rule. They make a desert and call it peace.' And Tacitus' father-in-law, Agricola, almost annihilated the Ordovices of central Wales. These were not isolated instances. A year after defeating the Macedonians in 168 BC, Roman armies swept through the Balkans, enslaving 150,000 people. Two decades later, in 146, after they had defeated the Achaeans, they burned the ancient city of Corinth to the ground, and sold its inhabitants into slavery.

Around the same time, during a twenty-year 'fiery war' in the Iberian peninsula, 20,000 Vaccaei from the Salamanca area were massacred after surrendering. Another Spanish tribe, the Celtiberians, fought so fiercely that at one point a Roman general had to make a treaty recognising their independence, but in 133 they finally surrendered. They were sold into slavery and their capital was razed to the ground. The Lusitanians, who lived in what is now Portugal, defeated a Roman army but were persuaded to make peace on the promise that they would be settled on fertile lands. When they appeared unarmed to claim their new territory, they were put to the sword.

In the same year that Rome devastated Corinth it committed perhaps its greatest act of destruction. From 153 BC onwards, Marcus Porcius Cato would end every one of his speeches in the Senate, on whatever subject, with the demand that 'Carthage must be destroyed'. Cato was the 'censor', in charge of Rome's morals. It was his job to crack down on fun, like wearing fine clothes or having big parties. He also had to make sure women did not get rich. In the previous century the Romans had received a terrible fright from the great Carthaginian general Hannibal, who had led his army on an epic journey from North Africa, up through Spain, across the Alps and down into Italy, winning victories right on Rome's doorstep, before he finally had to withdraw and Carthage was forced to accept a humiliating treaty. As a former ambassador to the city, Cato had been stunned by its beauty and grandeur, and came to the conclusion that the world was not big enough for Rome and Carthage. So Rome constantly supported Carthage's neighbours, the Numidians, as they stole territory and generally created a nuisance. Eventually, in desperation, in 151 the Carthaginians raised an army against their tormentors. The Romans threw up their arms in horror, declaring it a breach of the treaty. Carthage desperately tried to make amends, even executing the generals who had led their forces. They handed over hostages and then all their weapons. Only then did the Romans make their final demand – Carthage must be abandoned and its population moved to a new site inland. Even without arms, warships or allies, the Carthaginians decided they had to resist. Temples were turned into workshops; women cut off their hair so it could be twisted into bowstrings. When the Romans attacked the city walls, they were driven back, so they blockaded Carthage by land and sea, inflicting terrible suffering. For three years, the defenders defied Rome until finally, in 146, the invaders breached the walls and took the city street by street. Perhaps 200,000 were killed, and the 50,000 survivors were enslaved. Then the Romans burned Carthage to the ground, and sowed the site with salt to try to ensure nothing could ever grow there again.

But what goes around comes around, and it was from a rebuilt Carthage that the Vandals emerged in AD 455 to sack Rome. Twenty years later, the Western Roman Empire was no more.

## · ATTILA ·

Three years before the Vandals sacked Rome, its people had expected to meet a similar fate at the hands of a terrifying barbarian, Attila the Hun, who became known as the 'scourge of God' because many saw him as the human agency through which the Almighty enforced His punishments.

In 434 Attila and his brother, Bleda, inherited an empire stretching from the Alps north to the Baltic and east to the Caspian Sea. They treated the Western and Eastern Roman Empires with undisguised contempt. Even when they agreed to meet ambassadors from Constantinople they would not dismount from their horses. In 441 they complained that the Eastern Empire had not paid the tribute it had promised, and launched an invasion, destroying a number of important cities, including Belgrade. In 443 they resumed their attack, flattening Sofia, Plovdiv and Nis (in modern-day Serbia), the birthplace of Constantine the Great. The Eastern Empire had to buy them off with even more tribute. Around 445, Attila murdered his brother, then ruled alone. He attacked the Eastern Empire again in 447, devastating the Balkans and destroying Marcianople, the biggest city in Thrace, before driving southwards into Greece and taking more than 100 cities, according to the ecclesiastical chronicler Callinicus. He said there was such slaughter, 'the dead could not be numbered. Ay, for they took captive the churches and monasteries, and slew the monks and maidens in great quantities.'

A Gothic philosopher and historian named Priscus accompanied the Eastern Roman emperor's ambassador to Attila's camp in 448. They found the great king sitting on a wooden chair. His clothes were plain, and he drank from a wooden cup, while his guests used goblets of silver and gold. They consumed 'a luxurious meal, served on silver plate . . . but Attila ate nothing but meat on a wooden trencher'. Priscus says he was short, swarthy and broad-chested, with a big head, deepset eyes, a flat nose and a thin beard. He had a proud step and a haughty manner as though he considered himself lord of all, and would sometimes roll his eyes fiercely, enjoying the terror he inspired.

Two years later a Roman palace scandal played into Attila's hands. When she was sixteen, Honoria, the sister of the Western Emperor Valentinian III, had had an affair with her chamberlain and got pregnant. She was packed off to Constantinople for a dozen years of prayers and fasting. Now, thoroughly bored, she managed to smuggle her ring out to Attila, and asked him to claim her as his bride. The Hun already had plenty of wives, but he agreed to her request, and demanded half the Western Empire as her dowry. The Romans quickly married off Honoria to 'some obscure and nominal husband, before she was immured in a perpetual prison', as Edward Gibbon put it, but Attila pursued his claim. The Huns invaded Gaul in 451, sacking cities like Reims and Besançon as they went. According to the chronicler Gregory of Tours, Attila devastated 'the whole country'. At Metz, 'they gave the city to the flames and slew the people with the edge of the sword, and did to death the priests of the Lord before the holy altars'. At Troyes, Attila is supposed to have met Bishop St Loup, who had held office for more than fifty years. 'Who are you?' asked the bishop. 'I am the scourge of God,' replied Attila. The bishop rejoined pluckily: 'If indeed you are the scourge of God, do only that which God allows you.' Gregory says that, 'struck by these words and the saintliness of the bishop', Attila left Troyes alone, but when Bishop Servais of Tongeren (in modern-day Belgium) begged God to keep out the Huns, God apparently replied that they would not only enter his diocese but 'devastate it in the manner of a great hurricane'.

In the end, after the Huns had caused enormous destruction, the Romans and the Visigoths managed to defeat them at Chalons. As they retreated, Attila's allies, the Thuringians, massacred hostages and captives; 200 maidens had their bodies torn apart by wild horses or were crushed beneath rolling wagons, then they were left on the roads to be eaten by dogs and vultures.

The following year Attila invaded Italy and devastated Padua, which was reduced to 'heaps of stones and ashes', Verona, Brescia, Bergamo and Aquileia, then one of the richest cities on the Adriatic. The last was destroyed so comprehensively that 'the succeeding generation could scarcely discover the ruins'. People fleeing the Huns sought refuge in the lagoons of the Adriatic and founded what would become the city of Venice. With Rome seeming certain to be the next target, Pope Leo the Great went to meet Attila. Leo was apparently extremely eloquent, and he got a helping hand from St Peter and St Paul, who allegedly appeared alongside him and threatened Attila with instant death if he attacked the city. Whether because of the power of this vision or fear of the malaria then raging in Italy, Attila turned back.

In 453, as the Huns were planning another attack on the Eastern Empire, Attila took yet another wife, a beautiful Gothic maiden named Ildico. After the celebrations, he went to bed 'oppressed with wine and sleep'. The next morning it was thought best not to wake him too early, but as time wore on, according to the sixth-century historian Jordanes, 'the royal attendants suspected some ill and, after a great uproar, broke in the doors'. They found Attila covered in blood, 'without any wound, and the girl with downcast face weeping beneath her veil'. The great barbarian king was dead, apparently from a burst artery. The Huns forced a group of captives to bury his body secretly at night. Then they were massacred to keep its whereabouts a mystery.

## · GENGHIS KHAN ·

Genghis Khan came up the hard way. Born with the name Temujin in 1162 near Lake Baikal in Mongolia, he was said to have entered the world holding a clot of blood in his hand. When Temujin was nine his father was poisoned, and the boy was plunged into poverty, surviving on roots and fish instead of the usual nomad diet of mutton and mare's milk. He was captured by the faction that had killed his father and forced to wear a wooden collar, but one night while they were feasting, Temujin knocked down a sentry and escaped. As he grew up, there was no respite. At one point a rival clan raped his wife, but Temujin borrowed an army from a powerful friend of his father and routed them. Another clan was rash enough to plunder his property while he was away fighting the Tartars. Temujin exterminated their nobility and took the common people to be his soldiers and servants. Next he defeated the Tartars, and slaughtered all those taller than the height of a cart axle. By 1206, he had emerged as undisputed master of the steppes, welding the nomadic Mongol tribes into a disciplined state, and taking the title Genghis Khan – 'Universal Ruler'. Soon much of the world would tremble at the name.

First, his ambitions turned to China. In 1213 he managed to penetrate the Great Wall and dispatched three armies to overrun the north of the country. They took twenty-eight cities, including Beijing. By 1300, China is believed to have lost perhaps forty million people, though it is unclear how much of this can be directly blamed on the invaders. Next to face Genghis's wrath was the Khwarezmian empire, which ruled Central Asia and Iran. A caravan of merchants had gone there under his protection. When they arrived in the town of Otrar, they were robbed and massacred by the governor, Inaljuk Kair-khan. Genghis sent envoys to the emperor, Shah Mohammed, to demand the governor's execution. Instead, the shah had the chief of the embassy beheaded and cut off the beards of the rest. Incensed, Genghis attacked and routed the shah's forces, capturing Otrar after a five-month siege, killing Inaljuk and all his followers, then pillaging and razing the city. Next was Bukhara. On entering the town, he climbed the steps of the main mosque and announced, 'The hay is cut; give your horses fodder' – an invitation to his soldiers to plunder. The inhabitants were subjected to 'infamies worse than death', then the town was levelled. Samarkand and Balkh both surrendered, but Genghis's soldiers pillaged them anyway and slaughtered the inhabitants. Next he dispatched his youngest son Tule with a force of 70,000 to ravage Khurasan, and sent two flying columns to seize Shah Mohammed, who had taken refuge in Nishapur (in modern-day Iran). The shah managed to slip away, though he died soon after from pleurisy, but Tule took the city after an assault lasting four days. The Mongols made pyramids of the skulls of the men, women and children they had killed.

Merv was then claimed to be one of the greatest cities on earth, and its population was swelled by refugees who had fled from the fearsome invaders. The Persian historian Ala'iddin Ata-Malik Juvayni said when the Mongols took the city they decided to kill everyone apart from 400 skilled artisans. Each soldier was assigned more than 300 people to execute. Some claim that perhaps a million perished here. The Mongols then moved on to devastate Lahore, Peshawar and Melikpur. Herat in Afghanistan opened its gates and was spared, but later the city was foolish enough to depose the governor Tule had appointed. Furious, Genghis dispatched an army of 80,000, which laid siege to the city for six months. On taking it, the burning and murdering continued for a week. It is said that 1.6 million people perished. These exploits led the contemporary English chronicler Matthew Paris to call the Mongols a 'detestable nation of Satan that poured out like devils'.

Genghis died on 18 August 1227 in his travelling palace on the banks of Mongolia's River Sale. By then, he had conquered lands stretching from Beijing to the Caspian Sea. Unlike today's politicians, he never had to worry about his 'legacy'. Based on chromosome research, it is estimated that about one man in twelve in the territories he conquered is a direct descendant. Although he was incensed when his own wife was ravished, Genghis had no objection to rape in principle. He said: 'The greatest joy a man can know is to conquer his enemies and drive them before him. To ride their horses and take away their possessions. To see the faces of those who were dear to them bedewed with tears, and to clasp their wives and daughters in his arms.' The Mongols would frequently rape the women of their defeated foes, and the most beautiful would be reserved for the great khan himself.

## · TAMBURLAINE ·

Tamburlaine's name is derived from a contemptuous nickname – 'Timur the Lame' – given to him by his Persian enemies after his right leg was injured in battle. It is a fair bet that many regretted their impertinence later, as their lands were among the many he conquered and ravaged from Damascus to Delhi. Tamburlaine would ultimately lead thirty-five campaigns and amass twenty-seven crowns. Born in a village about fifty miles from Samarkand in 1336, he was a chief's son from one of the Mongol tribes that had settled in Transoxania (modern-day Uzbekistan) following the campaigns of Genghis Khan. Tamburlaine first tasted war when he was twelve, and a tribe called the Getes drove him into the desert with just sixty horsemen. The fugitives were said to have been overtaken by 1,000 of the enemy, whom they repulsed with extraordinary slaughter, but the action reduced Tamburlaine's retinue to just seven men and four horses, and he was eventually captured. He escaped by swimming across the River Oxus (the Amu Darya) and lived as an outlaw for months until he made his way back to his own people. Then he was able to defeat the Getes.

Perhaps not surprisingly, Tamburlaine had white hair from childhood. He grew very tall, with a large head. When he was twenty-five he was made chief minister to Ilyas Khoja, the governor of Transoxania. Three years later, with the help of his brother-in-law Amir Husayn, he attacked Ilyas and took over his lands. Next he turned on Husayn, who was assassinated. Tamburlaine then proclaimed himself restorer of the Mongol Empire. After wars with the Lithuanians and Russians, his troops occupied Moscow. In 1383 he began his conquest of Persia, and over the following eleven years his forces overran huge swathes of territory, including modern-day Iraq, Azerbaijan, Armenia and Georgia. As a warning to his enemies, Tamburlaine would camp in a scarlet tent. If cities he had conquered should dare to revolt, his response was ruthless: they were destroyed, their populations massacred and towers built of their skulls.

In 1398 Tamburlaine, now in his sixties, launched one of his most notorious campaigns. He invaded India, complaining that the Muslim rulers of Delhi were being too indulgent towards their Hindu subjects. Crossing the Indus on 24 September, he left a trail of carnage as he marched on the city. Waiting to fight the emperor, Sultan Nasir-u-Din Mehmud, outside Delhi, Tamburlaine grew concerned that his army had amassed more than 100,000 'infidel' prisoners. He ordered his men to execute them because, in his own words, 'these 100,000 prisoners could not be left with the baggage, and it would be entirely opposed to the rules of war to set these idolaters and enemies of Islam at liberty'. Therefore, 'no other course remained but that of making them all food for the sword'. Any soldier who did not murder his captives faced death himself. No wonder 'Maulana Nasiru-d din Umar, a counsellor and man of learning, who, in all his life, had never killed a sparrow, now . . . slew with his sword fifteen idolatrous Hindus, who were his captives'. Tamburlaine won the battle, then reduced Delhi to ruins. Some put the number killed at over a million. Tamburlaine's defenders claim he did not intend to destroy the city but could not control his troops; his critics say he gave his men free rein. Tamburlaine himself said: 'Although I was desirous of sparing them I could not succeed, for it was the will of God that this calamity should fall upon the city.' Delhi would not recover for more than a century.

While he was in India, Tamburlaine received news that the Mamluk Sultan of Egypt and the Ottoman Sultan Bayazid I had had the temerity to seize lands from some of his vassals. Incensed, he destroyed the fortified city of Suvas on the borders of Anatolia, and had the garrison of 4,000 Armenians buried alive. He took Aleppo in 1399, and engaged in a learned debate on law with some captured academics while his soldiers ran amok. In Gibbon's words, the city's streets 'streamed with blood, and re-echoed with the cries of mothers and children, with the shrieks of violated virgins'. Each soldier was ordered to produce at least two severed human heads, which would then be piled up in pyramids. In 1401 he persuaded the citizens of Damascus to let him in under a flag of truce. Once inside, he demanded a fortune in gold, then reduced the city to ashes, killing all its inhabitants except for the artisans, whom he deported to Samarkand. Returning to Aleppo, he burned it down. Then he took Baghdad, massacring its citizens, destroying its monuments, and erecting a pyramid of 90,000 heads on the ruins.

These atrocities led to Tamburlaine being publicly denounced as an enemy of Islam, but that did not stop him. Next he took the ancient city of Smyrna (now Izmir) after an obstinate defence by the Christian knights of Rhodes: 'All that breathed was put to the sword.' At the beginning of 1405, now approaching seventy, he set out to invade China with an army of 200,000, planning to restore the Mongol Empire there. After riding 300 miles, they pitched camp near Otrar in February, but Tamburlaine fell ill with a fever and died. His body was embalmed in an ebony coffin and carried to a sumptuous tomb at Samarkand, which stands to this day among some of the mosaic-covered architectural wonders he created. In his lifetime he was said to have sacked or destroyed 1,000 towns and cities.

### · THE THIRTY YEARS WAR ·

On 23 May 1618 a large crowd of Protestants broke into the royal castle at Prague, then capital of Bohemia, grabbed three of the Catholic king's henchmen, and threw them out of the window. None was seriously hurt, thanks to a pile of rubbish that broke their fall. The 'defenestration of Prague', though, sparked off three decades of misery, death and destruction for Central Europe as contending armies fought out the Thirty Years War. Religion was at its root. Bohemia was mainly Protestant, but its kings were Catholic Habsburgs. Historically, they had tolerated Protestantism, but the new king, Ferdinand, had started a crackdown. Now, after the defenestration, the Bohemian Protestants began laying waste to neighbouring Catholic Austria. Prague soon suffered, too. The Bohemians had replaced Ferdinand with a new Protestant king, Frederick, but in 1620 the city was taken by Catholic forces and plundered for a week.

The war was fought across a huge area, including modern Germany, Austria, the Czech Republic, Switzerland, Luxembourg, the Netherlands and parts of Poland and France. At the time, most of it was known as the Holy Roman Empire, although, in the words of Voltaire, it was neither holy, nor Roman, nor an empire. The emperor was elected, and the territory was divided into hundreds of rival cities and states, many of them very small. A century earlier the Reformation had opened up a religious fissure between those who had broken with and those who had stayed loyal to Rome.

Most of the soldiers who fought in the Thirty Years War were mercenaries contracted to their commanders, one of the most fearsome being Ernst von Mansfeld. 'God help those where Mansfeld comes' was the cry. In the winter of 1620–1 his men, supposedly allies of Frederick of Bohemia, crossed into Alsace, carrying plague and typhus with them. Anything they could not steal they would burn or destroy. For fifteen miles around Hagenau, they were said to have set fire to every house they passed. In just three weeks they destroyed thirty villages and a town. When they could not find anything more to destroy in Alsace, they moved on to Lorraine. Frederick observed plaintively: 'There ought to be some difference made between friend and enemy but these people ruin both alike . . . I think these are men who are possessed of the devil and who take a pleasure in setting fire to everything.' An English mercenary recorded that the people of Weisskirchen in Moravia refused to offer them shelter, so 'we entered killing man, woman and child; the execution continued the space of two hours, the pillaging two days'.

The other side was no less ferocious. In 1624 the armies of the Catholic League plundered Hildesheim, stealing treasure, livestock and women. Any cattle they could not drive off they slaughtered. They wrecked churches, dug up graveyards, and shot any peasant they found hiding in the woods trying to save some pathetic bundle of belongings. When a pastor protested they cut off his hands and feet, and left him bleeding on his altar. Not that being Catholic offered any great protection. They pillaged the convent of Amelungsborn, even ransacking the graves of the nuns. The official army of the deposed King of Bohemia, now Holy Roman Emperor Ferdinand II, was more disciplined under Albrecht von Wallenstein, but it would still demand food, drink, shoes, clothes, and lots of money. If the local bigwigs failed to raise it, the soldiers would drag them off as hostages.

As ever, the apocalyptic horseman War brought along his colleagues, Famine and Pestilence. In 1625 three years of hunger struck Franconia, Württemberg and the Rhine Valley. It was started by terrible weather, with snow falling in June, but aggravated by a growing reluctance of peasants to grow food simply for armies to steal. By 1630, in Nassau they were having to make bread from roots and acorns, while in Bavaria the bodies of those who had starved to death lay unburied on the roads. Now plague joined in, killing 16,000 in Prague alone. It would wipe out whole encampments of wretched refugees. The English diplomat Sir Thomas Roe said that in eighty miles he found 'not a house to sleep safe in; no inhabitants save a few poor women and children'.

In this dreadful war probably the most notorious atrocity came at Magdeburg, the 'virgin city'. Over its gate stood the wooden statue of a young girl with a virgin's wreath in her hand, and the words: 'Who will take it?' The population were nearly all Protestants. In May 1631 it fell to Graf von Tilly and Graf zu Pappenheim's Catholic League army after a six-month siege. There is some dispute over whether these two commanders tried to restrain their troops. Pappenheim rescued the wounded Protestant administrator, while Tilly was seen inexpertly nursing a baby he had salvaged from the arms of its dead mother. But whether they tried or not, it made little difference as Walloon and Croat soldiers in particular wrought havoc. In the words of the great German writer Friedrich Schiller: 'Here commenced a scene of horrors for which history has no language – poetry no pencil. Neither innocent childhood, nor helpless old age; neither youth, sex, rank, nor beauty, could disarm the fury of the conquerors. Wives were abused in the arms of their husbands, daughters at the feet of their parents; and the defenceless sex exposed to the double sacrifice of virtue and life.' When some of Tilly's officers remonstrated with him, it is alleged he replied: 'the soldier must have some reward for his danger and toils'. After burning Magdeburg to the ground, the troops carried off thousands of women to their camp. Tilly sent priests to tell them to do the decent thing, and marry those they had abducted or give them up for a reasonable sum. A few of the surviving men in Magdeburg were able to scrape together enough to ransom themselves and buy back their women, but those who could not had to march off with Tilly's troops as their servants. Perhaps 30,000 people were killed, and the city's population was said to have been reduced to just 400. The atrocity caused such horror throughout Europe that the emperor called off the planned victory celebrations. The statue of Magdeburg's wooden maiden was found charred and broken in a ditch. With grim humour, some spoke of the 'marriage of Magdeburg', but Protestant troops remembered it in a different way, and from then on, many a Catholic soldier crying for quarter would be met with the retort 'Magdeburg quarter!' and shot down.

The great Protestant hero was Gustavus Adolphus of Sweden, the 'Lion of the North'. In April 1632 his army crossed into Bavaria and Swabia, laying waste to the land as it went. Famine and sickness wiped out whole villages, while wolves came from the forests to eat the dead and dying. From the king's point of view, it was nothing personal – just the cold-blooded use of hunger as a weapon of war, a way of denying resources to the enemy. Catholic troops took a similar view. When the emperor's army captured Kempten, they burned houses, slaughtered men, women and children where they stood, or drove them into the river. It became known as the 'Magdeburg of the South'. The Jesuits of Hagenau tried to feed the poor from their own grain stores until French soldiers came along and stole the lot. In 1635 a dreadful famine struck from Württemberg to Lorraine. In Alsace they tore the bodies of criminals from the gallows and ate them; rats were sold in the market at Worms; and at Zweibrücken a mother admitted having eaten her child. At Bacharach poor people were found dead with grass in their mouths; at Mainz beggars would kill each other in ferocious battles for scraps of food. During the siege of Breisach in June 1638 rich burghers' wives were seen in the market bartering jewellery for a little flour, and mice became a delicacy.

By this time, what had begun as a war between Catholics and Protestants had become essentially a power struggle between Catholic France and Catholic Spain and Austria, but this made little difference to its victims. Increasingly, troops were not paid but were expected to rely on plunder. As the war went on, ever more ragged bands of soldiers crossed Germany, caring nothing for any cause other than feeding themselves, and increasing numbers of peasants gave up tilling the land to join them. It seemed to offer a better chance of survival. When the Swedes and the French invaded his territory in 1646, Maximilian of Bavaria did not dare arm his subjects for fear that, maddened by their privations, they would rise in revolt. Instead, he scorched the earth, destroying mills and stores, and starving his own people as well as the invaders.

By the time the war ended in 1648, the destruction was almost beyond belief. Bavaria alone was said to have lost 900 villages and 80,000 families, and Bohemia three-quarters of its people. In cities such as Württemberg and Chemnitz even bigger population losses were recorded, perhaps five-sixths. In Nassau a Swedish general declared: 'I would not have believed a land could have been so despoiled had I not seen it with my own eyes.' The overall loss of life is hard to assess, but according to one estimate the population of the Holy Roman Empire fell from around twenty-one million in 1618 to just thirteen million in 1648.

## · THE MANCHU CONQUEST OF CHINA ·

While the Thirty Years War was raging in Europe, an equally destructive conflict was devastating China. By the second decade of the seventeenth century, the Ming dynasty had lost control of much of the north-east, and a Manchu leader named Nurhaci began a bitter struggle to carve out his own kingdom, which would eventually supplant the Mings as the Qing dynasty. When Nurhaci took the town of Tsingho, he massacred 20,000. At Yangzhou his son Dodo allowed his men a free hand for five days, during which they killed 80,000 men, women and children. So fearful did the reputation of the Manchu become that there were a number of mass suicides. When the wife of a Ming official heard they had captured her husband she and forty-two relatives and retainers killed themselves. Her husband changed sides and survived.

A little later a man named Li Zeching appeared on the scene. Starting off as a robber, he eventually attracted half a million followers. Around 1640 he took Honan, where he perpetrated 'horrible outrages' on the townspeople. Two years later, while he was laying siege to Kaifeng, then said to be the strongest fortress in China, the governor demolished dykes so the Yellow River inundated Li's camp, drowning many of his soldiers. Its waters, though, are notoriously unpredictable, and the torrent suddenly got out of control,sweeping away the town's walls and flooding it. Thousands drowned, while many of those who tried to escape were cut down by the rebels. Many more would perish later from famine and disease. Altogether, 300,000, half the population, are said to have died, and Kaifeng never recovered its ancient importance. Now the former bandit was master of a third of China, so he declared himself Emperor Yongchang. As he approached Beijing in 1644 the last of the Ming emperors strangled himself before the city surrendered. But Li's triumph was short lived, as the remaining Ming forces and the Manchu combined to defeat and kill him.

There was widespread anarchy while the new Manchu emperor tried to establish himself. In Szchuen a rebel proclaimed himself Si Wang, King of the West. Posing as a patron of the arts, he invited 30,000 literary men to come to his capital to work for him; then he had them massacred. When a courtier got his complicated title wrong, Si flew into

a fury and had 3,000 people murdered. His worst atrocity was the massacre of Chentu, which is said to have cost 600,000 lives. He destroyed
cities and flattened forests, and when he learned that a Manchu army was
after him he ordered his followers to murder 400,000 women camp-
followers. As the Manchu attacked, Si was one of the first victims, felled
by an arrow. They quickly took Szchuen, pillaging the city of Canton. By
the time the Manchu dynasty finally won the war, it is estimated that
about twenty-five million people had perished in China, perhaps one-
sixth of the population.

## · THE RAPE OF NANKING ·

The Japanese took their first step towards building an empire in Asia in
1931, when they seized Manchuria. The following year they bombed
Shanghai, killing tens of thousands and provoking worldwide protests. In
August 1937 they took the city. In a suburb where 100,000 people had
lived a British journalist found 'hardly a building standing which has not
been gutted by fire'. The only living creatures he saw were five old men
hiding in a mission compound, and 'dogs unnaturally fattened by
feasting on corpses'. Many other Chinese cities were heavily bombed,
including Nanking, Hankow and Canton, and every town and village the
Japanese entered could expect brutal treatment, while the scorched-earth
policy pursued by the retreating Chinese ensured that millions died of
hunger. On 19 November 1937 the Japanese took the ancient city of
Suchow, known as the 'Venice of China' because of its many canals and
bridges. For days they plundered it, raping and murdering thousands of
women. According to the *China Weekly Review*, a population of 350,000
was reduced to just 500. As the Japanese neared Nanking, the capital of
Nationalist China, they would bayonet or club to death everyone in
sight.

On 9 December Japanese aircraft dropped leaflets on the city, saying
they would 'show no mercy towards those who offer resistance, treating
them with extreme severity, but shall harm neither innocent civilians
nor Chinese military who manifest no hostility'. When no one emerged
to offer the city's surrender the Japanese bombed and shelled it for two
days. Many Chinese soldiers then fled. To the Japanese, this seemed

deeply shameful. When they took the city on 13 December Chiang Kai-shek and his government had already left for Hankow, but more than 700,000 people remained, including perhaps 150,000 Chinese soldiers, some of them disguised in civilian clothes they had stolen from shops or torn from the backs of passers-by. The Japanese commander, General Matsui, was suffering from chronic tuberculosis, but he called his staff officers to his sickbed and reminded them that the army's behaviour would be seen by the world. Then he ordered: 'Let no unit enter the city in a disorderly fashion . . . Plundering and causing fires, even carelessly, shall be severely punished.' On 7 December, though, Emperor Hirohito had dispatched his uncle, Lt.-Gen. Prince Asaka Yasuhiko, to be commander-in-chief of the army around Nanking, and some orders seem to have gone out saying that all captives should be killed. Certainly, the Japanese 66th Battalion had received instructions to shoot all prisoners.

Little is known about many Japanese atrocities, but the 'rape of Nanking' was revealed to the world because there were foreigners there to witness it. If the Japanese did plan to avoid unnecessary bloodshed, they failed right from the start. As they entered the city some Chinese flew Japanese flags and cheered, believing their own government had abandoned them, but the invading army began shooting people randomly, including elderly women and children in the back as they ran away, until the streets ran with blood. As they began going house-to-house looking for Chinese soldiers, the Japanese troops murdered more systematically. They would demand shopkeepers open their doors, then gun them down and loot their stores, burning anything they did not want. Next they massacred all captured soldiers – mowing them down with machine-guns, soaking them with petrol and burning them alive, or using them for bayonet practice. Many Japanese officers believed getting their men to bayonet helpless captives in this way would toughen them up. One said that when he decapitated a Chinese prisoner with his sword, 'I gained strength somewhere in my gut.' A witness to a mass execution wrote: 'Those in the first row were beheaded, those in the second row were forced to dump the severed bodies into the river before they themselves were beheaded. The killing went on non-stop from morning until night, but they were only able to kill 2,000 people in this way. The next day, tired of killing in this fashion, they set up machine-guns.' A Japanese officer at the scene estimated that about 20,000 people were executed.

One Japanese reporter described seeing 100 Chinese silently dragging bodies from a 'mountain' of corpses and throwing them into the Yangtze. Some were 'still alive and moaning weakly, their limbs twitching'. When the 100 had finished their task the Japanese lined them up and machine-gunned them. They seemed constantly on the lookout for new methods of murder – roasting, burying alive, carving out organs, hanging victims by their tongues on iron hooks, burying them up to their waists then getting dogs to tear them apart – many of which appear to have been designed principally to provide amusement. Often the murders were photographed and made into postcards that soldiers sent home to their families.

Tens of thousands of children were killed. An American surgeon named Robert Wilson wrote to his family: 'They bayoneted one little boy, killing him, and I spent an hour and a half this morning patching up another little boy of eight who had five bayonet wounds including one that penetrated his stomach.' An eight-year-old girl saw her grandparents, parents and elder sisters shot before her eyes. She was bayoneted three times and left for dead but survived. Someone else not intended to live was a twenty-five-year-old shoemaker's apprentice, Tang Shunsan. He hid for days after the Japanese arrived but was finally overcome by curiosity and went outside. The Japanese spotted him and made him join hundreds of other Chinese they were herding along the street to a newly dug pit that already contained about sixty corpses. Tang thought of leaping in, but then he saw Japanese military dogs eating the dead bodies. The Japanese ordered them to line up in rows by the pit, and Tang went right to the edge. While one soldier stood guard with a machine-gun, the others started systematically beheading the prisoners. Some of the Japanese were laughing; others were taking pictures. One soldier tried to take away a pregnant woman to rape her. She began clawing at him, so he killed her by bayoneting her in the belly. As things got more chaotic, the body of a man who had just been beheaded banged against Tang and knocked him into the pit. No one seemed to notice, so he hid beneath one of the corpses. To speed things up, the Japanese switched from beheading to slitting throats, and soon dozens of bodies had fallen into the pit. Then the soldiers left, apart from one who kept plunging his bayonet into the corpses to ensure no one was left alive. Tang was wounded five times but managed to avoid crying out. Later, two Chinese people found him and pulled him out. He was the only survivor.

According to one Japanese war correspondent, the terrible events of Nanking were not an aberration, but standard practice for the invading army. He wrote that officers promised their troops 'three days to do what they like' as reward for taking a town. In Nanking, the three days extended to six weeks. In the stark words of one Japanese soldier who took part in the atrocities: 'We sent our coal trucks to the city streets and villages to seize a lot of women. And then each of them was allocated to 15 to 20 soldiers for sexual intercourse and abuse.' Some of the victims were younger than ten, others as old as eighty. Once the soldiers had finished with them, they would try to run away: 'Then we would – "bang!" shoot them in the back.' Some officers warned soldiers to dispose of their victims afterwards. One admitted: 'We always stabbed and killed them. Because dead bodies don't talk.' Many Japanese soldiers believed that raping virgins would make them more powerful in battle. Some even wore amulets made from the pubic hair of their victims, thinking it conferred magical powers against injury. Officers also participated enthusiastically. The commander of the Japanese Sixth Division was later found guilty of raping about twenty women in Nanking. Robert Wilson said it was a 'modern Dante's Inferno . . . Murder by the wholesale and rape by the thousands of cases. There seems to be no stop to the ferocity, lust and atavism of the brutes.' Some victims were disembowelled, others had their breasts sliced off, others were nailed to walls. The Japanese forced fathers to rape their daughters, or sons their mothers, while other members of the family watched. Monks who had sworn to be celibate were forced to rape women, and Chinese men were made to have sex with corpses. One German diplomat recorded that many rape victims not murdered by the Japanese threw themselves into the Yangtze. Women were attacked in nunneries, churches and Bible schools. If children cried while their mothers were being raped, they would be bayoneted; and many men were murdered trying to protect their loved ones. No one knows how many women were raped, but the Chinese claim it was up to 80,000. Over the last days of 1937 and the start of 1938, the number of non-combatants killed by the Japanese in Nanking was estimated by the International Military Tribunal of the Far East at more than 260,000, though some say the real figure was 350,000.

Members of the small foreign community in the city tried to set up an area, the Nanking Safety Zone, in which Chinese people could be protected. John Rabe, a German businessman and leader of the Nazi Party in the city, was chosen as its head. A quarter of a million managed to get into the zone, including several thousand Chinese soldiers, whom the Japanese came in and removed. They also took rickshaw pullers and manual labourers, claiming the calluses on their hands proved they must be troops. The YMCA representative in the city, George Fitch, saw them roped together in groups of 100 and marched off by soldiers with fixed bayonets. Many women were captured by the Japanese while trying to get into the zone, and Rabe confronted Japanese soldiers trying to attack women within it. Fitch noted that he always 'thrusts his Nazi armband in their face and points to his Nazi decoration'. This usually worked, but many women were still raped in the zone. Minnie Vautrin, an American missionary, recorded in her diary for 16 December: 'Thirty girls were taken from the language school last night, and today I have heard scores of heartbreaking stories of girls who were taken from their homes last night – one of the girls was but 12 years old.' She saw a truck carrying ten girls who cried: '*Ging ming! Ging ming!* – save our lives.' Three days later another foreign resident, James McCallum, wrote: 'Never have I heard or read of such brutality. Rape: we estimate at least 1,000 cases a night and many by day. In case of resistance or anything that seems like disapproval there is a bayonet stab or a bullet.'

General Matsui arrived in the city on 17 December, claiming he was unaware of what had happened up to that point. In a statement to the press he said: 'I offer my sympathy, with deep emotion, to one million innocent people.' He also told the *New York Times*: 'the Japanese army is probably the most undisciplined in the world today'. At a burial service for the Japanese dead, Matsui publicly rebuked 300 of his officers. One Japanese correspondent said: 'Never before had a superior given his officers such a scathing reprimand.' Within two days, though, he moved to

Prince Asaka's headquarters outside the city and seemed incapable of halting the atrocities. Matsui was hanged in 1948 for crimes against humanity. He told his Buddhist confessor that when he had expressed his anger about Nanking to Asaka, the prince just laughed, but he did not mention this at his trial. At the time of the massacre there were claims that Japanese officers in other places wept with shame, but many Japanese continued to insist that no massacre had taken place and that all the casualties were military personnel. Asaka was one, maintaining he never received any complaints about the conduct of his troops. Under the terms of the agreement signed by General Douglas MacArthur and Emperor Hirohito at the end of the war, all members of the royal family were exempt from prosecution for war crimes.

Although there was little evidence of genuine Japanese contrition for Nanking, they knew a public relations disaster when they saw one. While the world howled in protest, the Japanese hoped to dilute their soldiers' enthusiasm for rape by setting up a system of military brothels in which women from conquered countries would be forced to serve as sex slaves, or 'comfort women', as their captors delicately called them. The first was opened in Nanking itself in 1938, and by the end of war up to 200,000 women from Korea, China, Taiwan, the Philippines and Indonesia had been press-ganged into service. When the scandal was revealed the Japanese claimed the brothels had been run by private entrepreneurs, but official documents showed they had been set up by the authorities. Many of the women killed themselves, and after the war many survivors were too ashamed to speak out.

Japanese denials of the rape of Nanking might have been greeted with less scepticism if their soldiers had behaved better elsewhere. Sadly they did not. After taking Singapore, they murdered sixty Australian nursing sisters and beheaded 5,000 Chinese civilians. In Java 10,000 Dutch people died in their internment camps. More than 50,000 Burmese and 16,000 Allied prisoners were worked to death on the Burma–Thailand railway. When a British merchant ship sank in the Indian Ocean the crew of the Japanese heavy cruiser *Tome* rescued sixty-nine of them, then slit their throats one by one and threw them back into sea. And the Japanese seemed proud of their brutality. In occupied Manchuria they made schoolchildren watch newsreel films of people being cut in half or of prisoners being torn to pieces by dogs, with lingering close-ups of the victims' terror-stricken eyes.

As the war turned against them, the Japanese became, if anything, more brutal. With the Americans advancing towards the island of Tinian, they murdered 5,000 Korean labourers. When they took Bataan, at least 5,000 Filipinos died on the 'March of Death'. Any who stumbled or were too weak to walk would be bayoneted or clubbed to death on the spot. They would tie patients to hospital beds, then set fire to the building. As the Americans advanced on Manila, the Japanese murdered perhaps 100,000 people. Then there were the prisoners who were dissected while still alive and conscious after being deliberately infected with plague. Altogether, during the 1930s and 1940s, the Japanese are estimated to have been responsible for the deaths of about twenty million Asians.

Some apologised for what they had done. One young officer said Japanese troops were 'turned into murdering demons', and a soldier confessed: 'I beheaded people, starved them to death, burned them, and buried them alive, over 200 in all . . . I was truly a devil.' Even today, though, Japan is reluctant to acknowledge its crimes. In 2005, unusually, Prime Minister Junichiro Koizumi apologised for the suffering Japan had caused during the Second World War, but by then both China and South Korea had cancelled summits because of the prime minister's regular visit to Tokyo's Yasukuni shrine, where fourteen war criminals are buried. The following year forty-five former slave labourers and their families tried to bring actions against both the Japanese state and companies like Mitsubishi Materials. Mitsubishi's defence questioned whether the Japanese had really invaded China, and the Japanese court dismissed the case. In 2007 Koizumi's successor, Shinzo Abe, denied that Japan had forced women into prostitution.

## · THE SECOND WORLD WAR ·

On 1 November 1911 an Italian lieutenant named Giulio Cavotti leaned out of his monoplane and dropped a hand grenade on the oasis of Tagiura near Tripoli. It was the first bomb ever dropped from an aeroplane. The Italians were trying to conquer the last outpost of the

Ottoman Empire in Africa and had run into stiffer resistance than they had expected. Less than thirty years later, air raids had become a major new way of killing civilians. During the First World War Britain and Germany had bombed each other's cities, but the death toll in Britain was just 1,400. A few years later, though, the British Fire Prevention Committee warned: 'In the next war, cities will be bombed without warning; what has been done in the past will be altogether eclipsed by the horrors of future aerial bombardments.' And during the Spanish Civil War the world was given a foretaste of what might happen next: on 26 April 1937, in a bombing raid in support of Franco's Nationalists, German and Italian planes killed perhaps 1,500 of the 10,000 people living in the Basque town of Guernica.

On the day Hitler invaded Poland, forty German bombers attacked Warsaw, killing about a hundred civilians. A Polish schoolboy named Ben Helfgott had been taken by his father to a small village, supposedly out of harm's way, but soon he heard aircraft overhead. They started dropping incendiary bombs and 'Seconds later, this pretty village was a mass of flames.' People with their clothes on fire ran for the woods while the aeroplanes machine-gunned them. On 4 September, the day after Britain declared war on Germany, RAF bombers were sent to attack German warships in the Kiel Canal, but four bombs fell on Esbjerg in Denmark, more than 100 miles away, killing one civilian. Early on in the war, Chancellor of the Exchequer Sir Kingsley Wood opposed bombing even military targets in German cities because such action was 'bound to kill women and children and thereby provoke reprisals from the Germans', but the two sides drifted into an air war in which civilians became the main targets.

The first civilian casualties from enemy action in Britain came on 30 April 1940 when a German plane that had been laying mines crashed, killing two people at Clacton-on-Sea. Ten days later, thirty-six British bombers hit Moenchengladbach, killing four people, including one Englishwoman. When Hitler invaded neutral Holland, he met stronger resistance that he expected, so on 14 May he ordered the Luftwaffe to bomb bridges over the Rhine at Rotterdam, but many missed their targets and hit the city centre, completely flattening a square mile and killing more than 800 civilians. German planes also routinely machine-gunned refugee columns. Across the border in Belgium, one man described the horror as he tried to escape with his children: 'before our children's eyes other children were blown to bits . . . the planes began circling and swooping down, with their machine-guns singing out their merciless pursuit of any living thing – however small'. That same night, 130 British bombers targeted oil refineries and railway yards in Hamburg, but they also hit the city centre, killing thirty-four people. In retaliation, Hitler ordered the Luftwaffe to attack Britain, and by mid-August more than 700 British civilians had been killed. RAF aircraft continued to attack Germany, and Churchill warned the raids might 'attain dimensions hitherto undreamed of'. In his view bombing Germany was the 'most certain of all roads to victory'.

On the night of 24 August two German aircraft dropped bombs on the City of London, killing nine people. They had probably got lost looking for the oil storage depot at Thameshaven, but in retaliation Churchill ordered a series of raids on Berlin. Most did little damage, but one killed ten civilians near a railway station. On 4 September Hitler threatened terrible revenge, and it was exacted just three days later. London was the biggest target on earth, spread out over eighty square miles. To attack it, Germany had assembled the most powerful force ever directed against a single target – nearly 350 bombers escorted by more than 600 fighters. The sirens sounded at four o'clock on a beautiful afternoon, and as the aircraft flew towards London some of those who would be on the receiving end could not help admiring their 'majestic orderliness'. They unleashed what one fire-fighter described as 'a raging inferno against which were silhouetted groups of pigmy firemen directing their futile jets against the wall of flame'. On what became known as 'Black Saturday', 430 people were killed and 1,600 injured. It was the start of the Blitz. Over the next two days the Germans killed more of the capital's civilians than had perished in the whole of the First World War. And for the next seventy-six nights, with the exception of one when the weather was too bad, London was bombed.

By the end of October, nearly 6,400 British civilians had been killed in attacks on cities such as Liverpool, Cardiff, Swansea, Southampton and Manchester, as well as London. The RAF's raids on Germany had been less deadly, but on 9 September a bomb had landed in Goebbels's garden, and in November Hitler was driven into a fury when he had to reschedule a big speech in Munich to avoid a British raid. In revenge, he ordered a brutal raid on Coventry on 14 November that destroyed a hundred acres of the historic city centre and killed 554 people. The carnage was achieved by starting a firestorm. This happens when many fires merge into one, creating temperatures of 1,000 degrees with winds of up to 150 miles an hour. They draw the air out of shelters and suffocate everyone in them, and the flames become so intense that fire-fighting is completely ineffective. Sir Arthur 'Bomber' Harris, who would take charge of Bomber Command in February 1942, studied the tactic carefully: 'The Nazis entered this war under the rather childish delusion that they were going to bomb everyone else, and nobody was going to bomb them,' he said. 'At Rotterdam, London, Warsaw, and half a hundred other places, they put their rather naïve theory into operation. They sowed the wind, and now they are going to reap the whirlwind.' The Coventry raid disrupted important strategic industries, but the city's people proved extremely resourceful. When the Morris engine works lost its roof, the workers carried on in the open air, and in six weeks production was back to normal. Other factories brought in coke braziers for heating, and replaced damaged roofs with tarpaulins. By now, around 15,000 British people had been killed, compared to fewer than 1,000 from RAF raids in Germany. Indeed, until September 1942, you were more likely to die if you were a British civilian than if you were in the armed forces. No wonder one woman in a blitzed city remarked: 'I'm only glad my Jim is in the army and out of all this.'

In retaliation for the raid on Coventry, the British bombed Hamburg, killing 233 civilians. Hitler then launched further fearsome raids on London – one in May 1941 killed more than 1,400 and severely damaged the House of Commons. To the east, though, much worse things were happening. On 6 April German bombers had attacked Belgrade and 17,000 Yugoslav civilians had died, but the war on the Eastern Front showed that traditional ways of killing civilians could be more lethal than air raids. In June 1941 Hitler began his attack on Russia, with the German forces systematically burning villages as they passed through them. Meanwhile, Stalin ordered a scorched-earth policy – everything that could not be removed must be destroyed. In September the Nazis virtually surrounded Leningrad (St Petersburg), trapping 2.6 million people, who began to freeze or starve to death in large num- bers – 3,700 died on Christmas Day alone. People ate horses, dogs, cats, crows and rats; then glue, candles, paper and leather. During February 1942, 100,000 people died from starvation, frostbite or shelling. By the time Soviet forces lifted the siege after 900 days, approximately 950,000 people had perished. Meanwhile, the Japanese killed 240 in an air raid on Darwin in Australia, showing this was truly something approaching a 'world war',

Fortunately for Britain, the Germans did not possess a true heavy bomber (indeed, the Staaken R-39, which had attacked London in the First World War, was heavier than any they used in the Second). Britain, on the other hand, had been building big, four-engine bombers since 1937, and Churchill tried to take some of the pressure off his new Soviet allies by ramping up the raids on German cities. Lübeck had a factory making U-boat components, but it was also a fine medieval city. Being built largely of wood, it burned well when Bomber Harris sent over the RAF in March 1942: 80 per cent of it was destroyed at the cost of 312 lives – the highest total yet for a British raid. Hitler retaliated with the 'Baedeker' raids, named after the famous German guidebooks, and designed to 'raze English cultural shrines to the ground'. The Luftwaffe attacked Exeter, Bath, Norwich and York, killing 938. Then came the biggest British raid of the war so far on 30 May, when more than 450 people were killed at Cologne and 36 factories had to cease production. News of the raid reached the Warsaw ghetto, where 42,000 Jews a month were dying of starvation (see Chapter 11 – Adolf Hitler). The Polish Jewish historian Emmanuel Ringelblum wrote: 'Day in, day out in hundreds of cities throughout Poland and Russia, thousands upon thousands of Jews are being systematically murdered according to a preconceived plan . . . After the Cologne affair, I walked around in a good mood, feeling that, even if I should perish at their hands, my death is prepaid.' He would be shot by the Germans in 1944.

In January 1943 the Allies decided they could not invade Europe before the summer of 1944, so they resolved secretly that bombing would have to be their key weapon, aimed at the 'progressive destruction and dislocation of the German military, industrial and economic system' but also 'the undermining of the morale of the German people to a point where their capacity for armed resistance is fatally weakened'. Some leading Nazis were already becoming alarmed. The head of the Luftwaffe, Hermann Goering, commented: 'If the English are in a position night after night to attack some German city, one can easily imagine how Germany will look after three months.' The famous Dambusters raid on the Moehne and Eder dams in May 1943 brought the highest civilian death toll of any raid on Germany up to that point – 1,260 – mostly people drowned when the dams burst. Nearly 500 of them were forced labourers, mainly women from the Ukraine, but the major industrial dislocation that the RAF had hoped for did not materialise, and even sixteen major night raids on Berlin in the winter of 1942–3 generally disrupted the city's industry for only a short time. Civilian death tolls were mounting, though. Just over a fortnight after the Dambusters raid, the RAF started a firestorm in the narrow streets of the old town of Wuppertal, killing up to 3,400.

The following month Churchill was watching film of the raids when he suddenly shot bolt upright in his chair and exclaimed: 'Are we beasts? Are we taking this too far?' The Australian representative in the War Cabinet, Richard Casey, replied that the Allies had not started the bombing, and anyway it was a case of 'them or us'. With German aircraft sucked away to the Eastern Front, Luftwaffe raids on Britain were by now far less lethal, but the RAF's were growing ever more deadly. In July 1943 a raid started a firestorm in Hamburg. One British pilot said the city seemed 'like the glowing heart of a vast brazier . . . I looked down, fascinated but aghast, satisfied yet horrified.' Eight square miles of the city were reduced to blackened ashes and ruins, and about 42,000 people were killed. Albert Speer, Germany's minister for armaments and war production, got factories working again remarkably quickly, but he warned Hitler that if three or four cities were bombed in a similar fashion, it could mean the 'end of the war'. In fact, in spite of all the raids, the average number of single-engine fighters, for example, produced by Germany each month rose from 851 in the second half of 1943 to 1,581 the following summer. However, attacks on the Nazis' synthetic oil industry did begin to starve the Luftwaffe of fuel. Civilians in occupied territories also found themselves in the sights of the RAF and the United States Air

Force. In the run-up to D-Day 640 Parisians were killed in an attack on the marshalling yards at St Denis.

In the last year of the war the Germans unveiled two new weapons. The V1 was a flying bomb, a forerunner of the cruise missile. The first hit London a week after D-Day in June 1944, but the most deadly strike killed 119 people attending a Sunday morning church service. One survivor said, 'There was a noise so loud it was as if all the waters and winds in the world had come together in mighty conflict.' Then the chapel collapsed on them 'in a bellow of bricks and mortar'. By the middle of August 1944, V1s had killed nearly 2,000 people in Britain. They were followed the next month by V2 rockets, which travelled at twice the speed of sound. In November 168 lunchtime shoppers were killed when a south London Woolworth's was hit. The new weapon was also used extensively against newly liberated parts of Belgium: when one hit a cinema in Antwerp 567 people were killed.

Meanwhile, the Allies' more conventional weapons were proving far more deadly. To try to disrupt Hitler's plans to move more men to the Eastern Front, a huge raid was mounted on Dresden, an elegant baroque city that had not yet been targeted, but was now virtually defenceless. On the night of 13 February 1945 more than 750 British bombers attacked the railway marshalling yards, but they also started a ferocious firestorm that destroyed eleven square miles of the city. The next morning 450 USAF bombers attacked. Some fires burned for a week after the raid, and, although the death toll was never established, it was almost certainly more than 40,000. An inscription on a mass grave in the city's main cemetery reads: 'How many died? Who knows the number?' Rail services, though, were put out of action for only three days.

After the war, while most British military commanders would be revered, 'Bomber' Harris was often reviled. He was the only commander-in-chief not offered a peerage, and for a time he left Britain. He returned in 1953 to receive a baronetcy from Churchill, but when the Queen Mother unveiled a statue to him in 1992 she was jeered. Yet when Harris said in February 1945, 'I do not personally regard the whole of the remaining cities of Germany as worth the bones of one British Grenadier,' how many British people would have disagreed with him?

An estimated twenty million civilians died during the war through famine and disease. In conquered territories the Germans requisitioned food, so in some Dutch cities during the winter of 1944–5, for example, civilian rations fell to 500 calories a day, and Red Cross ships were prevented from bringing in supplies. About 30,000 people starved to death. Occupied countries could also face a relentless Allied sea blockade. At least 300,000 Greeks are said to have died of hunger before the embargo was relaxed. The charity Oxfam was formed to buy food that was allowed through the blockade. These might be regarded as incidental casualties of war, if sometimes inflicted by apalling callousness, but many civilians were deliberately murdered, especially by Hitler's Nazi regime (see Chapter 11). Similarly, when the Russians conquered Germany, the nation that had seemed intent on destroying them, they showed little mercy and thousands of women were raped. After the liberation of France, several thousand French men and women regarded as collaborators were executed without trial.

The Second World War was the greatest man-made disaster in history. The total number of civilians who lost their lives was around 47 million: China lost perhaps 16 million; the Soviet Union 11.5 million; Indonesia 4 million; Poland 2.2 million; Germany 1.8 million; Japan 600,000. Roughly 68,000 died in the UK. About 3.1 million prisoners of war died in Nazi captivity, many deliberately starved to death. At one point, Goering complained that Russian prisoners having eaten everything they could lay their hands on, including the soles of their boots, had turned to devouring each other, and, 'which is more serious, a German sentry'.

## · HIROSHIMA ·

A former stunt pilot, Lt.-Col. James H. Doolittle, masterminded one of the most audacious raids of the Second World War in April 1942, when he took sixteen B-25 bombers into the middle of the Pacific on a ship and then used them to bomb Tokyo, killing about fifty people. After the attack, the aircraft landed in China and civilians helped most of the airmen to safety. The Japanese soon exacted a dreadful revenge, devastating the area where most of the aircraft had come down, butchering perhaps a quarter of a million people. The raid notified the Japanese, who had no qualms about bombing civilians themselves, that they were no longer invulnerable in their home islands, but it was more than two years before the Americans had conquered islands sufficiently close to Japan to allow them to start bombing in earnest.

Tokyo was one of the most densely populated cities on earth. In one part, more than a million people packed into flimsy wooden buildings covering an area of just twelve square miles. It was also virtually un-defended, and had poor fire-fighting and medical services. On the night of 9 March 1945, 330 B-29s dropped incendiary bombs for more than two hours, creating the worst man-made fire in history. For the loss of just fifteen aircraft, they destroyed more than a quarter of a million buildings. Perhaps as many as 140,000 people died as the fires raged for four days. Over the next few days Nagoya, Osaka and Kobe were all laid waste, and during the following weeks nearly every major conurbation in Japan was attacked. America's joint chiefs of staff reported: 'Japan will become a nation without cities . . . and will have tremendous difficulty in holding her people together for continued resistance,' but perhaps no one had told the Japanese because, instead of giving in, they now seemed to be raising an army of 2.5 million to mount a fanatical defence of their main island of Honshu. The Allies knew all about fanatical defence: as US forces had advanced through the Pacific, on island after island the Japanese would fight virtually to the last man. When the Admiralty Islands had been over-run in May 1944, nearly 4,000 Japanese soldiers had been killed while just 75 surrendered. From October, their pilots were making 'kamikaze' suicide attacks on American ships. One killed 131 sailors on the US cruiser *Nashville*.

US medical staff calculated it would cost 900,000 US dead or wounded, as well as three million Japanese casualties, to conquer the country. The alternative of a blockade might kill millions of civilians from starvation. On 1 April 1945 the battle began for Okinawa, the final stepping stone for an assault on Japan's home islands. The Japanese defended ferociously, and took no prisoners. More than 12,000 Americans were killed, plus 120,000 Japanese military personnel and 80,000 Okinawans – over 200,000 deaths for one small island. It was also known that the Japanese had been developing chemical and biological weapons, stockpiling tons of germ-laden foam. They had also made plans to annihilate all their captives.

For years, German-Jewish scientists, refugees from their homeland, had been developing an atomic bomb for the Allies, and in 1945 the project was coming to fruition. (The Germans and the Japanese had been working on such a bomb too, but in November 1944 Japanese scientists reported there had been little progress since the previous February.) Apart from the bomb's military benefits, there were also political considerations. The United States was beginning to worry about the Soviet Union's post-war ambitions, and President Truman was anxious to defeat Japan without Russian involvement. The new bomb was tested successfully for the first time on 16 July. Now, said Churchill, the 'nightmare' of having 'to quell the Japanese resistance man by man and conquer the country yard by yard' could be replaced by 'the vision – fair and bright it seemed – of the end of the whole war in one or two violent shocks'.

Signals emanating from Japan were ambiguous. Its government had put out feelers via Sweden and the Soviet Union to discuss surrender terms. On the other hand, its official attitude seemed uncompromising. On 26 July the Allies demanded unconditional surrender, while saying Japan would be allowed to keep its four main islands, and warned that refusing this offer would inevitably result in 'the utter devastation of the Japanese homeland'. The Japanese prime minister, Admiral Kantaro Suzuki, immediately declared that his country would 'ignore' the demand 'and fight resolutely for the successful conclusion of the war'. The Allies decided not to target Tokyo again, because it was 'practically all bombed and burned out'. Hiroshima was seen as 'the largest untouched target'. Its rivers meant it was 'not a good incendiary target', but the hills around the city were 'likely to produce a focusing effect which would considerably increase the blast damage'. Truman wrote in his diary that he instructed his secretary of war, Henry Stimson, to use the atomic bomb, 'so that military objectives and soldiers and sailors are the target and not women and children,' though it is hard to see how this might have been achieved.

On 5 August a specially adapted B-29, *Enola Gay*, blessed by a Roman Catholic priest, took off from Tinian Island in the Pacific carrying a uranium atomic bomb 'Little Boy'. Early the following morning it detonated nearly 1,900 feet above Hiroshima. Those close to ground zero were instantly vaporised, while over the next two weeks 92,000 died, many from terrible burns. Of the city's 90,000 buildings, 62,000 were completely destroyed. Truman announced that if the Japanese continued to refuse to accept Allied terms, they faced 'a rain of ruin from the air the like of which has never been seen on this earth'.

The explosion produced shock and awe throughout the world, and the very next day the Russians invaded Manchuria. The Japanese, though, did not respond immediately. Truman had agreed that another bomb could be dropped if he did not receive the unconditional surrender by 11 August, but the weather forecast for that day was poor, so the date was brought forward to the 9th. In the early hours another B-29 took off from Tinian. Its initial objective was Kokura, but the pilot found the city wreathed in industrial haze. Their orders were to bomb only a clear target, so they flew on. (The phrase 'Kokura's luck' passed into the Japanese language.) At that very moment Japan's six-man Supreme War Council was discussing surrender. Suzuki advocated it but the council could not reach a decision. Meanwhile, the bomber had flown on ninety miles to Nagasaki and dropped a second atomic bomb, 'Fat Man'. Made from plutonium and more powerful than the one used on Hiroshima, it caused a greater blast but, thanks to superior air-raid precautions, killed fewer people. Even so, the initial death toll was 40,000. When the news reached Japan's War Cabinet it finally agreed to surrender. On 14 August 1,000 Japanese soldiers attacked the Imperial Palace to try to stop the capitulation. They killed the commander of the Imperial Guards but were driven back by troops loyal to the emperor. At midnight many Japanese citizens heard Hirohito's voice for the first time when he went on the radio to announce the surrender.

One of the first outsiders to enter Hiroshima after the bomb exploded was Captain Mitsuo Fuchida, who had led the attack on Pearl Harbor. He is said to have wandered aimlessly through the wasteland. The following May, the American journalist John Hersey gave many foreigners their first glimpse of the nuclear holocaust when he went to interview survivors. He discovered the city had been full of foreboding, with people convinced the Americans were saving something special for them. Many had started sleeping in the suburbs, including the wife and baby of the pastor of Hiroshima's Methodist church, the Reverend Kiyoshi Tanimoto. On the 'beautiful' morning of 6 August he had heard the air-raid siren, quickly followed by the 'all clear' as the Japanese detected only three aircraft. When the bomb exploded at a quarter past eight, the Reverend Tanimoto was in a friend's garden two miles from the epicentre. He saw a tremendous sheet of light flash across the sky, and flung himself between two huge rocks as debris rained down. When he finally dared to raise his head, he saw his friend's house had disappeared and there was so much dust that morning had turned to twilight. A tailor's widow, Hatsuyo Nakamura, was perhaps four miles from the blast. She was picked up and flung through the air, then buried up to her chest in rubble. Less than a mile from the epicentre, at the Red Cross hospital, one of the surgeons, Terufumi Sasaki, found himself surrounded by dead bodies and running, screaming patients. Another doctor, Masakuzu Fuiji, who ran a private hospital, was blown into the river. He managed to get out and saw wounded people with terrible burns scurrying around. Some had skin hanging off their hands and feet; many were vomiting. Only 1,400 yards from the blast a German priest, Father Wilhelm Kleinsorge, had been lying on his bed reading. He did not know how he had got out of the house, but he found himself wandering around the garden in his underwear, bleeding from small cuts. All of the buildings around him had collapsed, apart from the Jesuit mission house, which had been specially strengthened by a priest who was afraid of earthquakes.

The Reverend Tanimoto climbed a mound and saw the whole of Hiroshima covered with a cloud of dust, through which clumps of smoke were rising. Thinking of his wife, his baby and his church, he began running towards the city, while everyone else seemed to be heading in the opposite direction. Meanwhile, Mrs Nakamura managed to free herself and her children. They were unhurt, so she took them to Asano Park, the designated evacuation area. Everywhere fires were breaking out and she could hear cries for help from ruined buildings. By now, nearly all of Hiroshima's doctors were dead or injured, and only 100 out of 1,800 nurses were fit to work. At the Red Cross hospital Terufumi Sasaki was the only doctor unhurt, and casualties with dreadful burns were beginning to pour in. The Reverend Tanimoto found a tap still working in a ruined house, and he helped about thirty injured people who were begging for water. But as more and more appeared he was overwhelmed, and set off to Asano Park to see if he could find any members of his congregation. Fires, fanned by fierce winds, were closing in on the people who had taken refuge there. As the flames edged closer the crowd was forced towards the river; and some were pushed in and drowned. The pastor found a punt and used it to get some of the worst injured across the river, though when he took one woman by the hand her skin came off in huge pieces. After leaving the area, he found a medical aid station besieged by patients, and asked an army doctor why no one had come to Asano Park to help. Without looking up from the patient he was treating the doctor replied: 'The first duty is to take care of the slightly wounded . . . to save as many lives as possible. There is no hope for the badly wounded. They will die.'

The first official news came in a radio broadcast saying the city had 'suffered considerable damage . . . It is believed that a new type of bomb was used. Details are being investigated.' Everywhere in the ruins were messages on piles of debris – 'Sister, where are you?' or 'All safe and well at . . .' with an address. Years later, a schoolboy remembered seeing people with their skin 'peeling off', so red muscle was visible: 'Without exception they stretched their arms out in front of them and were walking very slowly, marching like ghosts.' A seven-year-old girl recalled sitting in the garden cleaning her brother's shoes when there was 'a bright green flash'. The house immediately collapsed, trapping her and her mother. Although her mother was slim and only five feet tall, she somehow found the strength to free herself then move heavy burning timbers and other debris to free her daughter. She tore her clothes to bandage the girl's injuries, then carried her through the ruins for a whole day, stepping over the dead and dying, trying to reach the outskirts of the city, where she hoped to find medical help. They saw many charred bodies of mothers who had instinctively thrown themselves on top of their children to protect them. Sometimes the children had survived, but with terrible burns. Eventually they reached an emergency dressing station in a school that was still smouldering. The next day soldiers started burning the bodies of the dead. More and more injured people kept appearing, and many of them died. The little girl contracted leukaemia.

Over the years, this and other consequences of radiation accounted for tens of thousands. The final death toll for Nagasaki was calculated at nearly 75,000; at Hiroshima it was at least 140,000. Today, what has become known as the A-bomb dome can still be seen – the remains of the Hiroshima Prefectural Industrial Promotion Hall, the closest building to the epicentre to survive in any form. It is now part of the Hiroshima Peace Memorial Park, but arguments still rage over whether the bombings were justified. In 2007, a furious row broke out when Japan's defence minister, Fumio Kyuma, said they 'couldn't be helped', and that through them the Americans believed they 'could prompt Japan's surrender'. Kyuma, who represented Nagasaki in the Japanese parliament, had to apologise for his comments and resign from the government.

# 11

## MURDER BY THE STATE

### · THE CONGO FREE STATE ·

For 23 years, a huge area of Africa, more than 76 times the size of Belgium, became the personal property of that country's king, Leopold II, a cousin of Queen Victoria. In 1877 Leopold paid Henry Morton Stanley, of 'Dr Livingstone, I presume' fame, to explore the Congo. Stanley managed to persuade local chiefs to provide land, labour or both to the king, so that by 1885 the 'Congo Free State' had been created. Wholly owned by the king, already one of the richest men in Europe, it represented one-thirteenth of the whole continent and had a population of perhaps thirty million. Leopold turned a third of it into a free trade zone in which European entrepreneurs were encouraged to buy monopoly leases on commodities like ivory, while the rest became his private domain. A tenth of the natives were effectively slaves, and others had to work part time for the authorities. They were not allowed to sell anything to anyone other than the government. They were also required to provide food for the Europeans and to deliver quotas of goods at fixed prices.

At first, the state wanted tens of thousands of porters, including children. An official described those who carried his luggage as 'a pile of poor devils, chained by the neck ... There were about a hundred of them, trembling and fearful before the overseer, who strolled by whirling a whip ... many were skeletons dried up like mummies.' The disciplinary instrument of choice, even for children, was the chicotte – a corkscrew whip made from hippopotamus hide – usually administered by Africans. A single blow left a permanent scar, and a sentence of 100 was not unusual, but was often fatal. Food was poor. One Belgian senator said porters received only a handful of rice and stinking dried fish. Many died 'along the journey, or, the journey over, headed off to die from overwork in their villages'. Of 300 porters conscripted on a 600-mile forced march in 1891, not one returned.

Leopold was initially disappointed with the proceeds from his acquisition, and at one point he offered to hand it over to the Belgian state. Then, in 1890 his fortunes were transformed, as the inflatable rubber tyre was invented. Soon rubber was also being used for hoses and tubing, and as insulation for cables and wiring. Exports from the Congo in 1897 were six times what they had been five years before. Wild vines from which rubber could be extracted grew everywhere, but the work was arduous, painful and dangerous. People had to stay in flooded forests for days on end, and climb high into the trees. An officer from Leopold's private army, the Force Publique, confided to his journal: 'The native doesn't like making rubber. He must be compelled to do it.' The Force, whose rank-and-file members were black, was much feared. The troops would burn any villages that were reluctant to supply forced labour. They flogged villagers, raped women and took them hostage. Their white officers, to ensure ammunition was not 'wasted' on hunting animals, required the soldiers to produce a human hand for each bullet they had used. So if a soldier had 'wasted' a bullet, he might need to cut off a living man's hand to get himself off the hook. Those soldiers who harvested most hands might get their term of service shortened. When a number of villages failed to deliver their rubber quota in 1894 one white official ordered drastic action: 'A hundred heads cut off, and there have been plenty of supplies at the station ever since.' On another occasion he made his men put ten natives in a net, then attach stones to it and throw it in the river. If another official found a leaf in a courtyard that women prisoners had been sweeping, he would order that a dozen be beheaded. If a path in a forest was not well maintained, he would have a child killed in the nearest village.

One woman told how virtually the whole of her village was marched off tied in groups of ten, with men and women separated. On the sixth day her husband could go no further, so the soldiers killed him. Many other men were also killed, while babies were thrown into the grass to die. One of the rubber companies working in the Congo reckoned that natives had to spend twenty-four days every month in the forest to satisfy the quota. When they slept there they risked being eaten by leopards. Once they had finished they might have to walk twenty miles or more to have their rubber weighed. Payment might be a few beads, or spoonfuls of salt. If they had cut their rubber with dirt or pebbles to make the quota, they might be forced to eat it. An entry from the diary of one Force Publique officer illustrates the routine brutality: 'A man from Baumaneh running through the forest shouting for his lost wife and child came too close to our camp and received a bullet from one of our sentries. They brought us his head . . . We burned the village.' Hundreds of thousands fled their homes. Soldiers retaliated by stealing animals and burning huts and crops. Villagers would abandon small children in case their cries gave away hiding places. Many starved to death.

An agent named Eugene Rommel was a terrifying procurer of forced labour. According to a Swedish missionary, he abducted schoolgirls to 'treat them in despicable ways' and imprisoned women when people refused to sell him goods below market prices, sometimes forcing them into prostitution. The missionary saw 700 women chained together and taken away. One said: 'Whether they cut off our heads or that of a chicken it is all the same to them.' Some chiefs took payment for providing forced labour, but others tried to resist. In 1893 one named Nzansu led a revolt and killed Rommel. There were also a series of mutinies by black soldiers, sometimes lasting several years. One group told a captured French priest how one white officer shot sixty soldiers because they refused to work on a Sunday.

Every so often, Leopold seemed to suffer a twinge of conscience, once declaring: 'These horrors must end or I will retire from the Congo.' But the mood soon passed. Eventually, though, his secret was revealed. In 1899 a British diplomat saw how the rubber quota was enforced. When the soldiers arrived in a village, he said, the inhabitants 'invariably bolted'. The soldiers 'commenced looting, taking all the chickens, grain etc. out of the houses'. Then they seized women who would be kept as hostages until the quota was delivered. Children and elders were often taken, too.

Once the rubber had been handed over, most of the women were returned, though some would have died by then from the harsh conditions and inadequate rations. Many more would have been raped.

A clerk named Edmond Morel worked at a Liverpool shipping company that had a lucrative cargo contract with the Free State. He began to realise that natives were being used as forced labour; it was 'legalised robbery enforced by violence'. Morel proved a skilled propagandist, and the British government sent Sir Roger Casement, then the British consul in Leopoldville, to investigate his claims. Casement found that the population at one mission station had fallen from 40,000 to 1,000. Sleeping sickness had played some part, but so had the forced labour regime. When the diplomat approached a village in his launch the natives would flee. Only once the missionaries had reassured them would they tell their terrible stories. Some said they were starving because they were forced to collect rubber and had no time to cultivate their own fields. Others were going hungry because they had handed over most of their food to the soldiers. One said a number of people had died in the forest – eaten by leopards or through hunger or exposure. 'We begged the white men to leave us alone, saying we could get no more rubber, but the white men and their soldiers said: "Go. You are only beasts yourselves. You are only meat."' When they failed to produce enough rubber, the soldiers returned: 'Many were shot. Some had their ears cut off; others were tied up with ropes around their necks and bodies and taken away.' An old man told Casement when the white men were dissatisfied with the yield they 'would put some of us in lines, one behind the other, and would shoot through all our bodies'.

In 1904 Casement produced a denunciation of the atrocities for the Foreign Office: 'Whole villages and districts I knew well and visited as flourishing communities in 1887 are today without a human being; others are reduced to a handful of sick or harassed creatures who say of the government: "Are the white men never going home? Is this to last for ever?"' The British newspapers reported his findings in a fury.

In a damage-limitation exercise the Congo Free State convicted a few low-ranking white officials and gave them short prison terms, but it was too late. By now, Leopold was a hate figure. Morel had caused a sensation with his photographs of Congolese natives with their hands cut off, so when the king's teenage mistress bore him a son with a deformed hand, *Punch* published a cartoon entitled 'Vengeance from on High', showing the monarch holding his son surrounded by Congolese corpses. Leopold was forced to set up his own commission of inquiry, and the following year it declared that there had been systematic abuse of human rights. Four years later the Belgian government took over the Congo, though Leopold was paid two million pounds in compensation, in addition to the fortune he had already salted away. He died the following year.

Casement, an Irish nationalist, later helped to run German guns to the rebels in his home island. He was hanged for treason in 1916. No tally was kept of African deaths in the Congo – they were not considered sufficiently important – but an official Belgian government commission in 1919 estimated that during the life of the Free State the population was reduced by about half.

## · THE ARMENIAN MASSACRES ·

'Who remembers the Armenians?' Hitler is supposed to have asked scornfully on the eve of his invasion of Poland. The failure of the victorious Allies in the First World War to call anyone to account for massacring this Christian minority in Turkey was said to have induced him to believe that he could literally get away with murder. Eighty years after the massacres, though, the answer to Hitler's question appeared to be: 'Quite a lot of people.' In 1994 three Turkish authors were prosecuted for translating a banned French text, *The Armenians: Story of a Genocide.* Twelve years later Orhan Pamuk, the first Turk to win the Nobel prize for literature, was prosecuted for insulting 'Turkish identity' after drawing attention to the killings, though the charges were later dropped, while the French National Assembly recommended it should be a criminal offence to deny the Armenians were victims of genocide. Then, in 2007, Hrant Dink, a Turkish journalist of Armenian descent, was shot dead outside his office in Istanbul. He had received a number of death threats after describing the mass killing as genocide. So what were these events that still provoked such fierce emotions nearly a century later?

By the end of the nineteenth century, there were nearly two million

Christian Armenians living in what was then the Ottoman Empire. They were treated as second-class citizens, and for centuries they had not been able to protect their property, their homes or their lives. Now some of them began demanding autonomy. Sultan Abdülhamid II, alarmed at the growth of separatist movements all over his decaying empire, tried to stir up the Armenians' neighbours, the Kurds, against them. In 1894 Turkish troops and Kurdish tribesmen killed thousands of them and burned their villages. Two years later Armenian militants seized the Ottoman Bank in Istanbul. In the mayhem that followed more than 50,000 Armenians were killed by Turkish mobs, apparently organised by government troops. Over the next few years the attacks continued. In 1900 Kurdish villagers working with the local Turkish military commander murdered up to 400 Armenians. When a group in one village took refuge in the church it was set on fire, killing all those inside. The Armenians rose in revolt in 1904, but Turkish troops and local Kurds suppressed the uprising, destroying a dozen villages and killing thousands of men, women and children. Five years later the so-called Young Turks seized power and converted the Ottoman Empire into a constitutional monarchy. For a time, some Armenians welcomed the change, but the faction that favoured equality for minorities lost out to a shadowy clique known as the Committee of Union and Progress, which effectively began to run the empire.

Russia's relations with its own Armenian minority had not always been happy – during the nineteenth century the tsars had closed hundreds of Armenian schools, libraries and newspaper offices, while in 1905 Muslim Tartars had attacked Armenian homes in Baku, Tiflis and Erevan. When revolutionary elements took the side of the Armenians, tsarist troops joined in on the Tartar side so that hundreds of Armenians were massacred and dozens of villages destroyed. But when the Ottoman Empire entered the First World War on the side of Germany and Austria, and began attacking Russia, the tsar tried to woo Turkey's Armenian minority, and Armenians began to hope that a Russian victory might mean independence. The Turks suffered a humiliating defeat, and their minister of war, Ismail Enver, tried to put the blame on the Armenians. The government's propaganda machine claimed they were planning to kill leading figures in the government in an uprising in Istanbul.

Massacres began, and by 19 April 1915 more than 50,000 Armenians had been murdered in Van province. They appealed to Germany and the United States for help, but to no avail. A brief respite came when Russian forces reached the town of Van and freed those who had been besieged for a month, but at Bitlis, a few miles away, 15,000 Armenians were killed in eight days, while Turkish troops murdered all but 100 of the 17,000 Armenians in the Black Sea port of Trebizond. Then, on 24 April, the Turkish authorities arrested 250 leading Armenians in Istanbul. Many would be killed.

A month later the government passed laws allowing it to deport Armenians and seize their property. Enver ordered that all Armenians in the Ottoman forces should be disarmed and assigned to labour battalions. Many were executed by Turkish soldiers or paramilitaries. Next, the government released thousands of criminals, many of them convicted murderers, to form a force to escort the Armenian deportees. These escorts allowed the Armenians to be robbed, raped and killed along the way, and often joined in themselves. The deportees were taken to more than twenty concentration camps in the deserts of Syria and Iraq, where tens of thousands died.

The American consul in Kharput said he had seen the bodies of nearly 10,000 Armenians dumped in ravines near Lake Göeljuk, in an area he referred to as the 'slaughterhouse province'. The USA, which had not yet entered the war, protested, but the Turks claimed they were 'retaliating against a pro-Russian fifth column'. The British writer and diplomat Gertrude Bell reported on 12,000 Armenians being guarded by Kurdish 'gendarmes' who were 'mere butchers; bands of them were publicly ordered to take parties of Armenians, of both sexes, to various destinations, but had secret instructions to destroy the males, children and old women'. Many caves were 'filled with corpses'. Germany was Turkey's ally, but even some Germans could not stomach what was happening. Armin Wegner, a military doctor, defied strict censorship and took hundreds of photographs of Armenians being deported and held in camps, which he smuggled out of the country. The head of Germany's diplomatic mission said in July 1915 that he believed the Turks were 'trying to exterminate the Armenian race' in the Ottoman Empire, while Major General Kress von Kressenstein, who was assisting the Ottoman Army, wrote that they were deliberately starving the Armenians.

Overall, during these years, it is estimated that 600,000 Armenians were massacred in Anatolia, at least 400,000 more died from the hardships and brutalities of the forced deportations, while another 200,000 were forcibly converted to Islam. Former US president Theodore Roosevelt called it 'the greatest crime of the war'. The Treaty of Sèvres signed between the Allies and the Turks in 1920 was supposed to give independence to Armenia, but Turkey's new leader, Kemal Ataturk, refused to accept it, and Armenia remains Turkish territory to this day, though the Russian Armenia won its independence in 1991. The treaty also required the Ottoman Empire to hand over those responsible for the massacres. Although there appeared to have been a systematic destruction of evidence in the Ottoman archives, a number of people were condemned to death in their absence, including Ismail Enver. He was killed in 1922 helping the Tajiks in an uprising against the new Soviet Union.


## · ADOLF HITLER ·

In the last months of the First World War, a twenty-nine-year-old German soldier, Corporal Adolf Hitler, was awarded the Iron Cross (First Class) for bravery. The officer who recommended the decoration was Captain Hugo Guttman, a Jew.

Hitler was born in Austria 29 years before. His dream of becoming an artist never came true, and after the war, he went to Munich and joined the National Socialist (or Nazi) Party, in which he took charge of propaganda. As early as 1919 he was writing that 'the removal of the Jews' was the 'final objective'. He became party leader in 1921, and served nine months in prison after a bungled attempt to seize power two years later. He used the time to write the first volume of *Mein Kampf*, expounding the idea that the German people were the saviours of the human race, and that their greatest enemies were Marxism and the Jews, describing them as 'a parasite within the nation'.

When the Great Depression made German business leaders nervous, they began funding Hitler. In the 1932 election the Nazis became the largest party in the Reichstag, and Hitler was installed as chancellor the following January. Within weeks he had begun setting up concentration camps, and by the end of 1933 at least 100,000 Germans were held in them or in Gestapo prisons. The prisoners were mainly members of the Social Democrat and Communist parties, priests, lawyers who had defended the wrong sort of clients, or Jewish shopkeepers and business-men, who had often been denounced by rivals for imaginary crimes. They were subjected to a brutal regime of forced labour, with sudden violent death a constant danger. Soon signs were appearing on German streets saying, 'Jews not wanted'. In 1934 Nazi stormtroopers marched into the village of Gunzenhausen, where nineteen Jewish families lived. Their leader dragged a woman through the streets by her hair and other Jews were beaten and whipped. The following day a seventy-five-year-old man was found stabbed and another hanged.

In August 1934, as Hitler took the title Führer, or leader, German vil-lages were competing to be 'free of Jews'. By September 1935, at least a quarter of all Jews had been sacked from their jobs, and that month the so-called Nuremberg Laws barred them from German citizenship, and banned marriage and sexual relations between Jews and Germans. Albert Einstein had already fled by then. He would play a crucial role in per-suading Germany's enemies to make an atomic bomb. After being arrested three times, Captain Hugo Guttman also eventually got away, but many foreign countries were unwelcoming. Nor did Germany have a monopoly on anti-Semitism. There was a spate of attacks on Jews in Poland in 1937.

When Hitler took over Austria in 1938, the Jews were immediately stripped of their rights to own property and to work; 30,000 were sent to German concentration camps, while as many as 10,000 are believed to have killed themselves. Then, on 28 October, 17,000 Polish Jews living in Germany were arrested. They were allowed to take only what they could carry, and many Germans happily helped themselves to whatever had been left behind. The Nazis took them to the river that formed part of the Polish–German border and forced them to cross it. The Polish border guards immediately sent them back. The stalemate continued for days in pouring rain, until the Polish government admitted the Jews to refugee camps, where the conditions were 'so bad that some actually tried to escape back into Germany and were shot'.

A seventeen-year-old named Herschel Grynszpan, who lived in Paris, was the son of one of those thrown out. When he heard from his family what had happened he protested several times to the German Embassy. They ignored him so he shot and fatally injured the third secretary. In response, Hitler ordered a massive attack on Jewish homes and synagogues in what became known as *Kristallnacht* – the Night of Broken Glass. More than 100 Jews were killed, and over the next few days 20,000 were arrested and sent to concentration camps. The Nazis then expelled Jews from old people's homes, hospitals and schools, and put public places put out of bounds. No foreign government protested.

Poland was home to more than two million Jews. When the Germans invaded in 1939 every army commander had a civilian working alongside him who was in charge of the 'racial extermination' programme. In the first days of the attack twenty Jews were killed in the border town of Wieruszow, but Nazi plans went far beyond Poland's Jews. After a discussion with Hitler's chief of staff, General Halder, one German officer wrote in his diary: 'It is the Führer's and Goering's intention to destroy and exterminate the Polish nation. More than that cannot be hinted at in writing.' In one diocese nearly a third of the Catholic priests were shot. About 25,000 civilians had been killed during the fighting, but thousands more were murdered by the SS. Any resistance brought ferocious reprisals. At Wawer, near Warsaw, two German soldiers were killed by two Polish criminals trying to avoid arrest. Two hours later the Germans rounded up 160 men and boys and shot them. On Polish Independence Day, 11 November, 350 people were murdered at Gdynia.

Meanwhile, in Germany on 20 September, Hitler signed a secret decree authorising the killing of any German found to be 'incurably ill'. Over the next two years more than 100,000, mainly babies and young children, would be gassed under this law. Similar policies were pursued in Poland. The Nazis also began a systematic programme of exterminating Poland's Jewish intellectuals and local leaders. They drove the rest into ghettos, allowing them to take with them only what they could carry on handcarts. A third of Warsaw's population was forced into one-fortieth of the city's area, with an average of nine people sharing each room. There was constant humiliation and brutality. Emanuel Ringelblum, who kept a diary of life in the ghetto, saw a German soldier spring out of his car and hit a boy on the head with an iron bar. The boy died. Hitler put the lawyer Dr Hans Frank in charge of much of Poland, with the instruction that the Poles were to become 'the slaves of the Greater German Empire'. It was also Nazi policy that 'their propagation must be curtailed in every possible way'.

Some Germans were distraught at what was happening. Major Helmuth Stieff wrote to his wife from Warsaw: 'It shames me to be a German!' Major General Friedrich Mieth, chief of staff of the German First Army, protested at the SS's mass executions which he said had 'besmirched' the honour of Germany. He was dismissed. Frank was more worried about the practicalities. He wrote in his diary: 'We cannot shoot 2.5 million Jews, neither can we poison them. We shall have to take steps, however, designed to extirpate them in some way – and this will be done.' In 1941, 15,000 people died of starvation in the ghettos of Warsaw and Lódz. If Jews left the ghetto to look for food, they were executed.

When the Nazis invaded Russia, murder moved up a gear, as SS special task forces followed the advancing forces and exterminated hundreds of thousands of Jews in the first few months, generally by taking them to the nearest ravine or wood and shooting them. Babies and small children would be flung alive into pits to join the dead bodies already there. One Austrian SS man wrote in his diary on the day they had murdered 100 Jews in a wood: 'We order the prisoners to dig their graves. Only two of them are crying, the others show courage. What can they all be thinking? . . . I don't feel the slightest stir of pity. That's how it is, and has got to be.' Overall, these *Einsatzgruppen* would kill more than a million people, most of them Jews. In September 1941, during the biggest massacre of the war to that point, nearly 34,000 Jews were ordered from Kiev and shot by the ravine at Babi Yar over the course of three days. German records were often very precise. The special task force at Kedainiai, Lithuania, reported on 28 August that it had killed '710 Jewish men, 767 Jewish women, 599 Jewish children'. The problem with this method of extermination was that even the most hardened Nazis could not keep it up for long, so the executioners had to be bribed with triple pay and long holidays, or kept half drunk. Heinrich Himmler attended one massacre but it turned his stomach, and thereafter he became a major advocate of murder by other means.

Back in June 1940 the German Ministry of the Interior had tried gassing mental patients: they would be taken to fake 'shower rooms' where they would sit on benches while poison gas was pumped in through the water pipes. And mobile gas vans had already been used to murder Serbian Jews in Belgrade. The euthanasia programme eventually provoked such disquiet in Germany that it was abandoned, but on 31 July 1941 Hermann Goering suggested gassing the Jews to Reinhard Heydrich, the head of the Reich Security Service. Tests using the commercial pesticide Zyklon-B were begun on Soviet prisoners of war at Auschwitz, which had been built as a punishment camp for Poles. It was guaranteed to kill in ten minutes.

By December, the first of the gas extermination camps had been opened in a forest near Chelmno in Poland, using vans. In addition to Jews, several thousand gypsies were killed there. The Nazis believed the latter carried disease and were 'unreliable elements who cannot be put to useful work'. The camp commandant boasted he could kill 1,000 people a day; and he did, until 300,000 had been murdered. The Germans ensured that 'all teeth, gold fillings and bridgework' were taken from the mouths of those they had murdered. The gold was taken to the Reichsbank, credited to the SS's account, and used to buy armaments from neutral countries like Spain, Portugal, Sweden and Turkey. German doctors and nurses who had worked in the euthanasia programme were now sent east to assist in the extermination of Jews. Dr Irmfried Erbel became commandant of Treblinka, where up to 900,000 Jews would die.

On 20 January 1942 Heydrich convened a conference of senior German officials at Wannsee, near Berlin, to address the 'final solution to the Jewish question'. SS Lt Col. Adolf Eichmann claimed Estonia was now 'free of Jews' and that the number in Lithuania had been cut from 135,000 to 34,000 in just six months. The conference minutes were studiedly imprecise, saying a 'possible solution' was 'evacuation to the East'. It was decided that Polish Jews should be told they were going to be resettled in the East, prior to transporting them to the death camps. Until then, most Nazi prisoners had been sent to labour camps, where they would toil for a few months until they dropped dead or were killed because they could not work any more. Some of these were near big factories, run by German industrial giants, like the one next to Auschwitz operated by IG Farben. Now, five death camps would receive specially designed gas chambers. With the help of Ukrainian and Latvian collaborators and prisoners of war, a few Germans would be able to kill tens of thousands of prisoners each month, without the psychological problems the mass shootings had caused. Goebbels considered there was 'a life and death struggle between the Aryan race and the Jewish bacillus'. He feared 'later generations' would not have the 'willpower' for the job: 'The task we are assuming today will be an advantage and a boon to our descendants.'

Jews arrived at Auschwitz from all over Europe in squalid cattle trucks. Those who did not die on the journey would be split up on arrival into those fit to work and those deemed unfit. Their bundles and suitcases were taken from them, and anything of value systematically removed. The unfit would be killed at once in a gas chamber – a fate that befell more than half of those who arrived. The fit ones were forced to work in the camp or the surrounding areas in harsh conditions that killed hundreds of thousands.

The Italian-Jewish writer Primo Levi gave a vivid account of the journey to Auschwitz, where he arrived in February 1944 after being captured fighting with Italian partisans. He was locked in a truck for four days: 'Through the slit, known and unknown names of Austrian cities, Salzburg, Vienna, then Czech, finally Polish names. On the evening of the fourth day the cold became intense.' Then the train stopped, seemingly in the middle of nowhere, and the door opened: 'the dark echoed with outlandish orders in that curt, barbaric barking of Germans in command'. They were told to leave their luggage by the train and SS men 'with faces of stone' interrogated them: '"How old? Healthy or ill?" And on the basis of that reply they pointed in two different directions.' Their manner, though, was reassuring. If someone asked about their luggage, they would be told 'luggage afterwards'. If a husband did not want to leave his wife, they were informed they would be 'together again afterwards', although a man who took too long saying goodbye to his fiancée was knocked to the ground with a single blow. In less than ten minutes all ninety-six fit men had been collected in a group. They were joined by twenty-nine women. Of the others on the train, none was alive two days later. As time went on, the Germans did not even bother to assess fitness. Those who exited on one side of the wagon went to work; those on the other were consigned to the gas chambers.

On 27 May 1942 Heydrich was assassinated in Czechoslovakia. Fearsome reprisals followed, including the destruction of two Czech villages, apparently selected at random. Every inhabitant was either killed or sent to a concentration camp. In December Allied governments issued a solemn condemnation of the mass murder of Jews. Two weeks later Himmler announced that more than 360,000 had been killed over the previous four months. In January 1943 the Jews of the Warsaw ghetto drove off Nazi deportation squads, but then they had to try to resist German machine-guns, heavy artillery and flame-throwers with pistols and Molotov cocktails. The revolt did not attract the support of other Poles, and nearly all the 50,000 Jews who survived were sent to their deaths in the camps. As the tide of war turned, the first German war criminals were put on trial in the Soviet Union, and in October 1943 the Allies set up a War Crimes Commission, hoping it might give the Nazis pause. It did not.

The grand design had been to settle Germans in Russia, and, as Hitler put it, 'treat the natives as redskins'. The defeated people would be denied any education: 'The least of our stable lads must be superior to any native.' Now, facing defeat, the Germans became even more murderous. Over thousands of square miles of Russia, they destroyed everything they could – towns, villages, buildings, machinery, railways, animals, people. In 1943, the Germans burned down more than 1,000 Greek villages in a year, and killed up to 10,000 civilians. Those under occupation, though, seemed to grow more adept at defying them. By the autumn of 1943, 7,000 Danish Jews had been spirited away to neutral Sweden by fishermen. Among them was the scientist Niels Bohr, who would work on the atomic bomb project in America.

In six weeks during 1944 more than a quarter of a million Hungarian Jews were gassed at Auschwitz. Four Jewish prisoners escaped and sent a plea to the Allies to bomb the railway line to the camp. This could only be achieved by US bombers in daylight, and the Americans rejected the idea as being too dangerous. But Churchill wanted something done, so the USAF bombed Budapest instead, and dropped leaflets warning that 'all those responsible' for carrying out orders to persecute the Jews would be punished. The Hungarian government told the Nazis they must stop; and with no troops available to enforce their will, they did, saving perhaps 100,000 lives. But some on the Allied side felt that not enough was being done to disrupt the Nazi extermination programme. An internal US Treasury memo in January 1944 complained about 'acquiescence to the murder of the European Jews'.

In July Soviet troops reached the Majdanek concentration camp near Lublin, where hundreds of thousands of Poles, Soviet prisoners and Jews had been murdered. Photographs of the gas chamber, the corpses and the crematorium were wired all over the world. The Russians hanged four SS men and two guards on a gallows at the camp, and an estimated 150,000 came out from the town to watch. The same month, Stalin held his forces back as the Poles of Warsaw rose against the Germans, allowing them to be defeated and massacred. When Warsaw was eventually liberated by the Soviets, of half a million Jews who had been living there before the war, only 200 remained. By now, the Germans were falling back everywhere, but the search for Jews never ended. Anne Frank was discovered in her Amsterdam hideout on 4 August. She would die in Belsen.

Hitler had imitators in other countries. When a fascist regime came to power in Romania hundreds of Jews were murdered in the streets of Bucharest by members of the Iron Guard terror organisation. And in a brief interval between the Russians leaving Lithuania and the German Army arriving, locals massacred more than 2,000 Jews. Norwegians, Swedes, Danes, Dutch and Belgians swelled the ranks of the SS.

There was also courageous resistance and obstruction, though. In 1942 Admiral Wilhelm Canaris, a senior German intelligence official, saved the lives of fourteen German Jews by sending them to Switzerland on the pretext that they were being employed as counter-intelligence operatives. It had taken twelve months of careful planning. The same year, the industrialist Oskar Schindler helped to save more than 1,000 Jews in Cracow by taking them into his factory. In Berlin Otto Weidt, who owned a small brush factory, employed several hundred blind Jews and successfully insisted that their work was vital to the German war effort.

Fearing Soviet forces would come across Auschwitz, Himmler ordered the whole camp to be dismantled. Of the hundreds of thousands of remaining prisoners, some were murdered. Others were moved west in freezing railway wagons, dying by the thousand, or were shot as they failed to keep up on forced marches, or were killed in Allied air raids, or perished in the camps to which they were sent. On 25 January 1945, with the Russians a few miles away, the SS shot 350 Jews at Auschwitz. Then they blew up the remaining gas chamber and the crematorium and left. By then, the camp had killed more than a million people. The next day the Russians entered to find about 6,000 Jews and 1,200 Poles. In April American troops entered Buchenwald and discovered 77,000 starving prisoners. The British reached Belsen at around the same time to find 30,000 prisoners living alongside 35,000 unburied corpses. Despite all the efforts of the liberators, 300 people a day died for the next week from starvation and typhus.

On 30 April Hitler shot himself. In his final testament he declared the Jews were 'the real guilty party in this murderous struggle'. Three days after his death SS men, Hitler Youth members and German marines killed 500 Jewish women who had survived Stutthof concentration camp.

In November 1945 war crimes trials began at Nuremberg, the site of many Nazi Party rallies. There was no building of sufficient size left in Berlin. Some leading Nazis – such as Goebbels, Himmler and Hitler himself – had already escaped justice by suicide, while Goering cheated the hangman by swallowing poison in his cell, but ten of the defendants were executed. Those who had committed war crimes in a single country could be tried and punished there, and there were further rounds of trials, but as Britain and America's former ally, the Soviet Union, turned into the new enemy, prosecuting war criminals became a lesser priority. In 1951 Oswald Pohl was hanged for his role in the concentration camps, as was Otto Ohlendorf for running death squads that had murdered 90,000 people in Russia. But the US High Command in Germany issued an amnesty to all generals and all convicted industrialists who had used slave labour. Still, in some countries, the hunt continued. In 1960 Eichmann was kidnapped in South America and taken to Israel, where he was tried and executed. And as late as 1998 Maurice Papon, who had been an administrator in German-occupied France, was found guilty of handing over more than 1,500 Bordeaux Jews to the Nazis. He was sentenced to ten years in jail, though he served fewer than three.

It is believed that up to seven million people died in the Nazi death and concentration camps from exhaustion, starvation, epidemics, medical experiments or murder. About half of Belgium's Jews and three-quarters of the Netherlands' were killed. Although terrible things happened to the Jews in Vichy France, where the race laws were in some respects even more strict than those in Germany, three-quarters of French Jews survived. On the other hand, a quarter of a million potential 'troublemakers' were deported to concentration camps, and only 35,000 of them returned after the war. The Germans also murdered an estimated 30,000 French hostages, often in retaliation for resistance activity. Until Italy tried to change sides and German forces occupied the country, Jews fared better under the Fascist regime than they did in most parts of occupied Europe because Mussolini declined to participate in the Holocaust. In contrast, of Romania's three-quarters of a million Jews, about two-thirds were murdered, mainly by the Romanian fascists themselves. Altogether, about 200,000 gypsies were also exterminated.

Overall, through genocide, the killing of hostages, reprisal raids, forced labour, 'euthanasia', medical experiments, starvation and other privations, some estimate the Nazis killed perhaps twenty million people. How did this happen? Did the German people turn into monsters for more than a decade? Primo Levi thought the answer was more mundane: 'Monsters exist, but they are too few in number to be really dangerous. More dangerous are the functionaries ready to believe and to act without asking questions.'

Fewer than 100,000 Jews survived the concentration camps. When they tried to return to their homes many found they had been taken over by other people and some were brutally attacked or killed, including more than 1,500 in Poland.


## · JOSEPH STALIN ·

In January 1923, a month after his second stroke, Lenin, the maker of the Bolshevik Revolution, urged his colleagues to sack the Soviet Communist Party's general secretary, Joseph Stalin, saying he would mount a major attack on him at the party congress in April. It was never delivered. Lenin suffered his third stroke on 9 March and would not recover. He died the following January. Two leading lights in the party, Grigoriy Zinoviev and Lev Kamenev, who were anxious to stop Leon Trotsky becoming leader, now joined forces with Stalin, and helped keep Lenin's views secret. Once his position was secure, Stalin broke with Zinoviev and Kamenev.

He had been born Joseph Dzhugashvili in Georgia in 1879, the son of a poor, heavy-drinking cobbler, who beat him savagely. For a time the young man studied at a seminary, but he started reading Karl Marx and other forbidden communist texts, and was expelled in 1899. Short, stocky, fierce-eyed and scarred by the smallpox he had suffered as a child, he was also strong, had prodigious willpower and patience, and was able to disguise his feelings. In the early 1900s he adopted the name Stalin – 'Man of Steel'.

Georgia had a tradition of blood feuds, and Stalin would be implacable against those who offended him. In the years up to 1913 he was arrested seven times for revolutionary activity and repeatedly imprisoned or sent into exile, but the mildness of the sentences and the ease with which he kept escaping led some to believe that he was a tsarist agent. He was looked down on by more intellectual rivals, like Trotsky and Zinoviev, but he outmanoeuvred them all to emerge as Lenin's successor, and for a quarter of a century he exercised virtually absolute power in the Soviet Union.

In 1928, as part of his first Five-Year Plan, Stalin decided to reorganise agriculture along communist principles, which meant getting twenty-five million rural households to turn over their land and livestock to the state and become workers on huge collective farms. The idea was that tractors would operate in vast fields, doubling the grain yield. More milk, butter and cheese would also be produced, while peasants would live in skyscrapers in 'agro-towns' and eat in massive communal dining rooms. There would be no more wages; instead, points would be awarded by the collective farms. When the government issued invitations to join this rural utopia, the response was a deafening silence. So the following year thousands of Soviet officials were sent into the countryside to speed things up, but rebellious villagers could only be dragooned into the collective farms at gunpoint, and even then they contributed as little as they could – slaughtering livestock, smashing tools and burning crops. In 1929 there were thirty-four million horses in Russia; by 1933, there were less than half that number. Nearly half of the cattle were lost, too, while the number of sheep fell by three-quarters.

About 1.8 million recalcitrant peasants were transported with their families to the Urals, Central Asia and Siberia. Up to a fifth died in cattle trucks or on forced marches. The writer Vladimir Tendryakov, then a child, saw some of them in the station square of Vokhrovo in northern Russia. They 'wandered along the dusty, sordid alleyways, dragging drop-sied legs, elephantine and bloodlessly blue, and plucked at every passer-by, begging with dog-like eyes'. They found little charity among people who had been queuing all night for bread themselves. Every morning the hospital stable boy came and piled up his cart with those who had died during the night.

Worst hit was the Ukraine, the most fertile region of the Soviet Union, which supplied about half its grain. Every year the state took a proportion of what the peasants produced. For 1932, it was planned to be nearly thirty million tons out of an expected harvest of just over ninety million. But with a drought compounding the shambles of collectivisa-tion, the harvest was less than sixty million tons and the state was able to seize less than nineteen million. That still meant the peasants had a third less grain than normal. On 7 August Stalin's government decreed that the death penalty could be applied to anyone found guilty of theft of public property, and soon scapegoats were found to blame for the disappoint-ing grain deliveries. By January 1933, 103,000 people had been convicted of stealing from the state. Many peasants were among the 5,000 sen-tenced to death and the 26,000 given ten years in jail. Meanwhile, on 9 November 1932, the government said that if there was no grain in Ukrainian villages, then other food should be seized. 'Shock brigades' enforced the new rules, and were told not to concern themselves with whether the peasants had enough grain to survive or enough seed to plant for the following year.

Lev Kopelev, at the time a loyal Bolshevik but later a dissident, was one of those who went searching for 'hidden' grain, poking the earth with an iron rod, emptying food stores, 'stopping my ears to the children's crying and the women's wails. For I was convinced that I was accomplishing the transformation of the countryside.' In the 'terrible' spring of 1933 he saw people dying of hunger everywhere: 'with distended bellies, turning blue, still breathing but with vacant, lifeless eyes. And corpses – corpses in ragged sheepskin coats and cheap felt boots; corpses in peasant huts, in the melting snow.' Peasants ate mice, rats, sparrows, ants and earthworms, ground bones into flour, or cut up skins and fur to make 'noodles'. The American communist Fred Beal was horrified: 'I had never dreamed that Communists could stoop so low as to round up hungry people, load them upon trucks or trains, and ship them to some wasteland in order that they might die there.' In Kharkov, then capital of the Ukraine, the Italian consul reported that human meat was being sold and that people were killing and eating their children.

At first, the government denied there was a famine and closed the region to foreign journalists, while peasants were forbidden to leave their villages. Many tried all the same. The writer Victor Serge saw railway stations full of 'filthy crowds . . . They are chased out, they return without money or tickets . . . They are silent and passive. Where are they going? Just in search of bread, or potatoes.' Some left their babies in stations, hoping someone would pick them up and take them to an orphanage. Doctors were forbidden to mention starvation as a cause of death, and any Soviet official brave enough to report truthfully on what was happening in the countryside risked being branded a 'right opportunist capitulator'. In Kharkov the police were removing 250 corpses every morning from the station, but when the secretary of the city's provincial committee tried to alert a closed party meeting in Moscow, Stalin cut him short: 'It seems that you are a good storyteller, you've made up such a fable about famine, thinking to frighten us, but it won't work. Wouldn't it be better for you to leave your post . . . and join the Writers' Union? Then you can write your fables and fools will read them.'

In spite of the blackout, though, news did begin to leak. The former Russian chargé d'affaires in Britain, E. Sabline, heard from a correspondent in Armenia: 'We receive only 100 grams of bread daily, which is uneatable . . . Nothing can save us; we must die soon. Scores of helpless people are dying in the streets every day.' Another man lamented: 'Today, my two little children died of starvation. I, myself, am doomed to die, and will have to follow soon.' Sabline castigated Stalin's government for refusing to ask for help from abroad. The Politburo did try to provide some emergency supplies in the first half of 1933, but they were wholly inadequate.

It was not only Ukrainians who suffered in this ideological experiment. Nomadic tribes like the Kazakhs were forced to settle down. Three-quarters of their cattle died, along with more than four-fifths of their horses and nearly all of their sheep. According to some estimates, perhaps one in four Kazakhs themselves died too. But while the people starved, the Soviet Union continued to export grain.

How many people perished in the famine of 1932–3? The short answer was given later by Stalin's successor, Nikita Khrushchev: 'No one was keeping count.' An official Russian estimate in 1990 put the number at four million, but it is widely believed to have been many more. In 2003 the Ukrainian parliament declared the famine an act of genocide deliberately organised by the Soviet Union, and more than twenty other countries have delivered a similar denunciation.

After 1934, Stalin was forced to ease back on the dogma, allowing each household to have a small plot on which to grow vegetables and raise a few animals, reckoning this was the only way in which the country could be fed. At the same time, alarmed by the revival of nationalism in the USSR he launched an attack on Ukrainian culture, with mass imprisonment and execution of intellectuals, writers and artists, 'eliminating' an estimated four-fifths of the cultural elite.

Paranoia among the Soviet leadership was understandable. After the revolution, various foreign powers, including Britain, had supported their enemies in a brutal civil war, and Lenin had been seriously injured in an assassination attempt in 1918. In the aftermath, the Bolsheviks had rounded up real and imagined opponents of the regime and executed 500 in a single day in Petrograd (St Petersburg). Stalin, though, took it to extremes, with an orgy of purges and show trials. The first Five-Year Plan ran into problems in industry as well as agriculture, so more scapegoats had to be found. The first show trial was held in 1928, with completely fabricated charges that engineers had sabotaged coal mines at Shakhty. Banners demanding 'Death to the Wreckers' hung from many public buildings. There was the edifying spectacle of the twelve-year-old son of one of the accused demanding the death penalty for his father. Confessions were shamelessly forced from the defendants, and five were executed. From then on, numerous industrial managers found themselves intimidated into confessing to imaginary crimes.

By the end of 1933, Stalin had purged more than 1,000 Red Army officers, and had thrown more than a million people out of the Communist Party. On 1 December 1934 a Politburo member and potential rival, Sergei Kirov, was assassinated in Leningrad (St Petersburg). The authorities said it was the work of Stalin's disgraced former colleagues, Kamenev, Zinoviev and Trotsky. Kirov was made a national hero and a plethora of things were named after him, including the Kirov Ballet, but the speed with which Stalin moved to eliminate his close associates as well as the assassin made some believe he had a hand in the murder. Whatever the truth, he quickly used it as an excuse to beef up anti-terrorism laws. In future, those accused of 'planning or carrying out terrorist acts' would have no right to defence counsel or appeal.

Those at the top of the party hierarchy were now in grave danger. Of 1,225 delegates at the 17th Party Congress in 1934, 1,108 were arrested within a year, and most died under interrogation or in the slave labour camps of Siberia. By 1936, there were five million people in the gulags (a Russian acronym for 'Chief Administration of Corrective Labour Camps'). One was the writer Ivan Uksusov. At Toblosk he saw a column of more than 100 people, including old men, women and children, who had been forced to walk 200 miles. As the prisoners came to a stream a woman bent down and started taking gulps of water. A guard dog pounced on her and ripped off one of her breasts. She was left to die. General Dmitri Volkogonov discovered what was happening in his home village of Agul in Siberia, near which there were a number of camps, from local people who kept seeing long columns of exhausted people arriving on foot from the railway, sixty miles away. Initially, they could not understand how the camps could accommodate so many prisoners. Then they saw long ditches appearing outside, where 'the corpses of dead prisoners would be taken on carts or sleighs, covered with tarpaulins, and buried at night'. Some had been shot; others had died from the appalling hardships in the camps. All over the most inhospitable parts of the Soviet Union, inmates would be sent to build canals or railways, or to work in mines. Food was inadequate, and summary executions frequent. Two hundred thousand are estimated to have died digging the White Sea–Baltic canal alone.

Among the many charged after Kirov's death were Stalin's former sponsors Zinoviev and Kamenev. Tried in secret, they denied any responsibility, but admitted that Kirov's assassin might have drawn inspiration from criticisms of the leader they had once made. That was enough. Kamenev got five years' penal servitude, and Zinoviev ten. It was only thanks to a direct appeal from Lenin's widow that they escaped the death penalty, but they were both executed the following year anyway. From now on, those suspected in any way, along with their families, were deported to Siberia. Leading generals, Politburo members and ambassadors were all put on trial. They would be charged with trying to assassinate Stalin, attempting to restore capitalism, plotting to poison masses of Russian workers, or entering into secret agreements with the Nazis. Many were tried in secret or executed without trial, but any who did appear in public would praise Stalin and confess their sins. Often they had been tortured or were afraid of the consequences for their families if they refused to cooperate, particularly when the age limit for the death penalty was reduced to twelve. When a general refused to sit in judgement on his colleagues he was arrested, his wife was sent to a labour camp where she died, and his daughter was imprisoned as a 'socially dangerous element'. By then, the general had shot himself. Apart from the prisoners' confessions, no other evidence was produced at the trials. Sometimes these confessions were demonstrably ludicrous, as when three defendants said they had met Trotsky in a Copenhagen hotel that had closed down years before. It made no difference to the proceedings. The prosecutor, Andrey Vyshinsky, would invariably sum up with fearful curses: 'Shoot the mad dogs! Mad fascist police dogs! Despicable rotten dregs of humanity!'

In the army perhaps 20,000 of 80,000 officers were purged, and thousands of them were shot. Stalin also liquidated two of the police chiefs who had arrested so many people on his behalf. Then, in 1937, the Politburo told the commandants of all labour camps that they had to identify a quota – set at 28 per cent – of their prisoners who were conducting anti-state agitation in the camps. Nearly 73,000 of those denounced were shot; the rest had their sentences increased by up to ten years. From exile in Mexico City, Trotsky saw what was happening. 'Stalin', he said, 'is like a man who wants to quench his thirst with salt water.' An assassin dispatched by the Georgian would kill him with an ice-pick in 1940.

While many were executed for making imaginary deals with Hitler, Stalin concluded a real one, and used it to overrun eastern Poland, the Baltic states and other territories. Just like the Nazis, the Soviets started deporting and massacring the inhabitants, and even when the USSR had its back to the wall during the Nazi invasion Stalin continued his purges. On 5 September 1941 he signed a death warrant for 170 people, including a seventy-three-year-old former Soviet ambassador. As in most of the territories Germany conquered, some people in the Soviet Union did collaborate with the Nazis, sometimes for ideological reasons, sometimes for self-preservation, so Stalin brutally deported many national groups, like the Chechens and the Ingush, whom he feared might rise against him. He sent up to 10,000 Poles who had been resisting the Nazis to labour camps because they were loyal to the Free Polish government in London. Then, in the dying days of the war, he launched a new purge of army officers accused of not being sufficiently enthusiastic about communism. Among them was Captain Alexander Solzhenitsyn, who was sentenced to eight years' hard labour. Later he would win the Nobel prize for books such as *One Day in the Life of Ivan Denisovich*, which exposed the horrors of Stalin's regime.

After the war, the Allies agreed to repatriate Soviet citizens found in Nazi territory. Most went willingly, but about 50,000 had to be forced. These were generally people who had worn German uniforms, often in quite humble occupations, and their families. When the British deported a group of Cossacks to Odessa the authorities would not allow any to come ashore on a stretcher, and even the dying were forced to carry their own bags. Fifteen minutes after they had been handed over, the sound of machine-gun fire rang out.

Stalin now imposed client communist regimes on the peoples of

Eastern Europe, and exported persecution to his new empire. In just four days in March 1949 special trains carried off 43,000 Latvian citizens to Siberia, part of an operation in which nearly 100,000 people were deported from the Baltic republics to join five million others in the camps. The most trivial matter could consign you to this terrible fate. One woman, whose son was serving with the Red Army in Vienna, was sentenced to ten years' hard labour for telling fellow shoppers in a Moscow milk queue that people in the West could get milk without queuing.

One day in 1950 former deputy premier Nikolai Voznesensky vanished. Khrushchev and a colleague tried to intercede for him, but Stalin snarled: 'Voznesensky has been unmasked as an enemy of the people; he has been shot this very morning. Are you telling me that you, too, are enemies of the people?' They beat a hasty retreat. Khrushchev said that in his later years Stalin's 'persecution mania reached terrifying dimensions' as he demanded of people: 'Why are your eyes so shifty today?' or 'Why are you avoiding looking me directly in the eyes?' He also claimed Stalin would personally supervise the interrogation and beating of prisoners.

On 3 January 1953 nine professors of medicine, mostly Jews and all serving as personal physicians to leading figures in the Kremlin, were denounced as agents of Britain and America, on whose orders they had allegedly murdered top communists. Many feared this would be the launch pad for yet another purge, but Stalin died two months later, before it could happen, raising suspicions that he had been helped on his way. It is impossible to say how many he had killed by then, but the figure might be as high as thirty million.

## · MAO ZEDONG ·

The third great tyrant of the twentieth century was Mao Zedong, and he may have been the greatest killer of all. He was born in 1893 in Hunan province, the son of a peasant who had come up in the world and become a rather prosperous farmer and grain dealer. Mao's father wanted him to work on the farm, but at the age of thirteen the boy ran away to continue his schooling. In October 1911 rebellion against the

Manchu dynasty erupted in Hunan's capital, Changsha, where he was studying, and he spent six months as a soldier in the Nationalist army until the Chinese Republic was proclaimed in the spring of 1912. Nine years later he was converted to communism, but he stayed loyal to the Nationalists until their leader, Chiang Kai-shek, broke with the Communist Party and massacred many of its members, including Mao's first wife.

In 1927 Mao led a few hundred peasants into the mountains of Jiangxi province and began the so-called People's War against the Nationalists. It was the beginning of a painful journey through the political wilderness that would last twenty-two years. During those two decades, he deserted his second wife, who had shared many hardships despite being seriously ill, and married a well-known film actress and socialite, Jiang Qing. By the time the Communists assumed power in 1949, he was party leader.

Back in 1927, Mao had said: 'We must create a short reign of terror in all parts of the countryside. A revolution is not like a dinner party.' The communists encouraged poor peasants to kill richer ones, while activists who were not sufficiently ruthless knew they might be killed themselves. They seized one wealthy landowner who had helped them against the Japanese, put an iron ring through his nose, then made his son lead him around the streets on a rope. In Henan rich peasants were nailed to the walls of buildings or buried up to their necks before having their brains smashed out. Altogether, up to five million landlords may have been killed.

On assuming power in 1949, the Communists' policy was that land should be given to those who worked it. Mao wanted the peasants them-selves to take the lead; but, just to make sure, government teams were sent out to 'educate' them. All peasants had to submit themselves for clas-sification. If they were found to be rich or a landlord, they would be allowed to keep only enough land to earn a living. The rest they would have to donate to those classified as poor peasants or landless labourers. Middle peasants would be allowed to keep all their land and property. A similar policy was pursued in the cities, with only the richest bourgeois families being dispossessed, while smaller entrepreneurs were allowed to stay in business. In areas where the Communists were strong, like the

north-east, peasants attacked landlords with gusto, and about two million were killed before the party cooled things down to avoid alienating
the middle classes. In other parts of the countryside, though, people
were reluctant to classify their neighbours as landlords or rich farmers,
so not enough land was liberated for redistribution. Mao also began to
wonder whether giving everyone their own plot of land was a good way
of developing socialism. Increasingly, he felt that collectivisation was the
only means by which the countryside would be able to produce enough
food to feed itself and the rapidly growing towns and cities.

Many peasants hated this idea, though, and they started slaughtering
their farm animals before the collectives could appropriate them. Those
that were handed over were often neglected and worked to death, as no
one felt responsible for them. In Hebei province it was calculated that
nearly a quarter of all working animals had died in 1956, and the following year the first secretary of the Henan Communist Party complained
that there were so few that women were having to yolk themselves to
ploughs. By then, some of Mao's senior colleagues had begun to order
the dissolution of thousands of cooperatives.

Feeling insecure, Mao championed freedom of speech – 'Let a
Hundred Flowers Bloom, a Hundred Schools of Thought Contend'. This
initiative was launched just as a poor harvest, and the effects of collectivisation, brought the first food shortages since the revolution, with
people dying of starvation in a number of provinces, and those who
spoke up kept saying the wrong things – like suggesting Mao should
resign. He responded by arresting half a million people. Students and
party members would be sent for 're-education' – which entailed hard
manual work to help them see things more clearly.

Then, in May 1958, Mao launched the 'Great Leap Forward' – his ver-
sion of Stalin's Five-Year Plan. It made things even worse in the
countryside, and Mao grew very worried about his position in the party,
so he started to build an alternative power base in the People's
Liberation Army. At the same time he denounced the emergence of
'new bourgeois elements' in the Communist Party, the bureaucracy and
the technical and artistic elite, saying they were putting their interests
above those of the masses. He foresaw a long 'and sometimes even violent class struggle'.

China's grain output was much lower than Russia's, and its risk of famine higher. Khrushchev warned Mao not to repeat the Soviet Union's mistakes, but he decided the Chinese leader 'thought of himself as a man brought by God to do God's bidding'. Under the Great Leap Forward cooperatives and collective farms were no longer sufficiently radical for Mao. Using local activists to bypass the party's central authority, he forbade peasants from cultivating any private land and amalgamated them into communes of up to 30,000 people, which would pool all private property and reward people according to their needs rather than what they did. For many peasants, this removed any incentive to work hard. Everyone would eat food from the communal kitchens, taking as much as they liked, while families were broken up, with men and women sent to separate dormitories and children raised in crèches. Official propaganda boasted that the family had been 'shattered for all time . . . the dearest people in the world are our parents, yet they cannot be compared to Chairman Mao and the Communist Party'.

Every county in China was ordered to build a giant reservoir, even if it meant evicting hundreds of thousands of people, some of whom starved to death. Then many of the dams collapsed because of shoddy construction, which led to devastating floods (see Chapter 4). Mao decided iron and steel production would transform China into a modern nation, so millions of peasants were ordered to stop tending fields and instead work to meet a steel production quota that was identical for every commune, regardless of resources. So the crops rotted, as 'backyard furnaces' fuelled by firewood sprang up, though often they did no more than melt down bicycles, bedsteads, pots and pans, and even agricultural implements. The steel they made was unusable. Peng Dehuai, the only government minister who came from genuine peasant stock, was horrified. In one village he asked the peasants: 'Hasn't any one of you given a thought to what you will eat next year if you don't bring in the crops? You're never going to be able to eat steel.' He was sacked. Other madcap schemes included planting seeds more closely together, which led to them choking each other, trying to squeeze more harvests out of the land, which exhausted it, and killing all the birds, which resulted in more insects and bugs attacking crops.

Mao's theories brought the same result as Stalin's – starvation. There was terrible weather in 1959–60, with more than half of all cultivated land hit by droughts, floods or both. In 1955, 170 million tons of grain had been produced; in 1960, the figure was 143 million tons. In a small village in normally fertile Henan one woman recalled seeing dozens of corpses lying unburied in the fields, while the living crawled among them, trying to find grass seeds to eat, or squatted in the mud, hunting for frogs. People would cut flesh from corpses to eat. An eerie silence reigned. The oxen had died, the dogs had been eaten, the chickens and ducks confiscated by the party because the village had failed to produce enough grain, and there were no babies crying because no woman had given birth for three years. Those who had been labelled rich peasants were given the least rations. Then, when they became too weak to work, they received nothing, so they died first. Some peasants hid grain at the risk of a savage beating, or worse, from party activists. The widow of one rich peasant was buried alive with her children. Of 300 people in the village, only 80 survived.

The famine came just as the delegation of powers to the communes undermined China's centralised planning and distribution system. Now those communes with enough food stockpiled it instead of allowing it to be sent to those in need. Not that the government knew what was happening. The State Statistical Bureau had been dismantled and replaced by 'good news reporting stations', and there was fierce competition between local activists to be the most Maoist, so they grossly inflated harvest figures and trumpeted many other fake achievements. The New China News Agency said peasants were growing pumpkins weighing ten stones, while cows had been crossed with pigs. Any local activist tempted to tell the truth was told to give Mao the story he wanted to hear instead. The leader's arch crony, Chen Boda, wanted to abolish money because he reckoned there was such plenty everything could be free. Peasants were urged to eat as much as they could, and in some villages they are said to have polished off rice that should have lasted six months in twenty days as they competed with each other to see who could devour most.

While his people starved, Mao cut food imports and doubled exports, handing out free grain to North Korea, Vietnam and Albania.

He refused to believe Chinese people were dying, and would not open up the state granaries because he thought the peasants must be hoarding grain. As real harvests shrank, the phantom harvests grew, with Sichuan declaring that its fields were producing ten times their normal yield. But the reality could not be hidden for ever, and peasants had to be encouraged to cultivate private plots again. Still, the famine continued. The 1959 grain harvest was at least thirty million tons lower than 1958's, but officials reported it was much higher, so more was taken from the villages, which often lost their whole harvest. Often the party activists simply took everything they could find, and the food searches became more brutal, with peasants beaten or tortured to death. Sometimes, activists would plant 'hidden' grain which they then 'found'. Some smashed cooking pots so the peasants would not even be able to make grass soup.

One local party secretary let 200 people starve to death, then sent the grain he had saved to the authorities. A grain relief train was turned back by a local official who was sure it had been sent as a trick, and that if he accepted it, he would be punished. Now the communal kitchens were serving up only gruel, and everywhere there were peasants in rags looking like concentration camp inmates. Cannibalism was widespread but often went unpunished, as it was considered less heinous than crimes against the state, though a fifteen-year-old girl who had survived by eating her younger brother's corpse was sent to prison and starved to death there. At Xinyang in Henan a mother survived by killing a pig that had run into her house at night and hiding the meat under the floor. She did not give any to her five-year-old son, because she was convinced he would blurt out the secret. He starved to death. Tens of thousands died in Henan, while one of its senior party officials ordered twenty-four-course banquets in some of the worst-hit communes. Communist Party members generally suffered least. They lived in separate compounds and ate in special canteens. The party did call for sacrifice, though, and Mao himself gave up eating meat. This was probably the first famine in history to hit the whole of China, but the worst-affected areas were those run by the most fanatical Maoists, like Sichuan, normally one of China's most fertile regions, which this time suffered the highest number of deaths.

Finally, in Henan at least, there was a change of heart. Some say it happened because an army colonel went home on leave and found his relatives starving. Anyway, early in 1961, 30,000 soldiers occupied Xinyang, arrested the party leadership and started distributing grain. Before China's hunger ended, though, between sixteen and forty million people had died.

Khrushchev said: 'I look at Mao, I see Stalin – a perfect copy.' Now China had to set up new penal colonies for the millions Mao was having arrested. Most were in the frozen wastes of Heilongjiang, and up to half the prisoners would die. The failure of the Great Leap Forward inevitably led to purges. Peng Dehuai, who had dared to tell the truth about the famine, was forced to write out a demeaning 'self-criticism' and was then put under house arrest. (Later, he would be tortured and killed during the Cultural Revolution.) Backsliders were dismissed or arrested as 'little Peng Dehuais'. On the other hand, some leaders were purged for having implemented Mao's policies too enthusiastically! He decided the Great Leap Forward had failed because the masses and even party activists did not understand his policies properly. As Oscar Wilde might have put it, the Revolution had been a great success, but the people were a total failure. Mao started to be eclipsed by less doctrinaire figures such as Liu Shaoqi and Deng Xiaoping during the mid-1960s, so in a desperate attempt to regain power he launched the Cultural Revolution. Short of support in Beijing, Mao tried to stir things up in the provinces, especially Shanghai, which was controlled by a group of fanatical Maoists led by his ex-film star wife Jiang Qing, whose commitment to communism was widely distrusted. In the spring of 1966, while Liu Shaoqi was away on a tour of South-East Asia, Mao urged students and the masses to seek out and destroy all those taking the 'capitalist road' at whatever level in the party. This tapped into a well of discontent felt by many at the privileges enjoyed by party members. Meanwhile, the army stopped Mao's opponents travelling to crucial meetings, and commandeered trains to bring in fanatics from the provinces.

When Liu returned home, he and Deng had to produce 'self-criticisms'. Two years later they were paraded in front of crowds to be vilified. Liu died in jail, having been denied medical treatment by his captors, while Deng took out his hearing aid so he could not hear his tormentors and told his children to condemn him to save themselves. He survived, but one of his sons was paralysed after being attacked by Red Guards. Now anyone who had ever been in the West, or owned foreign books or records, or wore Western clothes, or participated in the dreadful bourgeois habit of keeping pets was in danger. Indeed, anyone who was not sufficiently fanatical could be denounced as a 'class traitor', dressed up in a dunce's cap and tormented. Many were beaten to death, executed by kangaroo courts, or committed suicide. Powerful people would establish their own Red Guards for protection, rather like the private armies of Chinese warlords before the revolution, and there were often battles between rival groups, one of which nearly destroyed the city of Wuzhou.

While the Cultural Revolution resulted in the deaths of perhaps half a million people, Mao assumed the status of a god, with his picture everywhere. Loudspeakers blared out news of his latest achievements into schools, colleges, factories and even buses. People's political correctness was assessed by their ability to quote from his thoughts, and even the most mundane conversation had to be prefaced with a eulogy of him.

Eventually, though, the mayhem reached such a pitch that even Mao began to distance himself from it. He made Jiang Qing take a back seat, while Lin Biao, one of the chief agitators and for a time Mao's chosen successor, disappeared mysteriously, as did many of his supporters. By the time Deng was rehabilitated in 1973, Mao was crippled by Parkinson's disease, though some said the real problem was drugs and debauchery. He died in 1976.

His time in power cost at least fifty million Chinese people their lives, though some say the figure could be as high as seventy million. In 1981 the Communist Party Central Committee blamed Mao for 'theoretical and practical mistakes', declaring that the responsibility for the 'grave errors' of the Cultural Revolution 'does indeed lie with Mao Zedong'. Even so, thirty years after his death, Mao's body still lay in his great mausoleum on Tiananmen Square; his giant portrait adorned the Gate of Heavenly Peace; and every Chinese banknote carried his image.

### · POL POT ·

Mao Zedong provided inspiration for another murderous ideologue, Pol Pot, who killed millions in a reign of terror that gripped Cambodia for four years. Born Saloth Sar in 1925, the son of a landowner, he was a mediocre student, failed the entrance exam for high school, and ended up going to Paris to study radio electronics. There he met a group of young Cambodian left-wingers, who would become his colleagues in the Khmer Rouge. Again he failed his exams, partly because he spent so much time studying Marxism instead, and he was sent home in 1953, the same year Cambodia won independence from France. He taught at a private school in Phnom Penh, while secretly working with the underground communist movement, but in 1963 he feared the police were after him and fled into the jungle, where he formed the Khmer Rouge.

Taking the names Pol Pot and Brother Number One, he launched an uprising in 1968, but it was effectively the Americans who brought him to power. Embattled in neighbouring Vietnam, they started bombing and strafing Cambodia, complaining that the Vietnamese communists were using it as a sanctuary. Then, in 1969, they began carpet bombing the country. Prince Sihanouk's government was removed in a military coup led by Lon Nol, who was much more pro-American, so the prince joined forces with Pol Pot. As the US air raids continued, Khmer Rouge recruitment soared. After an attack on Kompong Cham province killed 200 people in 1970, one local peasant said: 'Some people ran away . . . others joined the revolution.' The CIA reported in May 1973 that the communists were 'using the damage caused by B-52 strikes as the main theme of their propaganda'. The Khmer Rouge would take local people to see the devastation, usually telling them the bombers were Lon Nol's rather than American. As one of their leaders reported: 'Sometimes the bombs fell and hit little children, and their fathers would be all for the Khmer Rouge.' In July and August 1973 the south-west of the country was attacked in the most intensive campaign so far. This tipped the balance of power among the revolutionaries in favour of Pol Pot, and he was able to purge moderates. By the time the USA called a halt to the bombing later in the year, its B-52s had dropped more than half a million tons of explosives on the Cambodian countryside and had killed up to 150,000 peasants.

The Khmer Rouge were ruthless. In areas they took over they would evacuate villages and kill local officials and anyone who crossed them. Two survivors told of one village massacre in which the Khmer Rouge killed 500: 'They tied people up together, young and old . . . then they sprayed arcs of fire at them.' The two escaped because the bullets cut the rope tying them and they managed to run for it. In March 1974, when the Khmer Rouge captured the old Cambodian capital Oudong, they sent its 40,000 people to an uninhabited region then burned their houses. Lon Nol fled to the USA on 1 April 1975, and sixteen days later the Khmer Rouge entered Phnom Penh, then a city of nearly two million people. Almost immediately, they began driving out the inhabitants and those of Cambodia's second city, Battambang, telling people to leave quickly because the Americans were about to bomb them. A hundred thousand were driven from the port of Kompong Som in three days, while in Pursat market people were fired on and told to leave immediately. There were arguments over the evacuation policy within the Khmer Rouge. In some parts of Phnom Penh people were allowed to pack and look for relatives; in others they were shot if they did not leave at once. Those allowed to gather up their possessions carried them on their backs, on bicycles, or in handcarts. 'Children cried out that they were being squashed in the crowd. Everywhere people were losing their relatives.' Patients driven out of hospitals were pushed in their beds with drips still attached to them by their relatives, who struggled 'like ants with a beetle'. Some people had to march for six weeks.

Pol Pot had witnessed Mao Zedong's Cultural Revolution on a visit to China, and wanted to model Cambodia along similar lines, 'purifying' it of religion, Western culture and any foreign influence. He closed embassies, newspaper offices and television stations, and attacked all aspects of urban life. In his utopia everyone would work together as labourers in a huge coalition of collective farms. Many of the soldiers charged with imposing his dream were young country folk who had never lived in a city and were, as one observer put it, 'scared of anything in a bottle or a tin'. They confiscated radios and even bicycles. The use of money was forbidden, and hospitals were closed down, as were factories, shops, schools and universities. 'Bourgeois' professionals like lawyers, doctors, teachers, engineers and scientists were murdered along with their families. Even wearing glasses might make you seem suitable for elimination under the Khmer Rouge slogan: 'To spare you is no profit, to destroy you is no loss.'

Driving people into the country was not only ideologically sound but made it harder for potential opponents to organise or even communicate with one another. People were forced into labour camps, where they were housed in appalling conditions and made to work long hours on minimum rations. Children were separated from their parents, and any form of close personal relationship or display of affection was severely discouraged. The city people died in droves from hunger. One of Pol Pot's main henchmen, Ta Mok, 'Respected Grandfather', operated in south-western Cambodia, putting doctors, teachers, writers and scientists to work as slave labourers on dams for twelve to fourteen hours a day, feeding them only rice or watery soup made from banana stalks. Many died from hunger or overwork; others were killed. Minorities like the Chinese, Vietnamese, Thais, Christians and Muslims faced particularly harsh treatment.

While all this was happening, Pol Pot and his colleagues remained shadowy, virtually unknown figures. In 1976 they renamed the country Kampuchea, and Brother Number One emerged as prime minister. Like Stalin, he believed that every setback was the fault of 'traitors' within the party, and set up the Tuol Sleng special interrogation centre for party members in a former high school in Phnom Penh. There more than 20,000 were tortured and executed. Many were people who had served the party loyally for many years, although 2,000 were children. Prisoners were kept in tiny cells and shackled by chains to the walls or concrete floors. Women were often raped by their interrogators, and all prisoners were frequently beaten or given electric shocks. The building is now a genocide museum.

The Khmer Rouge had initially been trained by the Viet Cong, but by the early 1970s there was mutual hostility and suspicion. By 1977, the two groups were at war. Although the Chinese tried to prop up Pol Pot's regime, the Cambodians were no match for the Vietnamese. In early

1979 Brother Number One and his cronies were driven out of Cambodia into Thailand, while the Vietnamese installed a puppet regime of former Khmer Rouge members who had deserted their extremist leader. It restored private property, reopened schools, allowed people back into the cities, and permitted religion.

In less than four years in power Pol Pot's regime had killed up to 1.75 million people – a quarter of the Cambodian population – from exhaustion, starvation, disease, torture or execution. The Khmer Rouge carried on fighting in the jungle until 1995, when many of them made peace with the new Cambodian government. Pol Pot was arrested by his remaining colleagues in 1997. He died the following year, perhaps of a heart attack, though some believe he was killed to prevent a trial that could have implicated some of those holding office in the new government. By then, huge communal graves were being found, and bones and skulls were collected to form a memorial in what had become known as the 'killing fields' on the outskirts of Phnom Penh.

Two decades after Pol Pot's fall, Cambodia's government finally agreed to work with the United Nations to bring those involved in the atrocities to justice. But there were endless wrangles over procedure, and it was only in 2006 that international prosecutors were finally able to start work. Ta Mok was arrested but died in detention. In 2007 other Khmer Rouge leaders – such as Pol Pot's brother-in-law Ieng Sary; and Kang Kek Ieu, who ran Tuol Sleng – were also detained and charged with crimes against humanity.


## · RWANDA ·

Rwanda, known as the 'land of a thousand hills', is the most densely populated country in Africa. It was inhabited by two bitterly antagonistic tribes – Hutus and Tutsis. The Hutus formed the majority, but when Rwanda became a German, and later a Belgian, colony, the new rulers ran the territory through the Tutsis, so they received a better education and had better jobs. In riots in 1959 Hutus killed 20,000 Tutsis, and when independence was granted three years later 130,000 Tutsis fled to neighbouring Burundi and Uganda. There they plotted against the new Hutu regime.

Early Tutsi guerrilla raids into Rwanda were largely ineffective, but in December 1963 they managed to seize military vehicles and weapons. Alarmed, the government rounded up twenty prominent Tutsi politicians and summarily executed them. It also ordered local officials to organise Hutu vigilante groups. Armed with machetes, spears and clubs, they killed perhaps 10,000 Tutsi men, women and children, while on the border with the Congo more than a hundred drowned themselves in the river rather than face the mob. Tens of thousands more fled. The persecution boosted President Kayibanda's popularity, and even though the exiled Tutsis stopped their guerrilla activities he kept stoking the Hutus' fears.

In neighbouring Burundi the boot was on the other foot, as a failed Hutu uprising in 1972 saw perhaps 200,000 killed by Tutsis, while a similar number fled to Rwanda. Kayibanda responded with a 'purification' campaign, limiting Tutsis to 9 per cent of school and university places and jobs, even though in some parts of the country they still formed up to 30 per cent of the population. This prompted another Tutsi exodus. It was not enough to keep the president in power, though, and in 1973 he was overthrown by a Hutu army commander, General Juvénal Habyarimana. The new leader made everyone carry an identity card showing their ethnic origin, but at first he did not step up persecution of the Tutsis. By the 1980s, though, his government was beset by problems – a drought, a world slump in coffee prices, and a land shortage as the population rocketed. Habyarimana's popularity collapsed, and in 1990 an army of exiles from the mainly Tutsi Rwandan Patriotic Front (RPF) crossed the border from Uganda. The president got troops from his personal friend, President Mitterrand of France, and from President Mobutu of Zaire. Mobutu's soldiers had to be withdrawn quickly after going on the rampage, but Habyarimana still managed to drive back the rebels. Then he imprisoned 13,000 people without trial, many of whom died after torture. At the same time, the minister of defence urged people to track down and arrest those inside the country who had helped the rebels, with the result that hundreds more Tutsis were killed.

Under pressure from Western supporters, Habyarimana made peace with the RPF, and even brought some of them into the government.

This enraged Hutu supremacists, who formed the Hutu Power organisation and recruited young men without jobs or prospects into death squads. Broadcasting stations like *Radio Television Libre des Milles Collines* (thousand hills) and extremists, like university lecturer Léon Mugesera, said the RPF planned to restore the Tutsis to power with 'the extermination of the Hutu majority'. In a rabble-rousing speech, he proclaimed: 'Wipe them all out! . . . Know that the person whose throat you do not cut now will be the one who will cut yours.' Mobs, sometimes including police, burned Tutsis in their homes or threw them into rivers. If women and children were the victims, this was justified as 'pulling out the roots of the bad weeds'. Once again, trouble also flared in Burundi, with Tutsis and Hutus killing each other. About 150,000 died, while 300,000 Hutus fled to Rwanda, carrying fresh tales of massacre and torture. Now Colonel Théoneste Bagosora, the Rwandan Army's head of administration, set up paramilitary 'self-defence' units all over the country, while the government imported half a million machetes. A United Nations peacekeeping force arrived but its commander, the Canadian general Romeo Dallaire, was not allowed to seize weapons.

In March 1994 an extremist newspaper predicted Habyarimana's death, while on 3 April *Radio Milles Collines* announced that 'a little something' was about to happen. Three days later the president was flying home from an African summit in his private jet (a gift from Mitterrand) with seven members of his government. As the aircraft approached the Rwandan capital, Kigali, two missiles hit it, killing everyone on board.

The Hutu extremists and the RPF accused each other of assassinating Habyarimana. No conclusive evidence to support either side's claims has ever emerged, but Bagosora, who had previously declared 'the only plausible solution for Rwanda would be the elimination of the Tutsi', now took charge. Handily, a list of those to be liquidated had been prepared in advance. It mainly featured moderate Hutus – politicians, including the prime minister Agathe Uwilingiyimana, senior government officials, lawyers, teachers, human rights activists and journalists. Gangs armed with clubs, machetes and knives tracked them down and killed them. They also tortured and killed ten Belgian peacekeepers who tried to protect the prime minister. And they murdered thousands of ordinary Tutsis. Those with money sometimes paid to be shot instead of being hacked to death with machetes. The identity cards that Habyarimana had introduced were a great help in selecting victims.

One peacekeeper saw a militiaman grab his victim by the shirt and hit him twice on the head with his machete. As the man fell dead, his attacker calmly wiped his machete on his buttocks before going through the victim's pockets. Tipper trucks began collecting the dead and dying, but *Radio Milles Collines* declared, 'The graves are not yet quite full,' and Hutu Power leader Froduald Karamira said the elimination of the Tutsis was 'everyone's responsibility' and called on ordinary Hutus to 'help the armed forces finish the work'. As the massacres spread across the country, thousands jogged through the streets chanting, 'Let's exterminate them all.' Some Hutus were offered food, money or Tutsis' land to join in. If incentives failed, they were threatened.

Government broadcasts encouraged the Tutsis to take refuge in churches, schools and sports stadiums, but this just made them easier targets. About 500 Tutsis went to a mission station in a Kigali suburb, but while they were at mass a death squad burst in and slashed at them for two hours with machetes. Belgium offered more troops, and tried to get the UN peacekeeping mandate extended to stop the killing, but the French blocked it, so UN soldiers had to stand by and watch as Tutsis were murdered on the streets or dragged from trucks when they tried to flee to the airport. On 10 April Médecins sans Frontières withdrew from Rwanda after a mob pulled fifty wounded people from the central hospital and killed them. General Dallaire's forces had no petrol, little food or water, and were scattered and vulnerable because of Hutu roadblocks. The UN kept telling him to plan for evacuation, but he refused to go. On 12 April Belgium announced it was withdrawing its contingent of peacekeepers. Two thousand refugees taking shelter at their base pleaded with the Belgians to shoot them before they went rather than leave them to the militias. Hutu death squads waited outside drinking beer and chanting, 'Hutu Power'. As soon as the Europeans had gone they went in and massacred everyone. The Belgians tried to slip away discreetly, but hundreds of desperate people ran after their vehicles, pleading, 'Do not abandon us.' Within hours nearly all of them had been slaughtered. Even a weakened UN force was still protecting about 30,000 civilians at its

bases, but Secretary-General Boutros Boutros-Ghali produced an ano-
dyne report on the situation, and the organisation decided that the force
was not viable without the Belgians. So it was reduced to a token
presence.

Roman Catholic and Anglican bishops had supported the new government, and church leaders did not speak out even against killings in
their own churches. Some junior clergy tried to help, but more people
were killed in church buildings than anywhere else. Sometimes the
slaughter sessions took several days; the killers would cut the Achilles
tendons of those awaiting death so they could not run away. Five thousand people were massacred in the church at Ntarama, but one man
survived by hiding under a pile of bodies. He said that among the murderers were 'young boys, about eleven to fourteen, carrying spears and
sharpened sticks', which they used to kill children. When researchers
from the African Rights organisation arrived two months later they
could not get into the church because the entrance was piled high with
decomposing bodies. Looking through the window, they saw the building was full of corpses. Another 1,500 people sought sanctuary in the
Catholic church in Kivumu, but the Hutus knocked it down with bull-
dozers and killed anyone who tried to escape. A local priest was later
convicted of genocide. African Rights said some of the most prolific
killers were doctors, who helped murder colleagues, patients and
refugees, while the British Medical Journal reported horrific massacres in
maternity clinics, 'where people gathered in the belief that no one would
kill mothers and new-born babies'. Even the chairman of a human rights
group would later be charged with involvement in the murder of 12,000
Tutsis.

Mothers were often forced to watch their children being killed before
they were murdered themselves, but a woman from Taba described
something even worse – how the militia came and killed all the men,
then forced the women to dig graves, throw their children in and bury
them alive. She said: 'I will never forget the sight of my son pleading with
me not to bury him alive . . . He kept trying to come out and was beaten
back. And we had to keep covering the pit with earth until . . . there was
no movement left.' Hutu men with Tutsi wives were forced to kill them
or be slaughtered themselves. Women and even young girls took part in

the massacres. A farmer said he was one of a group who had killed nine men: 'We were given a list of people to kill . . . I either had to do it or I would die myself. Many were killed for refusing.' One victim was his brother-in-law: 'He was an old man . . . He was dragged from the bedroom and killed in the sitting room.'

By now, RPF soldiers were advancing from the north, and a million Hutus, including leaders of the death squads, fled the country. The French insisted the events in Rwanda were not genocide but a civil war, and they tried to prop up the old government even as the RPF took over the country. They offered 2,500 soldiers to the UN, which accepted, although Dallaire was hostile. The Hutus welcomed them with tricolores and shouts of '*Vive la France*', but their arrival could not stop the RPF taking Kigali on 4 July. Soon the French began to find rotting piles of bodies that provided undeniable evidence of what had happened. Some soldiers claimed they had been deceived. One said: 'I've had enough of being cheered by murderers.' The RPF formed a government of national unity, with twelve Hutus among its eighteen ministers.

In just 100 days at least 800,000 people had been slaughtered – three-quarters of the Tutsi population. It was the fastest mass murder in history. Boutros Boutros-Ghali's successor, Kofi Annan, admitted: 'In their greatest hour of need, the world failed the people of Rwanda.'

Genocide trials in Rwanda began rather haltingly in 1996, but in April 1998 twenty-two people were executed, including Froduald Karamira. The UN set up the International Criminal Tribunal for Rwanda to deal with high-level members of the government and armed forces, and by October 2007, only fourteen of its ninety indicted suspects were still at large. Bagosora's trial began in 2002. The prosecution described him as an 'enemy of the human race' and said that the genocide had long been planned. Bagosora claimed the slaughter was beyond his control. The court retired to consider its verdict in June 2007.

# 12

## REBELLIONS, RIOTS & TERRORISM

### · THE NIKA RIOTS ·

The worst sporting riots in history happened in ancient Constantinople. The city's favourite sport was chariot racing, and two teams, the Blues and the Greens, enjoyed support as fanatical as any attracted today by Real Madrid, Boca Juniors or Manchester United, while the stars were as famous as Zinedine Zidane or Cristiano Ronaldo. The Blues' fans were thought particularly fearsome, because they had long hair and dressed like Huns. They broke into houses and churches, and at night they would murder the Greens' supporters or anyone they happened to come across with their daggers. Few from the forces of law and order dared to punish a delinquent Blue, so the Greens felt abandoned by the authorities. Some tried to retaliate against their rivals, while others fled into the countryside and preyed on travellers.

The contemporary historian Procopius considered the rivalry 'a disease of the soul', but all the city's powerful aristocratic families supported one team or the other. Before he became emperor in 527, Justinian the Great had cultivated the Blues and counted on their support, but once he assumed the throne he refused to tolerate the lawlessness of the two factions and ordered that any crimes committed by Blues or Greens should be punished impartially. This angered their aristocratic patrons. The situation was complicated by the emperor's wife, Theodora. Her father had been a keeper of the wild beasts used to entertain the crowds in the Hippodrome. After his early death, she had had to make her way as best she could, becoming an actress more notable for her beauty than her virtue. Edward Gibbon noted that her charms 'were abandoned to a promiscuous crowd of citizens and strangers', and considered it best to leave her amorous exploits 'veiled in the obscurity of a learned language'. During this difficult time in her life the Blues were kind, while the Greens treated her with disdain. She never forgot their insults, and tried to persuade her husband to favour the Blues.

In this explosive atmosphere clashes were common, and in 531 seven men – some Greens, some Blues – were sentenced to death for murder after a riot at a race meeting. On 10 January 532, though, the hangman bungled the execution of one man from each faction. As the ropes broke and they fell to the ground still alive the crowd cheered. Then monks from a nearby monastery put them in a boat and rowed them across the Golden Horn to the sanctuary of a church. Eudaemon, the prefect of the city, sent soldiers to guard it and stop them escaping, but they were quickly surrounded by an angry mob. Justinian commuted the men's sentences to imprisonment, but the two factions demanded they should be pardoned.

Three days later the next chariot races were held at the Hippodrome, adjoining the imperial palace. As Justinian watched from the royal box the crowd hurled insults at him, demanding the prisoners should be freed. Then, as the twenty-second race began, instead of shouting, 'Blue' or 'Green', the crowd chanted, '*Nika*' – Greek for 'conquer'. Both factions now seemed united against the emperor. In the evening a mob broke into the city's prison, released the inmates, killed some officials and set fire to the building. They then burned others and even tried to set fire to the palace, but only managed to destroy the entrance. As Procopius put it: 'Fire was applied to the city as if it had fallen under the hand of an enemy.' The next morning the rioters started more fires, and demanded the removal of Eudaemon and two other unpopular ministers.

Justinian now knew he was in serious trouble. The loyalty of the palace guards was doubtful, and he could only rely on a force of 1,500 Goths, which seemed too small to secure a decisive victory over the rioters. For two more days the mob rampaged while Justinian's enemies plotted to depose him in favour of Hypatius, the nephew of a former emperor.

Eventually Justinian appeared at the Hippodrome holding the Gospels. He swore to a big crowd that he would grant a full amnesty and comply with his subjects' demands, but many still shouted: 'Long live Hypatius!' The mob then moved on to their chosen leader's house, took him to the Forum and crowned him with a gold chain, while Justinian wondered whether he should flee. Many advised him to do just that, but then Theodora said: 'The present occasion is, I think, too grave to take regard of the convention that it is not meet for a woman to speak among men.' She continued: 'For one who has been an emperor it is unendurable to be a fugitive. May I never be separated from this purple, and may I not live that day on which those who meet me shall not address me as mistress.' She warned Justinian that if he fled, he might spend the rest of his life regretting it. Then added: 'As for myself, I approve a certain ancient saying that royalty is a good burial-shroud.' Procopius recorded: 'When the queen had spoken thus, all were filled with boldness.'

By now Hypatius was installed on the emperor's throne in the Hippodrome surrounded by a great crowd, but Justinian sent out a trusted eunuch with a purse full of money to try to win over some of the Blues, insinuating that Hypatius would favour the Greens and reminding them of his own past favours and the unwavering goodwill of Theodora. Most of the Blues withdrew, then the Goths charged the rest of the crowd from each end of the stadium. Panic ensued and more than 30,000 of the rebels were killed, according to Procopius.

During the rioting many churches and fine houses had been destroyed; some said nearly half the city had gone up in flames. Hypatius was executed the following day and his body thrown into the sea, while eighteen leading supporters were banished. It was the end of the rebellion. For many years after, wrote Gibbon, the Hippodrome was condemned 'to a mournful silence'. But eventually the races resumed, and fans of the Blues and Greens continued to fight each other for years to come.

## · THE AN LUSHAN REBELLION ·

During the first half of the eighth century AD Emperor Xuanzong of China fell madly in love with the beautiful Yang Guifei, who had been married at sixteen to one of his sons, Prince Li Mei. Five years later the fifty-five-year-old emperor made his son divorce her, and eventually took her as his favourite concubine. The eighth-century Chinese poet Bai Juyi wrote of Xuanzong's love for Yang in his *Song of the Everlasting Sorrow*:

> Those nights were too short.
> That sun too quick in rising.
> The emperor neglected the world from that moment,
> Lavished his time on her in endless enjoyment.
> She was his springtime mistress, and his midnight tyrant.

As the emperor lost interest in government, squabbling ministers battled for power. Yang used her position to advance her relatives and her favourite general, An Lushan, who was said to be enormously fat. In 755 he led a rebellion, taking the city of Luoyang, where he proclaimed himself emperor. Xuanzong had to flee, and the imperial bodyguard demanded Yang's death, blaming her for the rebellion. Fearing they might mutiny, Xuanzong agreed and Yang was hanged (or possibly hanged herself). On reaching Sichuan the broken-hearted emperor abdicated. He later returned to the place of Yang's death but could not find her body. (Today, a glamorous statue of Yang Guifei bathing can be seen in Huaqing Pool, near Xi'an.) Meanwhile, another of Xuanzong's sons, Suzong, had tried to grab the throne, while one of his brothers set up a breakaway kingdom in Nanking before being assassinated. China was in chaos.

An Lushan was murdered by one of his subordinates in 757, but first his son and then one of his generals, Shi Siming, continued the rebellion for the next six years. After paying out a fortune on mercenaries, the imperial forces finally crushed the rebels. By then, Xuanzong had died, still mourning his lost love. For eight years, the rebellion had brought warfare, destruction and famine, and cost an estimated thirty-six million lives.

## · TAIPING ·

Another bloody civil war broke out in China eleven hundred years later, in the aftermath of the Qing dynasty's humiliating capitulation to the British in the Opium War of 1842. Four years later, floods and famine brought widespread suffering. Then, in 1850, a rebellion began in Guangxi.

Seven years earlier, a man named Hong Xiuquan had flown into a rage after failing the Chinese civil service examination for the fifth time. He had been having a recurring dream in which a bearded man with golden hair, accompanied by a younger man, gave him a sword and taught him to slay evil spirits. Now he started reading Christian tracts, and decided they must be God the Father and his son Jesus, and they wanted him to found a new heavenly kingdom on earth. So Hong got to work, proclaiming himself the younger brother of Jesus. An illiterate former firewood salesman named Yang Xiuqing, who had been converted to Christianity after some visions of his own, became his main military leader. They won popularity by fighting bandits who had been making people's lives a misery, but by January 1851 the emperor was getting worried and sent his troops against them. The imperial army was routed, and in August Hong declared himself absolute ruler of the Heavenly Kingdom of Peace, *Taiping Tianguo*. The revolt quickly spread northwards, and a force of up to 800,000 rebels, including many women, took Nanking and made it their capital. In doing so, they slaughtered thousands of civilians.

The Taipings were against gambling, opium, tobacco and prostitution. Polygamy was also supposed to be banned, but Hong is believed to have had eighty-eight concubines, and many other high officials kept harems too. The Heavenly Kingdom took over much of south and central China, and Hong dispatched four armies which conquered even more territory. His supporters came almost exclusively from the lower classes, and they often murdered landlords in the lands they captured. By 1853, though, their leader began to withdraw from politics to devote himself to meditation and enjoyment of his harem. He named Yang as his prime minister, but they fell out three years later and Hong's followers murdered him and thousands of his followers. The civil war raged on for another eight years, during which time about 600 walled cities were captured by one side or the other, often with a massacre of the inhabitants. The armies lived off the land, and civilians starved. Meanwhile, the rulers of the Heavenly Kingdom tried to revolutionise society with policies eerily similar to some the Communists would espouse in the next century, such as strict segregation of the sexes, including husbands and wives.

By the early 1860s, though, the imperial forces were closing in. Hong announced that God would defend Nanking, but by June 1864 the city was starving and Hong himself died of food poisoning after eating wild vegetables. The emperor's troops took the city after vicious street-fighting and dug up Hong's body. First they burned it, then blasted the ashes out of a cannon. The victorious forces executed most of his leading supporters, but remnants of the Taipings led further rebellions over the next thirteen years. It is estimated that the total death toll during the main rebellion was twenty million, perhaps a twentieth of the population of China at the time.

## · THE INDIAN PARTITION RIOTS ·

Partly as a reward for India's loyalty during World War Two, on 20 February 1947, the British government instructed Lord Mountbatten to prepare it for independence. The population was then around 400 million, of whom about a quarter were Muslim. In parts of northern India they formed a majority, while over the whole of the country thousands of places had mixed Hindu and Muslim populations who had lived together for centuries. The main pro-independence organisation, the Congress Party, claimed to be non-sectarian, but Muslims grew increasingly wary of it as the century progressed. In 1924 hundreds died as Hindus and Muslims fought each other in Malabar, and the trouble spread to virtually every major city in northern India.

Nine years later a group of Muslim students at Cambridge proposed the creation of a separate country to be called Pakistan – 'Land of the Pure' – in the Muslim-dominated north-western and north-eastern provinces. The following year Mohammad Ali Jinnah, a secular Muslim dentist's son from Karachi, became leader of the Muslim League. He had been active in the Congress Party but left because he felt it was becoming increasingly dominated by devout, illiterate Hindus who idolised Mahatma Gandhi. Jinnah still hoped that agreement could be reached with Congress, but after the 1937 elections its leader, Pandit Nehru, refused to enter into coalition with the Muslim League. By now, the Indians were effectively running their own affairs at provincial level, but Muslims viewed Congress politicians as leaders of a new 'Hindu Raj', prejudiced and tyrannical, in which Muslims would swap being subjects of the British for being ruled by Hindus. Meanwhile, communal violence continued. In 1938 three Hindus and a Muslim playing cards in a public garden in Bombay started to quarrel. The fight escalated with alarming speed, and assaults, stone-throwing and stabbings continued for days, with fourteen people losing their lives.

In the first post-war election of February 1946 enough Muslims voted for Congress in North-Western Frontier province and Assam to give the party a majority in these predominantly Muslim areas, while in the Punjab Sikhs began demanding their own country of Sikhistan (or Khalistan). The following month the British government held two months of talks with Nehru, Gandhi and Jinnah, but no agreement was reached. Britain proposed splitting the country into three parts – roughly equivalent to modern India, West Pakistan and East Pakistan (later Bangladesh). Nehru rejected the idea, so in August Jinnah called on Muslims to launch 'direct action' to achieve an independent Pakistan. On the 16th fierce fighting began in Calcutta and 4,000 people died in four days. Tens of thousands of Hindus were then driven from their homes in mainly Muslim East Bengal, and many were murdered as they fled. In retaliation, Hindus killed more than 700 members of the Muslim minority in Bihar. The Sikhs feared Muslim rule more than Hindu rule, and a group of them attacked a Muslim village, killing sixteen. Within the next two weeks nearly 1,000 people perished in the countryside around Amritsar. The death toll in Lahore reached 100 a day; in Calcutta it was even higher. An American journalist, Louis Fischer, said: 'The inhabitants are squeezed together herring-barrel fashion in filthy slums . . . a little Moslem girl pulling a Hindu girl's hair or a Hindu boy calling a Moslem boy names might precipitate a mortal riot.' Working together to get rid of the British had helped to keep communal tension in check, but now the British were leaving.

Mountbatten arrived in India as its last viceroy in March 1947 with the brief of handing it over no later than June 1948, but he decided it would be too dangerous to wait even that long. Partition seemed the only option, and now Gandhi alone among the major political leaders still refused to accept it. Mountbatten quickly gained the confidence of Nehru, but lost that of Jinnah. Under his breakneck programme, the British Parliament passed the Indian Independence Act in July 1947 to free India and Pakistan on 14 August. That evening, to a crowd of more than 100,000 in Delhi, Nehru pronounced the famous words: 'At the stroke of midnight, when the world sleeps, India will awake to life and freedom.' The hastily drawn boundaries across the Punjab and Bengal were kept secret until two days after independence in an attempt to damp down trouble, but it did not work. Soon ten million Hindus, Muslims and Sikhs were on the roads in a desperate race to what they believed would be a safe haven on the right side of the new frontiers.

A British administrator found the bodies of Hindus in the town of Hasilpur lying as 'thick as autumn leaves', with men, women and children 'all jumbled up together'. In the Punjab Lt Col. James Bell, who had served in India for twenty years, saw thousands of towns and villages destroyed and thousands of people brutally slaughtered: 'Trains have been regularly stopped and everyone of the wrong community dragged out and hacked down including women – if they're not stripped, raped and then left to roam naked.' His own train was halted just outside Ludhiana, and every Muslim was murdered except for a handful Bell managed to hide in the washroom of his compartment. The arrival of survivors telling dreadful stories further inflamed the communal hatred, so when a mass of Hindu refugees reached Delhi local Hindus and Sikhs attacked Muslims. Within a few days most of those in the city had fled. Bihar had a population of thirty-one million Hindus and five million Muslims. The Hindus marched through the streets of Patna and other towns shouting, 'Blood for blood.' In just one week about 10,000 people were killed, mainly Muslims. A British lieutenant watched one of the endless columns of refugees: '120 miles of bullock-carts were moving, nose to tail . . . We saw lorries mow down whole families and the drivers press recklessly on. When millions die, what are a few more?' Sometimes columns moving in opposite directions on the same road would fight. In the Punjab trains would cross the border into India with carriages packed with dead bodies and marked 'A Present from Pakistan'. 'Presents from India' would move in the other direction. A British officer found 2,000 dead Muslims on a single train in Pakistan. It had been halted by stones on the line, then a horde of Sikhs had swarmed aboard to kill everyone. Sikhs in the Punjab, though, would suffer the highest percentage of casualties, and up to 200,000 were transfered to India in a single column escorted by Gurkha troops.

Mountbatten called Gandhi a 'one-man peacekeeping force'. When killing had broken out in East Bengal nine months before independence he had walked, at the age of seventy-seven, barefoot from village to village. Usually he went to a Muslim's hut first. He would stay in the village for a few days, praying and talking, then move on. On this pilgrimage he visited forty-nine villages. He said he was determined to get Hindus and Muslims to live together in peace or 'die in the attempt'. One observer commented: 'Relations had improved perceptibly but insufficiently.' The day after independence he pitched his tent in Calcutta and announced he would fast to the death unless the killing stopped. When he saw the devastation in the city he was overcome by 'a sinking feeling at the mass madness that can turn man into less than a brute'. He continued admonishing the bigots, consoling the victims and trying to rehabilitate the refugees. Such was his prestige that after three days the violence in Calcutta did subside, but even Gandhi could not halt madness across a whole subcontinent. In October he wrote about an incident in which a Hindu had tried to shelter his Muslim friend from a mob, and both had been murdered. He said there had also been many instances of Muslims sheltering Hindus 'at the peril of their lives'. On his return to Delhi Gandhi preached non-violence every day and shamed the city into a communal truce. But on 30 January 1948 he was shot dead by a young Hindu fanatic.

More than a million people are believed to have died in the upheaval – either murdered or from diseases contracted on the refugee marches. Fifty million Muslims continued to live in India under Nehru's determinedly secular leadership, and the tide of religious hatred and violence did recede inside the country, though the enmity between India and Pakistan persisted, turning to war on three occasions, while another million or more would die as as East Pakistan fought to win its independence from West Pakistan. The Sikhs were also left bitterly dissatisfied. One of their leaders complained: 'The Muslims got their Pakistan, and the Hindus got their Hindustan, but what did the Sikhs get?'

## · TERRORISM ·

International Terrorism is now one of the world's great fears, and in the name of combating it, we have accepted many restrictions on our liberty – like allowing people to be locked up without trial for longer and longer periods. Terrorists have slain their hundreds or, on one occasion, thousands, but, of course, they are way behind governments and tyrants (see Chapter 11) who have slain their millions – by some estimates more than 100 million over the last century.

So what is terrorism? As the saying goes, 'One man's terrorist is another man's freedom fighter.' Ex-SAS man Barry Davies, who spent much of his life fighting terrorism, wrote: 'Any sort of resistance movement is going to be viewed by those against whom they are fighting as a terrorist organisation.' The word 'terrorism' was first used to describe the state terror of the French revolutionary government in the late eighteenth century, which saw thousands of people sent to the guillotine. When it was first applied to resistance groups in the late nineteenth century their victims were usually powerful rulers, like Tsar Alexander II of Russia and King Umberto of Italy. Two Spanish prime ministers were assassinated around the same time – one as he sat on the terrace of a hotel, the other while he was browsing in a bookshop. Few modern politicians would leave themselves so vulnerable to attack; and because those in power have made sure they are well protected the terrorists have increasingly targeted ordinary people instead. One analyst summed up the modern terrorist's strategy as: 'Why attack a tiger when there are so many sheep?'

## · THE IRAN CINEMA FIRE ·

Many Western regimes now see Iran as a sponsor of terrorism, but in the 1970s it was the victim of an outrage surpassing any seen in the West before 9/11 (see below). In the dying days of the Shah's regime, on 20 August 1978, police officers saw smoke billowing from a cinema showing an anti-government film on the upper level of a commercial building in Abadan. The officers radioed headquarters to say a number of Islamic militants had gone inside when they had realised they were being watched. It was claimed they then started a small fire so they could escape in the crowd. The officers on the spot were told not to let anyone leave until the police chief arrived with reinforcements.

The entrance gate of the stairway leading to the cinema was locked – whether by the police or the militants is not clear. As the smoke and flames intensified, a man wanted to use his pick-up truck to break it down, but the officers stopped him. By the time the police chief arrived, the cinema was engulfed in flames. When the fire brigade reached the scene twenty minutes after the blaze had begun, they found none of the hydrants was working and their mobile water tanks ran dry before the flames could be brought under control. Witnesses accused the police of making no attempt to rescue those screaming for help inside, and 422 people died. The secret police were blamed for starting the fire, and thousands of weeping, raging mourners crammed the streets to shout anti-Shah slogans, claiming his men had targeted the cinema to kill the militants. Meanwhile, the authorities arrested six suspects, including the owner of the cinema, who was accused of negligence.

On 11 February 1979 the monarchy fell to an Islamic revolution. Just ten days later an army officer, Captain Monir Taheri, was put on trial by Iran's new rulers. He was convicted in short order of involvement in the fire, as well as other offences, such as torturing political prisoners, and was executed by firing squad on 23 February. It is unclear whether any evidence was produced against him, and many of the victims' families rejected the verdict, with some mounting a four-month sit-in at a government office.

Some Islamic militants opposed the film on doctrinal grounds, and some had already set fire to a number of Iranian cinemas, as well as restaurants and nightclubs. On 25 August 1980 the Revolutionary Tribunal tried another twenty-six people, including Hossein Takializadeh, who confessed to starting the fire with three other religious activists, all of whom had died in the blaze. He was put to death in public along with five others. The name of Captain Taheri never came up at the trial.

## · THE AIR INDIA BOMBING ·

The dealiest single terrorist attack on an aircraft came on Sunday, 23 June 1985, when an Air India 747 flying from Montreal to Heathrow exploded at a quarter past seven in the morning off the coast of Ireland.

On board were 22 crew and 307 passengers, including 82 children. A bomb had been planted in the front cargo hold. When it exploded, the Boeing disintegrated. Meanwhile, 6,000 miles away at Narita Airport in Tokyo, baggage containers were being taken off a Canadian Pacific 747 that had arrived from Vancouver. In one was a suitcase due to be loaded on to another Air India flight. It exploded, killing two baggage handlers. The police investigation showed that a passenger called Singh, the name used by millions of Sikhs, had checked in at Vancouver for the Canadian Pacific flight but had failed to board.

Five months after the bombing, Canadian police raided the homes of four suspected Sikh terrorists. The previous year, their holiest shrine, the Golden Temple in Amritsar, had been stormed by Indian troops pursuing armed Sikhs who were fighting to have their own state. Then Prime Minister Indira Gandhi was murdered by two of her Sikh bodyguards, resulting in Hindus massacring Sikhs in New Delhi. In response, one of the suspects in the investigation into the bombings, Ajaib Singh Bagri, a forklift truck driver from British Columbia, fulminated in a speech in New York that 'Until we kill 50,000 Hindus, we will not rest!' Two other suspects, Talwinder Singh Parmar and Inderjit Singh Reyat, were seen by Canadian surveillance officers going into woods on Vancouver Island, where they were thought to be testing explosives. The police heard a loud bang, but they could find nothing incriminating. The two men were accused of conspiracy and of possessing explosives, but the charges were dropped.

In 1991, though, Reyat was given a ten-year sentence for manslaughter and explosives offences relating to the Narita bomb. The following year Parmar, by now thought to be the mastermind behind the plot, was killed in a gun battle with Indian police in Mumbai. But it was October 2000 before the other two original suspects, Bagri and Ripudaman Singh Malik, a millionaire businessman, were charged with blowing up the Air India flight and the two baggage handlers in Tokyo. The following year Reyat was also charged with the Air India bombing. In 2003 he was sentenced to five years for manslaughter and helping to make a bomb. It was widely believed he was given a light sentence in return for promising to testify against Bagri and Malik, but in the witness box he claimed he could not remember anything about them. On 16 March 2005 the judge found Malik and Bagri not guilty on all counts, saying there had been 'cruel acts of terrorism' but that the prosecution's evidence was inadequate.

Claims were made that some Canadian Sikhs had refused to testify against the defendants because of fear of reprisals, and that one had been murdered before he could give evidence. A year later the Canadian government finally gave in to demands from the victims' families and set up a public inquiry into the bombing. In 2007 it reported that there had been numerous security lapses – warnings were ignored, unauthorised people were allowed to wander freely on the aircraft, and an explosives sniffer dog had arrived too late to search it.

## · LOCKERBIE ·

On 3 July 1988 an American warship, the USS *Vincennes*, fired two missiles at an Iran Air Airbus A-300 over the Straits of Hormuz, apparently believing it was an Iranian fighter. The aircraft crashed into the sea, killing all 290 people on-board, many of them pilgrims going to Mecca.

Five months later, on 21 December at seven o'clock in the evening, Pan Am Flight 103 was 31,000 feet above the Scottish town of Lockerbie, carrying 246 passengers and 13 crew from London to New York. The cabin crew were serving dinner as the first officer radioed air traffic control for clearance to begin the Atlantic crossing. Those were the last words heard from the aircraft. Almost immediately, air traffic controllers at Prestwick noticed something strange and terrible on their screens: the single box that represented the jumbo jet split into five, and each sweep of the radar showed them moving further apart. Pieces of the aircraft were descending on Lockerbie and its 3,000 inhabitants. The central section of the fuselage and the wings, containing 50,000 gallons of aviation fuel, fell on Sherwood Crescent, sending a great fireball 300 feet into the night sky, and leaving a crater 30 yards long and 40 feet deep. Fifty bodies, some still strapped in their seats, fell into a widow's back garden and part of the economy cabin crashed into her house, but she survived. A seventeen-year-old out for a walk had to run for his life, dodging 'bits of metal flying through the air at incredible speed'. On the nearby Carlisle to Glasgow road at least five cars were set on fire. Debris was found scattered up to eighty miles away, but the section containing the cockpit and first-class cabin was found lying intact on its side, providing the most memorable image of the disaster. Scores of people had to be evacuated from their homes and put up in community centres, schools and hotels.

Altogether, eleven people died on the ground, including four members of a single family, as did all 259 on board, 189 of them Americans. The American vocal group the Four Tops and the former Sex Pistols singer John Lydon should have been aboard the aircraft, but all of them missed it. It soon became clear that this was no accident: the worst air disaster in British history was also the worst terrorist outrage. A bomb containing a pound of Semtex explosive had blown the aircraft out of the sky. Britain's smallest police force, the Dumfries and Galloway Constabulary, now had to undertake its biggest criminal inquiry. A number of odd facts surfaced. Among the dead were four American intelligence officers, and two weeks before the attack the US embassy in Helsinki had received a warning from a man with an Arab accent who said that Flight 103 would be bombed before Christmas. Airlines constantly receive hoax bomb warnings, but this one was taken seriously enough for the US State Department to cable news of it to dozens of embassies.

A number of organisations claimed responsibility for the attack, including the 'Guardians of the Islamic Revolution', who said they had done it in retaliation for the shooting down of the Iranian airliner. In the wreckage investigators found small fragments of a suitcase in which they believed the bomb had been concealed, together with bits of a circuit board from a radio cassette player in which a timer and detonator were thought to have been hidden. These were manufactured by a Swiss company and were part of a consignment that had been exported to Libya. Also in the suitcase were baby clothes bought in Malta. A Maltese shopkeeper said he had sold them to a man from Libya, and the spotlight now switched to that country, which also had a grudge against the United States, thanks to a bombing raid in 1986 that had killed dozens of people, including President Gaddafi's adopted daughter. The US planes responsible for that attack had taken off from British bases.

In 1991 indictments were issued against two Libyans, Abdelbaset Ali Mohmed al-Megrahi, an intelligence officer, and Al Amin Khalifa Fhimah, but it was only in 1999, following tortuous negotiations with

Gaddafi, that the men were handed over to stand trial. Gaddafi's decision to give them up was part of a complex deal that included Libya agreeing to pay compensation to the families of those killed in return for its diplomatic isolation being ended.

The trial was held in the Netherlands with Scottish judges. The prosecutors claimed that al-Megrahi had got the bomb on to the Pan Am plane from a connecting flight from Malta, though they admitted they did not know how. The two defendants both denied all charges, and after nearly nine months of hearings, Fhimah was acquitted, but al-Megrahi was sentenced to twenty-seven years in prison. He appealed against his conviction, and new evidence was presented that there had been a breach of security at a baggage store at Heathrow eighteen hours before Flight 103 departed, so that it would have been possible for someone else to smuggle a bag on to the plane. Al-Megrahi's appeal was rejected, but some of the victims' families were among those who did not believe the Libyan was the real killer. Some have even campaigned for his release, and have demanded a public inquiry into such questions as who exactly was aware of the bomb warnings that were given, and why PA 103 was the only transatlantic flight during the holiday period that had empty seats. In June 2007 the Scottish Criminal Cases Review Commission said it feared al-Megrahi may have been the victim of a miscarriage of justice and asked the appeal court to look at the case again.

## · THE MUMBAI BOMBINGS ·

Mumbai, besides being the country's commercial capital, is often regarded as a 'mini-India' because of its religious and ethnic diversity. The winter of 1992–3 was a troubled time, with widespread communal rioting in which an estimated 900 people, mostly Muslims, were killed and about 40,000 fled the city. At half past one on the afternoon of 12 March 1993 a powerful car bomb exploded in the basement of the twenty-eight-storey Mumbai Stock Exchange. The blast was so strong that some traders were flung through windows to their deaths on the street below. Others were trampled in the stampede to escape. Altogether, about fifty people were killed, including street hawkers and pedestrians outside, and the building was severely damaged.

Over the next three hours another dozen bombs went off in the city. All were made of plastic explosives and detonated by timing devices. Targets included banks, a passport office, a theatre and a major shopping complex. An explosion at the headquarters of Air India, another high-rise landmark, flung glass, furniture and bodies into the road. The worst casualties were reported in the Worli seafront residential district, where about ninety people were killed by a device planted on a crowded double-decker bus. Others were in cars or on scooters, and three hotels were attacked by the simple device of leaving a suitcase in a bedroom. Another blast shattered the headquarters of Shiv Sena, Mumbai's most powerful radical Hindu organisation, which was widely blamed for instigating the winter's violence. The terrorists also threw grenades at Mumbai airport. Some saw the day's events as an attack on Hindus, others as an assault on the whole Indian nation. A local MP said: 'This is a conspiracy to sabotage India's growing economy.'

The official death toll was 257 but it could have been even higher as, a few days later, a number of unexploded car bombs were found at a railway station. Islamic terrorist groups based in Pakistan were suspected of being behind the bombings, with the help of a major underworld figure, Dawood Ibrahim. After the attacks he disappeared but hundreds of people were arrested, and eventually about a hundred were convicted, including top Bollywood actor Sanjay Dutt, who specialised in tough anti-hero roles. After telling him: 'Don't get perturbed. You have many years to go and work, like the *Mackenna's Gold* actor Gregory Peck,' the judge sent him to gaol for six years in July 2007 for buying weapons from the bombers. Dutt claimed he needed them to protect his family and said he would appeal. In November 2007, he was released on bail. Meanwhile, Ibrahim became India's most wanted man. The Indian authorities claimed he was in Pakistan, but Pakistan denied it.

## · THE EAST AFRICAN US EMBASSY BOMBINGS ·

Osama bin Laden first came to the world's attention on 7 August 1998. At a quarter to eleven that morning bombs went off almost simultaneously at the American embassies in Kenya and Tanzania. The attacks were quickly linked to the al-Qaeda terrorist organisation. The embassy in Nairobi was in a busy central area of the city, and at the time of the blast the US ambassador, Prudence Bushnell, was meeting the Kenyan trade minister on the top floor of a nearby building. She heard a loud bang, later identified as the stun grenade the terrorists had thrown at a security guard; then, as she went to the window to investigate, she was thrown off her feet by a massive explosion and knocked unconscious. When she came round she followed staff filing down the emergency staircase: 'A huge procession of people who were bleeding all over each other.' The embassy building survived the huge truck bomb, but behind it a seven-storey block was flattened. An eighteen-year-old Kenyan named James Muiruri who had been in a long queue for US visas said he heard a bang, then the lights flickered, the building shook, objects shattered and people screamed: 'The visa interviewers, separated from us applicants by a counter, died before our eyes when their computers exploded. They were completely still, looking at us over the counter.' Outside, 'Smoke covered the whole city. I thought it was war.' Two buses were on fire. He saw a man who had been badly burned, and his skin was peeling off. Everywhere people were trying to help the injured.

The bomb sent a mushroom cloud of dust and smoke rising above the city. Trees were ripped up by the roots, shop windows shattered for miles around and cars were hurled into the air or burned to a cinder with their drivers still inside. Thousands of people were running screaming through the streets. The chief administrator of Nairobi Hospital said that almost immediately they received 'a deluge of people streaming with blood'. Heavily armed US marines quickly took up positions around the shattered embassy and cordoned it off behind a screen of barbed wire and sheeting. Over the next few days some Kenyans complained the Americans would not help while they combed neighbouring buildings for signs of life. They claimed the marines brushed away requests for shovels and digging tools to leave them scrabbling in the debris with their bare hands. Of the 257 people killed, just 12 were Americans. The embassy in Dar es Salaam was further from the city centre and the death toll there was much lower – eleven people.

A previously unknown group calling itself the Islamic Army for the Liberation of the Holy Places immediately claimed responsibility for both bombings and said there would be more attacks to drive Americans from Muslim countries. They demanded the release of Sheikh Omar Abdel Rahman, the blind Egyptian cleric imprisoned in connection with the 1993 World Trade Center bombing in New York, which had killed six people. The USA was convinced the organisation was part of al-Qaeda. Less than two weeks after the bombs exploded President Clinton ordered cruise missile strikes on what US officials said were terrorist training camps in Afghanistan and a chemical weapons facility in the Sudan. The Taliban government in Afghanistan denied there were any training camps in their country while the Sudanese said the Americans had hit a pharmaceuticals factory.

In October 2001 four alleged al-Qaeda operatives were sentenced to life imprisonment in the United States for their part in the bombings. Mohamed Rashed Daoud Al-Owhali, a twenty-four-year-old Saudi, admitted he had driven the truck to the Nairobi embassy, and that he had thrown stun grenades at guards. The lawyer representing a thirty-six-year-old Jordanian, Mohamed Sadeek Odeh, said he was a 'soldier in the military wing of al-Qaeda' and that he considered the embassy attacks a blow against the USA for its support of Israel. The trial took place in New York, a few blocks from the wreckage of the World Trade Center, which had been destroyed in the world's deadliest terrorist attack just six weeks earlier.

## · 9/11 ·

The World Trade Center's Twin Towers, each of 110 storeys, were the highest buildings in New York. Ten people were convicted of attacking them in 1993, and eight years later they would be targeted again. On the warm, clear morning of 11 September 2001 the blue skies above America were as busy as ever with business travellers criss-crossing the country. Among the passengers that morning, though, were nineteen al-Qaeda terrorists in four teams who would each use box-cutter knives to take over aircraft en route to California from the east coast – American Airlines Flights 11 and 77, and United Flights 93 and 175. The hijackers also claimed they had bombs, but these were probably fake. Each team included a pilot who had been trained in the USA.

The first aircraft to hit its target was Flight 11, which flew into the North Tower, 1 World Trade Center, at 8.46 a.m. Seventeen minutes later, Flight 175 struck the South Tower, 2 World Trade Center. At 9.37 a.m. Flight 77 hit the Pentagon. Meanwhile, a struggle was taking place on Flight 93. Black-box recordings reveal that the crew and passengers tried to wrest control of the aircraft from the hijackers after learning through phone calls that the other hijacked planes had been crashed into buildings. The al-Qaeda pilot started rolling the plane and at about 10.20 a.m. it crashed into a field near Shanksville, Pennsylvania. (Khalid Sheikh Mohammed, who would be put on trial for organising the attacks, said its target had been the United States Capitol Building.) By then, the South Tower had collapsed, and the North Tower would fall twenty-five minutes later.

After the first aircraft hit the North Tower, an IT specialist who was on the fortieth floor of the building joined a long procession of people descending the stairwell. Fifteen storeys down they started to meet sweating firemen moving up, carrying oxygen and hatchets. As he stepped into the daylight there was flaming debris in the plaza between the two towers, and the heat was intense. Once he was at a safe distance he looked back. The towers had 'charred, massive holes in their sides, and bright red flames were coming out'. A few streets away he saw a piece of an aircraft's landing gear. Then there was a great roar behind him: 'Thousands of us turned around and we saw the upper floors of Tower Two give way.' All he could make out through the haze of smoke was a silhouette: 'it seemed to become thinner and thinner . . . Finally, there was nothing left but a thin spine of elevator shafts. And then that seemed to disintegrate. Everything shook.'

A woman working in the North Tower walked down seventy-seven floors only to find her way blocked by debris as she neared the ground: 'I remember thinking there is no way I walked down seventy-seven flights to die three floors from safety. We climbed back up to four where a fire-fighter punched a hole in the wall to get us out.' Two lift operators in the North Tower, a husband and wife, both survived, each believing the other was dead. A man at his desk on the sixty-fourth floor of the South Tower was told to get out when the aircraft struck the North Tower. When he and his colleagues reached the fiftieth floor they heard a huge explosion, and a woman fell on his back from one flight up: 'The building was shaking and the lights were flickering on and off. It was terrifying! Then it began to sink.' Around the twenty-fifth floor they started to smell jet fuel, and he had to wrap a shirt around his head to breathe. Further down they looked out of the windows, and saw piles of bodies. Both towers had 'flames shooting out of them about 100 feet high, and when I looked at Tower Two, you could still see the tail end of the jet hanging out of the building'.

Among the people who had amazing escapes was an engineer who was due to be working on the roof of the South Tower. As he sped up in the lift, around the seventieth floor the lights began flickering and the lift started to shake as the North Tower was hit. He shouted to the lift operator to evacuate as many people as possible. Next he went down to the basement, where his firm was based, and began guiding firemen through the underground concourse. Then the second aircraft hit the South Tower: 'All of a sudden, it sounded like gunfire – bang, bang, bang. Three big explosions.' He found himself in a lift shaft: 'I thought I was dead. I could not see one inch . . . I just started yelling at people, "Pull me out."' He managed to get out of the building and walked away. At that moment the South Tower came crashing down: 'There were people screaming, total panic, people yelling: "This is not my war."' He escaped with leg injuries.

It had been the world's deadliest single act of terrorism. Altogether, 2,992 people were killed, including the nineteen hijackers, and all the passengers and crew on the four aircraft. An investment bank, Cantor Fitzgerald, lost 658 employees, while about 400 members of the emergency services, most of them fire-fighters, were killed. According to the US government's 9/11 Commission, around 16,000 people escaped from the Twin Towers. An official government investigation concluded that the initial impact by the aircraft blew off fireproofing from the steel columns in the towers. The floor supports were weakened by fires, making them sag, and this pulled the columns inwards until they collapsed. At the Pentagon, 125 people were killed.

The commission said the attacks were planned and carried out by al-Qaeda. Of the nineteen hijackers, fifteen came from Saudi Arabia, two from the United Arab Emirates, one from Egypt and one from Lebanon.

Another eight people entered America planning to take part in the attacks but did not do so. President Bush said that 9/11 produced 'a quiet unyielding anger' in the United States, and announced his determination to find Osama bin Laden.

The son of a wealthy contractor who had worked for the Saudi royal family, bin Laden was raised as a devout Sunni Muslim, and at school and university he came into contact with fundamentalists preaching jihad (holy war) against the West. He married and divorced several times, and is said to have fathered more than twenty children. Described as soft-spoken and polite, in the early 1980s he began recruiting Muslim guerrillas to fight with the Afghan mujahideen against the Red Army. After the Soviets withdrew in 1989, bin Laden returned to Saudi Arabia, where he opposed the stationing of American troops. He was expelled from the country in 1991 and went to the Sudan. Later he claimed to be behind an attack that killed eighteen US soldiers in Somalia, which was followed by an American withdrawal. In 1996 he was forced to leave the Sudan and returned to Afghanistan, where the Taliban gave him shelter. He wanted to cleanse the Arabian peninsula of the American 'locusts, eating its riches', and to liberate Palestine from Israeli occupation. The attacks on the US embassies in Kenya and Tanzania in 1998 (see above) were blamed on him.

Bin Laden initially denied being involved in 9/11, but the USA was not convinced and demanded the Taliban hand him over. They refused, and America and its allies invaded Afghanistan in October 2001. But they were unable to find their most wanted man, who continued to taunt them in a series of videos. It was only in 2004 that he finally admitted that he had been involved in 9/11, saying he had directed the nineteen hijackers.

Zacarias Moussaoui had been arrested three weeks before the attacks for immigration offences. Dubbed the 'twentieth hijacker', in April 2005 he admitted being involved with al-Qaeda and claimed he was supposed to help hijack another aircraft and fly it into the White House, but he denied knowing about the 9/11 attacks beforehand. He was sentenced to six life terms without parole. Leading al-Qaeda figure Khalid Sheikh Mohammed was captured in Pakistan in 2003 and then subjected to 'harsh interrogation techniques' – which many civil rights organisations say is simply a euphemism for torture – while in custody. The United States claimed he confessed to masterminding 9/11 as well as the 1993 attack on the World Trade Center and the Bali nightclub bombing (see below). In June 2008 he was put on trial for his life with four others before a military tribunal at Guantanamo Bay. He said that he would welcome a martyr's death.

## · BALI ·

Thirteen months after 9/11, on the night of 12 October 2002, a suicide bomber entered a nightclub called Paddy's Bar on the main street of the holiday resort of Kuta on Bali – a predominantly Hindu island in the mainly Muslim nation of Indonesia. At five past eleven he detonated his bomb. As people rushed into the street to escape, a second, more powerful bomb exploded in a van parked outside the Sari Club on the opposite side of the street. The blast set gas cylinders exploding and caused a fireball that engulfed buildings and vehicles. The wooden walls of the Sari Club collapsed like playing cards, and the flimsy roof caved in, trapping people inside, while those who escaped were confronted by blazing cars and motorcycles. A New Zealander saw 'a procession of people covered in blood', with shards of glass sticking out of them. Some had burning hair.

A British tourist who had been in Paddy's Bar when the bomb went off said there was a blinding light, followed by panic: 'loads of people diving for the door trying to scramble over each other'. He was still inside when the second bomb exploded in the street. When he finally got out 'it was awful, like something you'd see out of Vietnam. There were bodies everywhere.' Many headed for the beach, where people were walking around shouting for their friends. Victims were ferried by local people on their mopeds to the hospital in Bali's capital, Denpasar, ten miles away. Soon the morgue was overflowing, and bodies had to be stacked in corridors or under sheets in the alleyways outside. Other clinics were also pressed into use, but the medical services were overwhelmed by the number of injured people. Many had to be flown to Australia for specialist treatment in an airlift organised by the Australian Air Force.

The final death toll was 202, including thirty-eight Indonesians, and eighty-eight Australians – for whom Kuta had long been a favourite haunt. A week after the explosions, al-Jazeera transmitted a recording allegedly by Osama bin Laden praising the bombings, and warning: 'Expect more that will further distress you.'

Police discovered the vehicle bomb had been made from ammonium nitrate, widely used as a fertiliser in Indonesia. In April 2003 Amrozi bin Haji Nurhasyim was charged with buying the explosives and the van. Dubbed the 'the smiling assassin' because of his calm demeanour during his trial, Amrozi denied being a member of the organisation blamed for the bombings – Jemaah Islamiyah, a group linked to al-Qaeda that wanted a fundamentalist Islamic regime in Indonesia – but said he had done his duty to God. He was found guilty and sentenced to death. Another participant, Iman Samudra, was said to have been a quiet, studious child before becoming a religious teacher and going to Afghanistan to fight for the Taliban. He had stayed in the Kuta area for several days after the attack to witness the devastation and was also sentenced to death. Amrozi's brother, Ali Imron, who had mixed and packed the explosives, broke down in tears and apologised to relatives of the dead. He was jailed for life. Another of Amrozi's brothers, Ali Gufron, told police he was head of one of Jemaah Islamiyah's cells and knew Osama bin Laden personally. He said the bombings were to avenge Muslims against American tyranny in the Middle East. Gufron was sentenced to death. Riduan Isamuddin, thought to be the operational chief of Jemaah Islamiyah and a friend of Khalid Sheikh Mohammed, was arrested in Thailand and taken into American custody. Altogether, thirty people were jailed for involvement in the attacks. The executions of the three men sentenced to death were postponed the day before they were due to face a firing squad as their lawyers launched an appeal. Abu Bakar Bashir, the alleged spiritual leader of Jemaah Islamiyah, was often accused of inspiring the attacks. In 2005 an Indonesian court found him guilty of conspiracy and sentenced him to two and a half years' imprisonment. He had denied involvement in the Bali attack, and claimed the bombs were planted by US intelligence agents. Foreign governments, including those of the United States and Australia, expressed disappointment at the shortness of the sentence, but Bashir was released even before completing it to be greeted by cheering crowds. In 2008, two other senior figures from the organisation were each jailed for 15 years.

## · THE BESLAN SIEGE ·

Hostility between Russians and Chechens, who are mainly Muslims, goes back a long way. During the Second World War, as some Chechens threatened to help the Germans, Stalin ordered the deportation of huge numbers to Kazakhstan and Siberia (see Chapter 10). Many died. Then after the war, he tried to suppress local languages and customs. When the Soviet Union began to fall apart in the 1990s Chechnya tried to seize independence, but by then the region was poor, rundown and increasingly controlled by warlords. The Russians sent in troops and the Chechens responded by crossing into Russia and taking hostages. Many were killed as Russian forces tried to liberate them. In 2000 the Russians took the Chechen capital, Grozny, but the Chechens continued to fight a guerrilla war, and in 2002 they took 900 people hostage in a Moscow theatre. After a three-day siege Russian troops sprayed a mystery gas inside to try to disable the terrorists. They were all killed, but so were more than 120 hostages.

The campaign continued. Two women blew themselves up at an outdoor rock festival in Moscow in 2003, killing sixteen people, and on 27 August 2004 two Russian passenger aircraft exploded within three minutes of each other, killing more than 100 passengers and crew.

Just five days later, School Number One at Beslan in Russia's North Ossetian Republic was packed for the first day of the new academic year, as many parents and other relatives had come in to take part in traditional celebrations for the 'Day of Knowledge'. The school had been used as a detention centre for Muslim Ingush people during a civil war in 1992, and a number had been killed by Ossetians. At half past nine, thirty-two armed Chechen militants wearing black masks and belts packed with explosives invaded the school, taking more than 1,100 hostages – pupils, teachers and parents. The police arrived and there was a gun battle. About fifty hostages escaped in the chaos, but only one of the kidnappers was killed. The Chechens then herded the remaining hostages into the gym and surrounded it with explosives, threatening to detonate them if the police attacked again. That night they murdered twenty men and threw their bodies into the playground. They would not allow in medicines, food or water, and even refused to allow medical workers to remove the dead bodies. The heat was intense, and many of the hostages became dangerously dehydrated. It was said that the Chechens raped some of the women and girls. But after negotiations with an Ingush leader they released twenty-six breast-feeding mothers and their babies. One baby was released without its mother because she refused to leave her other children. One of the women released said the terrorists had told them they would be let out only after the Russians withdrew their troops. Then they had been herded into the gym: 'Everyone was ordered to sit down, and they began to set up booby-traps around the perimeter, right in front of our eyes. They had lots of guns and explosives with them.' At first the hostages were allowed to drink water from the tap, but the guerrillas soon put a stop to that because they were angry that the presidents of North Ossetia and Ingushetia would not come and talk to them. They broke some windows but it was still sweltering. The Chechens kept telling them: 'Your government is not allowing enough water for your kids.' For much of the time, the woman said, the guerrillas were running around the gym, waving their guns in the faces of the hostages and shouting at them to keep still or be quiet. She had been allowed to take only her baby son with her, and had left behind her six-year-old daughter. The girl clung desperately to her, but the terrorists said: 'If you don't go now, you don't go at all. You stay here with your children . . . and we will shoot all of you.' The woman admitted: 'I heard all the time how my daughter was crying and calling for me behind my back. I thought my heart would break into pieces there and then.'

After a time the gunmen said they would allow the dead bodies to be removed, but then they shot dead two of the men who came to take them. They also started to fire at the security forces surrounding the school. On the afternoon of the third day a bomb went off in the gym and a wall collapsed. This allowed dozens of hostages to escape, but as Russian security forces stormed the building a gun battle erupted, with the army also using tanks and flame-throwers. It continued until the evening.

The Russians stated that only one of the terrorists survived, though the Chechens claimed more escaped. Altogether, more than 330 people were killed, including 150 children. Ten of the dead were members of Russian special forces. Two weeks later the Chechen warlord Shamil Basayev claimed responsibility for the attack, while the Russians alleged that some of the terrorists did not speak Chechen and tried to link it to al-Qaeda. The only person to be put on trial was a twenty-four-year-old unemployed carpenter, Nur-Pashi Kulayev. He had hidden under a lorry but angry parents found him and tried to lynch him. He claimed he was told he would be attacking a military target, and did not realise he would have to take children hostage. He said he had not shot anyone, and that he had saved a girl's life, but there were reports of him shouting curses at hostages and threatening them with his gun. After a trial lasting a year the court convicted him of murder and terrorism, and sent him to jail for life. His father was unrepentant about his son's actions, saying that in Chechnya thousands of children had perished. One of his own sons had been killed by the Russians, while the eleven-year-old brother of another of the terrorists had been seized on the streets of Grozny and was later found buried naked with his head split open.

In Beslan there was great bitterness over how the authorities had handled the siege, and when a ceremony was held on the first anniversary local people asked President Putin to stay away. Shamil Basayev did not survive for long. In July 2006 he was riding in a truck packed with explosives when they went off, killing him instantly. The Russians said their agents got him. The Chechens said it was an accident.

## · THE MUMBAI TRAIN BOMBINGS ·

Ten years after the attacks of 1993 (see above), Mumbai was bombed again, with the loss of fifty lives, but worse was to come on 11 July 2006. The city has one of the biggest and busiest commuter railway systems in the world, carrying millions of people to and from work every day. A bomb went off on a train during the evening rush hour, and six more exploded over the next eleven minutes. All had been placed in first-class compartments of trains running from Churchgate Station in the city centre to the western suburbs. One exploded as a train was nearing

Bandra Station. A passenger said: 'Our compartment was filled with thick black smoke. When it cleared, I saw the dead . . . People in my compartment jumped from the running train and fell on top of one another on the adjacent track.' (A number of people were killed when they were struck by trains coming in the opposite direction.)

The trains' routes take them past shanty towns, housing some of Mumbai's poorest inhabitants, some of them in tenements hanging over the tracks, some in shacks made from corrugated aluminium. These people, both Hindus and Muslims, were the first to rush to help the injured. One rescuer, covered in blood, said: 'People were screaming for help and jumping from the train while it was still moving. We all climbed over the railings and ran to help them . . . We just picked up everyone we could and put them in rickshaws to be taken to the hospital.' One of his neighbours added: 'The government is always trying to move us away, saying we can't live here, but we were the ones who helped. Some of us gave up our own bed sheets to carry the wounded in.' Fellow passengers also pitched in, giving first aid or guiding the walking wounded to ambulances, but the official rescue effort was hampered by flooding from heavy monsoon rains. Emphasising Mumbai's reputation as a tolerant and diverse city, Muslims queued for hours to give blood even though most of the victims were Hindus. 'We don't care who gets our blood as long as we can save them,' said one Muslim man. The final death toll was 209.

Within thirty-six hours the government had rounded up 350 people for questioning. On 14 July a group linked to the outlawed organisation Lashkar-e-Toiba (Soldiers of the Pure) claimed it had carried out the bombings in retaliation for persecution of Muslim minorities in India, though Lashkar-e-Toiba later denied any of its people had been involved, as did another banned group, the SIMI (Students' Islamic Movement of India). If the objective of the bombers had been to stir up antagonism between India and Pakistan, it seemed to work, because talks between the two governments on border disputes were cancelled, with India saying it had evidence that Pakistan was involved in the attacks, in spite of political leaders there condemning them as 'a despicable act of terrorism'. There were also some fierce newspaper editorials attacking India's neighbour as 'the jihad factory next door'.

In September Mumbai's police chief said that Lashkar-e-Toiba had carried out the attack but that it had been planned by Pakistan's intelligence agency, the ISI, and that the SIMI had helped. Pakistan again rejected the allegations, saying India had produced no evidence, and dismissing them as 'yet another attempt to malign Pakistan'. Its information minister said India should search 'at home' for reasons for the 'growing insurgency' it faced. The police claimed eleven Pakistani militants had crossed the border and then joined up with Indian terrorists. They had transported the bombs by taxi and put them on the trains.

In December 2007 thirteen Muslim men, all alleged to be members of Lashkar-e-Toiba, were put on trial. They denied taking part in the bombings and refused to recognise the authority of the court. Police said they were still trying to trace fifteen other suspects.

## · IRAQ ·

Ironically, it was only after the United States, the United Kingdom and their allies invaded Iraq as part of the 'war on terror' in 2003 that the country became a leading theatre of terrorist violence. Almost every day there were murders and bombings, as Saddam Hussein's repressive regime was replaced by bloody anarchy. The attacks became so common that smaller ones often went unreported in the Western media; but some were too big to ignore. In March 2004 suicide bombers murdered 140 people at Shi'ite festivals in Karbala and Baghdad. A year later 114 people seeking government jobs died as a car bomb exploded in Hilla. And in September 2005, 182 people perished in Baghdad. Some surveys suggested the number of civilians killed since the invasion might be as high as a million, though the British and American governments contested these figures.

One of the worst outrages came on 23 November 2006 in Sadr City, a crowded, rundown, mainly Shi'ite district largely controlled by the Mahdi Army, the best known of the Shi'ite Iraqi militias, which had been accused of carrying out many sectarian attacks. The explosions happened while people were commemorating the life of Grand Ayatollah Mohammad Mohammad Sadeq al-Sadr, who was murdered by Saddam's regime in 1999. A suicide car bomb went off at ten past three in the afternoon, hitting the Jamila market. Two more followed in the next half hour, devastating another two markets. At about the same time, two mortar rounds struck busy squares. Then two more bombs exploded – one on the edge of Sadr City and the other near the office of the radical anti-American Shi'ite cleric Muqtada al-Sadr, the Grand Ayatollah's son and creator of the Mahdi Army. People rushed to put out fires and tried to drag bodies from the mangled wreckage of cars. Hospitals were inundated with casualties, and dozens of injured people were left lying in corridors. Angry residents and Shi'ite militiamen came on to the streets, shouting curses at Sunnis. It was the single worst act of terrorism since the invasion, killing at least 215 people.

Shi'ites retaliated by firing mortar rounds at the Abu Hanifa mosque, the holiest Sunni shrine in Baghdad. The next day they dragged half a dozen Sunnis out of mosques where they had been praying, doused them in kerosene and burned them alive. More than thirty Sunnis were killed around Baghdad. Areas where Sunnis and Shi'ites had lived together peacefully before the invasion were now riven by murderous sectarian enmity. The prime minister, Nuri al-Maliki, appealed for calm, saying: 'We denounce sectarian practices that aim to destroy the unity of the nation.' Leaders of the Shi'ite, Sunni and Kurdish communities all called for restraint.

In post-invasion Iraq, though, there was never long to wait for the next atrocity. On 3 February 2007 a Baghdad market was again the target as a one-ton truck bomb exploded in a mainly Shi'ite area, killing at least 135 people. However, the bloodiest attack so far would be carried out not on Sunnis or Shi'ites but on an obscure minority living in the remote north-west of the country. The Yazidis, who are mainly Kurds, adhere to a pre-Islamic religion. They believe God created the world, then left it to be ruled by seven angels, and that after death our souls are transferred into other living beings. They also reject the concepts of hell and the devil. Muslims have often accused them of devil worship, and over the centuries they have been persecuted and massacred by groups including the Ottoman Turks and Muslim Kurdish princes. Saddam Hussein deported them to new 'towns', which looked very much like concentration camps. In 2007 a video circulated purporting to show a

Yazidi girl being stoned to death for converting to Islam, and tensions began to rise. On 14 August four suicide bombers struck Yazidis living in the Sinjar region, killing more than 500, making it Iraq's worst terrorist attack. It came during the US military 'surge' that was intended to reduce violence. Three weeks later the Americans claimed one of their air strikes had killed the man behind the attack, Abu Mohammed al-Afri, who was said to have connections with al-Qaeda.

# 13

## FIRES

### · ROME ·

Nero did not fiddle while Rome burned; the violin was not invented until the sixteenth century. He may, however, have played the lyre or sung while his capital was consumed by flames in AD 64, or at least that is what some Romans alleged.

The Great Fire of Rome started in the early hours of 19 July in a row of shops at the Circus Maximus, the main venue for chariot racing. It would be, in the words of the great Roman historian Tacitus, 'the most terrible and destructive fire Rome had ever experienced'. Breaking out in shops selling inflammable goods, and fanned by the wind, the fire quickly swept through the whole length of the Circus. Rome's hotch-potch of shops, temples, densely packed tenements and mainly wooden houses offered little resistance to the flames, which moved 'with a rapid-ity which outstripped all efforts to cope with them . . . Terrified, shrieking women, helpless old and young, people intent on their own safety, people unselfishly supporting invalids and waiting for them, fugitives and lingerers alike – all heightened the confusion,' wrote Tacitus. 'When people looked back, menacing flames sprang up before them or outflanked them. When they escaped to a neighbouring quar-ter, the fire followed.' Finally, in despair, 'they crowded on to country roads, or lay in the fields. Some who had lost everything . . . could have escaped but preferred to die. So did others who had failed to rescue their loved ones.'

Gangs of thugs roamed the city, preventing fire-fighters from combating the flames, and sometimes using torches to keep them going. In those crucial first hours 'Nobody dared fight the flames,' wrote Tacitus, and the ruffians claimed 'they acted under orders'. This supported the conspiracy theory that the emperor himself was behind the fire, but as Tacitus conceded, the thugs 'may just have wanted to plunder unhampered'. When the fire broke out, Nero was at Anzio, thirty-five miles away, and he rushed back just in time to see his palace go up in flames. Then he spent all the first night, unaccompanied by guards, directing efforts to quell the blaze.

After six days the authorities had buildings demolished to make firebreaks which 'confronted the raging flames with bare ground and open sky, and the fire was finally stamped out, but just as it was dying down flames flared up in other parts of the city'. Fortunately, these areas were less congested, but they had more temples and public buildings, and the damage was considerable. The Great Fire was finally extinguished after nine days. By then, thousands had lost their lives. Of the city's fourteen districts, only four escaped damage. Tacitus reported: 'Three were levelled to the ground. The other seven were reduced to a few scorched and mangled ruins.' Many artistic masterpieces were destroyed, as well as the Temple of Vesta, where the statues of Rome's guardian deities were kept, the 700-year-old palace of Rome's second king, Numa, and the Temple of Jupiter Stator, said to have been dedicated by Romulus himself. The historian Suetonius said the fire demolished 'every ancient monument of historical interest'.

Nero appears to have provided generously for the tens of thousands who had lost their homes. According to Tacitus, 'he threw open the Field of Mars, including Agrippa's public buildings, and even his own gardens'. He also brought in food from neighbouring towns and slashed the price of corn. 'Yet these measures, for all their popular character, earned no gratitude. For a rumour had spread that, while the city was burning, Nero had gone on his private stage and, comparing modern calamities with ancient, had sung of the destruction of Troy.' The emperor was known to hate the slums, the narrow streets and the haphazard layout of Rome. He wanted to rebuild it to his own design, but the Senate had been resisting his plans. Now the emperor could do what he wanted, and some viewed that as far too convenient to be a coincidence. On the other hand, about a hundred fires would break out in Rome every day, so the city always faced the threat of one of them getting out of control. Whatever the truth, Nero got to work energetically, closing off devastated areas even to people trying to visit their former homes, and demanding that the new city should have wide streets and plenty of open spaces. A number of spectacular buildings appeared: a new Temple of Vesta; a bigger Circus Maximus; and above all a much grander royal palace, including the Golden House, decked with gold, ivory and precious stones, temples, baths, gardens, woods, fields, fountains and a huge artificial lake, all dominated by a huge 120-foot gilded statue of the emperor himself.

Nero initially said that the disaster was the result of divine anger, so, to placate the gods, he ordered a strenuous round of religious ceremonies. Still the Romans seemed to blame him, so next he claimed the Christians had started it (there is some evidence that in the poorer districts of the city they had been circulating texts prophesying that Rome would be burned to ashes). Adherents of this new religion were sent into the arena, and, 'dressed in wild animals' skins, they were torn to pieces by dogs or crucified', wrote Tacitus. It was even said that Nero used some as human torches to light his garden at night, but none of this reduced the emperor's unpopularity as his excesses grew ever more alarming. Among those he had murdered were his mother and his pregnant wife. In 68 the Senate condemned him to a slave's death by flogging. Nero forestalled them by slitting his own throat.

## · THE FIRE OF THE LONG SLEEVES ·

The story goes that in Tokyo (then known as Edo) in February 1657 a Japanese priest was burning an unlucky kimono. It had been owned in turn by three teenage girls, each of whom had died before she had a chance to wear it. At that moment, a violent wind sprang up and fanned the flames until they were out of control. The resulting blaze turned into the 'Fire of the Long Sleeves', one of the most devastating the world has ever seen.

Like most Japanese cities of the time, Edo was built mainly of wood and paper, with narrow alleys, and because of a drought, everything was tinder dry. For two days, the wind drove the flames mercilessly, and Edo's fire brigade was helpless. On the third day the wind finally died down, but for another four the city was blanketed with thick, choking smoke, and it was a further two before monks and local people were able to start removing the bodies. The fire destroyed sixty-one bridges, 300 temples, 500 palaces and 9,000 shops – altogether perhaps 70 per cent of the city. Most of Edo Castle, the headquarters of the shoguns who then ruled Japan, was also burned down. Many people drowned in the Sumida River as they piled on to ferries in an effort to escape, and many more burned to death or suffocated. The overall death toll was estimated at up to 100,000 out of a population of 300,000.

## · MOSCOW ·

It was one of Napoleon's great triumphs. On the 'magical', bright morning of 14 September 1812, having defeated the Russians at Borodino, he stood on the Poklonny Hill overlooking Moscow. In *War and Peace* Tolstoy describes the emperor surveying the city which 'lay spaciously spread out with her river, her gardens, and her churches . . . glittering like stars in the sunlight'. When Napoleon's soldiers entered Moscow, though, they were in for a disturbing surprise. It was virtually empty: 'perhaps a fiftieth part of its former inhabitants had remained'. One of the troops wrote later: 'The absolute stillness around us made us keep silence and listen nervously for every sound. Even the bravest felt fear.' About an hour after entering the city some of the soldiers began to see flames, but they assumed they had been caused by comrades who had already started plundering.

Napoleon himself went into in the city the following day, and set up his headquarters in the Kremlin. But the next morning a strong wind started whipping up the fires even more, setting ablaze the stores on Red Square. Soon the streets around the Kremlin were also on fire, and the wind was picking up burning pieces of wood and dropping them on the complex itself, igniting one of the towers. Napoleon and his aides decided to seek new accommodation urgently, but they were hemmed in by flames whichever way they turned. They were only saved when a group of soldiers temporarily abandoned their looting to help them out of the city.

The next day the situation deteriorated. According to one French soldier, 'a hurricane' blew up and spread the flames alarmingly: 'Within an hour the whole city was ablaze, a sea of fire, waves rising sky-high, spreading desolation.' The looters now tried desperately to escape: 'Burning logs rolling through the streets and embers cascading, red-hot sheet metal falling from roofs, the intense heat makes it impossible to breathe, and impossible to run: the cobbles of the street are hot as a frying pan.' Many officers rushed to take shelter with Napoleon in the Petroff Palace outside the city, some of them exhausted after trying to fight the flames. At first they had felt guilty: 'We could not look at each other . . . we were an army of criminals.' Then reports began arriving that the Russians themselves were setting fire to Moscow. Napoleon exclaimed: 'What savages! To annoy me they burn their own history, the works of centuries!'

On 17 September rain began to fall, and the next day the fires were out. But by then three-quarters of the city had gone up in flames. According to one estimate, 120 churches and more than 8,000 shops and warehouses were destroyed. The Moscow State University, libraries, theatres and many priceless works of art were lost. An estimated 2,000 wounded Russians and up to 20,000 wounded Frenchmen perished in the flames. No one knows how many of the Russian civilians who had stayed behind were killed, but when Muscovites returned to the city after the war, there were 50,000 fewer.

So who started the fire? The Russians blamed the French, while the French blamed the Russians, and even executed a number for alleged arson. The retreating Russians had certainly burned depots with ammunition, food and forage to deny them to the French. If they had decided to burn down the city as well, it would not be the first time such a scorched-earth tactic had been used. On the other hand, French soldiers had been given licence to pillage the city, and it is possible that some decided to burn what they could not carry away, or perhaps their campfires just got out of control.

For a month, the French tried to live on in the ruins, but on 18 October Napoleon ordered his army to leave. The retreat from Russia would be a humiliating disaster and the emperor would later say: 'I should have died immediately after entering Moscow!'

## · THEATRE FIRES ·

The world's deadliest theatre fire came on 5 March 1845, when 1,670 people were killed in Canton, China. Details are sparse, but one contemporary account records the building was 'consumed', and that another thirty nearby were also destroyed.

Fires in theatres were not uncommon in the nineteenth century, and on 8 December 1881 another swept through the Ring Theatre in Vienna after a huge lamp had crashed on to the stage just before the evening performance of Offenbach's *The Tales of Hoffmann*. In the confusion the management failed to lower the iron safety curtain. A disaster might still have been averted if the water reservoirs above the stage had been used to douse the fire, but no one opened them. Soon flames were shooting through the roof, and the whole building was gutted. Some of the audience managed to climb down ladders that had been raised to the windows, others leapt from high windows into sheets being held in the street, but many were trapped. As the audience rushed for the doors, gas lights were turned off to try to prevent an explosion, 'and in the narrow and intricate passages,' reported *The Times*, 'amid the most profound darkness, a struggle for life ensued'. Firemen had been beaten back on their first attempt to enter the building, but then they tried again 'in spite of the scorching atmosphere and the stifling smoke'. The first man they found was alive, but after that they discovered only dead bodies: 'Nothing was to be seen but a confused mass of human beings, who in their hurry to escape from a fearful death had blocked up the doorway and had thus been crushed and trampled to death . . . several of the bodies were so interlocked that they could hardly be separated.' Then a huge gas explosion brought the roof down, and the firemen could go no further.

An estimated 620 people died. The Governor of Vienna's report criticised the theatre for negligence – for failing to drop the iron curtain, for turning off the gas before alternative oil lamps had been lit, and for not calling the fire brigade quickly enough. The director of the Ring was jailed for four months, as was the commander of the theatre's firemen. The man in charge of stage lighting received an eight-month sentence.

America's worst theatre disaster came two decades later. In December 1903 the newest theatre in Chicago, the Iroquois, which had been open for only five weeks, was staging the musical comedy *Mr Bluebeard*, starring Eddie Foy Sr. The afternoon performance on 30 December had drawn a record house of more than 1,700, and patrons must have been reassured as they entered the auditorium beneath a sign reading 'Absolutely Fireproof'. The cast was performing 'In the Pale Moonlight', with the moonlight effect produced by stretching gauze over a blue arc light, when the gauze suddenly caught fire. Stagehands tried to put it out, but there was no proper fire-extinguishing equipment backstage, and flames spread to the canvas scenery with 'incredible' speed. As the performers fled, the stagehands tried to lower the asbestos safety curtain, but it got caught on a wire. Flames began shooting out into the auditorium from under it 'with a roar', fanned by the draft coming through the stage door that the company had left open as they took flight, while two gas tanks exploded, firing shrapnel in all directions. The audience now made a dash for the exits, but they were poorly marked and the aisles that led to them were very narrow. Worse, some of the doors were locked to stop people moving into more expensive seats, and others opened inwards, which meant they got jammed shut in the crush.

Some people jumped down from the balcony only to be burned to death in the stalls. Others managed to get on to the fire escapes that ran down the back of the building, but some of these were unfinished. One ended fifty feet above the alley below. *The Times* reported: 'This escape was crowded with women whom the frantic crowd behind gradually pushed over the railings to their death on the flags beneath, to be themselves in their turn hurled down.' Others tried to jump, but just a few survived, and only because their fall was broken by the bodies of those who had gone before. About a dozen escaped by crawling along planks that people in the buildings behind had managed to push over the narrow alley. Many died waiting.

It was only ten minutes before the fire brigade arrived and managed to rescue some people with ladders. They soon doused the flames, but by then 602 people were dead, mainly from being crushed or trampled. There was a huge pile of bodies, primarily those of women and children and they were so tightly packed that 'it was necessary to seize a limb and pull them out by sheer force'. A woman who escaped said she saw others 'fall fainting almost within touching distance of safety'. Whole families were wiped out, and *The Times* noted: 'Members of some of the wealthiest and most prominent families in Chicago were among the victims.' Of the 500 actors, dancers, stagehands and other theatre staff, only a tightrope walker died. Eddie Foy was hailed as a hero for attempting to calm the crowd, as was the lift boy who went up to the top gallery behind the scenes to rescue chorus girls trapped there. One stagehand saved a dozen women by making them join hands and getting them to follow him through a coal-hole to the outside.

Far from the Iroquois being 'absolutely fireproof', it transpired that no fire drill had ever been held there, that the asbestos curtain had never worked properly, and that inspectors had been bought off with free tickets. Within days a law was passed introducing a national scheme for the inspection of theatres, and fifty were soon closed. There was enormous public anger, and a number of people were arrested, including Chicago's mayor, the chief of the Fire Department, the city's building commissioner and the theatre manager, but the only person ever convicted over the fire was a tavern keeper charged with robbing the dead.

## · SANTIAGO ·

The world's deadliest fire in a single building happened in the church of La Campania in Santiago, Chile, on 8 December 1863, as devout Catholics, mainly women and children, crammed into vespers on the festival of the Immaculate Conception, 'the flower of the capital of Chile', according to *The Times*. The church 'was hung from roof to floor with floating gauze and rich drapery, and lighted with festoons of innumerable paraffin lamps'. According to a contemporary account, 'the crescent of lights at the foot of the gigantic image of the Virgin over the high altar communicated fire to the drapery overhanging . . . and in a shorter time than we can write it the fire had spread over the building'. Ladies fainted and were trampled on: 'A rush soon choked the entrances with a wall of dead and dying twelve feet in height.' It is not clear whether the exits were inadequate or whether, in the panic, the congregation failed to notice some that were hidden by screens. A British diplomat recorded: 'In their terror some of the poor people who had first reached the entrance must have stumbled or fainted, others had fallen over them, and in an instant a living, struggling barrier had been formed which the desperate throng, pushing forward from the back, had surged up against and striven in vain to overcome.' Melting lead from the roof and blazing oil from lamps poured down on the terrified congregation, 'who could be seen from the windows of neighbouring houses rushing wildly to and fro'. The church quickly 'turned into a vast brazier' which it was almost impossible to approach. There was no organised fire brigade and little water, but 'some mounted men contrived to extricate a few victims from the threshold by lassoing their bodies from a distance and literally dragging them out'. Then 'the big bell of the church came crashing down into the midst of the dying and the dead'. This, said *The Times*, 'put an end to their agonies.'

Most of the 2,000 or more who died were 'ladies of youth, rank, and beauty'. A contemporary wrote: 'scarce a family but mourns some of its number . . . while whole families have entirely perished'. Shortly after this terrible disaster the city established its first companies of fire-fighters.


· THE PESHTIGO FOREST FIRE ·

In 1871 Peshtigo was a booming Wisconsin lumber town, on the banks of the Peshtigo River that flowed into Lake Michigan's Green Bay. Houses were constantly sprouting up around the local sawmill, which was fed by the immense forest of pine and spruce that lay at the edge of the town. The summer had been very dry, and September saw a number of forest fires. On 7 October the *Marinette and Peshtigo Eagle* reported that fires were 'still lurking in the woods . . . ready to pounce'. The correspondent added that unless it rained, 'God only knows how soon a conflagration may sweep this town.' People who lived in the forest, though, were not too alarmed: they would often see smoke rising from fires that might smoulder for weeks. So when a neighbour told the Mechand family he had seen flames in the wood, Mr Mechand finished his breakfast before going to investigate. When he reappeared, though, he was running, saying he had climbed to the top of a hill and seen the fire approaching 'at a tremendous pace'. His wife later told the *New York Times* that 'the air darkened; a violent puff of wind rushed upon us, and smoke poured in volumes about the house'. Then a 'wall of fire seemed to be pushed down almost upon us, and instantly everything was in flames'.

Mr and Mrs Mechand, their six-year-old son Louis and Mrs Mechand's mother all fled, choked and blinded by smoke, and 'stumbling and tripping almost at every step'. After running for three miles through undergrowth that was in some places 'as close and stiff as wire', Mrs Mechand was exhausted, and the fire was still on their tail. Mrs Mechand's mother, who was mentally disturbed, ran off, and Mr Mechand chased after her. Mrs Mechand went on, carrying Louis until her arms ached and her 'limbs were scratched, bruised and bleeding'. All the time, she could feel the fire's 'heated breath . . . among the tree tops, sparks and firebrands were whirling in the air'. At one point a pack of wolves crashed out of the woods, and she and Louis hid behind a tree as the terrified animals rushed past. By this stage, 'My shoes were stripped from my feet, and my ankles were torn and bloody. Fallen trees lay in my way, but I clambered over and crawled under them in my desperate flight.' Finally, she passed out, and when she came to it was raining. Mother and son then walked for another hour or two before taking refuge in a hollow, where they fell asleep. Next morning, they were found by men who took them to safety. Mrs Mechand's mother was also found safe and well, but there was no sign of her husband.

By the evening of 8 October, ashes were being carried into Peshtigo on a breeze. Before long, a red glow appeared over the treetops. A distant roar grew louder, and firebrands started to fall on the sawdust that always clogged the streets. By nine o'clock that night, the pine pavements were on fire, and the flames were spreading to the town's buildings. A throng of humans, horses, cows, dogs, pigs and wagons charged down the east side of the river. But when they came to the town bridge they ran into a similar throng escaping from the west side. Then the bridge began to burn and, in the chaos, people and animals were trampled underfoot or fell into the water. The sawmill exploded in flames, and logs in the millpond caught fire. Some people sought safety by standing in the river. Burning logs banged into them and the heat set their hair on fire, but hundreds survived this way.

Soon, the whole of Peshtigo had burned to the ground. Next the flames headed north-east towards another sawmill town, Marinette, where the citizens tried dousing their roofs. Most of the women and children were put on to steamers which sailed out into the lake. Two mills were destroyed, as was the Catholic church, but a range of sand dunes seemed to protect much of the town.

The morning of 9 October revealed Green Bay lined with charred trees, burning peat bogs, and towns where burned fragments were 'all that remained of hundreds of peaceful homes'. Altogether, more than a million acres were devastated, and sixteen communities destroyed or damaged. More than 1,150 people lost their lives.

## · CHICAGO ·

On the very night that Peshtigo was burning down, Chicago was meeting a similar fate. In 1871 the city was just forty years old and one of the fastest growing in America. But 40,000 of its 60,000 buildings were made of wood. It also had more than 650 miles of wooden pavements. There were lumber and coal yards, paint sheds and furniture factories, and wood shavings and kindling were kept in sheds in backyards or under the wooden floors of houses. At the best of times the city was an enormous fire trap, and this was not the best of times. As in Peshtigo, there had been a long dry spell, and in the first week of October the fire alarm was going as many as seven times a day.

At a quarter to nine on the evening of 8 October a fire began in a barn behind Patrick O'Leary's house in DeKoven Street on the city's West Side. Legend has it that O'Leary's cow grew restless while it was being milked by his wife, and kicked over a kerosene lamp, setting the barn alight. In sworn testimony, though, Mrs O'Leary insisted that she, her husband and their five children were all in bed when the blaze started. Fingers of suspicion were then pointed at their one-legged lodger, Dennis 'Peg Leg' Sullivan, who was accused of nipping into the barn for a secret drink and starting the blaze when he lit his pipe. He in turn swore that he had seen the flames from across the street, shouted 'fire', then rushed into the barn and tried to free Mrs O'Leary's horses and cows. He lost his wooden leg when it got stuck in a crack in the barn floor, but managed to hobble out clinging to the singed neck of a calf.

At about nine o'clock a neighbour ran to the nearest fire alarm box, but for some reason the warning did not get through to the city's telegraph alarm system. So another twenty minutes went by before a watchman in the tower at the local fire station saw the flames; and by the time fire-fighters arrived nearby barns and sheds were also alight. Many of the fire-fighters were already exhausted after tackling a big fire the previous night, though a less charitable suggestion was that some had overdone the celebrations after they had got it under control. To make matters worse, one of the fire engines failed to work. By ten o'clock, sparks carried on the wind had spread the blaze to the steeple of St Paul's church five blocks away, and then to the furniture factory next door, which was packed with inflammable materials. Winds were now reaching sixty miles an hour and flinging burning debris into the lake.

It was hoped that the south branch of the Chicago River would halt the blaze, but it was so polluted that it burst into flames in a number of places, and at half past eleven the fire got a foothold on the South Side. Soon it was sweeping through the saloons and bordellos of the Conley's Patch red-light area. Next to go was the downtown business district. The post office, the customs house, the mayor's office, Crosby's Opera House, the Fire Department and the headquarters of the *Chicago Tribune*, which had warned the city it consisted of 'miles of fire traps', were all destroyed. The courthouse, headquarters of the telegraph alarm system, also caught fire. At half past one in the morning the building was evacuated, and half an hour later the great bell used to sound the fire alarm crashed into the basement. Now the question was whether the main branch of the Chicago River would stop the blaze spreading to the

North Side. Again the river failed to provide a significant obstacle. Burning debris carried the flames and set the water works on fire. Despite its thick stone walls, it was soon ablaze, and by three in the morning its pumps has been knocked out of action. Firemen arrived from as far away as Cincinnati and Milwaukee, but there was little they could do without water.

Of the city's 335,000 inhabitants, an estimated 75,000 fled from their homes. Some waded out into the lake, keeping just their heads above water and ducking when blazing timbers fell. One man saved his wife and children by burying them in the sand and leaving air holes facing away from the fire for them to breathe. He then stood in water himself for seven hours. Others were drowned when the boats they had swum out to caught fire. The wealthy sent their servants to bury silverware and valuables, and the authorities started blowing up buildings to try to halt the fire's progress. All through 9 October, though, it continued its relentless progress north. At five o'clock in the afternoon the Chicago Avenue bridge caught fire and was soon reduced to a twisted heap of metal. It was only at eleven o'clock that night, when the wind died down and rain began to fall, that the fire finally burned itself out. By then, the city centre was a mass of ashes and rubble. Nearly 18,000 buildings had been destroyed over an area of more than 2,100 acres, leaving 100,000 people homeless. It was estimated that about 300 people were killed, but the true death toll was never known as many corpses had been completely incinerated.

The *Evening Journal* recorded: 'All the principal hotels, all the public buildings, all the banks, all the newspaper offices, all the places of amusement, nearly all the great business edifices, nearly all the railroad depots, the water works, the gas works, several churches, and thousands of private residences and stores have been consumed. The proud, noble magnificent Chicago of yesterday is today a mere shadow of what it was.' The very next day, though, the city fathers met to draw up a rescue plan. Within a couple of days all the major newspapers were back; a week later the water was on again; and within six weeks more than 200 stone and brick buildings were going up on the South Side. The new buildings were much sturdier and finer than the ones they replaced, and by the end of the decade a far more impressive Chicago had risen from the ashes.

For a few weeks after the fire there were problems with looters, and the mayor called in troops under the command of Civil War hero General Sheridan to restore order. Tales of community solidarity were also common, though: one bank lost all its records but paid out to depositors on their word alone; and butchers donated meat to the destitute.

Astonishingly, the O'Learys' home survived the blaze, but in spite of their protestations that it was nothing to do with them an angry mob tried to lynch Mr O'Leary and he had to flee Chicago in disguise.

## · HOBOKEN ·

Hoboken, New Jersey, was the headquarters of the North German Lloyd shipping line. On Saturday, 30 June 1900, the *Aller* had just sailed for Naples, and there would be no more departures that day. The tradition was that people were allowed to come and look around the liners on Saturdays, and the fine weather had drawn many to view the ships that were still in port. Most of the crews were on shore leave while coaling took place. This was a major operation involving about 500 stevedores loading the coal from barges into the ship's bunkers. The *Saale*, due to sail the next day, was already coaled and ready to go. It was moored alongside the *Bremen* at Pier Two.

Just before four in the afternoon a watchman notified the Hoboken Fire Department that there was smoke rising from Pier Three, which had been vacated by the *Aller* that morning. Like most of the piers, Three was made of wood. It was piled high with cotton bales as well as barrels of oil and turpentine. In sheds and warehouses by the piers dust and debris had accumulated over the years, so the flames found plenty of fuel. Fanned by a stiff breeze, they were soon engulfing the coal barges and other vessels in the river, and lapping at the liners. Within twenty minutes the blaze had spread a quarter of a mile along the shoreline, and smoke was rising so high it could be seen for miles.

Lloyd's chief inspector, Max Moeller, tried to organise tugs to pull the big liners out of harm's way. The crew of the *Saale* had cast off and she was drifting away from her pier, but she was already burning. The first officer said that when he reached the lower deck, he 'saw nothing but fire.

It was raging everywhere – red, black, horrible. The smoke almost blinded me.' When he thought everyone had abandoned ship, he jumped overboard himself, but then he looked up and 'saw figures moving about'. There had been a number of visitors on board. He and his crew mates swam around in the river for a long time before a tug picked them up. The *New York Times* reported that those on board 'sent up piercing shrieks for help' as they jumped overboard or tried to climb down ropes. Some were picked up by lighters, tugs or rowing boats, but many disappeared. Meanwhile, the inflammable goods on Pier Three exploded with a sound like 'a rapid-fire gun'.

By now, the *Bremen* was also adrift and burning, and the flames had spread to the pride of the North German Lloyd line, the *Kaiser Wilhelm der Grosse* – the last word in luxury and the fastest ship on the sea – from a burning coal barge lashed to her bow. When the cry of 'fire' went up, sightseers were herded off, and the crew cut her loose. One man had to slash the last steel hawser holding the liner and then run to safety through the flames engulfing the pier. He received a chorus of cheers from the firemen. But the *Kaiser Wilhelm* did not have enough steam up to get away from the pier, so Moeller ordered two tugs to tow her out. Now another cheer went up, as the tugs turned their fire hoses on the liner's burning woodwork. On board, the ship's officers and men used their uniforms to beat out smaller fires, while the captain stood on the bridge with two pistols drawn. Order was exemplary, and no lives were lost. Damage was also minimal compared with that suffered by other ships.

On shore, the fire had reached four big brick stores filled with merchandise, including many bottles of whiskey. At first their iron shutters protected them, but then they were loosened by the heat and the flames slipped inside. Two of the stores were completely destroyed, and two severely damaged.

The tugs next tried to fight the fierce flames engulfing the *Saale* and the *Bremen* as they drifted helpless. The *New York Times* described 'flames bursting out in every part of the ships, men jumping overboard and others caught as in traps, trying in vain to force their way through the small portholes, while the flames pressed relentlessly upon them'. The crews of some of the lighters and barges had to leap overboard too.

Many were pulled aboard the tugs, but some drowned. By now, huge crowds were watching from the shore, and the mail boat *Main*, a new ship moored at Pier One, was also caught 'in a cauldron of flames'. People were seen trying desperately to escape through portholes, when smoke obscured everything. When it lifted, 'bodies were seen hanging limp and apparently lifeless in the same port holes'.

At about five o'clock, when the *Saale* had drifted a quarter of the way across the river, three tugs caught her and brought her to a standstill. Above the hissing of the flames the crews could hear faint cries coming from the lower portholes. They shouted to those inside to jump – some were picked up; others disappeared under the water. A priest had gone aboard one of the tugs to try to give Extreme Unction to those trapped on the ship, but the liner was now a mass of flames, with her rigging gone, her decks bare and her smokestacks 'warped like twisted reeds'. Smoke poured from every porthole, 'and every minute brought fewer and fewer leaping overboard'. A man at one porthole had been shouting to the tugs for an hour, his arm horribly burned. Behind him, the would-be rescuers could see the flames raging. Now they were close enough to hear him say that more than forty people were with him, including a woman and two children. Eventually, the tugs managed to beach the ship, but by then all human sounds from within had ceased. It was estimated that seventy-five people had been burned to death on board, including the captain.

By eleven o'clock, the *Bremen* and the *Main* had run aground. With the *Main*'s hull still glowing fiercely, a tug captain noticed a small oil lamp shining from the side of the ship. Then he heard knocking from inside. The tug's crew cut a hole in the hull and found fifteen crewmen who had been trapped in an empty coal bunker. They had jammed their clothes into any openings to stop the smoke entering, and one man had pushed his arm through a porthole to signal with the lamp. Some of the tugs caught fire as they closed in to fight the flames, but one managed to rescue 104 people from the *Bremen* alone. A few, though, rather than rescuing people from the ships or the water, were lured away by the rewards on offer from saving barges filled with cotton and coal, as well as floating barrels of whiskey. *The Times* said there were even reports of the crews demanding money from drowning people.

The *Saale* was the worst damaged of the Lloyd ships, and was the only vessel not to return to service, although the *Main* and the *Bremen* also suffered severely. Twenty-seven barges, workboats and harbour craft were also lost. All four piers were destroyed. The final death toll is estimated at anything up to 400. The *Kaiser Wilhelm der Grosse* managed to sail for Europe the following Tuesday, passing divers who were still searching for bodies in the water. What exactly caused the blaze remains a mystery. The most popular theory is that it was a discarded cigarette or a spark generated by a piece of machinery.

## · A DANCE OF DEATH ·

At Easter 1910 a dance was held at a village inn at Okorito, Hungary, to raise money for the local church. A petroleum lamp exploded and ignited the decorations. People ran for the exit but found it had been nailed shut. Many were trampled or crushed to death in the panic; then the roof caved in, killing many more. More than 330 people died.

## · HAPPY VALLEY ·

The Happy Valley racecourse was opened in 1846 to provide entertainment for British people in Hong Kong, but it soon became even more popular with the Chinese. 26 February was the second day of the 1918 season, and thousands of people had gathered. But just as the ponies were lining up for the China Stakes, a huge fire broke out in highly inflammable temporary stands made of rattan and bamboo. They had waterproof roofs, so, in addition to those who burned to death, many were suffocated. It is not clear what caused the disaster, but it might have been an overturned coooking pot. The death toll was 614, nearly all of them Chinese.

## · THE OHIO PRISON FIRE ·

In 1929 the *Handbook of American Prisons* said the Ohio State Penitentiary in Columbus was the most overcrowded major jail in the United States. Built to accommodate 1,500 prisoners, on 21 April 1930 it held 4,300. At about half past five in the evening, just as the inmates were about to be locked in for the night, a fire broke out on the top floor of one of the cell blocks. Flames raced along the whole length of the roof, so the top two floors quickly filled with dense smoke, and in less than half an hour the whole block was engulfed. Then parts of the roof began to cave in. Some prisoners who still had not been locked up fought guards trying to force them into their cells, or tried to make them open the doors of those who had been locked up, while other guards did start trying to let prisoners out. There were reports that one guard had shot an inmate who tried to break open his friend's cell door with a chisel. It was also said that when the order finally came through to unlock the doors, there was a delay because some keys had been lost, while others had already been grabbed by inmates. In any case, the heat was so intense that some of the locks had melted, so sledgehammers, axes and crowbars had to be pressed into use. *The Times* reported that some prisoners 'displayed extraordinary heroism . . . returning again and again to the blazing block after carrying out numbers of the dead and injured'. Many still perished, though: 'Through the choking smoke could be heard the continuous screams and shrieks of the dying.' In the prison yard some prisoners, 'driven mad by the agony of their burns, ran raving to and fro. Others, infuriated by the disaster, charged the fire brigade as they entered the yard.' The fire-fighters withdrew until troops arrived armed with rifles and tear gas.

After the main fire had been brought under control several others broke out. It was claimed they were started by prisoners trying to use the confusion to escape. One got away by changing into civilian clothes and walking 'quietly out of the gates'. In the end, soldiers trained rifles and machine-guns on the survivors and herded them into a corner of the yard.

When news of the disaster reached the outside world relatives of the inmates tried to storm the prison and were beaten off 'with difficulty'. Four cell blocks had been burned down, and more than 320 inmates had been killed. The remainder now had to be crammed into the cells that had not been damaged, many of which were flooded. Prisoners demanded the warden's dismissal, and some threatened to kill him.

It was the worst fire in American prison history. The local fire chief said no one would have died if the inmates had been allowed out of their cells, and an official investigation said there was virtually no fire-fighting equipment in the jail. According to *The Times*, the warden admitted he had 'considered the menace of escape more pressing than the fire itself', and had left a subordinate in charge while he went to organise a cordon of armed men outside. The inquiry was told that while prisoners on the upper floors were screaming to be let out, the guards argued about whether they should open the doors. The chief guard said he refused to open them without orders in case he was suspended. The Roman Catholic chaplain, Father O'Brien, claimed: 'Soldiers and police were all intent on keeping any convicts from getting away, and apparently nobody gave any thought to their safety. Soldiers came into the yard with fixed bayonets and stood about doing nothing while the trapped men died.' The report concluded the most likely cause of the fire was a light bulb breaking and setting fire to wood stored in an area where a new block of cells was being built. To try to combat over-crowding, the prison administrators moved several hundred inmates to a prison farm. The following year Ohio set up a parole board that eventually released thousands of prisoners.

## · THE COCOANUT GROVE NIGHTCLUB FIRE ·

Boston's Cocoanut Grove nightclub had once been a speakeasy. On the night of 28 November 1942 it was packed with 1,000 or more people, well above its official capacity. The club was decorated in tropical style with paper palm trees and cloth drapes covering the ceiling – very romantic and very inflammable. Just as the band was about to play flames were seen. Waiters tried to douse them with water, but they soon spread to the decorations. People with blazing hair rushed for the main entrance, but it had a revolving door and only a few escaped before it jammed. Soon scores of bodies had piled up inside. Fire burst across the dance floor, and within five minutes the entire club was ablaze. Some people tried to get out through side doors, but most had been welded shut to stop customers leaving without paying their bills. The others opened inwards, so they were soon jammed too.

People had to crawl on the floor or feel their way along the walls through searing heat and choking, blinding smoke as they looked for a way out amid the chaos of overturned tables and broken dishes. One of the few to survive in the downstairs Melody Lounge was the bartender, who covered his head with a napkin doused in water and managed to crawl out through the kitchen. John Rizzo, a twenty-one-year-old waiter, recalled: 'Everybody panicked. I knew there was a door across the dining room, but about 150 people were headed for it, and everybody was pressed together, arms jammed to our sides. The flames came down the side of the dining room like a forest fire.' Rizzo suddenly found himself pushed through a door and fell head over heels into the kitchen, landing on top of other people. He tried to persuade the cashier to escape but she said: 'I can't leave the money.' Later he saw her charred body among the dead. About fifty people managed to get on to the roof then jump down on to cars parked outside. The manager led another dozen into a huge refrigerator in the basement. A man who had been repairing the sound system just before the fire broke out ran back to the club to help. He knew of a small window over the bar, so he climbed up, 'shoved away bottles and started hoisting people out, head first'. A chorus girl was worried about fur coats being destroyed.

The fire brigade were putting out a small fire a few blocks away when they saw smoke coming from the Cocoanut Grove, so they were on the scene very quickly. Eventually, more than 180 fire-fighters would join the fight against the blaze. However, as the night wore on the temperature dropped, water on the cobblestones turned to ice and hoses froze.

The next day the *Boston Globe* said it was the worst disaster in the city's history. For months after, the injured died in hospital, until the final toll reached 490, of whom more than 50 were soldiers, sailors or marines. Among them was a Hollywood Western star, Buck Jones. The Boston College football team had a lucky escape. They had been due to celebrate that night at the Cocoanut Grove, but they suffered a surprise defeat and cancelled their reservation. A coastguard spent ten months in hospital with severe burns but survived. He had returned to the inferno four times in search of his date, not knowing that she had already escaped. Years later he died in a fire following a car crash. The death toll might have been even worse, but hospitals had recently increased their stocks of plasma, oxygen tents and other medical equipment following America's entry into the war.

An investigation was unable to determine with any certainty how the fire had started, but the favourite explanation was that a young soldier in the intimate Melody Lounge had removed a light bulb to create more privacy for himself and his date. A sixteen-year-old busboy (who survived) was told to replace it, but dropped the bulb on the ground. It was so dark he had to light a match to search for it, and this ignited the decorations. It was clear, though, that there had been many violations of the fire safety code, and the fire service said 300 lives could have been saved if the doors had opened outwards instead of inwards. The blaze was followed by a major tightening up of safety regulations for clubs: exit signs had to be lit, and revolving doors had to have conventional doors installed next to them. The club's proprietor, Barney Welansky, was sentenced to fifteen years in jail for manslaughter, but quietly pardoned after serving four. Nine weeks later he died from cancer.

## · THE ASUNCIÓN SUPERMARKET FIRE ·

On Sunday, 1 August 2004, many families were eating in the food court of the huge Ycua Bolanos supermarket in Asunción, the capital of Paraguay, when there was an enormous gas explosion. Fire then spread through the building with such terrifying speed that firemen found cashiers sitting dead at their tills. Other victims were found hugging each other. Some were burned alive in their vehicles as the blaze swept through an underground car park. A newspaper reporter heard a little boy sobbing and shouting: 'I'm looking for my mother! Where is she? She's tall and has black hair.' As President Frutos rushed to the scene with his wife, people outside tried to break windows to let in air for those suffocating inside, and some got out by knocking holes in the walls.

Paraguay is one of the poorest countries in South America, and its emergency services were severely stretched. Television pictures showed fire-fighters using their feet to try to plug holes in hoses, and some survivors had to be taken to hospital in open trucks. A total of 432 people died, including many children, and several whole families perished.

After allegations that exits had been locked, three people were charged in connection with the fire – the two owners of the supermarket and a security guard. The prosecution demanded murder convictions, which might carry twenty-five year sentences, but on 5 December 2006 all three were convicted of involuntary manslaughter and imprisoned for five years. Families of the victims were furious and rioted, starting fires and ransacking the court and the headquarters of the supermarket chain. Police had to fire rubber bullets to disperse them.

# 14

# EXPLOSIONS & MASS POISONINGS

## · RHODES ·

In 1856 lightning struck the church of St John on the Greek island of Rhodes and blew up a forgotten cache of gunpowder in its vault. Eight hundred people died in one of the deadliest accidental explosions in history.

## · COURRIÈRES ·

In the early years of the twentieth century most of the 4,000 inhabitants of Courrières in northern France depended on the local colliery for their livelihood. On the morning of Saturday, 10 March 1906, about 1,800 men and boys went underground. Just after half past six, as three cages were going down the shafts, there was a violent explosion. It damaged buildings at the pit head, and soon afterwards, four miners appeared at the surface. They said they had clambered over the bodies of men and horses to reach the ladders they had to climb to escape. Almost at once, flames began pouring out of the pit.

Miners' wives and children flocked to the colliery. The police were called, but they found it hard to hold back the crowd as more flames rose from the pit. Rescue parties bravely went down the shafts and managed to bring up 650 men who had been working some distance from the explosion. They toiled all day and night in relays, but it grew harder as they neared the site of the blast. Every time they came back up a shiver of anxiety ran through the crowd. If they carried only dead bodies, wrote one eyewitness, 'there were heartrending cries of grief and disappointment'.

Late in the afternoon, a miner named Leon Cerf had emerged with a few others. He said that after the explosion the foreman had told them to lie down to avoid the first gust of poisonous air rushing through the mine. He could not describe 'the agony of the eight hours' waiting that followed. Eventually, at about three o'clock, the foreman had said: 'I feel I'm dying, let's try to get out.' They tried to follow but lost contact with him. On their hour-long trek, they passed many dead colleagues, some suffocated, others burned or crushed. Cerf had had to leave behind his fifteen-year-old son: 'I could only save my little nephew, whom I carried on my back . . . groping my way on my knees.'

Another man appeared at the surface with a broken arm. He had heard rumbling, then cracking, then a long reverberating sound, which grew louder and louder. They 'stood immovable from fright', then the chief overseer shouted, 'Firedamp!' – the miners' name for inflammable gases like methane. 'Ah! How we rushed,' said the miner. 'You would have walked over your father.' He had no idea how he reached the shaft, or how many of his comrades were left behind. When he first saw the sky at the top of the shaft he and his colleagues shouted and cheered, but a rumbling noise was increasing in volume below them. They experienced 'eternities of suffering before the cage began to ascend'.

One rescue worker said the mine was like a battlefield: 'Dead and wounded were everywhere . . . Bodies were found lying in heaps, and the groans issuing from these ghastly mounds showed that living men were there.' In many cases his team could not reach the survivors, and had to leave them to die. Eventually, so many of the underground galleries collapsed that the search had to be abandoned.

Then, astonishingly, on 30 March, a group of thirteen survivors emerged from the pit. They had survived for twenty days on food taken down by miners to eat during their breaks, and later by slaughtering a horse. Two were awarded the Légion d'honneur; the other eleven, three of whom were under eighteen, received the Médaille d'or de courage. They had lost all sense of time, and believed they had been trapped for only four or five days.

The final death toll was 1,099. Attention soon turned to the cause of the blast, but in his official report the general inspector of mines said it 'could not be determined with absolute certainty'. Even now, it remains a mystery. It seems clear that the disaster resulted from coal dust exploding, but it is not known what ignited it. Perhaps the explosives being used to widen a gallery or simply the naked flame in a miner's lamp? The company that operated the mine had won an industry award the previous year, but a left-wing deputy in the French parliament was unimpressed, claiming the explosion had been caused by its 'excessive parsimony'.

## · HALIFAX ·

What was said to have been the biggest man-made explosion in history before the atomic bomb was invented devastated Halifax, Nova Scotia, during the First World War. Halifax was Canada's main wartime port, and on the morning of 6 December 1917 the harbour was packed with shipping. The *Mont-Blanc*, a merchant vessel on charter to the French government, was arriving from New York City to join a convoy, carrying 2,700 tons of explosives, including gun cotton and TNT, as well as high-octane benzene fuel stored in drums on her decks. At the same time, a Norwegian vessel, the *Imo*, was leaving for New York to pick up relief supplies for Belgian civilians. At the harbour's narrowest point, they collided, and a number of benzene drums split on the French ship. A fire started, and the captain ordered all hands to abandon ship. Then the vessel drifted towards the harbour and collided with a pier.

A storekeeper who could see the *Mont-Blanc* on fire from his home called local fire stations at about a quarter to nine. Several turned out, but they did not know the ship was carrying munitions. The fire chief and his deputy also came, and a number of bystanders gathered as the flames began spreading to the docks. Just after nine o'clock, while the fire-fighters were unrolling their hoses, the *Mont-Blanc* exploded with a force equivalent to a quarter of the power of the Hiroshima atomic bomb (see Chapter 10). The fire chief, his deputy and half a dozen other firemen were killed instantly. The ship disintegrated, a giant fireball rose a mile into the air, and an estimated 3,000 tons of hot metal rained down on Halifax and Dartmouth.

An injured fire-fighter saw people hanging dead out of windows, or flung on to overhead telegraph wires. The hospital was snowed under with so many injured people that he had to lie on the floor for two days while waiting for a bed. A man working in a building on the waterfront said that after the explosion, 'a gust of wind swept through the shed, and down came pillars, boards, and beams'. He ran outside and saw people 'lying under timbers, stones, and other debris, some injured beyond recognition, others at the point of death'. He reckoned he pulled more than twenty men, women and children from the wreckage, but there was worse to come.

The explosion knocked over many stoves and lamps, starting fires that soon had whole streets ablaze: 'Some men, half-demented, dashed into the burning debris in the effort to rescue their wives and families while little children were running along, some covered with blood, crying for their parents.' An eyewitness who had served in France said the scene was more terrible than anything he had seen there: 'Many people with fractured skulls or broken bones were lying unattended in the streets.'

The explosion also generated a wave that rose fifty feet above the high water mark. It drowned many people, and dumped the *Imo* on the Dartmouth shore. Fire-fighters from surrounding communities rushed to help, but they were hampered by the fact that hoses and hydrants were not standardised. More than 325 acres of Halifax were flattened, and an eyewitness described one local hospital as 'a synonym for horror . . . broken bones, scalds, burns due to the contact with stoves or boilers . . . but undoubtedly the most ghastly wounds were those inflicted by the flying glass'. Windows were broken up to ten miles away, while the explosion could be heard for two hundred miles. Part of the *Mont-Blanc*'s anchor was found two and a half miles from the scene, a gun barrel travelled three and a half miles, and a railway coach was flung a mile. One man was said to have been hurled the same distance only to land in a tree and survive. Rumours spread that Halifax had been bombed by Zeppelins or bombarded by the German Navy, and survivors with German names were attacked. The following day, sixteen inches of snow fell, freezing to death many of those trapped in the rubble, but at least it damped down the fires.

The docks and the factories around them were largely destroyed, as were more than 1,600 homes. No one knows exactly how many people died, but it was at least 1,950. The death toll would have been even higher except for the courage of a train dispatcher named Vincent Coleman. He had been warned that the *Mont-Blanc* was on fire and was about to run for it. Then he remembered a passenger train from Boston was due in the next few minutes, so he returned to his post and sent a telegraph message to warn the crew. The train, which was carrying more than 700 passengers, stopped a safe distance away, but Coleman was killed by the blast. Doctors and nurses flooded into Halifax from all over the area and from the USA. Massachusetts also sent medical supplies, food, clothing, glass and glaziers. Every Christmas, Halifax still sends a giant tree to Boston in thanks.

### · OPPAU ·

'German town wiped out', thundered the headline in *The Times*. The town in question was Oppau, where poison gas had been made during the First World War. In 1921 the BASF chemical plant was making ammonium nitrate fertiliser, along with another chemical, in a 4,500-ton silo. The two products tended to get clogged together, so holes were drilled in the mass and small charges of dynamite inserted to loosen it. This might sound rather risky, particularly as ammonium nitrate is also an explosive – used, for example, by the Bali bombers (see Chapter 12) – but the technique had been employed on thousands of occasions without mishap. On the morning of 21 September, however, the ammonium nitrate had become dangerously concentrated in parts of the mixture.

At 7.33 a.m. – the precise time is known because all the church clocks stopped – there was a fearful explosion that devastated the plant. At the epicentre it left a crater more than 375 feet long and 60 feet deep. A train carrying workers to the plant had just arrived and was buried under debris. A *Times* reporter was soon on the scene to survey the damage: 'Three tall factory chimneys stand gaunt above the wreckage; of a fourth there is but a broken stump . . . Huge fragments of machinery lie about over a wide area.' Some of the debris had been flung into the town, where 'there is not a complete house left. Some are mere heaps of bricks.'

It looked as though Oppau had 'suffered a night bombardment or a stiff bomb attack'. People had been crushed in their homes, while children on their way to school were killed by falling masonry. Men who had survived the explosion would return home to find their houses blown to pieces and their loved ones dead or in hospital. About 80 per cent of Oppau's buildings were destroyed, leaving 6,500 people homeless.

The town was soon besieged by people seeking news of friends and relatives, and *The Times* reported that there was 'hardly a family that has not lost someone'. The nearby cities of Ludwigshafen and Mannheim were also severely damaged. Roofs were torn off up to fifteen miles away, and windows shattered over a twenty-mile radius, so that in Heidelberg traffic was stopped by broken glass in the streets. The explosion was said to have been heard in Munich, nearly 200 miles away. Altogether, 561 people were killed.

## · HONKEIKO ·

The worst mining disaster the world has ever seen happened on 26 April 1942 at the Honkeiko colliery in the Chinese region of Manchuria, in the period when it was occupied by the Japanese. As with the Courrières disaster (see above), this accident also seems to have been caused by coal dust exploding. A total of 1,549 miners were killed – about a third of those who had gone down the pit that day. The miners were treated as virtual slave labourers by the Japanese, and this may have contributed to the accident. On the other hand, Chinese mines still have a dreadful safety record to this day, with deaths running at 5,000 a year or more.

## · TEXAS CITY ·

Ammonium nitrate, which played such a devastating role in the Oppau explosion (see above), was also involved in the blast that devastated Texas City twenty-six years later. At the time, much of the United States was in the grip of a post-war recession, but the port of Texas City was booming. One of the vessels in its harbour on the morning of 16 April 1947 was the *Grandcamp*, which had served in the Pacific before being donated by the United States to France after the Second World War. She had come from Houston carrying machinery and small-arms ammunition, but the port authority there did not allow ammonium nitrate to be loaded, so at Texas City she was taking on nearly 8,000 tons. As stevedores loaded the fertiliser they noticed the sacks seemed warm. Also in the harbour, 200 yards from the *Grandcamp*, was the *High Flyer*, which was carrying 900 tons of ammonium nitrate and 1,800 tons of sulphur.

At ten past eight a fire was spotted deep in the hold of the *Grandcamp*. At first the crew tried to extinguish it with jugs of water and an extinguisher. Then the captain ordered them to batten down the hatches and cover them with tarpaulins, while they piped steam into the hold from the engine room to try to preserve the cargo. Unfortunately, the steam heated the ammonium nitrate and it began to give off inflammable gases.

The people of Texas City were used to the smells generated by its factories and plants, and even to the occasional fire. Most felt they were a small price to pay for their growing prosperity. If they saw flames, rather than running off alarmed, they were more likely to stop and watch. The *Houston Chronicle* said: 'It was like going to the picture show.' This time, the flames emerging from the ship's hold were bright orange and accompanied by dense black smoke. Quite a crowd had gathered, including workers from nearby refineries and children skipping school, while at the Monsanto chemical works staff congregated by a window to get a good view. By a quarter to nine, twenty-nine members of the Texas City Volunteer Fire Department were trying to spray the *Grandcamp*'s deck, but the ship was so hot that the water turned to vapour as soon as it came out of their hoses. The standard plan would have been to tow the burning vessel into the middle of the harbour, but no tugs were available.

At twelve minutes past nine the ship exploded. Her anchor weighed more than a ton, but it was still flung two miles. Burning wreckage caused fires for miles around, igniting oil-storage and chemical tanks, and setting Monsanto ablaze. The explosion created a wave that rushed fifty yards inland, sweeping away everything in its path. A longshoreman, George Sanders, was among those caught by it. He had climbed on a fence for a better view, and a boy he knew was watching next to him. The wild water hit them, rolling them over and over, pulling them down each time they tried to catch their breath, until finally the waves rolled back in the opposite direction. Sanders found himself by the local molasses factory, his hair caked black and sticky. There was no trace of the boy.

Some people, seeing the dirty orange mushroom cloud that rose 2,000 feet into the sky, thought the Russians must have bombed them. For a time a seismologist in Colorado thought the same, and the United States was said to have raised its state of defence alertness. The blast was so powerful that it knocked people off their feet in Galveston, ten miles away; and it broke windows in Houston, forty miles away.

Hundreds of people in Texas City were killed instantly: the curious bystanders, the ship's crew and all the volunteer firemen who had been trying to tackle the blaze. At the time it was the worst death toll for fire-fighters in a single incident in America's history. Survivors ran from the shoreline through streets littered with broken glass.

The blast had also blown the hatches off the *High Flyer* and made a small hole in her deck, but initially no fire was detected. Then poisonous fumes started to rise from its cargo, and the crew abandoned ship. They had been trying to cut the vessel from her anchor but without success. Two tugs finally arrived from Galveston but they could not shift her out of the harbour. The fire kept burning, and at one o'clock in the morning, fifteen hours after the *Grandcamp* had exploded, the *High Flyer* blew up even more violently, demolishing another nearby ship. Warehouses were destroyed, oil tanks set ablaze and yet more fires ignited so the sky looked as bright as if it were midday. This time the waterfront had been cleared, so far fewer people were killed. Two hundred fire-fighters were drafted in from as far away as Los Angeles, but fires were still burning five days after the explosion.

A garage and a school gymnasium were pressed into service as emergency morgues, and for days sad people filed through them looking for their loved ones. It took a month to recover all the bodies that could be found, and many were never identified. At least 581 people were killed, though many others, like travellers and foreign seamen on the ships, may have perished and never been counted. Texas City had a population of only 18,000, and it seemed no one escaped unscathed. The docks were completely destroyed and many industrial premises flattened, as well as 500 homes.

The cause of the disaster remains a mystery. Many experts believe it was spontaneous combustion, though the possibility of sabotage has also been considered, or it might have been something as mundane as a carelessly discarded cigarette. Today the *Grandcamp*'s anchor rests in a memorial park.

## · THE POISONED GRAIN OF IRAQ ·

Iraq was one of the first places on earth where wheat was cultivated, but in the twentieth century life there was tough for most farmers as they tried to eke out a precarious living on land baked by a pitiless sun. The summers of 1969 and 1970 were even drier than usual, so harvests were abysmal and stocks of grain shrank alarmingly. In a bid to stave off disaster, the following year the ruling Ba'ath Party decided to buy nearly 100,000 tons of foreign seed. (Saddam Hussein was then the president's deputy.) The authorities insisted it should be treated with a mercury fungicide, which was highly effective in combating plant diseases but also lethal to humans, and consequently had been banned in the USA, Canada and most of Europe. The treated seed arrived in September. It was vivid pink, and some sacks carried a skull-and-crossbones logo with a warning in English or Spanish that it should not be used for food, plus the words 'Poison Treated'. Unfortunately, few Iraqis spoke English or Spanish, although the government did drop half a million warning leaflets over agricultural areas. Distribution warehouses were supposed to get signed statements from customers saying that they understood the grain had been treated with mercury, but not all of them bothered.

In some areas the grain arrived too late for planting, so it was used to bake bread. Some people said the pink bread was the best they had ever tasted, and offered it to special guests, but those who ate it soon began to experience disturbing symptoms – a prickling sensation on the skin, blurred vision and violent vomiting. Then there might be uncoordinated muscle movements, blindness, deafness, coma and death. Mercury attacks the brain and the nervous system, so many victims would just collapse and lie helpless where they fell. The sacks in which the grain had been delivered carried information on what to do if it was accidentally swallowed, but again it was in English. A writer travelling through the country said there were victims in virtually every village. One was deserted except for a frail old woman who just pointed her stick towards a bigger town in the distance and shouted, 'Doctor! Doctor!' In another, a group of youngsters were trying to play football. Some lurched and reeled grotesquely as if they were drunk, while others stared vacantly. One boy who was clearly blind ran headlong into a bush.

By January 1972, the hospitals were inundated with poisoned peasants, and the government ordered that all the treated grain must be returned to the warehouses at once. It decreed that it must not be fed to humans or animals, and that anyone who disobeyed this instruction faced the death penalty. But some farmers had already been feeding it to their cattle. As the animals fell ill and lost weight, desperate owners sold them while they could, so poisoned meat began appearing in butchers' shops. The government closed all the abattoirs and even went so far as to ban the eating of meat for two months. It also restricted fish sales because some farmers had dumped the poisoned grain in rivers. Not surprisingly, there were serious shortages and food prices shot up.

Establishing how many people died is almost impossible, because many victims never left their villages and were buried in unmarked graves. Estimates range up to 6,000, with perhaps another 100,000 poisoned but surviving.

## · BHOPAL ·

The world's worst industrial disaster happened in the early hours of 3 December 1984 at the Union Carbide chemical plant about three miles from the Indian city of Bhopal. An underground tank holding forty-two tons of methyl isocyanate (MIC) gas, used to make insecticides, sprang a leak. The gas, which is heavier than air, burst out and rolled along the ground. Many locals died in their sleep. Those who woke up had a sore throat, a frothing mouth or burning eyes, or they felt dizzy. Some started vomiting. There was a pungent smell in the air, as though chillies had been thrown into a hot pan. A woman said she awoke coughing violently, unable to breathe. She drove towards the city with a neighbour: 'It was gruesome, a nightmare.' There were countless people on the road in the dead of night, blindly stumbling into one another.

A man told how his three-month-old son died in his arms as he ran, while a nightwatchman returned home to find his wife and two children lying dead. The bodies of hundreds of animals and birds carpeted the streets, and soon thousands of people were being ferried to hospitals in lorries, buses, cars and rickshaws or on scooters. Without this huge community effort, said one doctor, many more would have died. Those who had tried to run for it seemed to suffer more severe poisoning because the exertion caused them to breathe more quickly.

By the following day, *The Times* reported, 20,000 people had been treated, and at least 2,000 of them were seriously ill. In Bhopal's main hospital 450 doctors and medical students were working desperately. *The Times'* reporter saw many young children thrashing 'in agony on their beds, choking, vomiting and screaming to suck in air'. Mothers dabbed their babies' mouths with water as they lay with oxygen tubes in their nostrils. Doctors predicted at least half would die. To deal with the overwhelming numbers, the authorities had to erect tents in hospital grounds and run open-air clinics. One doctor said he was seeing 1,200 people each day: 'At first there was respiratory trouble, then fever, now they are coughing blood. We don't know what symptoms we will see next.'

Union Carbide's managing director in India said the gas escaped when a valve broke because of a build-up of pressure, but a spokesman in America said the tank was fitted with a device designed to neutralise the gas if there was any escape. The police arrested three senior officials at the plant and cordoned off Bhopal, stopping trains and flights and turning back cars. Thousands were still fleeing from the stricken area into the countryside in spite of assurances from the government that the leak had been sealed. One correspondent reported: 'Wailing women with babies in their arms and children clinging to their saris are moving out of Bhopal in any available means of transport.' In the rush to escape many people were run over by buses or cars.

Mortuaries were overflowing, and bodies were burned at mass cremations or buried in mass graves. Packs of dogs sometimes dug up the corpses. One father was seen vainly trying to chase them away from the body of his four-year-old son.

When volunteers broke down the doors of houses in Jayaprakashnagar, the shanty town closest to the plant, they found hundreds of dead bodies but no one alive. It seemed that the victims had bolted their doors to try to keep out the fumes. Outside, at least half of the dead were children, many of them too weak and undernourished to escape. An Associated Press reporter described the scene in Bhopal: 'Thousands of dead cattle lie bloated in the streets, babies cry for milk. The leaves on the trees are yellow and shrivelled . . . Ponds are discoloured and lurid. The stench of death hangs over the city, mingled with the smoke of funeral pyres.' *The Times'* reporter saw two women in tattered saris walking down the street. One, whimpering and holding a dirty cloth over her eyes, was being led by the other, who was holding a cloth over one eye. An eight-year-old boy was rubbing his eyes. His father said the doctors had told him his son would go blind.

Many locals thought the plant manufactured medicine, so they had no idea of the danger lurking there. A charity worker said most people 'are still asking me to explain what came in the night and blinded them and killed their families'. The chairman of Union Carbide, Warren Anderson, now flew to Bhopal to offer his help, but there was growing animosity towards the company. A band of young students who lived close to the factory threatened to burn it down. Anderson was arrested but was allowed to return to the United States on bail of £2,000. The chief minister of Madhya Pradesh then claimed there had been 'cruel and wanton negligence on the part of the Union Carbide management'. Two years before the accident a trade union had pasted 6,000 posters on the walls of Bhopal criticising the plant: 'The lives of thousands of people are at risk. The factory is making gas but does not use safety measures.' Now a union official said there were leaks 'every week', and that maintenance staff had been reduced.

Union Carbide admitted that 'approximately 3,800' people died in the immediate aftermath of the leak, and that 'several thousand other individuals experienced permanent or partial disabilities'. Pressure groups such as the International Campaign for Justice in Bhopal, though, claim the true figures are much higher – up to 20,000 dead (with the number rising all the time), and half a million exposed to the gas, more than 120,000 of whom continue to suffer from ailments such as blindness, cancer and breathing difficulties, with 50,000 so ill they cannot work. They also claim the gas has caused birth defects.

The company says, 'a large volume of water had apparently been introduced into the MIC tank and caused a chemical reaction that forced the chemical release valve to open and allowed the gas to leak'. It maintains this could only have happened through sabotage. Critics of Union Carbide, however, say that cost-cutting measures compromised safety. They claim the firm cut back on repairs and training, and that employees were forced to use instruction manuals written in English, which few of them understood. They also allege that the number of supervisors was cut, and that none were on duty on the night shift. One worker was said to have been sacked after going on hunger strike for fifteen days to protest. The company countered that an inspection in 1982 revealed 'some safety issues', but that these were resolved before the leak happened, and that safety standards were at least as good as those in the USA.

After years of legal wrangling, in 1989 Union Carbide agreed to pay about £230 million in damages. The original suit had claimed £1.5 billion. The company says it has also spent more than £50 million on other forms of help for victims. By the end of October 2003, compensation had been awarded to nearly 570,000 people, including relatives of the dead. The average amount paid to each bereaved family was just over £1,000. There remained a good deal of resentment among local people about how little of the money reached survivors, and the anger was directed not just at the company but at local politicians, whose effigies were sometimes burned along with that of Warren Anderson.

Union Carbide closed the plant in 1985. Six years later the authorities in Bhopal charged Warren Anderson with manslaughter, and the following year the city's chief judicial magistrate declared him a fugitive from justice. Union Carbide has since been sold to Dow, and the local state government has taken over the site. Environmentalists claim the area is still contaminated by toxic waste, and have demanded that Dow take action to clean it up. Not all activists, though, want the site to be cleared. One said it should remain a blot on the landscape, 'so that people remember, as they do at Hiroshima'.

## · CHERNOBYL ·

It became the most famous power station in the world, but the nearest town to 'Chernobyl' is actually Prypiat. Chernobyl itself is about ten miles away. The station's four nuclear reactors started generating electricity in 1977. On Friday, 25 April 1986, inadequately trained technicians conducted a test. They shut down number four's safety systems while they removed most of the control rods from its core, and allowed the reactor to go on running at 7 per cent power. At 1.23 the following morning, the chain reaction in the core went out of control. A series of explosions triggered a huge fireball and blew the steel and concrete lid off the reactor, hurling a mass of radioactive material into the atmosphere – up to forty times the amount emitted at Hiroshima and Nagasaki. There was also a partial meltdown of the core. The initial explosion killed only two people, but over the years that followed the fallout would account for thousands.

Workers at the plant risked their lives to extinguish the flames, and the Soviet government immediately dispatched an emergency response team. However, they were not told of the dangers from radiation or given adequate safety equipment or protective clothing. Besides, their dosimeters could measure only low levels of radiation; with anything higher, they just went off the scale. So staff did not know how radioactive the area was: in places, it was bad enough to deliver a fatal dose in a couple of minutes. The reactor crew chief, Alexander Akimov, made a couple of mistaken assumptions. One was that the reactor was intact, even though there were pieces of fuel lying around the building. Another was that a new dosimeter brought in at 4.30 must be faulty, so its reading showing the area was extremely dangerous was ignored. Staff therefore stayed in the building all night trying to pump water into the reactor. None wore any protective clothing. Most, including Akimov himself, were dead within three weeks. Also on the scene quickly were fire-fighters from the power station's own brigade.

By five in the morning, they had put out fires on the roof of the station and in the area around the reactor building. They received high doses of radiation, and many of them, including their commander, would also die soon. The fire inside the reactor continued to burn until helicopters extinguished it by dropping sand, lead and clay.

Olexiy Breus, who worked at reactor four, commuted to the power station on the bus that morning as usual. When he arrived he could not believe his eyes: the reactor was completely wrecked, and he could not understand why he had not been told to stay at home. Then he saw water pouring down, and realised that he and his colleagues would have to keep damping down the reactor to cool it. He and three others went into a room which had been partially destroyed and opened taps on the pipes that led to the reactor. Then they went to the control room. Outside was a puddle that Breus was told was 1,000 times over the safe radiation level. That was the last he heard about radiation. In the evening a government committee arrived to investigate, by which time fifty-two people were in hospital. On the morning of 27 April the committee acknowledged the reactor had been destroyed and ordered the evacuation of 40,000 local people, who were told they would be away about three days.

In the first few weeks after the explosion thirty-one people would die, mainly fire-fighters and those involved in trying to clean up the reactor. At first the Soviet government said nothing, but on 28 April Swedish monitoring stations detected abnormally high levels of radiation and demanded an explanation. Only on 4 May did the USSR admit there had been an accident at Chernobyl. In Kiev, which had received a huge dose of radiation, a sociologist named Natalia Khodorivska said the first she knew of the explosion was when friends and relatives began calling from Moscow to say, 'Run, hide your children, something awful has happened!' after seeing a story in one of the capital's newspapers. Soon local people began to hear stories of convoys of coaches travelling by night to Chernobyl with their lights switched off. Natalia Khodorivska claims the authorities tried to persuade families to stay in Kiev, but evacuated their own children. Only at the end of May was it decided to send Kiev's children away, and by then the damage had been done.

A lorry driver named Mykhailo Martinyuk from the Ukrainian city of Zhytomir was one of a group who helped remove cows from farms near the power station. They never knew how much radiation there was because they had no dosimeters. By 2005, only four of the fourteen drivers Martinyuk knew were still alive, and in that year he was diagnosed with leukaemia: 'Doctors have prescribed interferon, but finding the money for medicine is difficult here,' he said. Hanna Semenenko was evacuated from her village to another 100 miles away. 'Oh God, how they tricked us!' she said. 'They took us to the end of the earth. We handed over everything – cows, calves, pigs. We took nothing with us but our souls.' She spent the winter in her new home but did not like it, so she returned to her village, where there were now only thirty-six people, most of them old. 'Officials come and check us, they check our food and our clothes. There is nowhere as clean as here!' she insisted. In the autumn of 1986, along with many of his colleagues, Olexiy Breus was allocated a new flat in Kiev. When he examined it with a dosimeter the readings went off the scale. Most people, he thinks, never had their flats checked, and if they called the local housing department they were told: 'Your flat is within the norms.'

In December the mass of radioactive debris still inside the Chernobyl reactor was sealed beneath a huge reinforced-concrete sarcophagus, much of it built hastily by remote-control robots. In the years that followed the sarcophagus deteriorated badly. There were fears that if it collapsed, something that even a very strong wind might cause, another cloud of radioactive dust could be released. Water also kept leaking in, spreading radioactive material around the wrecked reactor building, and perhaps also into surrounding groundwater.

The radiation cloud from Chernobyl spread across much of Europe. Belarus suffered most, receiving more than 70 per cent of the fallout. Altogether, more than 300,000 people had to be resettled, while millions still live on contaminated land. Ukraine and southern Russia were also badly affected. In April 2006 a report from the World Health Organisation predicted up to 9,000 cancer deaths in those exposed to radiation after the explosion. Some consider this a gross underestimate. A Green MP from Germany, Rebecca Harms, commissioned an alternative report that concluded the explosion would cause up to

60,000 deaths from cancer. Greenpeace reckoned it might be as many as 200,000. In addition, a group of German scientists said it has caused 10,000 children to be born with deformities, and that 5,000 of them have died. At Gomel children's hospital in Belarus, a senior doctor claimed in 2006 that only one in four babies born in the region is healthy, while Ukraine's health minister said more than 2.4 million Ukrainians, including 428,000 children, suffer from health problems related to the disaster.

Lena Kostuchenko was pregnant when the explosion occurred. She and her husband were staying with her mother in the village of Kopachi, just south of the power station. While they were waiting for a bus on 26 April they saw lots of fire engines and troop carriers. Then a policeman told them there had been an accident, and there would be no buses. 'There had been small accidents before,' she said, 'so we did not worry.' The next day she had to go to work in Prypiat. There were still no buses, so she and her husband set off on foot, but soon she began to feel 'very ill', and her husband took her home. Eventually, a policeman told her that radiation levels were very high and that 'pregnant women should get out at all costs. At that time I did not know what radiation was.' Two days later she was in hospital with lots of other pregnant women. Doctors away threw her clothes, then 'decontaminated' her with a cold shower. At first the medical staff said the women must all have abortions, and a few were carried out. Then they changed their minds, and they said the women should give birth. Lena was evacuated to the Black Sea, where her daughter Anya was born two months prematurely. The baby had to spend the first eight days of her life in an incubator, and her haemoglobin count was only a quarter of the normal level: 'At that time you were not allowed to say it was because of Chernobyl – it could be anything except Chernobyl.' Much later a haematology professor told her the truth. Anya survived but her mother said she 'is like a house plant. She has a very rare blood disease and almost no immunity.'

In 1987 the power station's director, Viktor Bryukhanov was sentenced to ten years in a labour camp, along with two of his deputies, but he was released in 1991. The International Atomic Energy Agency's first report on Chernobyl blamed the disaster on mistakes made by the operators, but in 1993 they decided it was caused by faulty design. By then, there had been another accident at the site, when reactor number two caught fire and had to be shut down. The whole station was decommissioned in 2000.

Today just 500 people live close to the plant – mainly scientists and maintenance officials. Among the empty buildings is an occasional one bearing a sign saying: 'Owner of this house lives here'. Prypiat, which was home to more than 30,000 people at the time of the disaster, is deserted. Some buildings are flooded; some have trees growing inside them; others are starting to collapse. When they were evacuated, the inhabitants were told by the authorities that they would be allowed back in three days, so they left most of their personal belongings behind. Nobody expected them to disappear, because the town will not be fit for human habitation for centuries, but looters braved the radiation and systematically removed everything they could, right down to the toilet seats.

# 15

# STAMPEDES, COLLAPSES
# & MASS PANICS

## · ROME ·

The worst sporting disaster in history happened in ancient Rome's centre for horse and chariot racing – the Circus Maximus. It was one of the greatest buildings in the world, holding up to 300,000 people. Beneath was an arcade of wooden shops, where the fire of AD 64 (see Chapter 13) had started. That had destroyed the stadium, but by 103 it had been restored to its former glory.

During the reign of Antoninus Pius (138–61), though, the upper wooden tiers collapsed during a gladiator fight. According to a Roman chronicler, 1,112 people were killed. The Circus was repaired again, and continued to host events until 549. After that it fell into disrepair, and all that remains today is the layout of the track.

## · CHUNGKING ·

In their war against China in the 1930s and 1940s (see The Rape of Nanking, Chapter 10) the Japanese bombed Chungking no fewer than 268 times, so the authorities built one the world's biggest air-raid shelters, with a capacity of about 30,000. On 6 June 1941 Japanese aircraft once again attacked the city for three hours. During the raid, the shelter's ventilation system broke down, so during an apparent lull between the waves of aircraft, hundreds of people rushed outside for a breath of fresh air. At that moment, the alarm sounded, so those outside rushed back to the entrance, running into people who were still trying to leave. In the chaos up to 4,000 people were crushed, trampled or suffocated to death.

### · LIMA ·

On 24 May 1964 Peru were playing Argentina in Lima's National Stadium. At stake was a place in the Tokyo Olympics football tournament. With just two minutes left Argentina were leading one–nil, but then Peru seemed to equalise. As the referee disallowed the goal for a foul, a howl of anger erupted from the crowd of 45,000, and two spectators then climbed over the wire fence and attacked the official. The police quickly grabbed them, but soon supporters were leaping over the barriers all around the ground, and the referee and players had to run for their lives. Mounted officers charged into the rioters to try to disperse them, while their colleagues fired shots in the air, threw tear-gas grenades, or set dogs on the crowd. Many fans trying to escape ran into locked exits and were trampled to death in the panic. Meanwhile, gangs of youths swarmed through the stadium, stealing watches, rings and wallets from the dead and injured. The rioters later moved into the centre of the city, overturning cars, looting stores and starting fires. The final death toll was 318.

### · MOSCOW ·

Another football disaster happened at the Luzhniki Stadium in Moscow on 20 October 1982, though its magnitude remained a mystery for a long time. The huge arena had been the main venue for the 1980 Olympic Games, but on this cold, windy night so few tickets had been sold for the UEFA Cup match between Spartak Moscow and HFC Haarlem of the Netherlands that the authorities decided to put all the spectators in just one stand, closing the rest of the ground. As full time approached Spartak were leading one–nil, and fans began to leave through the only exit that was open – a narrow, icy staircase. Then, during injury time, the home side scored a second goal. Hearing the roar from the crowd, some fans who had been on their way out turned back to join in the celebrations, colliding with others who were trying to leave. Police were accused of pushing fans back down the stairs. On the dark, icy steps, barriers buckled and dozens of supporters were crushed or trampled to death, but a Soviet newspaper simply reported: 'An accident occurred. There are some injured among the spectators.' The authorities prevented people collecting the bodies of their loved ones for two weeks, and eventually said sixty-six people had died. The following February the commandant of the stadium was given an eighteen-month prison sentence. For the next few years no matches were played at the stadium in late October to stop relatives of the victims laying flowers.

It was only in the dying days of the Soviet Union that the true horror of that night began to emerge. In July 1989 *Sovietsky Sport* accused the authorities of a cover-up, saying that 'a human mincer at Luzhniki on that day pulverised 340 lives'. If that death toll is correct, this was the worst football disaster in history.

· THE HAJJ ·

All able-bodied Muslims who can afford it are supposed to go to Mecca during the week of the Hajj at least once in their lives. Two million were in the holy city for the climax of the festival on 2 July 1990, and up to 50,000 had crammed into a 500-yard-long pedestrian tunnel which leads to a tent city for the pilgrims at Mina. With the temperature at forty-four degrees, the pushing and shoving became so intense that a number of people fell. As a crush developed, some pilgrims tried to turn back, but they collided with others still trying to move forward. One survivor said: 'I was pushed and fell over about twenty corpses and others were still pushing in two directions and walking on me.' Rescue workers threw in sacks of ice-cold water, but witnesses said people continued to pour into the tunnel in spite of the screams of those trapped and injured inside.

The following day Saudi Arabia's interior minister confirmed that 1,426 pilgrims had been killed. He said a few people had fallen, which had 'spread terror, and the tremendous throngs of the pilgrims caused them all to tumble on to each other'. Then the bodies just kept piling up. King Fahd said those who died had been 'martyrs' and that the accident 'was God's will, which is above everything. It was fate. Had they not died there, they would have died elsewhere and at the same predestined moment.' He added, however, that the pilgrims had failed to obey Saudi safety rules, and that 'No one can blame this country for this accident.' Iran, though, which had been waging a long campaign to wrest control of the holy places from the Saudis, specifically did want to blame them. A few days later the Iranian president, Ali Akbar Rafsanjani, called it 'a bitter incident' for which Saudi Arabia 'must answer to the Islamic world'.

There have been a number of disasters at the Hajj since. In 1994 at least 270 pilgrims died in another stampede, while in 1997 a fire killed 343 at the Mina camp. Then, seven years later, 244 people died in a stampede as they flocked to the traditional ceremony of throwing stones at pillars representing the devil; and 345 more pilgrims died at the same ceremony in 2006.


· SEOUL ·

The Sampoong department store in Seoul, South Korea, was one of the country's most popular, attracting about 40,000 people every day. The four-storey pink concrete building had been built in 1987 on an old rubbish tip, and was made up of two wings with an atrium in the middle. It was originally designed as an office block, but was changed to a store during its construction, which meant removing some support columns to allow escalators to be installed. The contractors refused to do this, so the owner, Lee Joon, sacked them and hired his own building company. Later a fifth floor was added to provide a food court of eight restaurants. Once again, the construction company working on the project advised against it, saying the structure could not support another floor, but again they were dismissed, and another was brought in to do the job. The building's air-conditioning unit was also put on the roof, creating a load that was four times the recommended limit for the structure.

In April 1995 cracks began to appear in the roof of the south wing. Then, on the morning of 29 June, there were more, and managers closed the top floor and shut off the air conditioning. Civil engineering experts were called in to inspect the structure, and declared it was in imminent danger of collapse. The building was packed with shoppers, but still the store's management did not close it. At about midday loud bangs rang out as cracks in the concrete widened. At about five in the evening the ceiling began to sink. Fifty minutes later there were more cracking sounds, alarm bells rang, and staff finally started to evacuate customers. At about five past six the roof gave way, the main columns collapsed, and the south wing fell into the basement. Within twenty seconds the whole building had fallen down, trapping more than 1,500 people.

Nine huge cranes were brought in to lift blocks of concrete, while US armed forces stationed in Korea joined in the hazardous rescue effort, as debris constantly shifted and acrid smoke poured from cars on fire in an underground car park. 'The most heartbreaking moment was when we had to withdraw because of another possible collapse, although we could hear some survivors shouting "help" over and over,' said a building worker from the rescue teams. 'When we went back there later, there were no sounds.' Thirty-nine hours after the collapse, though, rescue workers located a group of survivors, and they managed to get a long steel pipe through to them to provide fresh air, water and food. For the next thirteen hours they used electric saws, car jacks and their bare hands to clear a hole through the jumble of concrete slabs and iron reinforcing rods. They found twenty-four people, mostly cleaners, who had sheltered in a dressing room in the basement. The last survivor, an eighteen-year-old, was pulled from the wreckage seventeen days after the store had collapsed.

In the aftermath staff said they had noticed a number of problems during the Sampoong building's final days. A maintenance worker claimed he had reported a gas leak two days before it collapsed and recommended closing the store while it was repaired, but his superiors refused. The store's president, Lee Han Sung (Lee Joon's son), was said to have called an emergency executive meeting at two o'clock in the afternoon on 29 June, but they had decided to keep the store open and had given no warning to customers. He and the other executives had escaped unharmed. The owner of one of the restaurants in the food court said he had told an official about sections of the roof collapsing during the morning, but he was informed that the store would remain open. When the final collapse began, he said people started running for the exits but many were trapped. He himself managed to reach the basement, find a hole and crawl out. Altogether, though, 501 people lost their lives.

A police investigation revealed that the store had been built with a sub-standard mixture of cement and sea water, and that it had been inadequately reinforced, with only half the number of steel bars needed. It also showed that the concrete columns were too small, and that moving the air-conditioning units to the roof had fatally weakened the structure. Ironically, though, the final straw that broke the Sampoong building's back was the installation of a safety feature – fire shields around the escalators – which meant the builders had to cut even further into the already overburdened support columns.

Lee Joon was convicted of negligence and sent to jail for ten years. His son got seven years. A number of city officials who should have overseen the construction of the store were also jailed for accepting bribes.

## · LAGOS ·

To the north of the centre of Lagos in Nigeria is a big barracks and storage area called the Ikeja cantonment. It was also a home for many soldiers' families. On the afternoon of 27 January 2002 a fire broke out in an open-air market there. By six o'clock, it had spread to the munitions store, causing an enormous explosion that killed many soldiers and their families, as well as flattening a number of nearby streets and starting fires. Shells, grenades and bullets were set off, causing more death and destruction. Further away, the blast wrecked many flimsy houses, trapping people and knocking over cooking stoves to start new fires, while windows shattered for miles around. One eyewitness described a 'mighty mushroom plume', followed by 'an ear-shattering blast'. A man who lived half a mile from the munitions dump said: 'We started running . . . the stampede was unimaginable. The sick and elderly were abandoned.' Terrified animals joined in. Another man visiting his aunt near the camp reported a series of 'monumental and deafening' blasts that 'seemed to stop your heartbeat'. The exploding bullets made one woman think she was hearing machine-gun fire: 'We concluded it was a military coup and started praying.'

An estimated 20,000 people fled their homes. As the streets grew ever more crowded, the explosions caused panic, and people who fell were trampled. Near the camp was a banana plantation that many fugitives thought might offer shelter against the falling missiles. Next to it was a swampy canal covered in water hyacinth, which in the evening darkness looked like solid ground. Hundreds fell in, while others drove their vehicles into the water. One man said he could hardly get out, 'because drowning people grabbed my body, expecting to be helped'. Those on the bottom were trapped by people behind who fell and piled on top of them. At least 600 died here in the kicking, struggling confusion, many of them babies being carried by their desperate mothers. Wild rumours began to circulate. Some said bin Laden's men must have entered Lagos. For one woman: 'It was almost like our own 9/11.'

The fires burned for most of the night, with missiles continuing to fly out of the arsenal until the following afternoon. There were not enough fire-fighters, and not enough hydrants, so much of the city's northern suburbs burned down. Hospitals were overstretched, and many of the injured had to wait hours for treatment. The following evening people began returning to the devastated area to look for loved ones from whom they had become separated.

The total death toll is hard to calculate. At least 1,100 bodies were found, but many believe the true total is nearer 2,000. The Nigerian president, Olusegun Obasanjo, appeared at the scene and publicly demanded answers from the military on why such a huge munitions dump was kept in a poorly maintained state so close to a heavily populated area. It emerged that there had been a small explosion at the base the previous year, and that city officials had asked the army either to move it or to modernise it, but then no further action had been taken. The commander apologised, saying, 'This accident happened before the high authorities could do what was needed.'

## · THE BAGHDAD BRIDGE ·

On 31 August 2005 about a million pilgrims gathered around the Kadhimiya mosque in Baghdad – one of the holiest sites for Shi'ite Muslims. Tension was high because Sunni extremists had recently targeted a number of Shi'ite gatherings, and earlier in the day a mortar attack on the crowd had killed seven people. Rumours began to circulate that a suicide bombing was imminent, and in the panic people started rushing towards the Al-Aaimmah Bridge across the Tigris, which links the staunchly Sunni area of Adhamiya with the Shi'ite district of Kadhimiya.

The bridge had been closed, but when the pilgrims arrived the gate on the Kadhimiya side suddenly opened and they were able to swarm through. At the far end, though, people were slowed down by a security check, and a crush soon developed. Many people suffocated, especially women, children and the elderly. A twelve-year-old boy, who had teeth marks on his calf, said later: 'I stood on faces and one of them bit me.' Then the railings on the bridge gave way, and many people fell thirty feet into the murky brown river below. A forty-one-year-old retired soldier jumped: 'I didn't want to die slowly,' he said. 'I wanted it to end fast.' Somebody hauled him out. Another man had been carrying his son on his shoulders, but said: 'I don't know where he is now. Everybody was suffocating to death so I eventually had to jump.' Others dived into the water to try to save people. On the Sunni side of the river calls went out from mosque loudspeakers appealing for help, and one teenage Sunni drowned from exhaustion after rescuing several people. Sunnis also donated blood. Despite these efforts, perhaps 1,000 people died.

At first, government officials said someone in the crowd had deliberately triggered the stampede by claiming to be a bomber, but later they tried to play down any suggestion that the disaster had resulted from sectarian enmity. The defence minister claimed no insurgents were involved – the 'sorrowful incident' was an accident. Some survivors, though, blamed the government, saying that police and soldiers had made no effort to marshal a huge crowd in a confined space. A Sunni group, the Army of the Victorious Sect, which had links to al-Qaeda, claimed responsibility for the earlier mortar attack that had contributed to the heightened tension in the crowd.

# 16

SHIPWRECKS

Andersonville was the most notorious Confederate prisoner-of-war camp during the American Civil War. The 45,000 Union soldiers incarcerated there suffered hunger, exposure and disease, and nearly 13,000 died. But in April 1865 the war was over, and the 1,700-ton paddle steamer *Sultana* was dispatched to bring the boys home. The *Sultana* had done sterling work for the Union during the war, ferrying troops and supplies up and down the great rivers. Now she was badly in need of an overhaul, but in the understandable eagerness to pick up the prisoners the work was postponed. Just before she was due to depart, though, she developed a leak in one of her four boilers, and engineers wanted to replace two plates. The ship's maverick captain, J. Cass Mason, ignored their advice, and made do with riveting a metal patch over the leak.

Colonel Ruben Heath, chief quartermaster of the state of Mississippi, told Mason that the government would pay any steamboat operator five dollars for every enlisted man and ten dollars for every officer they could take north. On the morning of 24 April the freed prisoners started coming aboard; some, little more than skeletons, had to be carried on stretchers. Up to 2,100 were packed into every available corner. In addition there was an escort of twenty-two soldiers, plus ninety paying passengers and a crew of eighty-eight. The *Sultana* also carried 2,000 hogsheads of sugar, each weighing half a ton, and a crate containing a ten-foot alligator that Mason had brought from New Orleans as a mascot. Some of the ex-prisoners expressed alarm, as the deck sagged under their weight, and the crew had to wedge a great beam beneath it. They could not understand why the *Sultana* was carrying so many people, as there appeared to be other vessels available.

The steamer struggled clear of the wharf at Vicksburg and went puffing upstream, fighting a strong current. Mason seemed a little nervous, and at a stop en route the ship nearly capsized. He issued a warning that passengers must not move towards one side of the ship when they docked. By the evening of 26 April, the *Sultana* had managed to limp to Memphis, where they unloaded the sugar. Some of the crew feared this might make the ship even more top heavy. Just after midnight she resumed her journey to Cairo, Illinois, where most of the soldiers were due to disembark. Over the next couple of hours, she made slow progress against a powerful current, with the boilers labouring dreadfully. Seven miles upstream, as the *Sultana* crawled past a cluster of islands known as the Hen and Chickens, there was a tremendous series of bangs that could be heard back in Memphis, and an orange column of fire lit the sky for miles around. The abused boilers had exploded – first the one that had been patched up, then the others, and half of the ship disappeared.

Passengers were hit by great chunks of twisted machinery and wood, railings, beams and red-hot coals that were flung into the air. Others were asleep one moment then awake in ice-cold, dark water the next. Many could not swim and some who could were too weak to keep themselves afloat. The *Memphis Bulletin* reported: 'Some clung to frail pieces of the wreck, as drowning men cling to straws, and sustained themselves for a few moments, but finally became exhausted and sank.' Those parts of the *Sultana* not instantly destroyed by the explosion were now ablaze, and many of those on-board were burned to death. One survivor recalled: 'Hundreds of my comrades were fastened down by the timbers of the decks and had to burn while the water seemed to be one solid mass of human beings struggling with the waves.' Another said the river 'seemed black with men, their heads bobbing up and down like corks, and then disappearing beneath the turbulent waters, never to appear again'. The ship carried only seventy-six life-vests and two lifeboats. What remained of her was drifting helplessly downstream, and as the deck collapsed at one end more men slid into the water. Then the smokestacks came crashing down, pinning men beneath them. At this point Mason's alligator, or at least its crate, proved useful. A soldier bayoneted the reptile, then rolled its wooden container into the water, jumped in after it, and clung on until a passing boat rescued him. The skipper himself was glimpsed for a moment on the burning deck, throwing shutters and doors to people in the water, before disappearing for ever.

Hundreds of horribly burned men still clung to the drifting, burning hulk, huddling in the last spaces the flames had failed to penetrate. 'The men who were afraid to take to the water could be seen clinging to the sides of the bow of the boat until they were singed off like flies,' said a survivor. 'Shrieks and cries for mercy were all that could be heard.' Senator Stowe from Arkansas had been asleep in his stateroom when the boilers exploded. He stripped down and was about to jump overboard when he realised 'it was impossible to leap without killing one or more' of the people already in the water. So he went to the other side of the ship, which was further from the shore. The river was still quite packed, but he dived in and managed to find a log to cling to for four hours until he was picked up by another steamer.

Finally the wretched hulk ran aground on one of the small islands, and about thirty men leapt down. They managed to construct a makeshift raft from broken timbers, and as they put off from the island what was left of the *Sultana* finally sank with a great hiss, sending a huge pillar of smoke and steam into the sky. As dawn broke survivors still dotted the river, clinging to logs, rafts, barrels or anything that would float. Many were badly burned. In the confusion some of the rescue craft were fired on from a Union fort by soldiers who had been warned to watch out for Confederate guerrillas. Fortunately, no one was injured. Some survivors who were picked up by another steamer insisted on travelling in its dinghy. Others were washed all the way back to Memphis and pulled from the waters by local people. One former Confederate soldier with a small boat is said to have rescued fifteen ex-prisoners single-handed, but bodies continued to be found in the river for months, some as far away as Vicksburg.

Up to 600 survivors were taken to hospitals in Memphis, but about 200 of them died soon after. It is hard to know how many people perished altogether, because there was no proper record of the number on the ship, but it is estimated to have been about 1,700, making this the worst maritime disaster in US history.

April 1865, though, was a month of momentous events – the surrender of Confederate armies, the assassination of President Lincoln and the hunt for his killer, which ended the day before the *Sultana* sank. As a result, the disaster became something of a forgotten event. Several theories emerged about what had happened. The first was sabotage by a Confederate bomb smuggled on-board, but that was quickly dismissed (although two years later a former Confederate agent allegedly made a deathbed confession that he had blown up the ship). Marine engineers pointed to more obvious causes – like the botched boiler repairs and the grossly overloaded, top-heavy state of the ship. An official inquiry blamed two men, Colonel Heath and a Captain Speed, for their role in cramming so many people on to the *Sultana*. Heath had left the army, so only Speed was court-martialled. He was found guilty on all counts and faced a dishonourable discharge, but the judge advocate general of the army reversed the verdict.

There is no memorial to the soldiers who died. Major William McTeer of the 3rd Tennessee Cavalry, which lost more than 200 men in the disaster, lamented: 'Flowers are strewn over graves in the cemeteries of our dead, but there are none for the men who went down with the *Sultana*.'

## · THE *GENERAL SLOCUM* ·

What is today New York City's East Village was known at the turn of the twentieth century as Little Germany, Kleindeutschland. Home to many of the city's German immigrants, it was full of their sports clubs, theatres, beer gardens and churches. Every year, St Mark's Lutheran church took children who attended Sunday school and their parents on an outing. In 1904 it chartered a wooden steamer, the *General Slocum*, for a day trip to Locust Grove on Long Island Sound. Now in her thirteenth year, she was not a lucky a ship. She had twice collided with other vessels and had run aground three times, once stranding her 400 passengers all night. At half past nine on the morning of 15 June, though, there was a festive atmosphere among the 1,300 people on-board as the ship began to chug up the East River, with a band playing and hundreds of children cramming on to the upper deck to enjoy the sights.

As the steamer passed East 90th Street smoke started to billow from a storage room, where a bale of straw had caught fire. It was a small blaze and some of the crew of twenty-two tried to put it out, but they had never done a fire drill, and when they tried to spray water on the flames their rotten hoses burst. It was ten minutes before they alerted the captain, William Van Schaick, and by then the flames were raging out of control. People on the bank were soon shouting at him to dock the ship, but there were oil tanks along the piers and he was afraid of causing an explosion, so instead he headed as fast as he could for North Brother Island, about a mile away. The faster he went, the more it fanned the flames. As they spread, passengers ran around the deck screaming, desperately seeking shelter. The lifeboats were tied down and could not be launched. The ship carried 3,000 life-jackets, but they were as decayed as the hoses, and many disintegrated as people tried to put them on. Others held together long enough for mothers to put them on their children, but the cork inside had rotted and lost its buoyancy. So when they threw their offspring into the water they watched in horror as the children quickly sank from view.

Some passengers jumped overboard, with men trampling down women and children to escape, while others clung to the rails for as long as they could before letting themselves down into the churning, forbidding waters. A *Times* reporter wrote: 'People were seen clinging to the sides of the steamer like flies, and dropping by twos and threes as their strength gave out.' Most of the passengers could not swim, and some who could were crushed by the ship's turning paddles. Only a few were lucky enough to be picked up by the small flotilla that was now following the *General Slocum*. By the time she beached at North Brother Island, she was burning from end to end. Some of those still aboard jumped safely on to the island, but others, paralysed by fear, cowered in the parts of the ship the flames had not yet penetrated. Nurses and patients from a hospital on the island ran up with ladders to try to help them down. Some caught children thrown off the steamer by their parents; others formed human chains to pull people from the water.

Altogether, 1,021 passengers were killed, making it New York City's biggest disaster before 9/11 (see Chapter 12). Two of the crew also died.

As word spread onshore, people rushed to St Mark's church to try to find out what was happening, and men from the boats that had taken part in the rescue told a depressing tale. They had managed to pull out some survivors, but mostly they dragged corpses from the water, usually those of young children. A temporary morgue was set up by the East River, and for the next week thousands filed past victims lying in open coffins that had had to be requisitioned from all over the city. For days on end, funerals were held every hour in Kleindeutschland, and a number of people killed themselves after losing all their loved ones.

Captain Van Schaick faced some searching questions. Why had he not docked the ship as soon as the fire was discovered, instead of allowing it to spread as he raced upriver? Why were his crew so poorly trained? How had he survived when so many had died? He was indicted along with a number of other people, including four senior officials from the Knickerbocker Steamship Company, which owned the *General Slocum*, the inspector who had certified her as safe just a month before the fire, and managers of the company that made the life-jackets. They had allegedly used sub-standard cork and had even put pieces of iron in the jackets to bring them up to the required weight. Only Van Schaick was convicted, though, for criminal negligence. He was sentenced to ten years in jail, but served only three and a half before he was released and pardoned. The steamship company escaped with a fine. The *General Slocum*'s remains were salvaged and she was converted into a barge, but that did not change her luck: she sank in a storm in 1911.

One legacy of the disaster was a major tightening of US safety rules for steamboats, requiring better life-jackets and fire hoses, as well as fireproof metal bulkheads. The tragedy is also commemorated in James Joyce's great novel *Ulysses*. The ship sank on the day before what became celebrated as 'Bloomsday' – 16 June 1904 – when all the action in the book takes place. 'Terrible affair that *General Slocum* explosion,' says one of the characters. 'Terrible, terrible! A thousand casualties. And heart-rending scenes. Men trampling down women and children. Most brutal thing.'

### · THE *TITANIC* ·

At the beginning of the twentieth century competition between transatlantic shipping lines was ferocious. So when Bruce Ismay took over White Star from his father in 1900 he decided to launch a new generation of luxury liners built by Harland and Wolff of Belfast. They would be fast and opulent, with a top speed of about twenty-two knots. The *Titanic* was to be the star of the show – the biggest and plushest ship on the sea. Her propellers were the size of windmills, and two trains could have passed each other in one of her funnels. At 46,000 tons, with nine decks, she was as high as an eleven-storey building. She could carry more than 2,500 passengers, and was one of the first ships to have a swimming pool. The *Titanic* had a double iron hull. The outer one was an inch thick, and at the flick of a switch on the bridge she could be divided in seconds into sixteen compartments, four of which could be flooded without endangering her buoyancy. The technical journal *Shipbuilder* said she was 'practically unsinkable', but White Star's record had its blemishes. Its liner *Atlantic* sank off the Canadian coast in March 1873, taking 546 people down with her. Its cargo steamer the *Naronic*, then the biggest in the world, disappeared in 1893, with the loss of all seventy-four on board. And six years later the *Germanic* sank in New York harbour under the weight of ice on her upper decks.

As the *Titanic* slipped majestically out of Southampton on her maiden voyage on 10 April 1912 her great bulk caused consternation. When she came abreast of the liner *New York* the American ship rocked and her thick mooring ropes snapped, but the *Titanic* stopped just in time, and tugs nosed the other ship back to her berth. A few minutes later another ship heeled over several degrees. After Southampton the *Titanic* made calls at Cherbourg and Cobh; then, on 12 April, she was off into the Atlantic, carrying 1,316 passengers and 891 crew. One passenger had left the ship after the near miss with the *New York*, but a list of those on-board reads like an extract from *Who's Who*: the mining magnate Benjamin Guggenheim; John Jacob Astor, said to be the richest man in the world, with his new teenage bride Madeleine; Isidor Straus, co-owner of the world's biggest department store, Macy's, and his wife of forty years, Ida. Another American millionaire, J.P. Morgan, who had funded the building of the *Titanic*, had been due to travel but cancelled at the last moment, ostensibly because of illness. (He would be sighted at Baden-Baden taking the waters with his French mistress.) Then there was Thomas Andrews, from Harland and Wolff, who was constantly jotting down notes on how to improve the vessel.

The *Titanic* was commanded by fifty-nine-year-old Captain Edward J. Smith. He had been due to retire, but Bruce Ismay persuaded him to stay on for the ship's maiden voyage. Smith had joined White Star back in 1880, and had skippered seventeen of the company's ships. Ismay described him as 'a man in whom we had entire and absolute confidence'. Although a stickler for discipline, the captain was still popular with his crews. The *Titanic*'s second officer, Charles Lightoller, called him 'a man any officer would give his ears to sail under'. Smith's officers were the pick of the bunch, and the captain himself brimmed with confidence, once remarking: 'I cannot imagine any condition which would cause a ship to founder . . . Modern shipbuilding has gone beyond that.' Still he had a somewhat chequered history, including three accidents in a year while in command of the *Titanic*'s sister ship, the *Olympic*. She had nearly crushed a tug on her maiden voyage, then had collided with a cruiser, and finally had run over a wreck, losing her propeller blade.

The *Titanic* could easily have carried enough lifeboats for all the crew and passengers, but as she was unsinkable, reasoned Bruce Ismay, why go to so much unnecessary trouble and expense? So she set off with only twenty boats, with enough room for 1,178 people. At Cobh, Ismay made sure there was enough coal on-board for the ship to go 'at full speed' if the weather was good. This did not amount to an explicit attempt on the record time for a transatlantic crossing; but if the *Titanic* were to break it on her first voyage, plainly that would be very good publicity. Charles Lightoller wrote: 'Each day, as the voyage went on, everybody's admiration of the ship increased; for the way she behaved, for the total absence of vibration, for her steadiness.' On 14 April extra boilers were lit and steam pressure increased.

There should have been a lifeboat drill that day, but Captain Smith postponed it. The sea was calm, though the temperature had dropped dramatically, and a number of other ships were reporting icebergs further south than they were normally seen at that time of year. The

*Titanic's* lookouts were specifically warned to watch out for them, but no extra men were posted. Nor did they have binoculars, an omission First Officer William Murdoch had already decided must be remedied when they reached New York. No one seems to have suggested slowing down as the ship pressed on at twenty-two knots. It had become customary on Atlantic crossings to continue in spite of ice, at least if the weather was clear.

That night's church service included the traditional mariners' hymn, 'For Those in Peril on the Sea'. Just before nine o'clock, Smith slipped away from the party he was attending and went up to the bridge to check on the ice. It was freezing but dead calm, making it harder to spot icebergs than if the sea were moving about and breaking against them. Still, visibility seemed good. The captain said that if it deteriorated, they would have to reduce speed. Then he retired to his cabin. At nine-forty the *Titanic* received a warning from another ship of a 'great number of large icebergs' in the vicinity, but the chief radio operator, Jack Phillips, was too busy sending messages from passengers to pass it on to the bridge.

Then, at twenty to midnight, close to the end of his watch in the crow's nest, a lookout named Fred Fleet screamed, 'Iceberg straight ahead!' and rang the alarm bell three times. On the bridge they tried desperately to avoid the collision, but less than forty seconds later the *Titanic* struck it a glancing blow before it disappeared into the night, leaving the deck covered in ice, and a huge gash below the waterline. Within a minute of the warning the bridge had flicked the switch to divide the ship into watertight compartments. In his cabin Smith felt a jolt and heard a grating sound. He dashed into the wheelhouse, where Murdoch told him they had struck ice. Almost immediately the ship's carpenter was up on the bridge to report: 'She's making water fast.' The problem was that the compartments were not actually watertight. The partitions did not go right to the top, and once water had filled one compartment it would spill into the next. Smith took Thomas Andrews with him into the depths of the ship, with both men trying to walk casually so as not to alarm passengers. They found the water already fourteen feet deep and the bow starting to dip. Andrews did a quick calculation on a piece of paper and said the *Titanic* would sink in an hour and a half, or two hours at most. Smith told the radio room to start calling for help, and ordered the crew to uncover the lifeboats.

A few passengers near the impact had been thrown from their bunks, but most were probably unaware of what had happened as the impact had seemed fairly slight. The quartermaster, George Rowe, thought it felt similar to what happens when a vessel touches the dock wall before berthing. One survivor said there was 'no sound of a crash or of anything else, no sense of shock, no jar'. On deck, some passengers had a snowball fight with the ice. A few asked why the engines had stopped, but stewards assured them there was nothing amiss. Meanwhile, the *Titanic*'s distress call was picked up by another liner, the *Carpathia*, fifty-eight miles away. Her master, Captain Rostron, twice asked his operator if he had got the message right. Once convinced that the 'unsinkable' *Titanic* was going down, he radioed that he was on his way and went full steam ahead towards the stricken vessel. Every available man was given a shovel to feed the boilers, and the ship was prepared to take on hundreds of survivors. No one had ever seen her move so fast.

On the *Titanic* stewards were now going from cabin to cabin, knocking on doors, and asking passengers almost apologetically to put on warm clothes and take their life-belts down to the boat stations. Some refused to go, believing it was just a drill, and even those who realised it was a genuine emergency were reluctant to leave the great liner for one of the flimsy-looking lifeboats. There was almost no panic, and an ugly scene among the steerage passengers was quickly quelled by the ship's officers. Smith had heard the *Carpathia* was only four hours away, and at first he ordered the lifeboats to be filled and lowered, but not dropped into the water. The *Titanic*, though, was sinking fast, and he realised that as the bow went deeper and the stern rose, it would become ever more difficult to launch the boats. Women and children were told to go first, but some wives refused to leave their husbands. Isidor Straus was offered a place because of his age, but he refused, saying, 'I do not wish any distinction in my favour which is not granted to others.' Ida then refused to leave him, saying to her husband, 'Where you go, I go.' As her maid climbed into one of the boats Mrs Straus handed over her coat to keep her warm. John Jacob Astor helped his wife into a lifeboat. He asked if he could join her, and when he was told that he could not he stepped back politely. A group of the ship's musicians had gathered on the deck, and as the boats were lowered they played 'Nearer My God to Thee'. Some male passengers joined in as they watched the faces of their loved ones disappearing into the darkness below. The band went on playing until the slant of the deck made it impossible. Thomas Andrews seemed to be everywhere, helping people put on life-jackets, though he had none himself, wearing a brave face, but quietly telling friends, 'She is torn to bits.' The manager of the first-class restaurant stood on the deck wearing a top hat and carrying a small suitcase. He and most of his staff would die, as would the musicians. Down below, three junior engineers were pumping furiously. When one fell and broke a leg the other two carried on until one of the 'watertight' walls gave way and they were drowned. Meanwhile, the radio operators kept on sending out distress calls until the power ran out.

Some survivors were astonished at how quiet it was during those final minutes on the ship. A priest took confession and gave absolution. Benjamin Guggenheim and his valet stood side by side in full evening dress. They had taken off their life-jackets and changed, saying they were 'prepared to go down like gentlemen'. The last thing one woman saw of her father was his cheery wave and a shout of 'I'll see you in New York' as he stood on the deck with a cigar and a brandy. By two o'clock, all the lifeboats had gone, but in the confusion 500 places had been left unfilled, so 1,500 people were left on the liner. No systematic search of the ship had been made, and some steerage passengers had been kept off the deck behind locked metal gates until most of the lifeboats had been lowered. The boats were crewed mainly by stewards and stokers. Every officer and nearly all the seamen stayed on-board. Now Smith ordered: 'Abandon ship. Every man for himself.' He was last seen standing on the bridge. Some people leapt into the icy water, while others crowded together on the stern, which was rising alarmingly. Fifteen minutes later water flooded into the forward compartments, lifting the stern right out of the sea, and the hull snapped. By then, the lifeboats were about 300 yards away. People in them said the ship's lights were still shining brilliantly as the stern went almost vertical. Then she seemed to remain motionless for a moment. The lights went out, there was a deep rumble as machinery broke free and rolled towards the bow, then the water closed over her.

The sea was very calm but extremely cold. A woman in one of the lifeboats wrapped her big sable stole around a stoker to keep him alive and made everyone row to get their circulation going and raise their spirits. In the water a bath steward was looking desperately for something to hang on to when a stranger pulled him up on a piece of the ship's panelling. Then his saviour exclaimed, 'What a night!' and fell dead into the sea. Charles Lightoller swam to an overturned lifeboat, climbed aboard, and eventually got thirty people balanced on it. The *Carpathia* had received her last message from the *Titanic* – 'The engine room is full up to the boilers' – at ten to two. Fifty minutes later Captain Rostron saw a green distress flare, but now the *Carpathia* too was surrounded by icebergs and it was not until four o'clock that she could pick her way through to the bobbing lifeboats. Over the next four hours the liner took aboard 705 survivors. She held a brief memorial service over the spot where the *Titanic* had gone down, taking 1,500 people with her, then she headed for New York, where a crowd of 30,000 was waiting.

It was the worst accident in transatlantic maritime history. Nearly all the women in first class survived, but fewer than one-third of the men. Of those who had been in steerage, more than half the women and six out of every seven men died. All but one of the children who had been in first or second class survived, while two out of three of those who had been in steerage died.

Captain Smith went down with the ship, as did Andrews, Astor, Guggenheim and both of the Strauses. Bruce Ismay climbed into a lifeboat and was saved. It would haunt him for the rest of his days. Smith was heavily criticised as commentators pointed to White Star's instruction to masters that 'No supposed gaining of expedition or saving of time on voyage is to be purchased at the risk of accidents.' A number of distinguished commanders of transatlantic liners, though, said that in the same circumstances they would have done exactly as he did. A British Board of Inquiry concluded that the captain had made a mistake, 'a very grievous mistake, but one in which, in the face of practice and past experience, negligence cannot be said to have had any part'. However, the inquiry called for other masters to learn from the disaster, warning that: 'What was a mistake in the case of the *Titanic* would without doubt be negligence in any similar case in the future.'

Ismay emerged as the villain of the piece. Some considered his presence on-board had pressurised Smith to keep up his speed in spite of the icebergs. Within a year he had resigned from White Star. The novelist Joseph Conrad, himself a seaman, wrote a savage attack on what he saw as the company's cavalier attitude to safety: 'If you can't get more boats, then sell less tickets. Don't drown so many people on the finest, calmest night that ever was known in the North Atlantic.' He was also scathing about the *Titanic*'s 'watertight' compartments: 'when we want to divide, say, a box, we take good care to procure a piece of wood which will reach from the bottom to the lid. We know that if it does not reach all the way up the box will not be divided.'

As so often happens after a disaster, the air was soon ringing with the sound of metaphorical stable doors being slammed shut. The first International Convention for Safety of Life at Sea was drawn up, requiring there to be enough lifeboats for everyone on-board, and an international patrol was introduced to give warnings of icebergs.

## · THE *EMPRESS OF IRELAND* ·

Just two years after the *Titanic* sank another transatlantic liner came to grief. Canadian Pacific's *Empress of Ireland* left Quebec City for Liverpool at half past four on the afternoon of 28 May 1914 with 1,477 passengers and crew. Her captain, thirty-nine-year-old Henry Kendall, was a rising star who had been promoted less than a month before. In the dead of night, as the ship approached the mouth of the St Lawrence River on her way to the Atlantic, he spotted the approaching lights of a 6,000-ton Norwegian collier, the *Storstad*, which was under the command of Captain Thomas Anderson. Kendall had altered course slightly, planning to pass the other ship starboard to starboard, when a great bank of fog rolled in. Being cautious on his first voyage, he ordered the engines put into reverse, then signalled to the collier that he had stopped. Just before two in the morning, to his horror, he saw the *Storstad* looming out of the mist, heading straight towards him. It was too late for evasive action, and just off the town of Rimouski the two vessels collided. The collier's hull was reinforced to protect it against ice, so the liner came off much worse. Indeed, the *Storstad* inflicted a mortal wound. Kendall shouted to the collier to keep moving forward to plug the hole, but within seconds the two ships had slipped apart, and water poured into the liner.

Passengers awoke to find themselves in complete darkness – the collision had knocked out the ship's power – but they could tell she was listing badly to starboard. In their nightclothes, on a strange ship they had boarded only a few hours earlier, many had trouble finding the stairs. A surviving passenger, Dr J.F. Grant, said he woke up only when the list was enough to roll him out of his berth. Then he heard 'screams of terror and the sound of rushing water'. The liner seemed to make an attempt to right herself, then canted over still further to starboard. Its slant was so bad that Grant could not walk along the corridor, so he scrambled along a wall. Getting his head out of a porthole, he was astonished to see 'the side of the vessel crowded with people, standing there as though it were the deck'. Some jumped into the freezing water to join others who had climbed out of their portholes, but hundreds remained trapped inside the ship. The list to starboard made it impossible to launch the lifeboats on the port side, and only five could be dropped from the starboard side. Grant said that as the first one hit the water, 'the sailors in it were thrown out and the boat was overturned'. With the deck seeming 'as steep as the walls of a house', according to another survivor, boats were flung across it and several people were crushed to death before the ship was pulled like a rug from under them, and they were all struggling in the water.

In pitch darkness, they clung to anything they could find, but 'many let go their hold and slipped into the water'. He managed to hang on, but as the ship sank: 'I felt myself in a whirlpool, buffeted by bodies living and dead, by wreckage, and by enormous waves. Twice I was dragged down, and all the time spars and heavy pieces of timber seemed to be grinding me to fragments. It seemed to go on for hours, but at last I found myself with my arms wrapped around a piece of floating wood.'

As an Ottawa man and his wife fell into the water a boat packed with survivors approached them, but a huge piece of the ship's superstructure fell and hit it 'with a terrible crash'. The man closed his eyes in horror: 'When I looked up again all that was left of the lifeboat and her occupants was a few stumps of wreckage.' The couple were eventually picked up by one of the *Storstad*'s boats. One passenger told *The Times* that neither he nor his wife had woken up until water began rushing into their stateroom. They escaped death by clinging to a piece of timber in the river. In spite of the terror many must have felt, though, Dr Grant said 'there was no disorder'.

Captain Kendall was thrown from the bridge and eventually hauled into one of the boats, but hundreds were still clinging to the ship when she sank just fourteen minutes after the collision. Grant recalled, 'As she heeled over they slid down into the water as though walking down a sandy beach to bathe,' but soon they were 'screaming for help and shrieking as they felt themselves being carried under'. The doctor saw the *Storstad*, now about a mile away, and swam towards her. He was picked up by one of the collier's lifeboats, which in all saved about 400 people. Many were in a bad state. Grant did his best to help but four women died from shock and exposure, and another perished as she was being taken ashore.

Altogether, 465 people were rescued, but 1,012 drowned, including 840 passengers, more than had died on the *Titanic*, where the number of crew killed was much higher. Among the victims were 314 children; only four survived. One of the survivors was a stoker named William Clarke. Two years before he had been saved from the *Titanic*.

Who was to blame for the tragedy became a matter of bitter dispute. If both captains were telling the truth, the collision happened as each vessel was stationary with its engines stopped. As it was, a Canadian inquiry found the *Storstad* was to blame, while the Norwegians said the *Empress* caused the collision. Canadian Pacific, however, successfully sued the owners of the collier. Kendall and Anderson both went on to serve in the First World War, and both survived being torpedoed. The *Storstad* was sunk, though all hands were saved. The wreck of the *Empress* still lies on the bed of the St Lawrence.

## · THE *WILHELM GUSTLOFF* ·

Named after a Nazi leader assassinated by a Jewish student, the 25,000-ton *Wilhelm Gustloff* was launched in 1937 as a prestige cruise liner for Kraft durch Freude (Strength through Joy) – the Nazi tourist industry.

However, once war came she was turned into a hospital and a barracks ship. On the evening of 30 January 1945, the twelfth anniversary of Hitler's coming to power, she was at Gdynia, on the Baltic, and thousands of Germans fled to her in panic as Russian forces advanced. No one knows exactly how many people got aboard but some estimates say 10,500, including more than 1,000 soldiers and sailors. The weather was dreadful, with freezing temperatures, high winds, poor visibility and ice on the sea, but many Germans feared that if they stayed, they faced rape and murder. There was also an argument about whether the *Gustloff* should put on her navigation lights. Some said they were necessary to avoid colliding with a German minesweeper convoy known to be in the vicinity, but others felt they would alert Soviet submarines to the liner's presence. Eventually, the captain reluctantly agreed to turn them on.

A navy doctor named Hans Rittner, who was on-board, said of the refugees: 'Most are silent, gaunt, hungry, sunken-eyed. They are ill-clothed, many without boots, wearing mufflers around their feet for warmth.' Many had dragged trunks and wooden chests with them, but these had to be left on the dockside because there was no room on the ship. Every cabin was full. Mattresses carpeted every passageway and lounge, and even the empty swimming pool. But the ship was warm and brightly lit, and the passengers seemed surprisingly relaxed. Left behind on the pier were desperate people for whom there was no room. Those on-board were not sure exactly where they were going – Kiel or Lübeck, perhaps – but surely it would be safer than where they were now.

Almost immediately after casting off, the ship started to roll. When Dr Rittner went on deck, the lights worried him because they were burning 'with inappropriate gaiety, like Yule trees'. The master of the *Gustloff* had been asked to zigzag to make the ship a more difficult target, but she was so fouled with seaweed and barnacles that she could barely make fifteen knots, even sailing straight ahead. Besides, the minefields sown nightly by the RAF made zigzagging very dangerous. As the sea grew rougher, passengers started to vomit. Loudspeakers relayed a speech from Hitler. There were a number of pregnant women on-board, and at about seven o'clock in the evening a baby boy was born. Shortly after, the doctor went to bed. At a quarter past nine he was awoken by three huge explosions which shook the whole ship. The lights went out, and people were flung about as the ship listed to port. Women shrieked, children whimpered. The doctor was sure they had struck a mine, but he thought the liner was strong enough to make it safely back to harbour. Then the list became more extreme. In fact, the *Gustloff* had been torpedoed by Soviet submarine *S-13*, taking three direct hits. She was twenty miles from shore and many of the crew had been killed instantly.

A distress call went out to other German ships in the area, but they too were carrying refugees, and it was too dangerous for them to approach the *Gustloff* in case the submarine was still lurking. On the ship there was 'a cascade of inrushing water, like Niagara Falls . . . unbelievable in its speed and volume'. People were trapped behind doors jammed shut by the explosions, and some seem to have shot themselves rather than face the freezing water. Rittner tried to dress the wounds of the injured, but the ship's list got so bad it became impossible. Women tried to soothe and reassure their children; some people prayed. They were packed so tightly that they could scarcely move. Suddenly the water surged up to the doctor's chest and he started swimming. He had to break free from people who kept grabbing him and dragging him down. When he reached the surface there was nothing to be seen of the ship, just bodies 'like dark rag bundles being tossed on the waves'. A few moments later he found a small raft and hung on to it, but soon so many people had scrambled aboard that it seemed likely to sink, so he jumped off and swam to a nearby lifeboat, which was carrying about a dozen people. He managed to pull aboard a little girl who had lost her mother. A woman handed him a shawl. Some tried to keep warm by waving their arms or slapping themselves. Others sat silent and motionless, and the doctor wondered if they had already frozen to death.

There were a number of boats and rafts on the waves, and just before midnight they saw lights in the distance gradually drawing nearer. There was an agonised wait before they discovered it was not an enemy ship but a German destroyer. Even then there was no cheering. The rescue was greeted with 'numbed stupefaction'. One man who tried to climb the ladder on to the ship was so stiff and cold that he fell into the water and drowned. The destroyer picked up perhaps 400 survivors but had to make a rapid escape as the captain saw torpedoes in the water. Many were left behind, along with some sailors, who had climbed down to help them out of the boats. Dr Rittner was one of the lucky ones to make it aboard. The little girl was still beside him, still asking for her mother.

The next morning they were put ashore at the small, bleak port of Sassnitz. The doctor waited by the docks for other ships with survivors to arrive, but none came. It is thought that not more than 1,000 of those on-board the *Gustloff* survived, making this the worst maritime disaster in history. The commander of the submarine that sent her to the bottom, Alexander Marinesko, sank another big German ship, the *Steuben*, a few days later, drowning about 3,000. Marinesko was a renegade who had narrowly escaped court martial a few weeks earlier after going AWOL to pursue a liaison with a Swedish woman. The destruction of the *Gustloff* and the *Steuben* meant that he had sunk more tonnage than any other Soviet commander. He felt this entitled him to be decorated as a 'Hero of the Soviet Union', but the authorities gave him a lesser award. Marinesko was furious, and when officials approached to make the presentation he ordered his submarine to submerge. After the war he was discharged from the navy for alcoholism and indiscipline, and was later jailed for theft. Marinesko died in 1963. He was made a 'Hero of the Soviet Union' posthumously in 1990. There are now a number of monuments to him in the former Soviet Union.

Many other sinkings during the Second World War resulted in heavy civilian casualties. In September 1944, off Sumatra, a British submarine hit the freighter *Junyo Maru* – one of Japan's so-called 'hell ships'. Among those crammed on-board were Dutch, British and Australian internees and Asian slave labourers. Nearly 4,900 drowned. Many of the 700 survivors were sent to the Pakan Baru–Muaro railway in Sumatra to be worked to death. On 16 April 1945 up to 6,000 died when the German freighter *Goya* was torpedoed by a Russian submarine in the Baltic. She had been carrying troops and civilians fleeing from the Red Army. On 3 May 1945, four days after Hitler killed himself, the liner SS *Cap Arcona*, with former concentration camp prisoners and SS guards aboard, was attacked by the RAF in the Bay of Lübeck. As the ship sank SS units on shore tried to shoot any prisoners who escaped, although about 350 did manage to survive. The final death toll was around 7,000.

## · THE *DOÑA PAZ* ·

The world's worst peacetime maritime disaster happened in the Philippines just before Christmas 1987. On the evening of 20 December 1987 the ferry *Doña Paz* was on her way from the island of Leyte to Manila in the Philippines. She was supposed to carry only 1,518 passengers, but this was the last sailing before the holiday and lots of people wanted to travel. No one knows how many were on-board, but it was certainly many more than 1,518. Back in 1979, when she had been called the *Don Sulpicio*, the ferry had been gutted by fire after a cigarette end was thrown into the hold, but everyone on-board was rescued. Now, just over 100 miles from her destination, the rebuilt vessel was threading her way through the busy Tablas Strait, close to where another ferry, the *Don Juan*, had collided with an oil tanker seven years earlier, and 100 passengers had drowned.

Also in the area was a small, poorly maintained coastal tanker, the *Vector*, with a crew of thirteen, carrying 8,800 barrels of petroleum products. At about ten o'clock the two vessels collided. The tanker immediately caught fire, and the flames quickly spread to the *Doña Paz*. The first vessel on the scene was the ferry *Don Claudio*. Her master, Captain Melecio Barranco, saw flames as high as a seven-storey building. The fire was 'overwhelming', and even through binoculars he could not distinguish the two ships. Still, Barranco managed to pick up two junior crewmen from the *Vector* and twenty-four passengers from the *Doña Paz* – some of them badly burned. None of the passengers was wearing a life-jacket, and they complained that the life-jacket cabinets on the ferry had been locked. The captain scanned the area several times but could find no one else. There had been no time to lower the ferry's lifeboats, and the survivors all seemed to have escaped by swimming underwater long enough to avoid the deadly flames. No one else got out alive. One nineteen-year-old said the sea was teeming with the bodies of children and old people. As he struggled to keep afloat he swallowed gulps of sea water that tasted like petrol. He reckoned he had swum about two miles when he saw the two ships go down. His cousin also survived, but ten other members of his family died. Forty-two-year-old Paquito Osabel was asleep when he heard an explosion.

The blaze engulfed the *Doña Paz* in seconds and everyone was screaming: 'The smoke was terrible . . . I could see flames on the water below,
but I jumped anyway.' He clung to a plank and swam for more than an
hour before being picked up. Another survivor jumped holding his girl-
friend's hand, but she slipped from his grasp and he never saw her
again. Others could not jump because they had children with them. A
fifteen-year-old boy who lost his mother and two sisters said: 'There
were no lights, there were no life-vests. Nobody was giving orders.' One
survivor heard anguished shouts of 'mother' and 'father' in the water
around him. He searched desperately for his two children and his wife,
but to no avail.

According to the ship's manifest, there were 1,568 passengers on the
*Doña Paz* (still more than the maximum allowed), but all the survivors
said the ferry was full to bursting, with corridors packed with passengers
and people sleeping four to a bed. It emerged that as many as 1,000 children may not have been included on the manifest; nor were many
passengers who bought tickets after boarding. Sometimes only the name
of the head of a family was recorded, irrespective of how many people he
had travelling with him. According to survivors, at the time of the collision the captain of the ferry was watching a video while the first and
second mates were drinking beer. There were also reports that an
apprentice mate had been left alone on the bridge. The company denied
these claims and that the ferry was overloaded. At the official inquiry, a
lawyer speaking for the registered owner of the *Vector* said he had sold it
in 1985. There was no one representing the alleged current owners.
Captain Barranco said his radio operator did not pick up any distress
calls from either vessel, and that the two tanker crewmen he rescued
told him they had been asleep when the collision happened: 'They said
that when they woke up their ship was already on fire and they immediately jumped into the water.'

The official report that followed blamed the *Vector* for the accident,
calling it a 'floating hazard to navigation'. It had a steering defect, there
was no radio operator, and it had sailed without a valid certificate of
inspection. It also found the ship's master did not have the required
licence, and that there was no lookout on duty. The tanker was 'solely at
fault and responsible for the collision'. She had rammed the *Doña Paz* on

the port side, immediately knocking out her engine and generator. Oil from the tanker burst into flames, and both vessels disappeared in a huge fireball.

For all the denials of overloading on the *Doña Paz*, most estimates put the number drowned at between 3,000 and 4,375, making this the worst peacetime maritime disaster in history. The following October, another of the company's ships, the *Doña Marilyn*, sank during a typhoon, taking up to 390 people down with her.

## · THE *JOOLA* ·

Overcrowding also inflated the death toll when a Senegalese ferry, the *Joola*, capsized in 2002. Built in Germany in 1990 and owned by the government of Senegal, she set sail from the southern port of Ziguinchor on 26 September for the sixteen-hour coastal journey to Dakar. The *Joola* was designed to carry 44 crew and 536 passengers, but everyone agrees there were far more on-board. Many were travelling to sell mangoes and palm oil in the capital; a long-running rebellion had made the overland journey too dangerous. As it was the low season for tourism, there were few cars at the bottom of the *Joola*, which made her more top heavy than usual.

At about eleven o'clock at night the ship sailed into a storm. Passengers on the top deck were hit by wind and torrential rain coming in from the starboard side, so they rushed to port to take shelter. The overloaded ferry capsized almost immediately, throwing people and cargo into the sea. One survivor said he managed to grab a life-jacket and escape through a half-open window into the cold, choppy water. A student clung to a corner of the ferry until he could climb on to the upturned keel. He said: 'We were thrown about by the wind and huge waves until about four in the morning.' Then, as the storm started to die down, they were rescued by fishermen. Survivors paid tribute to their bravery, acknowledging that they were risking their lives. Two non-swimmers wearing life-jackets were saved after four hours in the sea.

Meanwhile, the official emergency services were nowhere to be seen. They did not respond until more than eight hours after the sinking. One man who managed to cling to a piece of wood until they appeared said if they had come even two hours earlier, the four people who had been sharing it with him would have been saved. Instead, they drowned. Altogether, only sixty-four people survived. Senegal's president, Abdoulaye Wade, declared three days of official mourning, saying everyone would know someone who had died. He conceded that the ferry was overloaded, which made the government's responsibility for the disaster 'obvious'.

Other disturbing facts emerged. The *Joola* was not supposed to go more than twenty miles from shore, but she was well beyond that when she capsized. She had returned to service after repairs only a fortnight before the disaster, and journalists who had travelled on her said there seemed to be a number of technical problems. Officially, there had been 1,034 people on-board, but children under five were not counted, and nor were many adults. Poor people were often allowed to travel free, and badly paid officials would also take kickbacks to allow on passengers who had not bought tickets, so most estimates put the number travelling at between 1,600 and 2,000, meaning that up to 1,940 perished.

It was also revealed that the *Joola*'s captain was scheduled to make a routine check-in call at midnight. When that call was not received, the authorities should have investigated immediately. In fact, the rescue operation was not launched until eight o'clock the next morning. There were reports that people supposed to be on duty at the air–sea rescue service had taken the night off. Two inquires concluded the disaster was caused by overloading, failure to observe safety procedures and bad weather. President Wade lamented: 'The vices at the heart of this catastrophe are based in our relaxed attitudes, our lack of rigour, irresponsibility and even greed.' The ministers for transport and the armed forces resigned, and the president fired the commander of the navy. He later sacked the prime minister and the entire cabinet.

## · THE *AL-SALAM BOCCACCIO 98* ·

The year 2006 saw yet another major ferry disaster. The *al-Salam Boccaccio 98* was a roll-on–roll-off vessel, built in Italy in 1970 and sailing under a Panamanian flag. She was built to carry 500 passengers, but in 1991 her superstructure was raised, increasing capacity to 1,300. Eight years later she was bought by El Salam Maritime Transport of Cairo, the largest private shipping company in the Middle East.

On the night of 2 February 2006 she was crossing the Red Sea from Duba in Saudi Arabia to Safaga in southern Egypt. The sea is known for its strong winds and tricky currents, and over the preceding few days there had also been dust storms. The *al-Salam* was carrying ninety-six crew and 1,312 passengers, mostly Egyptians working in Saudi Arabia or pilgrims returning from the Hajj. The were also about 220 vehicles, and a couple of hours into the voyage a fire broke out on the car deck. An engineering student said she smelled smoke and asked the crew what was wrong. They said it was just a small fire down below and it was being dealt with, but the smoke kept seeping up. One crew member who had tried to extinguish the fire said afterwards that they kept spraying water on to it but it continued to flare up. Soon, thick smoke was pouring out, and passengers went to the upper deck, only to be told: 'Relax, go to your rooms.' Many ignored the advice and started to put on life-jackets. Still there was no word from the captain, and soon the crew started to don life-vests too. Some passengers asked why the ship was not returning to Duba.

At about one o'clock in the morning the ferry began to list alarmingly to starboard. The captain and crew ordered passengers to gather on the port side, but in about ten minutes she sank. The engineering student said none of the bigger lifeboats, each of which could hold 100 people, was launched, so they had to try to get away in rubber dinghies. 'The crew and captain never said "abandon ship." They kept reassuring us until the end. By then, it was every passenger for himself.' Another survivor complained there were not enough life-jackets to go round.

A young Egyptian man jumped overboard when he saw the ship was sinking. He swam around for hours before making it to a lifeboat. He saw another lifeboat sink. A waiter said he clung to a rail as the ship went down, but people were grabbing his legs and scratching his face: 'I held on and asked God for strength.' He joined about twenty others in a dinghy, but as more people clambered aboard the dinghy began to sink, so he swam to a raft. The engineering student said that while she was in the water a ship came tantalisingly close, but it did not seem to spot anyone. The captain had sent out an SOS which was picked up by at least one other ferry, but none of the coastguard services reported any call.

Bad weather certainly hampered the rescue effort, but some survivors claimed rescue helicopters saw them, then flew on. Some spent more than twenty hours floating in rubber dinghies or clinging to life-belts. Eventually, they were pulled to safety by Egyptian naval ships and boats sent by the *al-Salam*'s owner. Meanwhile, at Safaga, hundreds of passengers' relatives and friends were storming the port, demanding information. They ransacked the shipping company's offices, threw furniture into the street and set fire to it. Riot police had to be called to disperse them.

In the end, 388 people survived but more than 1,000 died. An official investigation found the ferry did not have enough lifeboats, and that firefighting equipment was inadequate. It said 'wicked collaboration' between the company and the maritime safety agency had allowed the ferry to sail even though it failed to meet minimum safety standards. The authorities wanted to try five people for negligence, including the ferry's owner, Mamduh Ismail, but they had all been allowed to leave the country before the investigation finished. Four months after the disaster, Ismail, who denied responsibility, agreed to pay more than £25 million into a compensation fund for the victims in return for the Egyptian government's lifting a freeze on his assets.

In July 2008, all five defendants were acquitted, even though Ismail and his son, a senior executive in the company, were still in hiding abroad. The captain of another ferry was sent to jail for six months for failing to help the *al-Salem*.

# 17

## TRAIN CRASHES

### · MODANE ·

It was 12 December 1917 and French troops were looking forward to home leave at Christmas, away from the hell of the trenches. More than 1,000 who had been fighting in Italy were due to return in two trains from Turin. Because of the heavy demands of the war effort, though, there was only one locomotive available, so the two trains were coupled together to make one of nineteen coaches – four times what the engine would normally be allowed to pull. Only the first three coaches had automatic brakes controlled by the driver; the rest had either hand-brakes that a brakeman would have to operate or no brakes at all. The line went through the Alps via the Mont Cern tunnel before emerging on the French side near Modane, where it descended in a series of steep gradients. The driver protested that the train was a death-trap, but this being wartime, he was under military discipline. An officer drew his gun, and that settled the argument. The train climbed through the tunnel just before midnight, then began its descent. As it gathered speed the driver applied the brakes, but they seemed to have no effect. The train just went faster and faster. With the brakes glowing white hot and starting fires under the coaches, they careered on for four miles until they reached about seventy-five miles an hour. As they came to a bridge, the first coach derailed and the rest piled up behind it. The wooden coaches immediately caught fire, and it is estimated that up to 800 soldiers were killed. Because of wartime censorship, the facts remained hidden until fifteen years later, when the driver told his story.

## · THE TORRE TUNNEL ·

On 3 January 1944 the Madrid–Corunna mail train, the *Galicia Express*, was passing through a long tunnel near the village of Torre de Vierzo in Spain's Leon province when it collided with a coal train. Six wooden coaches caught fire and were burned to ashes. For two days the flames were so fierce that rescue squads could not get into the tunnel. Between 500 and 800 people died, among them hundreds of naval cadets returning from their Christmas holidays.

## · THE 'BLACK MARKET EXPRESS' ·

Just two months after the Torre disaster came another rail accident – one of the most bizarre in history. In 1944 food was so short in Naples that many of its one million residents could survive only thanks to a flourishing black market to which the authorities had to turn a blind eye. Train 8017 ran between the city and Potenza every Thursday night and was always packed with illicit traders carrying cigarettes and other goods to exchange with farmers for meat, milk and eggs, all of which were rationed in Naples. It was known as the 'Black Market Express'. Normally, it would have been hauled by electric locomotives, but the electrification system had been damaged, so on the night of 2 March two steam engines were pulling the four coaches packed with 521 passengers. There were six train crew and forty-two empty goods wagons – well above the maximum weight allowed, and there were hills to climb and, in places, ice on the tracks.

After he had gone about sixty miles, the driver made a stop for water at Balvano-Ricigliano station in the Apennines. Once it had left, the assistant stationmaster, Giuseppe Salonia, settled down to read his newspaper because the next train was not due for an hour, but he grew more and more anxious as no ticker-tape message came in from the next station up the line, Bella-Muro, just four miles away, to say 8017 had arrived. Eventually, he was told it was running late, so he would have to hold the next train. When it turned up at twenty to three in the morning, Salonia got the crew to detach the engine so he could go up on it to find out what had happened to 8017. Almost at once he saw a man by the rails swinging a red lantern and shouting. When he got closer the man collapsed, murmuring, 'They're all dead.' Salonia was baffled. The night was very still. If there had been a crash or a derailment, he would certainly have heard the noise. By now the man was sobbing bitterly, and Salonia wondered if he was out of his mind. They took him back to the station to try to coax the story out of him.

He was Michele Palo, a brakeman from 8017. He said that two miles out of Balvano the train had come to a stop after entering the curving Galleria delle Armi tunnel. All the coaches were inside apart from his brake van at the back. The driver had not sounded the whistle to say anything had gone wrong, so Palo had assumed they must have stopped for a signal. It was very cold, but after a while he opened a window and popped his head out. Nothing was stirring, so he got out. As soon as he saw dead bodies he ran back towards Balvano.

Having heard Palo's story, Salonia set off again in the borrowed engine. It was nearly four in the morning before he reached 8017. An eerie silence reigned as he climbed down and made his way to the first carriage inside the tunnel. He slid open the door and shone in his lantern. The passengers were all sprawled out, looking very relaxed, and dead. Every coach was the same. There seemed no one left alive. In the engine the driver was still standing, his head resting on the window. Now it was Salonia's turn to break down, but after a while he pulled himself together, unlocked the brakes, hitched the back of the train to his borrowed locomotive and towed it back to Balvano.

In total 521 people had died, and the police had the grim task of laying them out on the station platform so they could be identified. One of the corpses, though, came to life. He was an olive oil salesman who had left the train to get a breath of fresh air when it had stopped at Balvano. Perhaps because of this, he was one of the few passengers not to drop off to sleep. When the train halted in the tunnel something made him start coughing, so he wrapped a scarf around his mouth. Then he climbed down from the carriage and picked his way unsteadily along the tunnel. He tried to climb into another coach but collapsed by the side of the track. Later he was picked up by two police-men who assumed he was dead and carried him to the makeshift mortuary at the station, where he came round. Another survivor suf-fered severe brain damage. The only others to escape death were three black marketeers who were taken to the stationmaster's office for treat-ment then melted away.

Now the police had to work out what had happened. They concluded that the wheels probably started to slide on the icy track as soon as the train was in the tunnel. The driver could have backed down the hill but he decided to press on. The four crewmen in the locomotives fed the fire-boxes desperately, but that just made the wheels spin faster while the train stayed where it was. The coal was lower grade than usual, and the crew failed to realise how much carbon monoxide they were producing. The gas is deadly, but colourless and odourless, and it spread silently through the train, killing almost everyone in its path. Again wartime censorship threw a blanket of silence over the disaster. Only one news-paper was allowed to publish a short official report of the 'mishap', and it was seven years before the full story was revealed.


· BIHAR ·

India has one of the biggest rail networks in the world, used by thirteen million people every day. Its safety record is less impressive, though, with about 300 accidents every year. On 6 June 1981 a desperately over-crowded train was going from Samastipur to Banmukhi in the northern state of Bihar. As people travelling without tickets clung to the sides and sat on the roof, seven of the train's coaches plunged off a bridge into the swollen Bagmati River.

What caused the accident is unclear. Did the driver brake suddenly, perhaps to try to avoid hitting a cow on the track? Or was the train blown off by strong winds? However it happened, between 800 and 1,000 people died, many of them members of wedding parties travelling on the train. At the time, this made it the worst rail disaster in history. (More people would die twenty-three years later on the Sri Lankan train *Queen of the Sea* during the Boxing Day tsunami – see Chapter 3.)

## · THE TRANS-SIBERIAN RAILWAY ·

One Saturday night in 1989 engineers on the trans-Siberian gas pipeline noticed the pressure had suddenly dropped. The reason was a rupture in the pipe close to the industrial city of Ufa in the Urals that was releasing a highly explosive mixture of propane, butane, benzene and other gases into a valley about half a mile from the Trans-Siberian Railway. The engineers, though, seemed oblivious, even when local people called to complain about the smell. Regulations required them to investigate the cause of any drop in pressure but instead they just turned up the taps.

Early the next morning, 4 June, Train 211 was travelling from the West Siberian town of Nizhnevartovsk to the Black Sea when the driver began to smell gas. So did the driver of Train 212, coming in the opposite direction. They passed between Chelyabinsk and Ufa, and the aerodynamic effect of their combined movement sucked up the gas from the valley. Seconds later there was a huge explosion as a spark, or perhaps a discarded cigarette, ignited the lethal cocktail. It derailed one train, sending it crashing into the other, which then caught fire. It was said the explosion created a wall of flame a mile and a quarter wide. Up to three miles from the blast trees were flattened to a wasteland of stumps and ash, while windows shattered in the small town of Asha seven miles away. A number of coaches melted, others were reduced to twisted metal, and debris flew half a mile.

One of the drivers, who survived the accident, said that as he entered a gully in the forest he had seen a huge cloud of gas in his headlights. Another survivor, an army officer, remembered noticing an acrid smell while he was standing by a window. Then there was a glow and 'a thundering explosion. I covered my face with my hands, but then there was another explosion and I fell.' Fortunately, he did not lose consciousness and managed to climb out of the burning carriage through a broken window.

Between them, the two trains had been carrying 1,200 people, including many children going to or returning from summer camp. One rescue worker said: 'In the old days, when something like this happened, the only people who ever found out it had occurred were the people who were hurt and their relatives and some government officials.' Now

President Gorbachev's drive for openness, *glasnost*, had changed all that. The official Soviet news agency, Tass, said at least 800 people were missing in a 'huge catastrophe' and 'a terrible tragedy', while Soviet television reported 'hundreds and hundreds' of deaths.

Gorbachev declared a day of national mourning and went to the scene himself, describing it as a 'real hell'. By this time he was horrified and exasperated at the number of accidents occurring in the Soviet Union. Chernobyl (see Chapter 14) had happened just a year after he had come to power, while 1986 also saw a collision between two ships in the Black Sea, killing 400. Since mid-1987 there had been at least nine other serious rail crashes, which in total had killed about 300 people. He told a television crew that behind many of the accidents were 'negligence, irresponsibility and a lack of proper organisation'. It emerged that earlier in the year another leak had been reported in the four-year-old pipeline, but in an uninhabited region.

At least there was praise for the efficiency of the rescue operation, with the most seriously injured being flown to hospital by helicopter while a field hospital of tents was set up close to the scene for other casualties. It was difficult to establish the exact number of people killed, because children under eight did not need tickets, and because many bodies were vaporised by the fireball, but estimates range from 575 to 800.

## · FIROZABAD ·

Another serious Indian train crash happened at about a quarter to three on the morning of 20 August 1995. The Kalindi Express was devouring the miles between Farrukhabad in Uttar Pradesh and India's capital, Delhi, when it came to a sudden stop outside Firozabad station. Kaushal Chand Pathak was playing cards with his five brothers in one of the carriages. He jumped out to investigate and discovered the locomotive's brakes had jammed after it had hit an animal on the tracks. Reassured that nothing major had happened, he returned to his card game. Suddenly, though, there was a bang. A student living close to the track ran out, and with other local people immediately started trying to free the injured, 'tripping over corpses all the time'. One passenger said: 'The entire area was reverberating with cries and shrieks.' He kept stepping on bodies, not knowing whether they were living or dead.

The Puroshottam Express had ploughed into the back of the station-ary train at nearly seventy miles an hour. A dozen coaches were derailed and some toppled down a thirty-foot embankment to be crumpled like balls of paper. The impact also snapped power lines so that some pas-sengers who survived the impact were electrocuted. Kaushal found himself pinned inside his coach at the bottom of the embankment. He suffered head injuries and a broken leg, and was trapped for three hours before being pulled out.

A total of 358 people were killed. The crash had happened at one of the busiest junctions on the rail network, and an inquiry put it down to a signalman's error at Firozabad. He should have checked that the Kalindi Express had reached the next station, Haripura, before he let the Puroshottam Express proceed. Some argued, though, that the sig-nalman had not been properly trained, and that the system was antiquated.

The idea that the Indian railway system was not fit for purpose was given further credence by two later accidents. In 1998 about 200 passen-gers were killed in the Punjab when a passenger train was first derailed, then hit by another coming in the opposite direction. The following year, at least 285 people died when two trains collided at Gaisal station in West Bengal.

· EGYPT ·

The sixteen-carriage Cairo–Luxor service was packed with people returning home for the Eid al-Adha festival as it sped along on 22 February 2002. At two o'clock in the morning, forty miles out of Cairo, there was an explosion which started a fire, but in the third-class car-riages there were no smoke alarms and no way for the passengers to notify the driver of an emergency. So he raced on for four miles and the flames spread, fanned by the draught from the open carriage windows. It was only when he reached the village of Reqqa al-Gharbîya in Giza province that the driver realised what had happened, and slammed on the brakes. Even then the flames burned for hours. Each carriage was supposed to carry a maximum of 150 people, but more than 300 had crammed into some.

Witnesses said that when the fire started the lights immediately went out, so people had to try to scramble out in darkness. One said the train became 'a tunnel of death'. A villager at Kafr Amar watched the burning carriages flash past, with people hurling themselves from doors and windows, producing a stream of dead and injured. He picked up a soldier who moaned: 'My friends, please help my friends.' There were bodies everywhere, which the locals tried to cover as best they could, as well as a melancholy trail of burned shoes, luggage and clothing. A construction worker who managed to jump from one of the carriages said he had not heard an explosion, just people shouting, but when he smelled smoke he knew he had to get out or die.

An estimated 383 people, all Egyptians, were killed. By the time the flames had been extinguished, seven coaches were just charred ruins, and the rescue services spent hours carrying away the dead and injured on stretchers, while villagers brought blankets and food, and mosques opened their doors to the survivors. A hundred of the dead were so badly burned that they could not be identified.

Almost immediately, the authorities said the fire had been caused by a cooking stove brought on-board by a passenger, but many people pointed to poor safety standards on the railways, which had been starved of investment for years. Over the previous decade there had been four other major accidents that killed at least 211 people. The opposition newspaper *al-Wafd* said the government should find out who was responsible and 'hang them in public squares'. The transport minister and the head of the railway authority both resigned.

# 18

## AIR CRASHES

### · PARIS ·

In June 1972 a McDonnell Douglas DC-10 had to make a crash landing in Detroit after its rear cargo door flew off while the aircraft was in flight. An official investigation concluded that the door had not been properly locked, though the indicator on the flight deck had said it was. Now the manufacturer revealed there had been 100 reports of problems with the doors. The United States Federal Aviation Administration (FAA) ordered all doors to be modified so it would be impossible for them to open in flight, and McDonnell Douglas suggested installing a small peep-hole that would allow an observer to ensure the bolts were fully closed.

Less than two years later, on 3 March 1974, a Turkish Airlines DC-10 was ready to take off from Paris's Orly Airport for London Heathrow. It was carrying eleven crew and 335 passengers, including a number of people who had attended the France–England rugby union international the day before, forty-eight Japanese management trainees, and the British 400-metre runner John Cooper, a double silver medallist at the 1964 Olympics. The aircraft had had the peep-hole fitted, and a modification had been made to the locking pin. However, rather than increasing the distance the pin had to travel to indicate the door was 'locked', it had actually been reduced. Not only that – the 'door open' warning light on the flight deck was prone to go out even when the door was unlocked. Ground staff had been warned they must not force the door shut, and they were supposed to look through the peep-hole to check the pin was in the correct place, but some of the staff at Orly could not speak English, and there were doubts over whether they understood the placards indicating safe and unsafe positions. The airline had had problems with closing the door in the past, but this time it seemed to work perfectly, although it seems no one checked the peep-hole. At half past twelve the aircraft took off.

It was a warm Sunday afternoon, so many people were enjoying a stroll in the Ermenonville Forest north-east of the city. Some of them noticed an aircraft apparently in difficulty at low altitude, as the pilot kept trying to lift its nose. Air traffic control picked up a distorted transmission in which the DC-10's co-pilot seemed to be saying, 'The fuselage has burst!' Then the flight disappeared from the radar. As the controller kept trying to raise the crew, walkers in the forest saw the plane crash to the ground and dig out a furrow half a mile long and 100 yards wide. It fell apart as it went, scattering debris over a wide area. Miraculously, no one on the ground was hurt.

It transpired that as the aircraft ascended to 11,500 feet the door burst open and tore off part of the fuselage. The cabin floor collapsed, and the last two rows of seats were sucked out, taking six passengers with them. Just seventy-two seconds later the DC-10 hit the ground at nearly 500 miles an hour. The emergency services were on the scene quickly, but all they could do was clear up the wreckage. All 346 people on-board were killed, making this by far the worst accident up to that point in civil aviation history. It was also the first involving a fully laden, wide-bodied jet. All over the crash area small fires were burning where parts of the engine or the fuel system had fallen, while pieces of fuselage and passengers' belongings had been flung everywhere, leaving trees that had escaped destruction festooned with scraps of clothing. Many dead passengers were found still strapped in their seats.

The flight recorder showed that during the airliner's last seconds, there had been a muffled explosion followed by the sound of the cabin depressurisation warning horn. The captain asked what had happened, and his first officer replied: 'The fuselage has burst.' As the aircraft's floor collapsed, it damaged many of the cables and hydraulic lines the crew needed to control the aircraft. Another warning sounded, and the captain asked: 'Hydraulics?' The co-pilot replied: 'We've lost it . . . oops, oops.' Then the captain was heard saying: 'It looks like we're going to hit the ground.' His last word was: 'Oops!'

At first, it was thought a bomb had exploded on-board, but soon it became clear that, as in the Canadian incident, the rear cargo door had come off while the aircraft was in mid-air. The official inquiry was highly critical of the fact that although faults in the design of the cargo doors had been known about for more than eighteen months, 'no efficacious corrective action had followed'. An FAA inquiry revealed that there had been 1,000 separate incidents involving cargo doors on DC-10s between October 1973 and March 1974, and the United States House of Representatives criticised the lack of action by regulators, saying, 'Thousands of lives were unjustifiably put at risk.'

After the accident DC-10s had their cargo doors redesigned, but that was not the end of the aircraft's problems. On 25 May 1979 all 271 people aboard an American Airlines flight died when an engine fell off one minute after it had left Chicago's O'Hare Airport. After that crash all DC-10s were grounded for a time.

## · TENERIFE ·

The deadliest air crash in history happened on Tenerife in the Canary Islands on Sunday, 27 March 1977. It all began with a bomb going off in the passenger terminal at Las Palmas airport on Gran Canaria, injuring eight people. This was followed by a warning that there was a second bomb. A Canary Islands separatist movement was thought to be responsible. The authorities closed the airport while it was searched, and diverted all flights to Los Rodeos on Tenerife, which was soon severely overcrowded. Among the flights arriving there were a Pan Am Boeing 747 from Los Angeles on charter to a cruise line and a KLM jumbo from Amsterdam. On the Pan Am flight there were 380 passengers and sixteen crew, while the KLM aircraft had 234 passengers and fourteen crew. It was captained by KLM's chief training pilot for 747s, Jacob van Zanten. He had been with the airline for more than twenty-five years, and was the pilot whose picture they liked to use in publicity material, but he had not flown recently. Van Zanten was worried that if he got stuck for too long in Los Rodeos, the crew might not have enough hours of duty left to complete the trip back to Amsterdam. The Pan Am flight was captained by another veteran pilot – Victor Grubbs. He had asked for permission to circle Los Rodeos without landing in the hope that Las Palmas would soon reopen, but air traffic control refused. When Las Palmas did reopen he found himself stuck in a queue of aircraft, boxed in by the KLM jet. To make things worse, mist and light rain were drifting across the airfield, reducing visibility at times to 300 yards. The main runway at Los Rodeos had a parallel taxiway, to which it was joined at either end, as well as by four slipways, but the taxiway had become so congested that aircraft could not pass all the way along it. So any ready to take off were having to make a complicated manoeuvre – going along the main runway for part of its length, before leaving by one of the slipways to rejoin the taxiway beyond the parked aircraft, and then swinging around at the end on to the runway for take-off. After it had been on the ground for more than two hours the KLM jet was told it would face further delay. Van Zanten decided to refuel now rather than in Las Palmas, which would take another thirty minutes, and the Pan Am crew grew irritated because they could not leave while the KLM jumbo remained where it was. The refuelling finished about five o'clock in the evening. Both crews were now told to take their aircraft on to the main runway. The KLM would have to taxi about two miles, all the way to the end, then make a 180-degree turn and come back down to take off. Captain Grubbs was told to follow the Dutch aircraft, but to leave the runway by the third slipway and join the taxiway. Unfortunately, the slipways were not numbered, and by the time Grubbs received the instruction the Pan Am jet had already passed the first of them. There were only two controllers in the tower, and in the poor visibility they could not see the aircraft at the far end of the runway, while two of the airport's three radio frequencies were out of action, meaning that the pilots heard a lot of babble on the one being used.

Van Zanten's deadline for being able to get back to Amsterdam was fast approaching when visibility improved just enough for him to be able to take off, but the Pan Am crew was finding it hard to spot the slip-ways in the gloom and missed their designated exit. Van Zanten could not see the American aircraft still approaching him, and nobody in the tower could see either of the two jumbos. Having made his 180-degree turn, the Dutch captain was given air traffic clearance but not permission to take off. Instead of waiting for it, though, he opened his throttles and said either: 'We are now at take-off' or 'We are taking off.' In the radio babble, the controller was confused, and replied: 'Stand by for take-off. I will call you.' At the same moment the Pan Am crew told the controller: 'We are still taxiing down the runway.' The KLM flight engineer then asked, 'Is he not clear, that Pan American?' Van Zanten replied, 'Oh yes,' and continued with the take-off run. The Pan Am crew were horrified to hear messages suggesting the KLM jumbo was heading towards them on the runway, and Grubbs said, 'Let's get the hell out of here.' The controller reassured him and told him to say when he was clear of the runway, as Grubbs searched desperately for a slipway.

Almost immediately, his co-pilot saw the lights of the Dutch jet loom up out of the mist, travelling at 150 miles an hour. Grubbs threw his aircraft to the left and opened the throttles to try to get clear. By the time Zanten saw the other jumbo his only option was to try to 'hop' over it, so he pulled hard on the control column in an attempt to get airborne early. The nose lifted so dramatically that the tail struck the tarmac, and he managed to leave the ground just as the Pan Am was crossing his path. He got his nose wheel over the top of the other aircraft, but one of his engines grazed it, and his main landing gear smashed into it, ripping off the first-class lounge and most of the top of the fuselage, while the tail section snapped off. Grubbs had managed to get the front of his aircraft off the runway, and as the left side of the fuselage began to break up some passengers escaped through the gaps on to the wing and jumped down on to the grass. The flight crew also got out, through emergency hatches in the cockpit roof, and slid to the ground on steel cords. But the left-hand engines were still turning, there was a fire under the wing, and explosions were going off.

The KLM's landing gear sheared off, and the plane crashed back on to the runway about 150 yards past the collision, then skidded for another 300, scattering debris. A fierce fire engulfed the wreckage. The controllers could hear the blasts, but only when a gust of wind blew the fog clear did they see what had happened. According to a passenger in the Pan Am's first-class cabin, 'All hell broke loose.' He tried to get his wife out with him, but people began falling on them from the lounge above, along with pieces of ceiling. An explosion hurled him on to the runway. Then, he said, 'I was running back towards the plane to try to save her when I saw a body falling out. It was my wife.' A former Pan Am mechanic was thrown clear and suffered only minor cuts, but he said: 'I will never get the sound of the screaming out of my ears.' The plane's purser, Dorothy Kelly, was given an award for her bravery. After the impact she recalled there was nothing 'that looked like anything had looked before – just jagged metal and small pieces of debris'. She leapt down twenty feet and started to move away to safety, but then she returned to the aircraft. She found the captain on his knees, grabbed him under the arms, and tried to pull him away from the jumbo. Then there was a huge explosion and she said: 'We've got to move faster.' She managed to drag him to the runway and dropped him there before going back to pull other dazed survivors from the wreckage. Explosions continued to rip through the aircraft until a final series of blasts enveloped it in flames, making it clear there was no hope of getting anyone else out alive.

The controllers' first thought was that there had been another terrorist attack, while fire crews tried to reach the crash site through the misty, congested airfield. With the KLM aircraft apparently beyond help, the emergency services concentrated their efforts on the Pan Am. Airport staff bravely rushed to help, while fire-fighting teams were called in from other towns, but it was not until the next day that all the fires were put out.

Of the 396 people aboard the Pan Am aircraft, seventy escaped, though nine died later from their injuries. Most survivors had been in the forward section, and they owed their lives to Grubbs's desperate swing off the runway. Five of those who lived were members of the crew, including Grubbs himself, the first officer and the flight engineer. All 248 people on the KLM jumbo were killed, making 583 deaths in all. It was the worst aviation disaster of all time, and it had happened on the ground.

Crash investigators from Spain, the Netherlands and the United States examined what had gone wrong. If Captain van Zanten had not been one of the victims, he probably would have headed the Dutch branch of the inquiry. The cockpit voice recorder clearly showed that he thought he

had been cleared for take-off, while the controllers believed he was stationary at the end of the runway, waiting for clearance. The inquiry
concluded that the KLM jet took off without permission, and that van
Zanten failed to interrupt his take-off even when the Pan Am crew
reported they were still on the runway. It said that radio congestion contributed to the disaster. The investigators reckoned that if van Zanten
had managed to get just twenty-five feet higher, he might have cleared
the Pan Am jet.

## · RIYADH ·

A Saudia Lockheed Tristar en route from Riyadh to Jeddah on the night
of 19 August 1980 was only six minutes into its flight when the crew saw
warnings of smoke in the aircraft's cargo compartment. For the next
four minutes they tried to check whether it was a false alarm. The captain
decided to return to the airport, but the thrust lever for the tail engine
was stuck as the fire had burned through the operating cable, so he had
to shut it down. Still, he landed safely on Riyadh's main runway, then
taxied to the end of an older runway nearby. For some reason, though, he
did not order an immediate evacuation, and he did not shut down the
engines for another three minutes. Just as he told the control tower he
was trying to get his passengers down the emergency chutes, radio contact was lost.

Fire now swept through the Tristar. Helicopters tried to attack the
flames from above but rescue services on the ground could not get
the plane's emergency doors open, and it was another twenty minutes
before they could get into the aircraft. By then, all fourteen crew and
287 passengers, many of them pilgrims on their way to Mecca, were dead
from burns or smoke inhalation. Everyone was found in the front half
of the aircraft, some jammed against the exit doors. A statement from
the Saudi Arabian Directorate of Civil Aviation said: 'It became impossible to open the doors from outside or inside.' The cockpit voice recorder
revealed the captain had failed to delegate responsibility to his colleagues
on the flight deck. Instead, he tried to fly the aircraft and fix the problem,
too. The first officer had very limited experience on the Tristar and did not
appear to help the captain, while the flight engineer, who was thought to be

dyslexic, searched through the aircraft's manual and constantly repeated 'no problem' to himself.

Within days of the accident the Saudi authorities announced that they had found two small gas stoves in the burned-out fuselage, and that there was a used fire extinguisher near one of them. The stoves were the kind often used by pilgrims camping at Mecca, and the authorities pointed to them as a possible cause of the fire, but years later, it was suggested the fire might have been started by an electrical wiring fault.

## · THE JAL CRASH ·

The worst ever accident involving a single aircraft was also one of the most chilling in aviation history. On the evening of 12 August 1985 Tokyo's Haneda Airport was packed at the start of a three-day Buddhist holiday. At twelve minutes past six a Japanese Airlines Boeing 747 took off for the hour-long flight to Osaka, carrying fifteen crew and 509 passengers, many of them families with children. The aircraft had climbed to 24,000 feet when air traffic control in Tokyo received a message from the crew asking for permission to return. The captain said he was getting no response from his controls, and the airport radar showed he was following an erratic course – going in different directions, then turning a full circle, while losing height, all at a dangerously slow speed.

In fact, just twelve minutes after take-off the jumbo had been rocked by a huge explosion towards its rear which had blown off a section of the ceiling. A white mist had filled the cabin, oxygen masks had dropped down and passengers had clutched at them as the air rushed out. Some with heart problems may have died then. Most of the flight controls were now useless as all four hydraulic lines had been ruptured, and with the aircraft pitching and rolling a door came off. Captain Masami Takahama managed to check his speed by lowering the undercarriage. He was flying at 10,000 feet with the throttles eased back to prevent strain on the damaged tail when the aircraft began to stall. He tried manipulating the flaps but he was fighting a losing battle. Twenty-three minutes after the explosion a Tokyo controller asked him: 'Can you control now?' Takahama replied: 'Uncontrollable.' Ominously, there were mountains ahead.

Nine minutes later the aircraft disappeared from the radar, and no more was heard from it. The crew had kept the shattered jumbo in the air for over half an hour after the explosion, a feat many considered amazing. It finally crashed into a 5,000-foot-high ridge near Mount Osutaka, seventy miles north-west of Tokyo, and burst into flames. A Japanese military helicopter spotted it but the visibility was too poor and the terrain too rough to attempt a landing. The pilot reported no sign of survivors, and it was nine o'clock the next morning before fire-fighters managed to reach the still smouldering wreck, while paratroopers slid down ropes from helicopters. They discovered that the jumbo had almost cleared the ridge but had brushed into trees that tore off the tail and one of the engines.

Incredibly, the rescuers found four people alive: a twenty-five-year-old off-duty stewardess, who had a broken arm and pelvis; a thirty-four-year-old woman and her eight-year-old daughter, who had broken bones; and a twelve-year-old schoolgirl, who was found sitting on the branch of a tree and had suffered only cuts and bruises. The three passengers had all been sitting in the same row. They said they had heard groans and cries around them at first, but that these gradually ceased during the night. Among the 520 people who died was the singer Kyu Sakamoto, whose whose hit record 'Sukiyaki' was the only one sung in Japanese ever to top the American music charts.

Perhaps the most heartbreaking items found at the scene were the farewell messages that passengers had scribbled to their loved ones on tickets and scraps of paper during the pilot's half-hour battle to keep the Boeing in the air. A shipping company executive had written to his son and two daughters: 'Be good to each other and work hard. Help your mother. The aircraft is nosediving. White smoke is coming out of the back. We may have only five more minutes. I don't want to get on an aircraft ever again. Please God, help me. To think that our dinner last night was the last time.' Some who did not have pens had cut themselves and written notes with their own blood, like the man who left the message: 'Bang, we're starting to fall. Be brave and live.' Another passenger wrote to his wife: 'Machiko, take care of the kids,' then slipped the message into his driving licence.

At first, the aviation industry feared the crash might have been the first sign of a fatal weakness in 747 design or construction, but then investigators found a clue to what had really happened – a blurred amateur photograph of the jumbo flying with its vertical tail fin and rudder missing. A Japanese Navy destroyer found them in Sagami Bay, close to where the 747 had first reported problems. The flight recorder revealed there had been a thud, followed by the decompression warning, and the alarm indicating that all hydraulic systems had been lost. Next it emerged that a pilot landing the aircraft at Osaka back in 1978 had misjudged the approach and scraped the tail along the runway, cracking the rear pressure bulkhead. The airline had carried out repairs under the supervision of Boeing engineers, who had replaced the lower half of the bulkhead, but they had failed to insert a reinforcing plate, so just a single line of rivets was left to carry the load. Routine inspections over the years had failed to uncover the error in this inaccessible part of the aircraft, so it must have been flexing in flight for seven years before it finally broke. When the bulkhead gave way it ruptured the lines of all four hydraulic systems. JAL's president said he took full responsibility for the disaster and resigned. A maintenance manager committed suicide to 'apologise'.

## · THE WORST MID-AIR COLLISION ·

The world's worst mid-air collision was between a Saudi Arabian Airlines Boeing 747 and a Kazakhstan Airlines Ilyushin Il-76 on 12 November, 1996 over the Indian town of Charkhi Dadri. The jumbo was flying from Delhi to Dhahran, while the Kazakh aircraft was coming into the Indian capital. The Ilyushin was normally used for cargo, but it had been converted to carry passengers. There were twenty-eight, who were going on a shopping expedition, plus ten crew. The 747 carried 312 crew and passengers, many of them Indian labourers on their way back to Saudi Arabia. It took off at half past six in the evening, and seven minutes later it was cleared to climb to 14,000 feet. At the same time the Ilyushin was told it could descend to 15,000 feet on its final approach. Then the pilot was supposed to loop around the airfield to land, but sixty miles west of Delhi air traffic controllers saw the radar blips of both aircraft disappear from their screens. Witnesses on the ground said a great flash turned the sky red, then there was billowing black smoke. The commander of a US Air Force transport plane flying nearby said he 'noticed a large cloud lit up with an orange glow', then saw two fireballs plunging to the ground.

Debris rained down on the mustard and cotton fields surrounding Charkhi Dadri, but there were no casualties on the ground. Villagers said the Saudi pilot seemed to have kept some control of the aircraft after the collision, and managed to guide it into an open field, where it dug a trench sixty yards long. 'It's the pilot's mercy that ensured the villagers were not harmed,' said one local man. There were few telephones or roads in the area, which delayed the emergency services, but villagers worked by the light of oil lamps, carrying away bodies on carts hauled by tractors or bullocks, the only vehicles that could negotiate the fields and farm tracks. Four people are said to have survived the crash but died on their way to hospital. The Kazakh aircraft came down near another village about seven miles away. There were no survivors, bringing the total death toll to 350. Bodies and personal belongings like handbags, toys, glasses, passports and wallets were scattered across the fields.

The official inquiry decided the accident was the fault of the Kazakh pilot, who had descended below 15,000 feet until he was on a collision course with the jumbo. It said the crew's poor command of English was the probable reason for this, though there was also a suggestion that they might have been distracted by turbulence. Air traffic controllers at Delhi had been complaining for some time about the standard of English among crews from the former Soviet Union. Before the disaster one had written in his duty log: 'Are we waiting for an accident to take place?' The investigation recommended that in future pilots and co-pilots should have a good knowledge of English.

# 19

## OTHER TRANSPORT DISASTERS

### · CALI ·

Cali is the third biggest city in Colombia. On 6 August 1956 a convoy of army lorries loaded with more than forty tons of dynamite arrived there on its way to a building site in Bogotá. Seven of the trucks parked near barracks housing soldiers and police. In the early hours of the next morning there was a deafening explosion, and the barracks, the old railway station and eight whole blocks were flattened. The blast left a huge crater and debris was flung for miles.

At least 1,300 people are believed to have been killed, but what caused the explosion was a mystery, and heavy government censorship kept details sparse. At first, General Rojas Pinilla, who had been Colombia's military dictator since 1953, declared it was sabotage and said he would not rest until the culprits had been brought to justice. Others believed the blast might have been triggered by the trucks overheating or by an earlier explosion in the barracks. Whatever the cause, there was widespread anger that the army had brought so much explosive into a densely populated area. Pinilla decreed three days of national mourning, but he had to call in troops and police to prevent looting. He resigned and left the country nine months later.

## · LOS ALFAQUES ·

Most of the 780 tourists at the Los Alfaques campsite in the little Spanish resort of San Carlos de la Rapita, near Tarragona, were having lunch outside their tents or caravans, settling down for a siesta, or sunbathing at half past two on the afternoon of 11 July 1978. Meanwhile, a tanker loaded with twenty-five tons of highly flammable liquid propylene was on its way from Tarragona to a refinery in central Spain. As he took a long bend behind the camp, the driver lost control and skidded. The tanker overturned, then rolled over the wall into the tents.

The propylene exploded, spewing rivers of fire across the site. Flames engulfed the holidaymakers and climbed hundreds of feet into the sky, then set off a new series of blasts in butane cookers and petrol tanks. About 100 caravans were destroyed in seconds, and tents vaporised while campers fled into the sea to try to escape the flames. A French tourist said: 'It was like napalm . . . People were running everywhere, screaming, some of them on fire.' More than 100 were killed almost immediately, most of them burned beyond recognition, while another 150 were seriously injured. Most of the victims had little or no protection from the flames because they were wearing swimming costumes. Debris and bodies were flung 150 yards into the sea, and several entire families were wiped out. At least a dozen children were orphaned. A policeman said: 'We were helpless. I'll never be able to get rid of these horrible sights, no matter how long I live.' The blast demolished a shower block and a discotheque opposite the site, as well as a dozen nearby houses, killing the occupants. No trace was ever found of the tanker driver. *The Times* described it as 'the worst road accident since the invention of the wheel'.

Ambulances and private cars ferried the injured to Tarragona, Valencia and even Barcelona, 120 miles away, while German and Swiss aircraft took their nationals to specialist burns units back home. For a time, the remains of the tanker lay in the camp, 'like a giant tin can which had burst along its seam and blown out both its ends'.

Altogether, 217 people died. Three and a half years later six men from the tanker company were put on trial. The investigating magistrate said the vehicle had been defective and overloaded, but also that the campsite had been overcrowded. Four of the defendants were acquitted; the other two were given suspended sentences.

## · THE SALANG TUNNEL FIRE ·

The world's worst road crash in a tunnel remains shrouded in mystery. Was it an accident or a deliberate attack? How many people were killed? What exactly happened? It took place in Afghanistan's only road tunnel on 3 November 1982, when guerrillas were engaged in a bitter struggle against Soviet occupying forces.

The 1.7-mile-long Salang Tunnel, built in 1964, is 11,000 feet up in the mountains, seventy miles north of Kabul. A Red Army convoy was travelling through it when the disaster happened. Fearing a rebel attack, the Russians sealed off the tunnel after receiving reports from inside or possibly seeing smoke coming out. In the tunnel motorists stayed in their cars to shelter from the freezing cold and were either burned to death or suffocated by fumes.

Some Afghan refugees said a fuel tanker in a military convoy had collided with another military truck, and that an explosion and fire had followed. Other reports claimed that a munitions lorry had blown up. One eyewitness said he was on a bus about twenty yards from the entrance when he heard the blast, and that 'black, oily smoke started pouring out'. He said passengers on the bus were overcome and at least one died. According to some accounts, vehicles continued to enter the tunnel after the explosion, before the army sealed it off. Some said they saw half a dozen trucks driven away laden with bodies, mainly of Soviet troops. A man who went back the next day to pick up his belongings said he saw drivers, both military and civilian, slumped over the wheels of their vehicles.

There had been persistent rumours that Afghan rebels were planning to blow up the tunnel, which would have severely hampered deliveries of military supplies to the 100,000 Soviet troops then stationed in the country. Shortly after the disaster an insurgent group claimed responsibility, but other rebels denied any involvement. The size of the fire and the total number of vehicles involved remain unknown, but some estimates put the death toll as high as 2,000. Certainly, in the days after the disaster Kabul was said to be a city in mourning, with every family having lost a friend or relative.

The tunnel was reopened but fell into disrepair after the Soviets withdrew in 1989, and nine years later it was partially destroyed in the civil war between the Northern Alliance and the Taliban. It reopened again in 2002 but driving through it remained a terrifying experience. The ventilation system was not working, and there were huge gashes in the road. A BBC correspondent reported: 'I could see no more than a metre in front of the car. The lights were on but they made no difference through the cloud of dust and noxious fumes.' A few weeks later a number of people died – either suffocating or freezing to death – when one end was blocked by a landslide.


## · IBADAN ·

Nigeria suffers from plenty of traffic jams, and on 5 November 2000 a particularly bad one was clogging the motorway from Ife to Ibadan, the country's second-biggest city. Every lane was blocked, and pedestrians were weaving their way in and out of the cars. Suddenly, the driver of an approaching petrol tanker saw the stationary vehicles ahead of him and tried to brake, but it was in a poor state and it ploughed straight into them. The tanker came to rest on its side, with petrol leaking on to the road. Within seconds it ignited, and the vehicle disappeared in a huge fireball that devastated a wide area. Newspaper reports said that in no time hundreds of grieving people had appeared at the roadside.

The police and other rescue services were slow to help, so many bodies were removed by relatives and buried, while others were cremated in the inferno. Because of this, no one knows exactly how many perished. The official total of bodies recovered was ninety-six, the police reported that at least 115 vehicles were destroyed, and many believe the real death toll could be up to 200. Many hospitals were overwhelmed by hundreds of badly burned victims, and there was anger over what was seen as the authorities' dilatory response. Local people also claimed the gridlock had been caused by state police putting up a roadblock so they could demand money from motorists. The police denied these accusations, saying the hold-up was caused by roadworks, but officers who tried to visit the scene the following day were attacked and beaten.

It was Nigeria's fourth deadly road accident in just three months. In August seventy people had been killed when a lorry crushed three buses after its brakes failed. Then a fuel tanker had smashed into a market, killing more than twenty. And in October fifty people had died in a collision between a bus and a tanker.

## · BAKU ·

The world's worst underground railway disaster happened in Baku, the capital of Azerbaijan, on 28 October 1995, when fire broke out on a packed train. Survivors described seeing sparks flying from high-voltage cables just after the train had left the busy Ulduz station. 'Then,' said one, 'flames enveloped the carriage, there was a sound of breaking glass, and the lights went out. People started breaking windows to get out. We were beginning to suffocate.' The train had juddered to a halt with its doors jammed shut. A passenger in the second carriage said they could not break the windows, so he climbed out through a ventilation duct: 'I got out through the tunnel by grabbing a cable . . . People were dying all over the rails.' Another said fighting broke out on the train: 'A soldier standing near the door tried to break the glass, but he could not because of the crowd crushing him . . . I don't know how I got out. I fell on the rails and people started walking over me. In the darkness someone grabbed me and helped me away from the burning carriage.' It took him two hours to reach the next station through the smoke-filled tunnel, as people vomited all around him. Rescuers battled the flames for hours, while security forces kept away reporters.

The death toll was put at 337. Some of the victims had been crushed to death in the panic, but most were poisoned by carbon monoxide or other toxic gases. The previous year twenty people had been killed in two terrorist attacks on the Baku underground system, and some reports claimed a bomb had caused the fire, but government officials insisted an electrical fault was to blame.

## · THE *KURSK* ·

The world's worst peacetime submarine disaster happened in 2000 with the sinking of the *Kursk,* one of the first naval vessels built in Russia after the collapse of the Soviet Union, and the biggest attack submarine ever.

After the end of the Cold War Russia's Northern Fleet suffered ferocious cutbacks, with submarines left to rust and sailors unpaid for months. Towards the end of the millennium, though, the fleet enjoyed something of a revival, and the *Kursk* carried out a successful spying mission against the Americans in the Mediterranean in 1999. August 2000's training exercise in the Barents Sea was due to be the biggest since the end of the Soviet Union. At half past eleven on the morning of Saturday, 12 August, the submarine was firing a series of dummy torpedoes when there was an explosion on-board. She immediately sank to a depth of 325 feet about eighty-five miles off the coast. Then, two minutes later, a second explosion ripped through her.

The *Kursk* was located at five o'clock the next morning and Russian rescue vessels soon arrived, while a number of foreign countries – including the UK and the United States – also offered to help. The Russians launched a submersible, but a fierce storm was raging and it was unable to dock with the *Kursk.* Most of the submarine's crew had been killed by the explosions or by the first inrush of water, but a few were still alive on Monday. President Putin was on holiday in southern Russia and he said nothing about the disaster until Wednesday, when the Russians finally asked for help from Britain and Norway. By then, all the crew were dead. On Friday the president arrived back in Moscow, but it was only three days later that Norwegian divers managed to get into the *Kursk,* and the Russian Navy announced that none of the 118 men aboard had survived.

At first, the Russian Admiralty suggested that most of the crew had died within minutes of the explosions, but then a note written by Lieutenant Commander Dmitry Kolesnikov was discovered, and it became clear that twenty-three submariners survived the blasts and took refuge at the stern of the *Kursk.* It read: 'It's too dark to write here . . . It seems we have no chance – no more than 10 to 20 per cent. I hope at least that someone will read this.' At Kolesnikov's funeral the commander of the Northern Fleet said: 'His fate will become an example of serving the fatherland for everyone.' It emerged that the survivors were eventually killed when their oxygen-generation canisters came into contact with the rising sea in the compartment where they were sheltering. This generated enough heat to set fire to an oily film on the water, and cause an explosion. Anyone who survived that would have suffocated as the fire consumed the remaining oxygen.

The Russian press savaged Putin's handling of the disaster. The front page of *Izvestia* declared: 'The reflexes of the Russian elite have not changed . . . The first thing they want to do is to conceal the truth.' It listed what it claimed were lies, inconsistencies and cover-ups regarding the course of events, the number of casualties, the causes, the situation on-board and the rescue operation. Then two journalists smuggled themselves into a meeting between the president and 500 relatives of the victims. The families howled at Putin and demanded to know why they had been fed so much contradictory information. In response, the president launched a furious attack on the media and threatened Boris Berezovsky, who controlled the main state television channel. Berezovsky fled to Britain.

Blaming the messenger, though, did not convince those who had been bereaved. On the first anniversary of the disaster they met to throw flowers into the water at the *Kursk*'s home port of Vidyayevo. 'They took us for imbeciles,' said Ljudmila Zafornova, the mother of a twenty-six-year-old navigation officer on the submarine. 'They started to tell us the crew was still alive, that they had oxygen and power, but they knew the true situation from the beginning.' She was furious that the Russian authorities did not immediately request foreign help. President Putin chose not to appear at the commemoration service, just sending a message of sympathy. Mrs Zafornova said: 'At the same time that the whole world was worried about our children they were showing pictures of our president lying down under the sun.'

The wreck of the *Kursk* was raised in October 2001, and it became clear that the heat generated by the first explosion had detonated the warheads on four torpedoes, causing secondary explosions that fatally damaged the vessel. The Russians had originally suggested the *Kursk* was sunk after a collision with a foreign submarine or by hitting a Second World War mine. Once the truth was revealed the commander of the Northern Fleet was demoted, and eight admirals and three captains sacked, although the chief of staff of Russia's armed forces said the dismissals were not connected with the disaster.

It was only in July 2002 that the Russian government finally admitted that the first explosion was caused by a leak of hydrogen peroxide torpedo fuel, a highly unstable propellant that most navies have discarded as too dangerous. There was a criminal investigation but no charges were brought.

## · THE KAPRUN FUNICULAR TRAIN ·

The Gletscherbahn 2 was a funicular railway that carried skiers from the town of Kaprun on a ten-minute journey to the top of the 9,800-foot Kitzsteinhorn glacier in the Austrian Alps. It ran through a tight, two-mile tunnel which rose at an angle of nearly forty-five degrees. While one carriage went up, the other came down, and each could carry about 180 passengers.

At nine o'clock on the fine morning of 11 November 2000, 161 passengers and a conductor boarded the train to go to the slopes. When it was 600 yards into the tunnel a fire began in the empty conductor's compartment at the back and melted plastic pipes carrying hydraulic fluid for the braking system. The train stopped automatically. The conductor at the front realised a fire had started and reported it to the control centre. Next he tried to open the sliding doors, but as they were operated by the disabled hydraulic system they remained firmly shut. Then he lost contact with the control centre as the fire burned through a power cable running along the track, and the tunnel was plunged into complete darkness. Passengers tried to smash windows to escape, but they were made from break-resistant glass. At the back of the train, though, a group of twelve did manage to force one open. Among them was a former volunteer fire-fighter, and he saved the others' lives by getting them to go down narrow stairs running beside the track, instead of climbing up, which meant the wind was blowing the smoke and flames away from them up the tunnel. A German survivor said passengers trapped inside 'screamed as they tried to prise open the doors and smash the windows . . . I only managed to escape by the skin of my teeth because a window was kicked open, letting me battle my way out.' Those who did escape emerged retching for breath.

Eventually, the conductor managed to unlock the doors, and passengers who were still conscious forced them open. But many had already passed out because of toxic fumes, and a lot of those who now got out headed upwards, as did the conductor. Unfortunately, the tunnel acted like a giant chimney, sucking oxygen from the bottom and sending up poisonous smoke, heat and flames, so everyone who chose this escape route was killed.

Meanwhile, the train coming down the mountain was also caught in the fire. It carried only a conductor and one passenger, but both died from smoke inhalation. The smoke surged right up to the Alpine Centre at the top. Two staff members saw it coming and escaped via an emergency exit, but they left the exit doors open, increasing the chimney effect in the tunnel, and three skiers waiting for the train down were killed.

Within minutes of the alarm being raised helicopters took emergency crews to the tunnel entrance, and more than 200 rescue workers tried to reach the stranded train. At first they were driven back by the thick smoke, then their rubber boots melted. Indeed, four hours after the fire began smoke was still billowing out of the top of the tunnel. By then, all that was left of the train was its metal base.

Overall, 155 people died, including ninety-two Austrians, thirty-seven Germans, ten Japanese and one Briton. Nearly forty of the victims were under twenty, many of them on their way to a snowboarding competition. Business for Austrian funiculars had been booming, but safety standards had been criticised. It emerged that there was no sprinkler system, no fire extinguishers in the carriage, no fireproof emergency refuges and no evacuation tunnel. Nearly a year later an official inquiry concluded that the disaster had been caused by an electric heater in the rear conductor's compartment, which was not meant to be used in a moving vehicle. It had overheated and caught fire, and then ignited a slow leak of highly flammable hydraulic fluid, which in turn had melted the plastic pipes, further feeding the flames and disabling the train.

The funicular never reopened, and the tunnel was sealed up. It was replaced by a gondola lift. In 2004 sixteen people, including company officials, technicians and government inspectors, were tried for negligence, but a judge decided there was insufficient evidence to convict them. A mother who lost her only son in the disaster said tearfully: 'This is a slap in the face for all the relatives of the dead. I can't believe no one can be found who was responsible for one hundred and fifty-five deaths.'

# INDEX